Rice Talks

Rice Talks

FOOD AND COMMUNITY IN A VIETNAMESE TOWN

Nir Avieli

Indiana University Press

BLOOMINGTON AND INDIANAPOLIS

This book is a publication of

Indiana University Press
601 North Morton Street
Bloomington, Indiana 47404-3797 USA

iupress.indiana.edu

Telephone orders   800-842-6796
Fax orders   812-855-7931

Manufactured in the United States
of America

Library of Congress Cataloging-
in-Publication Data

Avieli, Nir.
  Rice talks : food and community in a
Vietnamese town / Nir Avieli.
      p. cm.
  Includes bibliographical references and index.
  ISBN 978-0-253-35707-6 (cloth : alk. paper)
  — ISBN 978-0-253-22370-8 (pbk. : alk. paper)
  — ISBN 978-0-253-00530-4 (e-book) 1. Food
habits—Vietnam—Hội An. 2. Food—Social
aspects—Vietnam—Hội An. 3. Gastronomy—
Vietnam—Hội An. 4. Cooking, Vietnamese.
5. Hội An (Vietnam)—Social life and customs.
I. Title.
  GT2853.V5A85 2012
  394.1'2095975—dc23
                                    2011028385

1 2 3 4 5 17 16 15 14 13 12

To my parents Elyakum
(1937–2004)
&
Aviva

Contents

Preface

Food, like the air we breathe, is vital for our physiological survival. Food is also the most perfect cultural artifact, the outcome of a detailed differentiation process, whereby wheat grains are transformed into French baguettes, Italian pasta, or Chinese steamed buns, each encompassing a world of individual, social, and cultural identities: "The way any human group eats," Claude Fischler (1988: 275) points out, "helps it assert its diversity, hierarchy and organization ... food is central to individual identity, in that any human individual is constructed biologically, psychologically and socially by the food he/she chooses to incorporate."

The power of food is epitomized by the process of incorporation (literally, "into [the] body"), in which culturally transformed edible matter crosses the borders of the body (ibid. 279) and breaches the dichotomy between "outside" and "inside," between "the World" and "the Self." No other cultural artifact penetrates our bodies with such immediacy and thoroughness. As Brillat-Savarin's aphorism "You are what you eat" suggests, when we eat we become consumers (and reproducers) of our culture, physically internalizing its principles and values. Hence, when Brahmins partake of their vegetarian meals, they express their commitment to the sanctity of life and to the principle of nonviolence; equally, when Argentinian gauchos bite into their bloody steaks, they reaffirm their masculinity and the violent vitality that distinguishes their lifestyle.

Yet it is precisely the nature of food as a constant and necessary part of life, consumed habitually and often nonreflexively, that consigns the culinary sphere to banality, unworthy of sustained scholarly attention. Anthropologists tend to give far more weight to "substantial" aspects of culture, such as kinship, religion, or language, and mention foodways only as a secondary phenomenon. If overlooking the importance of food seems to be rather the norm in anthropology, when it comes to the anthropological study of Vietnam by foreign and local scholars alike, the neglect is almost complete: Huard and Durand (1954),

Hickey (1964), Popkin (1979), Jamieson (1995), Kleinen (1999), Malarney (2002), Hardy (2005), Fjelstad and Nguyen (2006), and Taylor (2004, 2007), in their important ethnographies of Vietnam, rarely mention food practices and hardly ever suggest that they may be meaningful in themselves. Even Thomas (2004) and Carruthers (2004), who highlight the importance of food in Vietnamese culture, are mainly concerned with globalization and the diasporic dimensions of Vietnamese cuisine, and overlook daily food habits and their meanings. In this sense, Krowolski and Simon-Baruch's (1993) ethnography of domestic food and eating in Danang is a salient exception.

In this book I approach food and eating differently: focusing on the cultural and social dimensions of the culinary sphere in the small town of Hoi An and emphasizing the motivations and meanings of eating that transcend physiological needs or ecological constraints, I show that looking at foodways allows us to approach Vietnamese society and culture from a unique perspective. This, I demonstrate, is a powerful analytical lens that allows for new insights regarding the phenomenology of "being Vietnamese."

As a culinary ethnography of Hoi An, a prosperous market town of some 30,000 people in Central Vietnam, this book describes the local foodways and analyzes their social and cultural features. Hence, *Rice Talks* is first and foremost intended as a significant contribution to the anthropology of Vietnam, addressing the dearth of studies on Vietnamese foodways and, in particular, the neglect of the complex culinary sphere of Hoi An, a town that has been involved in global trade and cultural exchange for centuries.

Rice Talks is also a theoretical project that seeks to understand the unique position and qualities of the culinary sphere as a cultural arena. As such, it goes beyond the conventional anthropological understanding of food and eating as reflections of other social and cultural phenomena by conceiving of the culinary sphere as an autonomous arena, where cultural production and social change are *initiated and elaborated*. I focus on the ways by which differing facets of identity such as gender, class, ethnicity, religious propensities, and even political orientations are constructed, maintained, negotiated, challenged, and changed within the culinary sphere.

The ethnographic data presented in this book result from an ongoing project that began in 1998. While my initial twelve months of fieldwork in 1999–2000 laid the foundations for this book, repeated shorter stays of two to three months each year since 2001 have allowed for a close tracking of the powerful processes of development and change that characterized life in Hoi An during this period, and which still continue. Though change is an essential feature of every society and culture, taking it into account has always been problematic in anthropology, as the "anthropological moment," as extended as it might be, is limited and not many ethnographers have the privilege of returning time and again to the field.

Repeated periods of research also facilitated a systematic elaboration of ideas that evolved as I was writing the ethnography. Many colleagues point out that while writing, quite a few questions that "should have been asked in the field" come to mind, but then it is usually too late. I, however, could note down these questions and raise them again when I returned to meet my Hoianese friends and interlocutors. Importantly, my data, findings, and analyses were periodically updated and scrutinized by the same friends and other informants, who were also my harshest critics. Our disagreements and variant interpretations have allowed for the nuanced understanding that this book conveys.

This book is therefore multidimensional and seeks to engage with a variety of questions, some theoretical and some ethnographic, concerning the culinary sphere of Hoi An. It also raises methodological questions and shares some important limitations with its readers: the final chapter is dedicated mainly to the specific problems that arise when studying foodways. But a brief biographical note is in order now.

I first went to Vietnam as a backpacker in late 1993 and fell in love immediately, and for all the wrong reasons, according to my anthropological training. It was warm, green, exotic, and beautiful, and after several months of backpacking in China, it was a relief to feel welcome again. I was struck by the beauty of the country, the endless rice fields, and countless hues of green, the cliffs of Ha Long Bay, the temples and pagodas in the small Red River Delta villages, and the eclectic architecture, lively streets, and colorful markets of Hanoi. I was lucky enough to arrive in Vietnam just before Tet, the Vietnamese New Year Festival, which was one of the loveliest events I had ever witnessed. Above all, I was impressed by the kindness and friendship shown by so many Vietnamese toward a wandering stranger, by their resilience and determination, and last but not least, by their keen sense of humor. The friends I made in Hanoi on that first visit have remained close and significant to this day.

But it was only when I hopped off a 1954-model Renault truck in Hoi An, a small town in Central Vietnam, early in March 1994, that my enchantment and wonder changed to a sense of possible deeper engagement. After exploring the streets of Hoi An's ancient quarter—transported to the Imperial China of my childhood books—and cycling the winding paths of the lush, green delta, which was the most beautiful place I have ever seen, I told my traveling companion, "You know, I am coming back here, to Hoi An, to write a Ph.D. thesis in anthropology." My friend smiled and said, "Sure you will."

That evening, we left the government-run Hoi An Hotel (originally the French governor's mansion, later the headquarters of the U.S. Marines and the only hotel allowed to host foreign guests in the early 1990s), in search of dinner. We walked down the dark empty streets toward the market and ended up in Cafeteria Ly 22, one of the first hole-in-the-wall eating places catering to the few foreign tourists who ventured into town. I ordered *ca xot ca chua* ("fish in tomato sauce") and was served a huge slice of the freshest fish I had ever eaten, seasoned lightly with a sauce made of fresh tomatoes and spices, served with a steaming bowl of rice and a plate of unfamiliar fragrant herbs. It finally dawned on me that Vietnamese cuisine (which was, and still is, virtually unknown in Israel), consisted of much more than the ubiquitous spring rolls, fried rice, and *pho.* This understanding broadened while I traveled down south to Ho Chi Minh City and the Mekong Delta, where I discovered new dishes and tastes on every street corner and a new cuisine in every town.

My first visit to Vietnam lasted three months, and when I returned to Israel I began developing tour programs and led the first Israeli group that traveled beyond Hanoi and Saigon and the first Israeli group ever to visit Hoi An. I also spent a month traveling up and down the country with an Israeli photographer who was putting together an exhibition on Vietnam. These projects further enhanced my interest in the country and its people. Returning to Israel in November 1995 to start graduate studies in anthropology at the Hebrew University of Jerusalem, I was determined to do something in Vietnam, preferably in Hoi An.

My academic interest in food began to take shape while I conducted interviews for a paper on the ways in which Israeli chefs define Israeli food. I was struck by my finding that chefs discussed food in terms of the most pressing sociopolitical problems of Israel: tensions between Jews and Arabs and between Jews of different ethnic, social, and economic backgrounds; conflicts regarding Jewish dietary laws; and even Israeli domestic politics. This research, and my discovery of the anthropological literature on food, coalesced into my decision to work on a culinary ethnography of Hoi An.

My Ph.D. dissertation in anthropology, supervised by Professor Erik Cohen, was followed by postdoctoral research at the Asia Research Institute, National University of Singapore, in 2004 and 2005. In 2006 I joined the newly established Department of Sociology and Anthropology at Ben Gurion University in Israel, where I continue my study of the Hoianese culinary sphere.

When I reflect on the question posed to me several years ago by a friendly woman in New York, who approached me after a lecture and asked: "What's a nice Jewish boy like you doing studying Vietnamese food?" I think I know the answer: as an Israeli, Jewish, Ashkenazi, left-wing humanist (at least, wannabe), married, and a father of three, I find the lively culinary sphere of Hoi An so attractive because it offers hope, optimism, and a promise of peace and gentle, refined cultural pleasures, which are so hard to find in Israel. Vietnam has emerged from more than a century of warfare as a vibrant nation whose citizens are eager to leave behind memories of hardship, sacrifice, scarcity, and hunger and are determined to improve their lot. And though prosperity is as central to the Vietnamese as it is to everyone else, an improved lot for most of my Hoianese friends means that more time and more money can be invested in leisure and fun, with family and friends, in the refined pleasures of *van*—the Confucian notion of culture and cultivation that highlights peaceful, intellectual, and aesthetic activities—and, most significantly, in the sharing of food. In Hoi An, this optimism is expressed and nurtured in the booming culinary sphere and food industry, which feature dishes both familiar and exotic, cheap and expensive, local and imported. While scarcity, poverty, hunger, and the struggle over resources have not disappeared from Hoi An, it is the everyday effort invested in creating and nourishing, rather than denying and destroying, that I find so appealing.

Acknowledgments

How can I thank all those who have helped me along the years with writing this book? I have met with so much good will and generosity, and they made all obstacles and difficulties meaningless.

I am forever indebted to my adviser, mentor, and friend Professor Erik Cohen, who taught me the secrets of the trade, whose door was, and still is, always open, and whose advice is always sound.

My research in Vietnam would not have been possible had I not had the support of Professor Phan Huy Le from the Vietnam National University in Hanoi. I am obliged to the chair and members of the People Committee of Hoi An for bearing with me for so many years. I guess they realize by now that, just like them, I love Hoi An very much.

There would have been no book but for the endless help, support, knowledge and friendship of my Vietnamese teachers Nguyen Tran Thi My Thuy and Ngo Minh Hien who, along with their family members, were extremely generous and incredibly patient. In Vietnam we never forget our teachers.

Mentioning the names of all those Hoianese who kindly shared their food and thoughts with me and my wife, Irit, is impossible. I am especially grateful to my wonderful friend Trinh Diem Vy, her family members, and her employees for taking care of us so well, for always making us feel at home, and for sharing so much good food and so many good ideas with us; to Ngo My Dung and her family members for all the help and for so much fun; and to Le Nguyen Binh and Mai Thi Kim Quyen and their family members for their long-standing friendship. Le Quynh Thi Giang was my first friend in Vietnam and I cherish this friendship.

I am grateful to my parents, Elyakum and Aviva, and to my sisters, Merav and Hila, for their love and for believing in me. My children, Zohar, Gilad, and Noam were born and grew up with this book, whose pages are stained with fish-sauce and milk. It is hardly appropriate to thank someone for what is essentially hers. Irit, this book is yours just as it is mine.

Fieldwork in Vietnam was sponsored by the Schaine Institute and the Truman Institute at the Hebrew University in Jerusalem, by the Asia Research Institute in the National University of Singapore, and by Ben Gurion University. My colleagues in the department of sociology and anthropology at Ben Gurion University, and especially Fran Markowitz, were always willing to discuss my ideas and comment over the chapters. Dayaneetha de Silva did a great job editing the text. Rebecca Tolen and the editorial staff at IUP were professional and helpful throughout the publication process. This book was published with the support of the Israel Science Foundation.

Note on Transliteration

Vietnamese words, phrases and terms are italicized throughout the text.Names of places and of persons are not, so as not to disturb the flow of reading. I have used the Vietnamese mode for writing names of places (that is, each syllable as a word, as in "Hoi An," and not "Hoian"), with the exception of places whose names are internationally well known (e.g., Hanoi or Saigon), where the Vietnamese mode (Ha Noi, Sai Gon) might lead to confusion.

Throughout the chapters, short sections are set off as indented paragraphs. These are descriptions of events that I attempt to present as comprehensively and as vividly as possible, without the interruption of explanations, comments, and interpretations. These texts are not primal excerpts from my field notes but, rather, processed textual units, based on the field notes as well as on the other means of documentation that I used. These descriptive sections are intended to allow readers to get as close as possible to the events and thus to develop their own perceptions, which would enable them to approach my analysis in an informed and critical mode.

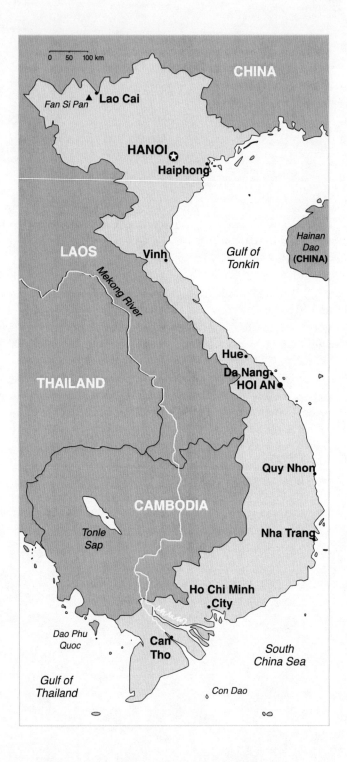

Rice Talks

⚜ Introduction

Breakfast in the small riverside town of Hoi An is never a simple matter, as the choice and variety can seem overwhelming. There's something to suit everyone and every budget, and having breakfast at a street stall is a common way to begin the day. At dawn, hundreds of food stalls come to life, catering to a diverse local clientele, young and old, rushing to work or study. Noodles are popular, mainly *mi quang* ("the province noodles"), *bun* (rice vermicelli), *pho* (Hanoi-style beef noodle soup), *mi ga* (chicken noodle soup), and Chinese *hu tieu* (flat rice noodles). Some prefer to have *banh mi* (Vietnamese baguette) filled with pork *pa te* (paté), "La vache qui rit" cheese spread, peanut butter and sugar, or condensed milk. Baguettes are also served with sizzling fried eggs (*op la*) or with a mild breakfast *ca ri* (curry).

And then there are the steamed rice pancakes with shrimp paste (*banh beo*), glutinous rice garnished with ground peanuts, sugar, meat, and chili paste (*xoi*), and various kinds of rice porridge (*chao*). Some opt for local specialties: crab wontons, "white rose" dumplings, or *cao lau*, Hoi An's own noodle dish. There are vegetarian versions of almost all these dishes, as well as soy or mung-bean milk or strong Vietnamese *ca phe* (coffee), drunk black or white, hot or iced, customarily served along with a glass of green tea.

This list ignores the entire array of special dishes for the tourists who flock to the town now, as well as the freshly baked croissants, sponge cakes, and taro and green bean tartlets, popular with locals and tourists alike—and the roasted sweet potatoes, yams, peanuts, coconut pancakes, and clam porridge (*chao ngeu*), sold to those who exercise on the beach at dawn. The list goes on and on, and this is only breakfast. Lunch, dinner, and snack foods available through the day vary considerably.

While such a culinary range may not seem unusual for someone living in any cosmopolitan city, Hoi An is a provincial town with a permanent population of some 30,000 people, the hub of a rural district of some 70,000 inhabitants, who are mainly rice farmers, fishermen, and laborers with an average daily income of roughly US$2–4.

Beyond culinary variation, sophistication, and ingenuity, these breakfast dishes also convey a sense of the town's history and ethnic composition. They speak of local religious propensities and preferences. They remind us of the Chinese, Cham, Japanese, Indian, and French presence and influence and the repeated waves of internal and external migration. They also express class, gender, and age differences, as well as those of education, income, and status. They suggest spatial orientations, define aspects of the local, regional, and national identities, and hint at political dispositions.

The list of breakfast foods one can have in Hoi An is dynamic and ever-changing. It has expanded to reflect rising incomes and a degree of affluence, and from time to time includes new dishes from other regions of Vietnam and beyond, often fused with local elements into hybrid culinary creations.

WHY HOI AN

One of the main dilemmas in contemporary anthropology concerns the question, "Whom do we study?" Do we follow our totemic ancestors and go to the ends of the earth looking for exotic isolated indigenous peoples, where ethnographers are constantly in awe due to the huge differences between their own culture and the ones they are studying, or do we accept the postmodern premise that everyone is a stranger and, therefore, any social group is a legitimate target for anthropological query, inclusive of the anthropologist's own culture? While the debate continues, in practice there is an increasing inclination toward "homework," that is, toward studying "others" who live among "us" or very close by, or simply even studying "us" ourselves.

While the advantages of research done at home (such as the ethnographer's familiarity with the studied culture, which is far greater than any anthropologist who studies a foreign culture can expect, even if he or she devotes an entire career to this end) are considerable, I have decided to conduct my own research within a place and culture remote and substantially different from my own, opting for what might seem to be a more "traditional" or "classic" approach to anthropology. Even though much of my initial interest in Hoi An had to do with an emotional and aesthetic "Orientalism" (as recounted in the preface), I quickly realized that remoteness and strangeness notwithstanding, Hoi An offers a unique opportunity for conducting an up-to-date and potentially cutting-edge anthropological study of (post)modern life.

Though remote, strange, and, as far as I am concerned, exotic, Hoi An and its dwellers are anything but "simple," "pure," "uncorrupted by foreign influence," "frozen in time" or any other description that early anthropologists or tourist brochures might have attributed to it. Hoi An and its predecessor communities were a regional hub for international maritime trade and migration for at least two millennia. They experienced constant intercultural interaction and exchange, and were transformed time and again by what we now term globalization and hybridization of the kind we rarely attribute to provincial towns in less developed economies.

And even though time–space compression, the presumed prerequisite for hypermodernity and for the so-called "condition of postmodernity" (Harvey 1989), has reached Hoi An only recently and only to a certain extent, the notion of "liquid" social spaces, coined by postmodernist guru Bauman (2000), seems to be compatible with the social and cultural features of this town. The postmodern stress on consumerism and economic activities as the main venue for producing and reproducing identities is also well suited to addressing the centrality of trade and the entrepreneurial spirit that have characterized this town for thousands of years. Hoi An, then, seems to have had "postmodern" qualities long before the term was conceived. Put differently, Hoi An does not only accommodate postmodern questions but, in some sense, challenges postmodernism's presumptuousness by suggesting that there is nothing revolutionary about it.

In short, doing research in Hoi An meant that I could ask the most up-to-date anthropological questions while studying a culture that was very different from mine in Israel, enjoying the benefits of being a stranger while pursuing issues that are as important in Hoi An as they are in my own society or in societies that are deemed more modern and developed than both Vietnam and Israel.

THE SETTING

Hoi An sits in a small, lush river delta, some 30 km south of the city of Danang and 5 km west of the beach in the central Vietnamese province of Quang Nam. The Thu Bon River emerges from the Central Highlands near Dien Ban District and winds its way to the sea, making up the main artery of a maze of streams, ponds, and irrigation canals that form its tiny delta. Six large islets are part of the silting river, and a narrow lagoon separates the beach from the inland fields.

Hoi An District includes the town, composed of the neighborhoods of Cam Pho, Minh An, Son Phong, the new neighborhood of Tan An (established in 2006), and six villages: Cam (islet) Thanh, Cam Chau, Cam Ha, Cam An, Cam Nam, and Cam Kim. The tiny Cham Archipelago nearby is also administered by the Hoi An People's Committee. In 2000 the total population was 80,000, of which only 20,000 were classified as town dwellers. In 2007, following administrative reorganization, the urban population rose to 60,000, while 25,000 were classified as rural dwellers.[1] Significantly, it was estimated in 2007 that there were some 35,000 "nonregistered" residents[2] from neighboring districts and provinces living in Hoi An and working in the booming tourism industry.

The town and villages are interlinked in a socioeconomic system of reciprocity. Cam Ha is known as the "pottery village" due to its numerous kilns, where, until recently, bricks, tiles, and home utensils were produced for the rest of the district. Kim Bong (Cam Kim) is famous for its carpentry, as it produces fishing boats, wood carvings, and furniture for townsfolk and better-off farmers. Cam Thanh, near the estuary, features extensive shrimp farms as well as

FIGURE 0.1. Signboard showing map of Hoi An's ancient quarter.

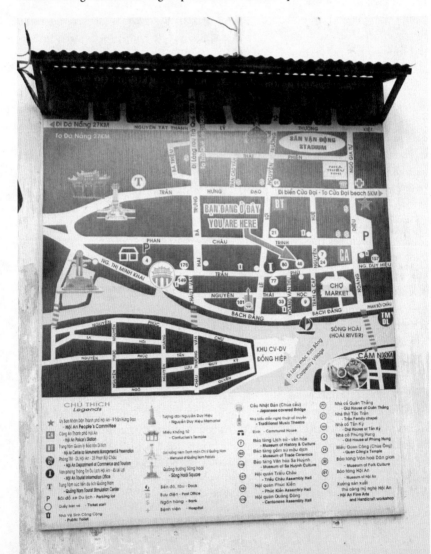

dua nuoc (water-coconut or nipa palm) plantations, which thrive in the marshes there. Nipa palms make for superior thatching material in comparison to the coconut palm and are used mostly by the poorer dwellers of the district to build roofs and walls. The hamlet of Tra Que (in Cam An village) specializes in intensive farming of high-quality, cinnamon-scented greens and vegetables, which are fertilized with marsh weed compost.[3]

Apart from the fishing and tourist-oriented Cam An, all the villages grow rice as their main agricultural product, supplemented with fishing and aquaculture. There are duck farms near the ponds, reservoirs, and irrigation canals, as well as lucrative areca palm gardens, which provide the essential component of the mildly narcotic betel quid, harvested mainly for export to China and Taiwan. Other cash crops include kumquat bushes (potted for sale during Tet, the Vietnamese New Year) and flowers for various ritual purposes. Since 2007, some farmers have also been growing turf grass for the lawns of the numerous hotels and tourism projects.

Most rural families farm corn, beans, sweet potatoes, and cassava in small garden plots, and raise pigs, chickens, and cows. Many farmers own water buffalos, which are indispensable for rice farming. Though machines are sometimes used, most rice cultivation is still powered by these gentle bovines whose enormous grey bodies dot the rural landscape. Each village has its own small daily market for fresh produce, dried food, and domestic wares. Larger transactions, and most importantly, wholesale fish and rice marketing, take place at Hoi An's central market.

The ancient quarter, Minh An, most of which was designated as a UNESCO World Heritage site in 2000,[4] stretches between the river and Phan Chu Trinh Street and includes the central market. Due to the strict conservation rules for World Heritage sites and soaring real estate prices, this part of town is gradually being deserted by its original dwellers, who turn their homes into tourist-oriented souvenir shops, tailor shops, art galleries, or restaurants, or who sell them to entrepreneurs from the town and elsewhere in Vietnam. The neighborhoods of Cam Pho and Son Phong are both semi-rural, though this situation is quickly changing as smaller houses are torn down and are being replaced by larger, often commercially oriented town houses.

To ease some of the increasing pressure on the ancient quarter's infrastructure, the northern extension of Nhi Trung Street and its vicinity were designated as a new tourism development zone. In the early years of the twenty-first century, this part of town became a fashionable neighborhood for the emerging middle class, with many former Min Anh families who had been making a living from tourism moving out into huge new houses that often accommodated extensions or replacements of their original businesses. A very large tract

of sand dunes beyond Cam Pho was also designated for suburban development, and extensive building of more modest private houses began in 2000.

Tran Phu Street, the hub of the ancient quarter, was built along the Thu Bon
River by Chinese immigrants. The five Chinese community halls, as well as the
"All-Chinese Community Hall," are therefore located at the northern side of
the street, which used to face the river. The Japanese quarter, linked by the
"Japanese Bridge," stretched beyond Hoi An stream, a channel of the Thu Bon
River, around present-day Nguyen Thi Minh Khai Street. The "Japanese
Bridge" or *chua cau* ("temple bridge," because it houses the god of storms), is
the official symbol of Hoi An.

As the river silted, the ancient quarter gradually expanded southward and is
now composed of three streets: Tran Phu, the original river-facing street;
Nguyen Thai Hoc; and Bach Dang. The central market is located at the eastern
end of the old town, just below Quang Cong Temple (Chua Ong), and is clearly
the pulsating heart of town. Plans to move the market out of town were can-
celed and a new two-story market was built in 2008 next to the old one. The
"government complex" comprising the People's Committee building, hospital,
central police station, post office, and bank are located to the north of the market, just beyond the ancient quarter.

A HISTORY OF MULTICULTURALISM, GLOBAL TRADE, AND ENTREPRENEURSHIP

Archaeological remains in the Hoi An area indicate that its inhabitants were
members of the prehistoric Sa Huynh culture,[5] contemporaneous with the
Dong Son culture of the Red River Delta (Nguyen, K.V. 1993: 14). Like Dong
Son, Sa Huynh was part of a wider Southeast Asian trading and cultural net-
work that expanded to Laos, Thailand, the Philippines, and Indonesia.

The Malay-Polynesian Cham had a significant influence in the Hoi An area.
They set up Indic principalities[6] between the first to sixth centuries along the
coast of central Vietnam (Wheeler 2006a; Chandler 1993: 14), which eventually
coalesced into the Kingdom of Champa. The Kingdom's capital was established
at Simhapura, present-day Tra Kieu, just 30 km upriver from Hoi An. Its religious center, the great temple complex of My Son, dedicated to the Cham kings
as incarnates of the Hindu deity Shiva, was built further along the river. In its
heyday, Champa prospered through international trade in eaglewood, minerals, spices, and jungle products (Nguyen, V. X. 1998: 5; Hoang and Lam 1993: 69;
Burns and Brown 1993: 65–66; Nguyen, K.V. 1993: 113). Hoi An was built in the
vicinity of the great Cham port, Cua Dai Chiem, on the estuary of the Thu Bon
River. The Cham also introduced significant agricultural advances: specifi-

FIGURE 0.2. The Japanese Bridge over Hoi An stream.

cally, a superior hydraulic system and a revolutionary rice variety that matured in three months, which the Chinese obtained and subsequently adopted in all their southern provinces, which then included the Red River Delta (Nguyen, K. V. 1993: 113).

While relations between the Cham and indigenous Vietnamese were characterized by intermittent territorial skirmishes, both were held at bay by their powerful respective neighbors: the Chinese and the Khmer. Only in the aftermath of the Mongol conquest of China—and their subsequent failure to reconquer the Red River Delta—were the Vietnamese able to seriously attempt to take over the central coastal plains (Keyes 1977: 183). When the Cham Empire eventually collapsed in 1471, the area was taken over by Dai Co Viet (the Great Viet Kingdom) emperor, Le Loi.

As with many details of Cham history, controversies remain about whether the Cham were decimated, dispersed, or displaced (Wheeler 2006a). In any case, the triumphant Vietnamese who had occupied lands south of the Hai Van Pass since the beginning of the seventeenth century set about creating "a brave new *Kinh* [ethnic Vietnamese] world" (ibid.). Charles Wheeler, in his historiography of Hoi An, suggests a multidirectional process of assimilation, whereby Cham and Kinh cultures were fused into a hybrid entity: while the Cham elite was possibly decimated (or deported; see Taylor 2007), the local population was mostly unharmed and the Cham gradually intermarried with the new Kinh settlers (Keyes 1977: 183; Wheeler 200ba). Many cultural differences between the North, Center, and South of Vietnam can be explained by variations in this intermingling of Kinh, Cham, and Khmer (Keyes 1977: 184; Taylor 2007).

Wheeler (2006a) argues that the Cham were not deported wholesale, mainly because the Vietnamese still needed them to develop Hoi An as a trading port. It should be noted, however, that Hoi An's prosperity came from exporting its land and sea produce just as much as from international trade (ibid.). Here again, it is the commercial spirit of the town that seems to have prevailed as the main thread of continuity in a constantly changing polity and society.

The next phase of Hoi An's history was marked by its rise in importance as an entrêpot. During the sixteenth and seventeenth centuries, tensions between Ming China and Japan led to the banning of direct trade between the two countries. Commerce continued, however, via "free-trade" ports set up in several neutral locations along the Southeast Asian coast, where Chinese merchants could trade indirectly with the Japanese (Nguyen, V. X. 1998: 7). In the early decades of the seventeenth century, the Nguyen lords who ruled the center and south of the country reestablished Hoi An as a major entrepôt (ibid.; Nguyen, D. D. 1993: 117) frequented by Chinese, Japanese, and Portuguese (and later Dutch, English, and French) merchants.

The Chinese and Japanese traders became ever more involved in Hoi An's economy, partly because they had to stay for a few months each year to wait for the trade winds to change direction and carry them home. In time, these traders built warehouses, installed permanent representatives, and built shop houses (for which the town is famous). They also married local women and settled down. Most prominent were the southeastern Chinese traders, who established five communities and built a market and a Chinese community hall (Nguyen, D. D. 1993: 118). The Japanese created their own quarter across Hoi An Stream and in 1639 linked it to town with the Japanese Bridge (Nguyen, V. X. 1998: 13).

By the early seventeenth century, Hoi An had two trading streets (*pho khach* or "guest streets"): Chinese and Japanese. The town was referred to in Vietnamese as *Hai Pho*—"two trading [*hai*] streets [*pho*]," or, possibly, "the street [*pho*] by the sea [*hai*]." This name probably led the French to name the town *Faifo*, which was replaced by the original name "Hoi An" only after national reunification in 1975.[7]

Thus Hoi An was cosmopolitan from its inception; indeed, the town displayed its propensity for incubating innovation and hybridization when Alexander de Rhodes, a Jesuit who lived there between 1624 and 1627 and who compiled the first Vietnamese–Portuguese–Latin lexicon, developed *quoc ngu*, the romanized national script, into a usable means of communication. Hoi An was not only de Rhodes's point of entry into the country, but was also where he himself, like many other foreigners, first encountered the Vietnamese language and culture.[8]

Another important wave of southern Chinese immigrants arrived during the second half of the seventeenth century, with the collapse of the Ming Dynasty (Hucker 1978: 147–51). These were Ming loyalists who refused to accept the rule of the Manchu Qing, left by boats, and spread throughout the trading ports of Southeast Asia. In Hoi An they were referred to as *Minh huong* (Ming worshipers), and later on, as *Minh an* (the pacified Ming), which reflected their changing status from refugees loyal to a deposed monarch, to a localized and assimilated group. Most of the streets and houses in the ancient quarter (*pho co*), were built by these newcomers and their descendants, who also renewed and expanded their community halls. Thus, Hoi An is one of the few places in the world where Southern Ming architecture can still be found not only intact but also continuously inhabited, which is the major reason that the ancient quarter was awarded its UNESCO World Heritage status.

Hoi An declined in the nineteenth and twentieth centuries. Many traders left for the newly established Nguyen capital of Phu Xuan (Hue), while the French conquest of the South attracted many wealthy Chinese traders down to Saigon. Moreover, the new larger trading ships could hardly navigate the shallow Hoi An River, and the French developed the new deep water port of Tourane (Danang), 30 km to the north of Hoi An. When extensive logging upriver led to siltation and further restricted maritime trade, Hoi An ceased to be an entrepôt and reverted to a prosperous market town.

Marginal to the political struggles of the twentieth century, Hoi An was somehow spared the worst horrors of the Indochinese wars. There was a small French settlement in the vicinity of Hoi An Hotel and People's Park, and a cathedral was built in that area for French and Vietnamese Catholics.[9] During the American War (as it is called in Vietnam), the town itself was controlled by the Army of the Republic of Vietnam (ARVN) and a small American garrison (whose decaying fortifications can still be seen in Cua Dai Street). The town's male population was conscripted, willingly or unwillingly, to the ARVN. However, the countryside—and the nights—were controlled by the National Front for the Liberation of Vietnam (NLF, or Viet Cong), who were hiding in the mangroves around the estuary, enthusiastically supported by impoverished farmers and fishermen. Several people recounted the night of the Tet Offensive of 1968, when what they first thought were the customary very loud New Year firecrackers turned out to be gunshots, as countryside refugees swarmed into town and many people were massacred.[10]

In the aftermath of the war, after reunification in 1975, Hoi An suffered its greatest decline. The anti-Confucian and anti-Chinese campaigns targeted the Hoianese Chinese, even though their families had been in Vietnam for hundreds of years and had no real ties with China. The policy of radical collectivization further devastated trade and commerce. As Hoi An was a market town, the cessation of trade was a deadly blow to the local economy, and caused widespread poverty and unemployment. I was also told of political persecution, inseparably mixed with personal vendettas, greed, and corruption. The result was an exodus of "boat people," who chanced the rough South China Sea to seek refuge in other countries. Indeed, almost everyone living in the ancient quarter, who were targeted as "Chinese" and/or as rich traders, has relatives in *Ca Li* (California) today.

My Hoianese friends[11] recalled that by the late 1980s, Hoi An was "a dead place." There was no work and no future and the young people wanted only one thing: to escape. Yet this period was also described by some as a time of blissful innocence: ". . . everyone was poor, and no-one even bothered to lock their doors. . . . [on] hot summer nights, everyone would sleep on the sidewalks, to get some fresh air, as there was no regular electric supply, nor money to buy electric fans. There were no tourists, no shops, no restaurants or cafés, no motorized vehicles and no TVs, but people were more relaxed and friendly." Even the pervasive hunger under the strictures of collectivization is tinged with nostalgia: one resident recalled diving under a flock of ducks swimming in the river, tying a brick to a duck's leg and returning at night to pick up the drowned bird for a secret family feast.

By the early 1990s, *doi moi* (economic renovation policy), had reached the town. Since then, Hoi An has experienced another glorious renewal thanks to tourism. First "discovered" by Western backpackers, Hoi An has become one of Vietnam's key tourist attractions. The town received some 660,000 tourists in the first four months of 2005, of which some 150,000 were foreign, a 70 percent increase from 2004 (Ngoc 2005). Local officials told me that there had been 800,000 visitors in 2006, 50 percent of whom were foreign, and that the target for 2007 was to double the numbers. Even allowing for some doubts about the accuracy of these statistics, these numbers are indicative of the huge and ever expanding volume of visitors.

Indeed, tourism in Hoi An has acquired a life of its own, radically changing its economy, daily life, and, most pertinent to our enquiry, culinary sphere. The ancient quarter is overwhelmingly tourist-oriented: there are art galleries, wood-carving workshops, "traditional" ceramics, antiques, and souvenir shops, with merchandise and artisans from all over the country (often presented as local). A booming industry is tailoring: there are literally hundreds[12] of small shops that offer to sew up anything and everything quickly and cheaply. Another recent product are the ubiquitous "Chinese lanterns," now handcrafted by dozens of families, who present themselves as "traditional lantern producers of Chinese origins." These lanterns are churned out in huge numbers, shapes, and colors, and also are sold elsewhere in Vietnam and around the world.

Tourist accommodation was dominated by the monopolistic government-run Hoi An Hotel until the mid-1990s. When I arrived in October 1999, there were sixteen hotels and mini-hotels, and when I left twelve months later there were more than twenty-five, including three seaside resorts. By 2007 there were seventy-eight hotels, with some three thousand rooms, and more under construction.

Food outlets have also changed radically: the few pre-1975 restaurants and cafés were replaced by a government canteen and an empty market during the collectivization period. These gradually gave way to a huge number of restaurants and eating venues. In 1994, there were fewer than a dozen tourist-oriented restaurants in Hoi An and several noodle shops and other food stalls and cafés catering to the locals. In 1999, there were more than sixty tourist-oriented restaurants, four bars, dozens of cafés, and more than one hundred food stalls of all sorts. In 2007 it was estimated that there were more than two hundred tourist-oriented restaurants, as well as hundreds of eating establishments of different kinds that catered mainly to the locals and Vietnamese tourists. In 2007, there were some ten markets in the entire district, with the lively central market boasting the biggest fish trading volume in the region.

This huge food industry caters to an ever-increasing influx of tourists and visitors: initially *tay* (Western)[13] backpackers, followed by other Westerners on adventurous package tours of Vietnam. But with the development of facilities, up-market companies routinely include Hoi An in their itineraries today. The weekly stopover of a Malaysian luxury cruise ship, for instance, floods the town with hundreds of Southeast Asian day-trippers, who are processed through the town's wonders, shops, and restaurants. The bulk of visitors, however, are the ever-increasing number of domestic Vietnamese tourists who are especially keen on sampling the town's *dac san* (culinary specialties).

The deluge of tourists has led to unprecedented prosperity, and many Hoianese have enlarged their houses, built new ones, established new businesses and shops, and purchased an increasing range of consumer goods.

FIGURE 0.3. Early morning scene at Hoi An's central market on
the Thu Bon River viewed from Cam Nam bridge; on the right
are fisherfolk selling their catch directly to fishmongers.

While in 2000 one of my more knowledgeable acquaintances suggested that
"though only some 10 percent of the Hoianese are directly involved with tourism, 90 percent are affected by tourism economically," in 2007 a local government official pointed out that "85 percent of the local economy is directly
linked to tourism." A friend pointed out that Hoi An's mayor recently refused
the position of vice-chairman of Quang Nam Province, "as Hoi An is clearly
the richest and most important town in the province, and its mayor has a lot of
power."

Hoi An is by no means in an isolated cultural bubble, nor is it some remnant
of the past, as it is sometimes depicted in tourist brochures. Hoi An always was,
and still is, a place where people, artifacts, and goods from all over the world
come together, where ideas are exchanged, and where cultural fusion and innovation take place. Indeed, the name "Hoi An" (peaceful congregation)[14] reflects a social sphere where Vietnamese, Chinese, and others have managed to

live together peacefully for centuries and to produce a remarkable and distinguished local culture.

All in all, Hoi An has unique qualities that made it an ideal site for my fieldwork on the most pressing issues in contemporary anthropology in a setting small enough to allow for a deep and intimate familiarity.

TOWARD A DYNAMIC ANTHROPOLOGY OF FOOD

I began my fieldwork in Hoi An more than a decade ago, assuming that the culinary sphere was akin to a mirror of culture. Conceiving of the culinary sphere as reflecting "other things" (such as religion, kinship, ethnicity, or gender) has a long tradition in anthropology. Early functionalists such as Durkheim (1915), Mauss (2005 [1925]), or Frazer (1963 [1922]) conceived of festive meals as expressions of the relations between people and their gods and between the living and the dead, while later functionalists (Malinowski 1935; Richards 2004 [1932], 1937, 1939; Radcliffe-Brown 1922; Evans-Pritchard 1982) pointed out that food practices reflect relations among the living members of society. Structural anthropologists (Levi-Strauss 1966, 1970, 1973, 1987; Douglas 1966, 1975, 1984; Tambiah 1969; Sahlins 1976, 1982; Barthes 1998), despite their pronounced attention to the culinary sphere, perceived foodways as mere reflections of the basic human patterns of thought and behavior in which they were actually interested. Food and foodways were, and still are, treated by many anthropologists as Geertzian "*models of*" artifacts and events "manipulated so as to reflect reality" (Geertz 1973: 8), miniature and schematic replicas of the "real world."

As my fieldwork evolved, however, the culinary sphere emerged in its own right as an arena in which cultural production was taking place. Indeed, the post-structural emphasis on agency and praxis explains much of the emerging anthropological interest in this sphere. As the anthropology of food was gradually acknowledged and "legitimized" (Mintz and Du Bois 2002; Watson and Caldwell 2005; Holtzman 2006), increasing attention was paid to the generative capacities of the culinary sphere. Culinary systems and practices were gradually recognized as arenas and processes that produce culture (Goody 1982; Mennell 1985 and 1989; Mintz 1985) and where differing ideas and ideologies evolve (Ohnuki-Tiernei 1993, 1995; Watson 1997; Caplan 1997; Counihan 1999, 2004; Ashkenazi and Jacob 2000; Sutton 2001; Scholliers 2001; Wilson 2006). Cooking and eating are treated at times as Geertzian "*models for*" symbolic systems "under whose guidance physical relationships are organized" (Geertz 1966: 8), practical attempts at manipulating, affecting, recreating, and changing the "real world."

But when I realized that even this paradigm was not complex or dynamic enough to deal effectively with issues that arose from my fieldwork on Hoi An's foodways, I turned to Handelman's (1998) scheme of "models, mirrors and re-presentations," devised for the analysis of public rituals. Handelman argues against the tendency of many anthropologists (especially Clifford Geertz), to view all ritual performances as texts or narratives that reflect the prevailing social reality (ibid. xvii–xviii) and makes useful distinctions among three kinds of public events: "events-that-model," "events-that-mirror," and "events-that-re-present."

Events-that-model (*models*) are intended to act upon the social world and transform it. A "model" is "a *microcosm* of the lived-in world—a simplified specialized closed system that operates in parallel with the indeterminate world that it models" (ibid. xxii, original emphasis), and which "regenerate[s] a healed self, a new social being, a rejuvenated community" (Handelman 1997: 387). Models "contract the lived-in world in order to give causal shape to certain of the world potentialities, while excluding others" (Handelman 1998: xxiv), while "[t]he world is altered radically within the model, to enable determinate transformation" (ibid. xxii).

In contrast, events-that-mirror (*mirrors*) "present the lived-in world" as it is and serve as "statements, mirror-images [and] reflections" (ibid. 41) of the fundamental characteristics of the existing social order (Cohen 2001). *Mirrors* say: "Look, this is how things should be, this is the proper, ideal pattern of social life" (Skorupski 1976: 164, quoted in Handelman 1998: 44).

Handelman defines yet a third type of public event: "events-that-re-present" (and note the hyphen, distinguishing *re-presentations* from "representations," which are essentially "mirrors"). While *mirrors* reflect the social reality and *models* are intended to transform it, *re-presentations* "do the work of comparison and contrast in relation to social realities . . . rais[ing] possibilities, questions, perhaps doubts, about the legitimacy or validity of social forms, as these are constituted within the lived-in world . . . whether through the juxtaposition and conflict of contraries, through the neutralization of accepted distinctions, or through their inversion, the more hidden or controversial implications of the prepositional character of the world are exposed" (ibid. 49). *Re-presentations* question the existing social order, challenge it, and negotiate it by outlining and enacting alternatives.

Re-presentations, whether in the form of inversions, juxtapositions, or their neutralization, do not discard the existing social order, nor are they aimed at transforming it. In fact, they have no material effect on the lived-in world and their outcome is actually "the reaffirmation of norm and custom" (ibid. 57). While "models" are explicitly aimed at changing the lived-in world, "re-presentations" do the opposite: by allowing for the expression of doubts, challenges, and alternatives, they release social pressures and ensure social stability and cultural continuity.

Contemporary food anthropology seems to be all about *re-presentations:* by showing how different facets of identity are negotiated and reconstructed through culinary choices and eating preferences, they highlight food's ability to bear multiple and even contrasting meanings, and by stressing fluidity and change, they convey a sense of instability and dynamism (Belasco and Scranton 2002; Lien and Nerlich 2004; Watson and Caldwell 2005). Ethnographies such as those of Rasmussen (1996), Counihan (1999, 2004); Cusack (2000); Pilcher (1998, 2001); Poe (2001); or Howell (2003) demonstrate how continual processes of interpretation, negotiation, and reinterpretation attribute different and even opposing meanings to food, even when it comes to a single dish shared by several diners (cf. Appadurai 1988; Noguchi 1994, Narayan 1997; Wu and Tan 2001; Cheung and Tan 2007). In this book I use Handelman's paradigm as a launching point for a dynamic anthropology of food. I apply "models, mirrors and re-presentations" to define the questions that underlie my research: How do food and foodways reflect the social order and cultural arrangements of the Hoianese, and how do they reproduce, help negotiate, or alter them? I further use this paradigm in order to make sense of the foodways and food events that I document in Hoi An and argue that this scheme defines a culinary sphere within which food and eating partake in processes of cultural production, reproduction, and negotiation.

THE OUTLINE OF THE BOOK

Rice Talks is composed of seven chapters. The first three deal with home-eaten meals, daily culinary practices, and everyday dishes. These are followed by four chapters that center on festive eating and extraordinary food events. The culinary sphere of Hoi An is therefore presented from its most private manifestations all the way to the most public ones; from its daily and mundane dimensions to the unique and extraordinary, and from profane moments to the most sacred.

The first chapter, "Deciphering the Hoianese Meal," features the basic structure of the Hoianese daily, home-eaten meal. My analysis links it to the Vietnamese cosmological principles of *am* and *duong* (*yin* and *yang*) and the theory of the "five elements," suggesting that the home-eaten meal is a model of the cosmos. The chapter emphasizes the ecological and nutritional foundations of Hoianese foodways and lays the material foundation for the rest of the book. The second chapter, "The Social Dynamics of the Home Meal," concerns the dynamics of the home meal and focuses on preparation, presentation, and consumption. The emphasis here is on the Vietnamese social structure, mirroring the priority of the collective over the individual and pointing to the prominence of age and gender hierarchies. Domestic foodways are also shown to accommodate contradictory and even subversive individualistic expressions. The culinary arena is never simple; in certain instances modern ideas challenge the traditional social order. The third chapter, "Local Specialties, Local Identity," opens the discussion of the culinary politics of identity.

Chapters 4 through 7 are dedicated to feasts and their meanings. I show that the meals in such events are organized according to a single "culinary scenario": a general formula that arranges the structure and content of all Hoianese feasts and defines their meaning. I also point to culinary nuances: slight modifications in the culinary scenario that express specific, context-dependent cosmological and social ideas.

In the fourth chapter, "Feasting with the Dead and the Living," I look at the feasts offered at ancestor-worship ceremonies and suggest that these communal meals create, organize, and maintain the relations between the dead and the living and among the living themselves. The fifth chapter, "Wedding Feasts: From Culinary Scenarios to Gastro-anomie," is dedicated to wedding feasts, and I emphasize the ambivalent role of festive food as facilitating both social cohesion and social competition. I suggest that due to this ambivalence, wedding feasts sometimes become events where the social order and prevailing norms are explicitly challenged and where new norms and values are initiated.

The sixth chapter, "Food and Identity in Hoianese Community Festivals," discusses the meals served at the annual gatherings of different communities in Hoi An. The varying dishes hint at the specific qualities, tendencies, and wishes of each community, while the magnitude of the feast is shown to indicate the relative cohesion and vitality of the group. In the seventh chapter, "Rice Cakes and Candied Oranges: Culinary Symbolism in the Big Vietnamese Festivals," I turn to the special dishes that are prepared for the most important events celebrated throughout the country. This chapter focuses on the meanings of "iconic" festive dishes, which I conceive of as "key symbols" that express some of the most fundamental Vietnamese values and concerns. Such iconic dishes are also shown to express local and contemporary ideas that often challenge the explicit national(istic) message. I suggest that these dishes have an important role in concretizing the abstract and imagined notion of "the nation."

In the concluding chapter, titled "Food and Culture—Interconnections," I return to the issues and questions outlined at the beginning of this enquiry, first pointing to the ways in which the foodways of Hoi An serve as *models, mirrors* and/or *re-presentations* in different instances and contexts. I then suggest that due to several specific qualities of food, the culinary sphere is especially susceptible to processes of cultural and social negotiation, contest, and experimentation.

Finally, the book contains an epilogue that details the pleasures and perils of food-oriented anthropological fieldwork in Hoi An. This is largely a methodological chapter, dealing with fieldwork practices and dilemmas. But the purpose of this chapter is to reflect further on my experiences of studying the Hoianese and their food and practicing/experiencing anthropology in Hoi An.

1 ～ Deciphering the Hoianese Meal

It was 11:30 AM and Quynh said that lunch was ready. We sat on wooden stools around the circular table: Quynh, her husband Anh, his mother, sister, Irit (my wife), and I. The dishes were already on the table: a small plate with three or four small fish in a watery red gravy seasoned with fresh coriander, a bowl of morning-glory soup *(canh rau muong)* with a few dried shrimp, and a mixed plate of lettuce and herbs. There was also a bowl of *nuoc mam cham* (fish sauce diluted with water and lime juice, seasoned with sugar, fresh ginger, and chili). An electric rice-cooker stood on a stool by the table. We each had a ceramic bowl and a pair of ivory-colored plastic chopsticks.

Anh's mother sat next to the rice cooker, and as we handed her our rice bowls in turn, she filled them to the brim with steaming rice with a flat plastic serving spoon. I asked Quynh what we were going to eat. Quynh pointed at the dishes: "*com* [steamed rice], *rau* [(fresh)] greens], *canh* [soup], *kho* ['dry,' indicating the fish]." Then she pointed to the bowl of fish sauce, adding "and *nuoc mam.*"

THE BASIC STRUCTURE OF THE HOIANESE HOME MEAL

The basic structure of the Hoianese meal is that of a dyad: steamed rice (*com*), served with an array of side dishes: *mon an,* literally "things [to] eat." This structure is similar to that of the Chinese meal (Chang 1977: 7): a combination of *fan* (steamed rice) and *tsai* (side dishes; literally "vegetables"). While steamed rice is the basis of the meal, *mon an* are of a more varied and dynamic nature. Distinct from the Chinese *tsai,* usually made of vegetables, soy products, and/or small quantities of the flesh of domesticated animals, Hoianese *mon an* consist of raw and cooked vegetables and a small amount of animal protein, usually fish.

TABLE 1.1. The "twofold-turned-fivefold" structure of the Hoianese daily meal

RICE			"THINGS TO EAT"	
Rice	Soup	Greens	"Dry" dish	Fish sauce

Mon an are not prepared arbitrarily, but adhere to the four categories mentioned by Quynh: *rau*—raw greens, *canh*—boiled soup, and *kho*—the "dry" dish (fried, stir-fried, cooked in sauce, or grilled), which are always accompanied by *nuoc mam* (fermented fish sauce). The outcome is more complex than a simple dyad of rice and "things to eat"; in fact, it falls into five categories: steamed rice, raw greens, boiled soup, fried/grilled/cooked dishes, and fermented fish sauce (see also Krowolski and Nguyen 1997: 154).

The basic structure of the Hoianese home-eaten meal is therefore that of a dyad of rice and "things to eat," which further develops into a five-fold structure encompassing five levels of transformation of edible ingredients into food: raw, steamed, boiled, fried/grilled, and fermented. Table 1.1 shows a schematic representation of this idea of a "twofold-turned-fivefold" structure.

It is important to note that this "twofold-turned-fivefold" structure is not a rigid cultural matrix but, rather, a Weberian ideal type. Ashkenazi and Jacob suggest that such basic meal structures should be viewed as "schemes" for a meal "which individuals may or may not follow, but which most will recognize and acknowledge as a representation of the ways things should be" (2000: 67). This reservation is important: though Hoianese home-eaten meals routinely adhere in one way or another to the structure outlined above, in practice, there are innumerable permutations and combinations.

Exposing the basic structure of the Hoianese meal in this way barely exhausts the process of "deciphering" its meanings. A fundamental shortcoming of any structural analysis of food lies in its disregard for material and nutritional constraints (Harris 1987: 9). Therefore, I first return to the basic ingredients and dishes that constitute the meal: rice, fish, and greens, and show how they conjure into a solid nutritional logic, which in turn is embedded in the Vietnamese and, specifically, Hoianese, ecology. This materialistic contextualization does not undermine the structural analysis but rather expands and supports it, moving the structure from the thin air of theoretical speculation to the firmer ground of material considerations. As we shall see, this grounding adds new dimensions to our practical and cultural understanding of the meaning of the Hoianese meal.

Com (Rice)

"Would you like to come and have lunch at my house?" asked Huong, a salesgirl in one of the clothing shops, with whom we had been chatting for a while. I looked at Irit and following our working rule of "accepting any invitation," I said, "Sure, why not!"

It was a sunny and cool December morning in 1999, following almost two months of nonstop rain and a couple of devastating floods. The sun sparkled in the puddles and warmed the mold-blackened walls of the houses in the ancient town. Women were hanging sleeping mats and quilts over their front fences and some elderly men were sitting basking in the sun in front of their houses after the long spell of wet and cold weather. We followed Huong's bike toward the little market near the Cao Dai temple and turned into a paved alley that soon became a sandy path ending abruptly in front of a gate. "This is my house!" Huong exclaimed proudly, pushing her bike through the gate and into the yard.

The small, pale blue house looked surprisingly new. Huong invited us into the front room and offered us green tea. She told us that her parents had left the country several years ago and had settled in the United States. Huong and her brother, both over eighteen at the time, were not eligible for "repatriation" (to the United States), and had had to stay behind. Huong was waiting for her parents to arrange for her immigration papers while her younger brother was about to marry his Hoianese girlfriend and was planning to stay in Hoi An. The newly built house, with its ceramic tiled floor, new wooden furniture, and double-burner gas stove, had been financed by their parents. We browsed through some photo albums, sipping tea and chatting. Shortly before 11:30 AM, Huong said that it was time for lunch and went to the kitchen. I followed her to see how a "real lunch" is prepared.

In the small kitchen, the brother's fiancée was sorting some fresh greens. Rice was ready, steaming in an electric rice cooker. On the gas stove there were two tiny pots, one with a couple of finger-sized fish simmering in a fragrant yellow sauce, and the other with a single chicken drumstick, chopped into three or four morsels, cooking in a brown sauce. There was nothing else. "Is this all the food for lunch for the three of you?" I asked Huong, feeling surprised and embarrassed. "Yes," she replied.

I returned to the main room and told Irit in Hebrew that there was very little food in the house, certainly not enough for guests, and that we shouldn't stay and eat the little they had. We apologized and said that we hadn't noticed how late it was and that we had to leave right away. Huong seemed somewhat surprised for a moment, but then walked us to the gate and said goodbye. She didn't look angry or offended, so I thought that she was relieved when we left, as she had avoided the humiliation of offering us the meager meal.

That afternoon, we recounted this incident during our daily Vietnamese lesson. I remarked that the house didn't look poor at all, so I couldn't understand why this family was living in such deprivation, with three working adults having to share two sardines and one drumstick for lunch. Our teacher, *Co* (miss/teacher) Nguyet, looked puzzled for a while and finally asked: "Why do you think that this was a small lunch? Didn't they have a whole pot of rice?"

Rice is the single most important food item in the Hoianese diet. When I asked a definition of the most meager diet that could sustain a human being, I was told that boiled rice with some salt "can keep a person alive." Rice is the main source of calories and nutrients and constitutes the bulk of a meal. In a survey of the eating patterns that I conducted in 2000, the ten families who reported daily for six months on their eating practices had steamed rice (*com*) or rice noodles (*bun*) twice daily (for lunch and dinner), six to seven days a week. In addition, most of their breakfast items (noodles, porridge, pancakes) as well as other dishes and snacks consumed in the course of the day (sweetmeats, crackers, etc.), were made of rice or rice flour.

Cultivating rice is the single-most-common activity in Vietnam (Nguyen, V. H. 1995: 218). Some 80 percent of the population lives in the countryside and roughly 80–90 percent farm rice. The rural landscape shows endless green expanses of rice fields. Though on average roughly 125 days per year are spent directly on rice production (Nguyen, D. N. 1993: 316), most other rural activities revolve around the exploitation of rice by-products (Jamieson 1995: 34) and/or in overcoming its nutritional deficiencies: peanuts, beans, and coconuts are cultivated to supply protein and fat; leafy greens and aromatic herbs provide the vitamins, minerals, and fiber lost in the process of polishing the rice; pigs are fed with rice bran and leftovers (mostly rice); and ducks are herded over the newly harvested rice fields so that every grain ends up in the human food chain. Even the dogs, whenever fed, eat rice.[1] Traditionally, when a farmer died, he was buried in his own rice field, returning symbolically and physically into the "rice chain" that is the source of human life.[2]

Rice has been grown in Vietnam for thousands of years. Grains of *Oryza fatua,* the earliest of Asian rice species, were cultivated by the proto-Vietnamese Lac[3] long before the arrival of the Chinese (Taylor 1983: 9–10). Rice has been at the center of Vietnamese farming and culture and has featured prominently in meals since its earliest days.

Taxonomically, there are three subspecies of *Oryza sativa* (Asian rice): the hard, long-grained tropical *indica;* the round, short-grained temperate *japonica;* and the intermediate, insular *javanica* (Nguyen, X. H. 2001: 12), all of which originated from the same ancestral *fatua* swamp rice, which has branched into thousands of varieties (ibid.).[4] In Vietnam, where the *japonica* and *javanica* are rare imported luxuries, a basic distinction exists between *gao te,* ordinary or "plain" rice, and *gao nep,* "sticky" glutinous rice (ibid. 11; Huu 1998: 186). Sticky rice (*Oryza sativa glutinosa*), the staple food of many of the numerous ethnic minorities in Vietnam (Dang, Chu, and Luu 2000), was domesticated and cultivated thousands of years before the development of the hard-grained "plain" rice (*Oryza sativa dura*). However, plain rice is now cultivated on a much larger scale because it thrives in less fertile soils and yields much bigger crops (Huu 1998: 186).

The distinction between plain and sticky rice in Vietnam is so important that the term *nep–te* (sticky rice–plain rice) is used to express binaries such as "good–bad," "right–wrong" and even "boy–girl." Interestingly, although plain rice is the overall staple in Vietnam, sticky rice is still considered the "real" rice (Nguyen, X. H. 2001).

The centrality of rice is evident in the language. Like the Inuit, who have more than thirty terms for snow (Atkinson et al. 1990: 326), the Vietnamese use a wide variety of terms for rice in its different states of cultivation, processing, and cooking. Rice seedlings are called *lua,* paddy is *thoc,* husked rice is *gao,* sticky rice is *nep* (and when boiled, *com nep*), steamed sticky rice is *xoi,* rice porridge is *chao,* and steamed (polished) rice is *com. Com* means both "cooked rice" and "a meal." *An com,* "[to] eat rice," also means "to have a meal," and this term is used even in cases when rice is not served. *Com bua,* literally "rice meal," means "daily meal" (as in "daily bread").

It is tempting to compare "rice" to "bread" in the biblical sense. However, this comparison would not do justice to rice, as *com* also means "flesh" and "pulp": coconut meat, for instance, is *com dua* (rice of the coconut) in Vietnamese. Hence, *com* encompasses the cultural meaning of both bread and meat in the Western context and is therefore a metaphor for all that is food.[5]

Another important aspect of Vietnamese rice culture is the quantity of the grain consumed daily, both in relation to other types of food and dishes and in terms of sheer volume. Though the total amount of food eaten in a meal is far smaller than that consumed in a parallel Western meal, the proportion of rice eaten is large: two to three bowls of cooked rice per adult per meal. As pointed out by Nguyen (2001: 1), the national target for domestic consumption is 300 kg of polished rice per person annually and the actual numbers reach over 250 kg, that is, approximately 700 grams of dry grain daily, or roughly 1.5 kg of cooked rice daily, exceeding 2,000 calories out of the recommended 2,500 calories per day (Mintz and Schlettwein-Gsell 2001).

Cooking rice, though rather simple, is done in a serious and calculated manner. The rice is rinsed thoroughly so as to wash off the dusty residue of the polishing process. If left to cook, this dust would make for a sticky cement-like texture that would disturb the balance between the distinctiveness of each grain and the wholesomeness of each mouthful of rice. Water is added to the washed rice in a 1:2 ratio (though personal preferences play a key role) and the pot is placed over the fire. When the water boils, the pot is covered, the heat is lowered, and the rice is left to cook for about twenty minutes. The rice is then "broken" or stirred with large cooking chopsticks and left to steam in its own heat for a few more minutes before serving.

The advent of electricity as an almost regular feature of life in Hoi An in the late 1990s has meant that most Hoianese, urban and rural alike, have adopted the electric rice-cooker. These utensils take care of the proper temperature, humidity, and duration of cooking. The more advanced cookers feature options for specific kinds of rice and even for specific tastes and textures. I have observed, however, that people tend to rely on their own expertise and experience even when using such advanced cookers. In the suburbs of Hoi An, inhabited mostly by farmers shifting into blue-collar and lower-middle-class urban jobs, I witnessed how traditional wood-fed hearths were gradually substituted by gas stoves and electric rice-cookers; rice was no longer served from large, smoke-blackened pots, but from smaller, lighter, bright aluminum ones.

Many of my friends claimed that they could tell the kind and quality of the cooked rice by its mere fragrance (*huong thom*) and taste (*vi*). They further said that they could distinguish between rice from different regions, counties of origin, and even harvest years, all determinants in the great price range among different kinds of rice. They certainly could distinguish subtle tastes and fragrances that were beyond my senses.

Although rice is undoubtedly the centerpiece of the meal, parallel to "meat" in Western culture, without which a "food event" would not be considered a meal at all, rice does not seem to be "stressed" in the same way that meat is. Ashkenazi and Jacob suggest that "because of its constant presence at most meals and because of [its] unchanging nature [and] methods of preparation that are restricted intentionally to preserve its pristine nature . . . [rice] is an element that, no matter how significant, does not call attention to itself in the same way a roast does" (2000: 78; for the "central yet unstressed" position of rice in Japanese meals, see also Allison 1991: 2). While the white, relative blandness, and lukewarm temperature of cooked rice, along with its subtle fragrance and fluffy consistency, are all characteristics conducive to this description, for the Vietnamese, rice undoubtedly constitutes the essence of a meal. This attitude is expressed in ways as subtle as the nature of rice:

> We went down to have lunch with the guesthouse staff. They have their lunch in the small "dining room," where a few tables are set for the guests' breakfast. Two tables were set together to create a table large enough for all of us. It was 11:30 AM and the meal was already placed on the table: steamed rice, two slices of pan-cooked mackerel (*ca thu*), a plate of boiled water morning-glory (*rau muong*), a plate heaped with fresh lettuce leaves torn to chopstick-size pieces and mixed with green herbs, a bowl of greenish soup (*canh*, actually the water in which the *rau muong* had been boiled), and a bowl of fish-sauce dip (*nuoc mam cham*). We were sitting and chatting as Ly, the cook, served the rice, carefully filling each bowl to the brim and adding a little extra to the men's bowls.
>
> Now everything was ready. We picked up our bowls and chopsticks as the younger ones mumbled *xin moi* (please), inviting the others to start eating. A moment of hesitation followed, everyone looking at each other and waiting for someone, preferably senior or older, to be the first to eat. Then, almost at once, but in a carefully timed order, from old to young, the chopsticks were lowered into the bowls and a chunk of fresh, lightly steaming, white rice was brought up to the mouths. Only then did we start helping ourselves to the other dishes with our chopsticks.

The everyday event described here illustrates (among other things) the respect that people feel toward rice. If eating is timed according to Confucian regulations of seniority and social status (Hucker 1978: 53), food items are treated similarly: though a basic rule of Vietnamese etiquette is that the eater should sample equally from all the side dishes without showing a preference for a specific dish (which would imply a dislike for the others, and see also Chang [1977: 41] for a similar Chinese notion), rice is qualitatively and quantitatively superior to any of the *mon an* (side dishes) and is eaten first and foremost. Despite the emphasis on restraint, everyone is encouraged to eat more rice, and if children are present, they are expected, indeed forced, to finish each and every grain in their bowl.

Rice and Nutrition

In densely populated monsoon-dominated Southeast Asia, growing rice as a staple is an ecologically sound (Huard and Durand 1998: 163–64) and "practical" choice (Popkin 1979; see also Reid 1988: 18–25). Irrigated, transplanted, labor-intensive paddy rice grown in the major river valleys and deltas is the most efficient crop (Phan, Nguyen, and Nguyen 1997: 8, 77–78; Taylor 1983: 12) under the conditions of limited arable soil, abundant water, high temperatures, perennial humidity (Le 1997: 72), and a huge number of available working hands, "permitting each year the production of sufficient quantities of carbohydrate . . . assuring the future of humans and . . . of their culture" (Huard and Durand 1998: 163).

Consuming rice as a staple, however, can result in major nutritional deficiencies that have to do with its protein composition and with the process of polishing, which drastically reduces the fiber, mineral, and vitamin content of rice (Harris 1987: 28). The rice grain is protected by two shells: a thick, rough outer husk that is easily stripped by threshing (usually right in the field during the harvest) and numerous finer layers, which are much harder to remove. In earlier periods (and among some of Vietnam's ethnic minority peoples today), these were removed by pounding the husked rice in large mortars (Dang, Chu, and Luu 2000: 203, 247; Condominas 1977, 1996), a process that was quite inefficient and, hence, left some of the essential fiber, minerals, and vitamins, ensuring proper nutrition.

Rice-eaters have long identified the shortcomings of the diet and through long-term observation, trial-and-error, and, perhaps, biologically based preferences and deficiency-resulting "hunger" (Harris 1987: 22), have developed a culinary system that compensates for the missing nutrients. Thus, while rice-eaters can extract most of their calories out of the rice, they must supplement it with proper amounts of other nutrients, notably protein, vitamins, and fiber. Generally speaking, the Indian rice diet is complemented with lentils, beans, and milk products. The Chinese supplement their rice-based diet with soybeans (transformed into soy sauce and tofu) and (mostly cooked) leafy greens, such as cabbage and broccoli (ibid. 125). The Vietnamese, much like the Cambodians, Thais, and other Southeast Asians, overcame the deficiencies of their rice-centered diets with products that abound in their unique ecological setting: marine and freshwater fish, seafood and aquatic animals, coconuts, groundnuts, and a variety of leafy vegetables and aromatic herbs (e.g., coriander, mint, and basil), as well as the leaves of wild and domesticated trees (e.g., lime, mango, and acacia).

Modern rice mills, which use long strips of sandpaper (hence the term *polished rice*), are much more effective (or, rather, over-effective), thereby exacerbating the nutritional problem: the polished grain, unlike traditional pounded rice, is completely stripped and composed mainly of pure starch, lacking essential proteins, amino acids, vitamins, and minerals, as well as the bran and fiber that are present in the whole grain (Anderson 1988: 115; Helman 2000: 38). Historically, the introduction of rice mills into Southeast Asia by the colonial powers during the eighteenth century had a disastrous affect, as a widespread beriberi epidemic is estimated to have killed millions.

While Dutch doctor Christian Eijkman accidentally discovered the importance of leafy greens for curing beriberi, for which he was awarded the Nobel Prize (the nutritional deficiency was identified later as lack of thiamine or vitamin B1 that is abundant in rice husk [Zilber-Rosenberg 1996: 107]), the locals seem to have realized that their meal structures should be reworked and by further increasing the amount and centrality of leafy greens were able to restore nutritional balance while maintaining their preference for polished rice.

As my analysis takes into account rational, empirically based choices within specific ecosystems, the question that immediately came to my mind was why the Vietnamese and, for that matter, all rice-eaters, strip their rice to such a degree. They could overcome many of their dietary deficiencies by husking only the outer, indigestible shell and eating wholegrain or brown rice. This would not only remove some of the "protein pressure" (Harris 1987: 25) that haunts overpopulated societies and would allow for an increased fiber intake, but would also save the work invested in polishing the rice and, more importantly in producing or otherwise supplementing the lacking protein, vitamins, and bran.

This question can be addressed from two directions: the practical and the cultural (Sahlins 1976). The practical aspect has to do with cooking time and energy consumption: wholegrain rice requires roughly forty minutes of boiling for proper cooking, while polished rice calls for only twenty minutes. Polishing the rice therefore saves roughly 50 percent of the fuel/energy and work invested in cooking it. Moreover, polished rice can be preserved for years while wholegrain rice molds within a few months. But while longer shelf life and savings in energy and working time are important practical considerations, it is the cultural significance that I would like to highlight.

When I raised the issue of eating *gao* (brown rice) on several occasions, I was repeatedly told that "*gao* is not edible." My Hoianese friends were quite surprised when I insisted that brown rice can be consumed, that it had considerable nutritional and health benefits, and that it is quite popular among health-oriented Westerners. I was told several times that no one would consider eating unpolished rice because "this is food for animals . . . humans eat polished rice and pigs eat bran." Indeed, polished rice is sold in special rice stores in the market and around town while wholegrain rice, along with bran and several other low-grade, nonhusked grains, is sold in stalls specializing in animal fodder.

I was also told by quite a few people that brown rice "is not tasty," even as they admitted that they had never tried it. We can observe here Bourdieu's (1984) principle of distinction at work: "taste" is a mechanism that distinguishes between different social groups or, in this case, between humans and (domesticated) animals. Unpolished rice, though perfectly digestible and certainly more nutritious, is rejected because "it isn't tasty." Taste here is used as the reason for culinary choices that have very little to do with nutrition or sensory experience and is actually applied to establish social categorization.

However, if polished rice, despite its nutritional deficiencies, is chosen as the staple and the basis of the meal for practical and sociocultural reasons, it is essential for it to be nutritionally complemented by other ingredients and dishes. These complementary nutrients and dishes must be embedded in cultural arrangements that would be powerful enough to confront, so to speak, the centrality of rice and to acquire an independent status in the realm of "taste," one that would be always taken into account when eating.

The nutritional deficiencies of rice are complemented in Vietnam by a wide range of raw and cooked leafy and aromatic greens, as well as vegetables and fruits, and with animal protein, mainly of aquatic source. Water, the often overlooked nutrient, is also a basic ingredient that is always included in the meal in the form of *canh* (soup). Along with *nuoc mam,* the ubiquitous Vietnamese fish sauce, these ingredients are the variables in the dynamic matrix of the Hoianese meal.

In the following pages, I discuss the two other most important categories of ingredients in the Hoianese meal: fish and fresh leafy greens. Though greens and vegetables are as important as fish, in terms of the nutritional qualities and relative proportion of the meal, fish are more salient by far. This can be observed in the popular saying that celebrates the special relationship between rice and fish in the Vietnamese diet:

| Khong co gi bang com voi ca | Nothing is [better than] rice with fish |
| *Khong co gi bang me voi con* | Nothing is [better than] a mother with a child |

Ca (Fish)

Vietnamese culture emerged along riverbanks and waterways and expanded along the South China Sea coast. The country has more than 3,000 km of coastline (Phan, Nguyen, and Nguyen 1997: 13), several large rivers, and an endless system of irrigation canals, ponds, and reservoirs. These provide a fertile habitat for the rich and diverse variety of fish, seafood, and aquatic animals such as frogs, eels, and snails, both in the sea and in freshwater bodies.

The intimate relationship the Vietnamese have with water and waterways can be discerned from the very early stages of their history. Beyond the fact that the early Vietnamese named themselves *Lac* (canal), the Vietnamese terms for a "country" are *dat nuoc* ("land [and] water"), *nong nuoc* ("mountains [and] water"), or simply *nuoc* ("water"), while government is *nha nuoc* ("house [and] water"), singling out the centrality of water in this polity. Constitutive myths, such as the legend about the nation's ancestor, the sea dragon Lac Long Quan, or the story of the "genie of the mountains and the genie of the water" further stress the aquatic context, as does the unique Vietnamese art of water puppetry, which evolved by village ponds (Nguyen and Tran 1996: 10–11) still widely used as reservoirs, for raising fish, washing, and as swimming pools and meeting places. It is easy to understand why under such socioecological conditions aquatic fauna are essential components of the diet.

Despite the history, ecology, and the obvious potential, however, Vietnam's fishing fleet is small and underdeveloped. Most boats are wooden and lack refrigeration and navigational and safety equipment.[6] Fishing is therefore mainly restricted to the overexploited coastal waters. Officially, there were just 24,000 fishermen in the entire country in 1997 (Le 1997: 580). Yet, in 2008 there were 100,000 fishing boats in the country, according to Deputy Agriculture Minister Nguyen Van Thang,[7] which suggests that there are approximately 500,000 fishermen.

Both numbers are misleading, however. First, many boats are too small to be registered. This is certainly the case in the coastal village of Cam An in Hoi An, where more than one hundred families make a living out of fishing, using unregistered coracle-type woven, tarred bamboo "boats" (some of which have engines). Moreover, many farmers are part-time fishermen (Keyes 1977: 185) and some have recently turned their rice fields into shrimp ponds.[8] More importantly, almost all farmers exploit aquatic resources that are by-products of rice farming, regularly trapping the frogs, snails, eels, fish, and crabs that inhabit the reservoirs, canals, and rice terraces and that often feed around the rice seedlings in the flooded paddies. Fishing nets and crab traps are regularly positioned in the water systems, and pole-and-line fishing is very popular. Every evening, the small lights of those who practice "electric fishing" are visible: spears are attached to car batteries to shock and collect the stunned fish and amphibians at night (at great personal danger, according to the fishermen, who risk poisonous snakebites as well as the hungry ghosts that roam the swamps at night).

I have often observed much time and effort invested in catching a few, miniscule fish. During the Hoianese flood season (November and December), I have witnessed many of my neighbors spending a couple of hours every afternoon pole fishing in the raging drainage canals. They never caught more than a handful of little fish, yet were obviously content with their catch, which was promptly cooked for dinner. This led me to pay attention to the relative proportions between the fish and the rice eaten at every meal. For Israeli or Western diners, serving such a small amount of fish would probably seem insulting; in Hoianese terms, however, half-a-dozen fingerlings, approximately equivalent to a single sardine can, were clearly perceived as sufficient for a family meal.

In 2004, I was invited by a neighbor to go fishing "just for fun" (*cho vui*). We cycled down to Cam An lagoon and pole-fished from a small boat. We caught a dozen finger-sized fish or so, which we took home. My neighbor's wife cooked these with tomato and pineapple into a sour fish-soup (*canh chua*), which we had with rice noodles (*bun*). Altogether five adults and two children shared the meal, in which each ate some 10 or 20 grams of fish flesh.

Fish are consumed fresh or preserved, dried or in the form of *nuoc mam*, Vietnamese fish sauce. Fresh fish, bought at the market early in the morning and eaten as soon as possible so that one might enjoy their freshness and delicate taste, are an essential ingredient in the Hoianese home-eaten meal. Mackerel (*ca thu*, "autumn fish") is very popular in Hoi An, although rather expensive (prices soared from US$2 per kg in 2000 to US$7 in 2007), similar to the price of chicken and more expensive than pork.[9] Although large fish, such as swordfish, tuna, and even stingrays and sharks ("shark embryos in fresh turmeric and green bananas" is a famous local specialty) are found almost daily in the market, smaller and much less expensive fish are the common fare for home meals. Shrimp and squid are also common, available in a variety of sizes and prices. Crab is also popular, but has become extremely expensive (roughly US$1 a piece in the market and US$2–3 in a restaurant in 2007) and exceedingly rare due to overharvesting and ever increasing demand from the tourist industry. Crabs are therefore mostly sold to wholesalers from out of town and to local tourist-oriented restaurants.

Due to a lack of advanced and/or reliable means of refrigeration at the point-of-catch and transport of the fish, seasonality is still a key factor when it comes to the choice of fish eaten at home. In April, *ca com* ("rice fish" or long-jawed anchovy) is the most popular catch, often cooked in turmeric and eaten rolled (*cuon*) in rice paper with fresh herbs. Even the prized mackerel, although available almost year round, "is best in the autumn, when it tastes sweet."[10]

Fish is commonly cooked either in a "dry" dish or soup. As a "dry," home-eaten Hoianese dish, fish (and other kinds of seafood) can be fried and then broiled in a tomato sauce, with lemongrass or garlic, steamed or grilled (another local specialty is grilled fish in banana leaves, but this is rarely prepared at home). Small fish and shrimp are often cooked with leafy greens into *canh* (soup). The most popular method of fish consumption in Hoi An (and in Vietnam), however, is actually in the form of *nuoc mam*.

Nuoc Mam (Fish Sauce)

Nuoc mam is not only the most important source of protein and minerals in the Vietnamese diet and the second-most-common ingredient after rice, but also the essential marker of Vietnamese cuisine and the key agent that defines the unique taste of Vietnamese food.

Lanh lives with her husband and daughters in her in-laws' Chinese merchant mansion opposite the pier, just by the municipal market. Her husband is a descendant of one of the Chinese families who settled in Hoi An in the nineteenth century and her mother-in-law used to trade in commodities; locally the family surname is still synonymous with high-quality trade (Lanh's daughters are nick-named *Gao*—"rice" and *Mi*—"wheat"). Nowadays, Lanh runs a large shop, where she sells souvenirs.

Lanh was quick to realize where my interests lay and would often invite me to come for a meal. We would go to the market, shop, and cook lunch together. Returning from the market, we would walk through the shop, climb the few stairs to the front room (elevated to avoid the seasonal floods), and continue into the kitchen. Well prepared, climbing up the stairs I would take a deep breath and hold it for as long as possible. When I couldn't hold my breath any longer, I would silently empty my lungs and then, slowly and cautiously, breathe through my mouth. I knew it wouldn't help. The thick, salty stench of fermenting fish would hit me. On my first visit, I had almost fainted: the stench was so overpowering and so inappropriate in a kitchen (as I felt at the time).

At the corner of the room, on a heavy stone tripod, stood a large cement vat with a tap. Amber liquid slowly dripped from the tap into a large ladle. "This is my mother's *nuoc mam*," said Lanh proudly, "the best in Hoi An!"

Lanh's mother-in-law buys a few kilograms of *ca com* each spring and mixes them with a large amount of salt. The salt extracts the liquid out of the fish, while the tropical heat and humidity facilitate the fermentation of the resulting brine. After three or four weeks, the brine mellows and clears. Normally, this would be the end of the process and the liquid would be bottled and consumed. In order to improve the quality of the sauce, however, Lanh's mother-in-law keeps the liquid "alive" by pouring it over and over again into the vat, allowing for a continuous process of fermentation that deepens its flavor and smell. This results in an especially potent *nuoc mam nhi* (virgin fish sauce), considered the best kind. Lanh told me that "only Vietnamese people can make *nuoc mam* because only they can understand! . . . Now you know why my dishes are so tasty," she added; "the secret is in the *nuoc mam*. Don't worry, when you go home, I'll give you a small bottle. My mother always gives some to our relatives and close friends for Tet."

Nuoc mam is the cultural marker of Vietnamese cuisine, just like soy sauce is in Chinese cuisine (Anderson 1988: 113, 123–24). Despite the fact that Vietnamese cuisine is based on rice, its taste is defined by *nuoc mam*. While the combination of rice and fish has sound ecological foundations throughout Southeast Asia, the tropical weather means that fresh fish and seafood spoil very quickly. Hence, practicality partly underlies this culinary icon, which is a way of preserving fish. However, *nuoc mam* embodies much more than nutritional and practical advantages as, according to many people I consulted and virtually every Vietnamese cookbook (Nguyen, T. T. 1997: 33; Jackson-Doling, Choi, Isaak, and von Holzen 1997: 10), *nuoc mam* is emphasized as the most important taste marker of Vietnamese cuisine.

Nuoc mam is used during three stages of the preparation and consumption of food: as a marinade before cooking, as a condiment while cooking, and as a dip when eating. In each mode, the fish sauce influences the taste in a different way: in a marinade, it softens the ingredients and starts the process of transformation from raw into cooked. Marinating is sometimes conducted in stages. For example, a local restaurant owner told me that when preparing green papaya salad (*goi du du*), it is very important to add the thinly sliced cucumbers to the shredded green papaya marinated in *nuoc mam* only a few minutes before serving, to retain the crispness of the cucumbers, which is essential for this dish. While the meal is cooking, *nuoc mam* is added to most dishes in order to perform several tasks: to enhance the flavor of the dish, like monosodium glutamate; to add saltiness; and, most importantly, to give the dish a crucial extra "fishy" quality.[11] At mealtime, *nuoc mam* is always present on the table, served in a dipping bowl, as an essential element in the pentagonal structure of the meal. As a dip, it is diluted with water, lime juice, sugar, crushed garlic, black pepper, and red chili, which are mixed into it just before the food is served so as to create a less pungent yet highly complex sauce. The five spices that are mixed with the fish sauce can also be adjusted into the "five-element" paradigm and actually make for the basic taste agents of Vietnamese cuisine.

Using their chopsticks, each diner dips a morsel of the "side dish" into the sauce before placing it on the rice and raking in a mouthful. Since it is impolite for diners to adjust the taste of a dish with condiments, as this implies that the dish is not perfect, providing a complex dipping sauce allows for a polite and acceptable personal adjustment of the taste of a dish.

Nuoc mam, like the gravy in the British meal (Douglas 1975: 253), is a mediating agent that breaks the binary oppositions and makes for the wholeness of the "gastronomic morpheme" (Dann 1996: 235–38). The ability to achieve this task stems from fish sauce's liminal, "betwixt and between" position (Turner 1967: 93–111): two "solids" (salt and fish) are processed into a liquid, which is an extract and an essence of both. Hence, at all levels of the meal, *nuoc mam* is the element that combines the different substances into a whole, while adding its own distinctive qualities to create a gestalt of taste.

Finally, the *nuoc mam* bowl is the real agent of commensality in the family meal: rice is dished into individual bowls and the side dishes are picked out of shared vessels, but everybody dips their morsels of food into a shared saucer of *nuoc mam* just before putting them into their mouths. In tourist-oriented restaurants, *nuoc mam* is served in small individual saucers (Cohen and Avieli 2004) and the symbolic binding interaction is thus reversed, expressing individuality and social distance.

This further elucidates the centrality of *nuoc mam* in the Vietnamese meal: beyond providing essential nutrients, contributing to the distinctive taste of Vietnamese food and being a "cementing agent" for the different dishes in a meal, it allows for individual preferences to be expressed without breaching etiquette or causing offense while simultaneously enhancing commensality and sharing.

Green Vegetables and Aromatic Herbs

While rice is the staple and centerpiece of the Hoianese meal, and fish in various guises are its distinctive culinary markers, no Vietnamese dish and certainly no Hoianese meal is served without accompanying raw and cooked leafy greens, such as stir-fried or boiled *rau muong* (water morning-glory), a plate of lettuce and aromatic leaves (*rau song*), or just a sprinkle of chopped coriander over a bowl of noodles. But greens are essential, contributing to several dimensions of the meal: nutrition (adding fiber, vitamins, and minerals), texture, color, fragrance, and taste.

For the rice-eating Vietnamese, the consumption of greens, and especially of raw or lightly cooked ones, is essential for balanced nutrition (see also Mintz and Schlettwein-Gsell 2001: 43). As has been pointed out, a diet based solely on polished rice and fermented fish would lack fiber and some essential nutrients.

Lack of fiber causes constipation in the short term and might contribute to serious digestive maladies, including stomach cancer (Guggenheim 1985: 278–82), in the long run. Lack of vitamin C can cause, among other maladies, scurvy (ibid. 176); and lack of thiamine might result in beriberi (ibid. 201).

The importance of raw greens in Vietnamese cuisine demonstrates an interesting contrast to Chinese cuisine, where vegetables are rarely eaten raw. While the relatively colder weather might explain the prominence of greens and vegetables of the Brassicaceae (mustard) and Cruciferae (cabbage) families, which require cooking to eliminate their toxins, another problem is the wide use of human excrement as fertilizer in Chinese vegetable gardens. Cooking the vegetables is therefore an essential hygienic measure, especially with regard to hepatitis (which is endemic in China). It is obvious, then, why the Chinese express deep suspicion about raw vegetables and unpeeled fruit ("Are you not going to cook it?" I was once asked by a Chinese friend when I served a fresh vegetable salad). In Vietnam, where the use of human excrement as fertilizer is less common, the threat of contamination is lower and raw greens are safer. Since cooking destroys some of the vitamins, raw greens are a sound long-term nutritional choice.[12]

A variety of fresh, mostly aromatic, greens is served as a side dish called *rau song* ("raw/live vegetables"). There are regional variations in the composition of the greens. In the North, the purple, prickly *la tia to* (perilla) and dill are often served. In the Center and South, lettuce leaves (*xa lach,* and note the French influence) are mixed with bean sprouts (sometimes lightly pickled), coriander, and several varieties of mint and basil. In the south, raw cucumber is sometimes added, resembling the Thai and Indian custom. In Hoi An, *ngo om* (rice-paddy herb) and *dip ca* ("fish leaves," a dark green herb with heart-shaped leaves with a somewhat fishy taste) are often included in the platter, too. In the countryside, farmers tend small plots of greens right next to the house, creating convenient kitchen gardens. Those who live in town buy their greens at the market just before mealtime.

Ba Tho (Grandma Tho), mouth red from the constant chewing of *trau cau* (betel quid), handed me a plastic bag of *rau song* fresh from the market and told me to wash them. The greens are harvested young and tender: a lettuce head is no bigger than a fist and the other greens are not higher than 10 cm and have only a few leaves on the stem. Ba Tho bought the herbs at different stalls and mixed them up herself: lettuce, mint, coriander, *ngo om,* bean sprouts. . . . She said that the ratio between the different greens depends on seasonal prices: when lettuce is cheap, there is plenty of it in the mix, but when the price goes up (usually during the flood season in November–December), she substitutes them with other cheaper greens.

I squatted on the cement floor near the tap, filled a plastic basin with water, and soaked the greens. Squatting on one's heels "Vietnamese-style" demands a painfully acquired flexibility. I was already sweating profusely as the temperature and humidity were close to the midday peak. I splashed some cool water on my face. Ba Tho, noticing my distress, grunted and handed me a miniature plastic stool to support myself. She set another basin near me, placed a plastic strainer in it, and told me to carefully clean the leaves and throw away anything that was black, torn, looked old, or seemed to be pecked at.[13] If the leaves were too big for one mouthful, I should tear them into smaller bits. Only the good parts should be put in the strainer for a second wash.

I don't think that the bag contained more than one kilo of leaves, but it took me a while to go over it thoroughly. The mound of rejected leaves grew larger than the pile of perfect, crunchy green leaves in the strainer. I was somewhat relieved now, as the cool water in the basin was comforting in the stifling heat.

Grandma Tho, obviously dissatisfied, now asked me why I was taking so long and why I was throwing away so many good greens! She picked up the pile of rejected leaves and went to the back of the kitchen. There, at the narrow space between the toilet wall and the fence stood her beloved chicken coop. She threw the leaves in and contentedly watched the chicks fight over them.

Greens are served fresh and crunchy, fragrant, cool, and bright, and their contribution to the taste, texture, and color of the meal is substantial. Diners pick them up with their chopsticks, dip them in *nuoc mam,* and sometimes combine them with rice or another morsel to have in one bite.

It would seem obvious that the greens are there for their taste and smell. However, the free mixing, changing, and substituting of the different herbs suggest that a *specific* taste is not the main objective. The prominence of the bland nonfragrant lettuce and bean sprouts further hints at other aspects of the greens. Here I recall my own eating experience: the cool crunchy greens adjust and balance the texture of the meal. The soft rice and the slithery fish are counterbalanced, "charged with life," so to speak, by the crisp fresh greens. When chewed, a crunching sound emerges that contributes to the total experience of eating (see chapter 2). The aromatic greens cool the dishes, not only by reducing the temperature (in any case, dishes are served lukewarm), but also by adding a soothing quality that smoothes away some of the sharp edges of the other tastes.

The taste aspect should not be ignored either. It is precisely the random mixing of aromas and tastes that adds a new aspect to every bite. Though the dishes are served spiced and seasoned, and are further dipped in the multileveled fish-sauce dip, the presence of a wide array of distinctive taste agents allows for an infinite number of taste combinations within a single meal: the same bite of rice or fish would taste completely different when eaten with mint as opposed to basil. The explosion of sharp new tastes in the mouth makes for a new experience in every bite. The taste of a piece of mackerel cooked in turmeric is altered when eaten with a crunchy lettuce leaf or with some aromatic coriander leaves. We see again how the structured rules of etiquette, which prevent personal seasoning and stress common taste, are subtly counterbalanced by a setting that allows for personal modification and constant, endless variation and change.

MEAL STRUCTURES AND COSMOLOGY

Chi, a local chef and one of my most valuable informants and cherished friends, suggested on several occasions that the basic dyad of "rice" and "things to eat" "is *am* and *duong*," relating food to two of the most important Vietnamese cosmological principles: *am* and *duong* (*yin* and *yang*) and *ngu hanh* (the theory of "the five elements"). A similar point was made by Canh, another prominent Hoianese restaurateur, when discussing the medicinal and therapeutic qualities of his cooking, while Tran, an experienced tour guide, also suggested that *am* and *duong* shape the ways in which dishes and meals are prepared.

Yin and *yang* is an all-encompassing Chinese Taoist principle that champions a dynamic balance between the obscure, dark, wet, cold, feminine energy of *yin* and the hot, powerful, shining, violent, male energy of *yang* (Schipper 1993: 35). This cosmic law maintains that harmony is the outcome of the apparent tension between these opposites, which are not merely the two sides of the very same coin, but also existentially dependent upon each other, as there would be no "white" without "black," no "cold" without "hot," no "men" without "women," and so on. Neil L. Jamieson, in his insightful *Understanding Vietnam* (1995), claims that the principle of *yin* and *yang* is the key to understanding Vietnamese society, culture, and history. He particularly points out that "Diet could . . . disrupt or restore harmony between *yin* and *yang*," stressing the essential relationship between this cosmological principle and the culinary realm.

It is tempting to briefly compare this ancient Taoist principle to the Lévi-Straussian structure, as both seem to assume a binary opposition that underlies

and arranges the universal, cosmological, and social orders. Yet these principles are actually very different: for Lévi-Strauss, thinking in binary oppositions
is an intrinsic human quality, whose outcome is the static, permanent structure
(e.g., 1966a: 38–40) in which humans as thinking beings are incarcerated, so to
speak. In contrast, *yin* and *yang* are external, metaphysical concepts that govern and harmonize the natural, the cultural, and the cosmological orders by
allowing a dynamic, ever changing balance between these two apparent oppositions. While opposition is the main feature of the Lévi-Straussian structure,
balance and harmony underlie *yin* and *yang*. When coming to understand the
Hoianese meal, it seems that the dynamic, flexible, and ever changing nature of
am and *duong* works much better then the rigid binary opposition that toler-
ates change in content but does not allow movement and dynamism and, hence,
denies agency, which is an essential quality of food events.

White, rather bland, and neutral rice is said to be compatible with the notion of *am* (with rice practically related to femininity, as the senior female is the
one who serves rice to the others), while the colorful, savory, varied *mon an*
adheres to the definition of *duong* as flamboyant, savory entities to which men
have privileged access. Moreover, the meal is wholesome only when both rice
and *mon an* are present on the table/tray, making for a material representation
of *am* and *duong*, with the plate of rice and *mon an* actually looking like the
famous graphic symbol of *yin* and *yang*.

Am and *duong*, however, were actually mentioned only by highly skilled
cooks and/or educated professionals, while the popular and common discourse
was mainly concerned with the therapeutic qualities of food, within the medical "cold–hot" paradigm, according to which all dishes, ingredients, and seasoning and cooking techniques are either "heating" or "cooling." According to
this theory, a dish should be balanced, combining hot and cold elements (as in
the case of sweet-and-sour dishes) so as to maintain the physical and emotional
harmony of the diners.

In some cases, heating or cooling are desired, usually due to some health
problems, as in the case of colds and flus, and ginger is often used to "heat" up
the dish and, as a consequence, the eater, to help him overcome his condition.
In other cases excess is sought after, as in instances where enhanced masculine
sexual potency is desired. In such circumstances, aphrodisiacs such as snake,
he-goat meat, or duck embryos, which are extremely "heating," are consumed
to enhance the level of *duong*.

While the hot–cold paradigm for food was mentioned often—and by people
from various echelons of society—very few were aware that it is actually an
implementation or implication of the *am* and *duong* theory. It seems, then, that
in between abstract cosmological notions and lived experience there exists a

third, mediating level, which is theoretical in a sense, but concerned directly with practical knowledge of the body and its well-being. While very few people talk confidently about *am* and *duong* (or, as a Vietnamese student put it, "Maybe old people know about this [*am* and *duong*], but we have no idea . . ."), the "hot and cold" paradigm is often evoked when discussing food.

The important point is that though the Hoianese only rarely linked the meal structure directly to *am* and *duong,* they did refer often to its practical implications of "hot and cold." Thus, even if most Hoianese are probably unaware that their meals are formulated along the lines of a cosmological theory, the fact that the hot–cold principle is widely recognized supports the idea made by the more knowledgeable few, who argued that the basic structure of the Hoianese home-eaten meal is a manifestation of *am* and *duong.*

It follows from our discussion that if the twofold structure of the Hoianese meal is a manifestation of the cosmic principle of *am* and *duong,* it would be reasonable to argue that the fivefold structure into which this meal develops also stands for a cosmological notion. Here, I would like to suggest that this fivefold structure is a representation of the cosmological theory of *ngu hanh.*

The five elements (or phases)—water, fire, wood, metal, and earth—are finer subdivisions of the *am* and *duong* and "represent a spatio-temporal continuation of the *Tao*" (Schipper 1993: 35), standing for the cardinal directions, the seasons, the planets, the viscera, and, actually, for everything else that exists. Hence, "like the *yin* and *yang,* the five phases are found in everything and their alternation is the second physical law [the first being *yin* and *yang*]" (ibid.). The elements are interrelated in cycles of production and destruction (e.g., water produces wood and extinguishes fire) and their relations and transformations generate the movement that is life.

While my informants never said that the five components of the Hoianese meal are representations of the five elements, when I suggested that this was the case, several of the more knowledgeable ones thought that I was probably correct. However, they were not able to help me with formulating a comprehensive explanation on the correspondence of each dish (or category) to the different elements. The only clear reference was to rice, which is the centerpiece of the meal and, as such, corresponds to the "center" and the "earth" element. I assume that the soup corresponds to "water" and the greens to "wood," but I am not sure which of the other two, the fish sauce and the "dry" dish, corresponds to fire and which to metal. As fish sauce is a fermented substance used in different stages to transform other ingredients, however, I am inclined to attribute it to the "fire" phase and the "dry" dish to "metal."

Ngu hanh inform a few other pentagonal culinary sets: the five possible states of transformation of edible matter into food—raw, steamed, boiled,

TABLE 1.2. The "twofold-turn-fivefold" structure of the Hoianese meal as expressing the cosmological principles of *am* and *duong* and *ngu hanh*

AM			DUONG	
Rice			"Things to Eat"	
Bland			Savory	
Pale/Colorless			Colorful	
Mother			Father	

EARTH	WATER	WOOD	METAL	FIRE
Rice	Soup	Greens	"Dry" dish	Fish sauce
Steamed	Boiled	Raw	Fried/Grilled	Fermented
sweet	salty	sour	spicy	bitter

fried/grilled, and fermented; the five tastes (*ngu vi*)—spicy, sour, bitter, salty, and sweet, which correspond to metal, wood, fire, water, and earth respectively; and the five textures—crispy, crunchy, chewy, soft, and silky.

The "twofold-turned-fivefold" structure of the Hoianese daily home-eaten meal presented in Table 1.2 is both an outcome and a representation of the two most important Vietnamese cosmic laws. The Hoianese meal is actually a *model* of the universe: an abstract, condensed version of the ways in which the universe looks and operates. Along similar lines to Mircea Eliade's (1959: 5) claim that "all the Indian royal cities are built after the mythical model of the celestial city, where . . . the Universal sovereign dwelt," and to Erik Cohen's (1987) suggestion that the cross pattern employed by the Hmong in their textile design, as well as specific patterns of face piercing applied by devotees during the vegetarian festival in Phuket (Cohen 2001) are cosmological schemes, I argue that the Hoianese meal is also a model of the universe and of the ways in which it operates.

Whenever the Hoianese cook and eat their daily meal, they make a statement about the ways in which they perceive the universe and, when physically incorporating it, reaffirm the principles that shape their cosmos, endorsing them and ensuring their continuity. In this respect, these daily food events, precisely because of their routine and ongoing nature, are probably the most common expressions of cosmology in Hoi An's everyday life.

As with royal Indian cities, Hmong embroidery patterns, or Thai piercing, most Hoianese are unaware of the cosmic meaning of the food they prepare. Cooking and eating, just like piercing or architecture, is an embodied practice that encompasses "embodied Knowledge" (Choo 2004: 207), which certainly exists, but not always intellectually and reflexively. Indeed, one of the main arguments of this book is that the unconscious nature of culinary knowledge, which is often embodied and rarely reflexive or verbal, allows for the culinary sphere to engage with ideas and notions that seldom find expression in more intellectual, explicit, and self-aware cultural arenas.

CANH CHUA (SOUR SOUP): EPITOMIZING THE HOIANESE HOME-EATEN MEAL

Finally, I turn to Hoi An's most common home-eaten meal: *canh chua* or "sour [fish] soup," eaten with *bun* (rice vermicelli), fresh greens, and *nuoc mam cham*. This meal epitomizes the structural, eco-nutritional, and cosmological principles outlined in this chapter, a fact that probably explains the dish's extreme popularity. Yet sour soup is a distinctive culinary artifact, typical and unique, different from any kind of dish or dish-combination described so far. It is a good example of the variety and dynamism characteristic of Hoianese cuisine. Yet before discussing *canh chua,* a few words are due concerning soups and, particularly, soups in East and Southeast Asia.

Soup is probably the most economical mode of cooking, as the amount of food actually increases with cooking and the addition of water: not only are the ingredients used with literally no waste, but the water is "charged," as it were, with nutritional and cultural value (Lévi-Strauss 1966b: 937–38). While Western-style soups, boiled for a long period, are time- and energy-consuming and, as a consequence, are often of inferior nutritional value, in Vietnam (as well as in other parts of East and Southeast Asia), soups are boiled for a few minutes or so, maintaining the freshness and texture of the ingredients and much of their nutritional value. Even when a chicken or duck is cooked into Western-style soup (in this case, termed *xup* in Vietnamese, with a clear French reference), the cooking period does not exceed twenty minutes and the flesh seems chewy and tough.

Though there are many kinds of soups in Vietnam, *canh chua* (sour soup) is the most popular by far in Hoi An (different versions of sour soup are popular in the rest of the Center and South, as well as in other parts of Southeast Asia). Cooking this soup is simple and quick: gutted whole fish is brought to a quick boil (in just a few minutes, depending on the size of the fish) with sliced pineapple, tomatoes, and several souring agents such as green tamarind pulp and lime juice added just before mealtime. A live fish, still jumping in the plastic bag it was placed in at the market, is consumed some fifteen minutes after the redemptive blow from the pestle. The quick processing helps preserve much of the nutritional value of the fish and other ingredients, as well as their fresh taste and texture.

The most valued fish for Hoianese sour soup is *ca loc,* "snake-headed mullet" or "mud fish." This fish has much in common with the carp, the most popular Chinese fish (and, in some senses, with the domestic pig, another Chinese favorite): it does not require a clean environment and can survive easily in polluted water. In fact, it prefers muddy, murky ponds and thrives in sewage. Like the pig, it can eat almost any organic substance, including animal and human excrement, and transform it efficiently into flesh. Snake-headed mullet is also preferred since it can survive for hours out of water and, therefore, is easier to transport and market and safer as it does not spoil so fast. It also has fewer bones, connected to a sturdy backbone, making it easier to handle and safer to eat. Finally, it is very strong and feisty, implying that much vital energy may be transmitted to the eater.

Although *ca loc* is the most sought-after fish for sour soup, it is only rarely used because it is expensive. Cheaper fish are usually used for *canh chua,* mainly small, fatty, freshwater fish that are bland and have plenty of bones. Three or four of these are ample for a bowl of sour soup for an entire extended family of several adults and children.

Though based on fish, *canh chua* is distinguished by its sourness, derived from several vegetal ingredients. The main souring agent is tamarind pulp. The other sour ingredients are tomatoes, pineapple, okra, lightly pickled bean sprouts, and bamboo shoots. The soup is further seasoned with lime juice, fish sauce, sugar, and black pepper.

Beyond the common lettuce and aromatics, the plate of fresh greens (*rau song*) used in *canh chua* also features sliced green bananas and unripe starfruit. In Hoi An, another kind of aromatic green is served: *ngo diec* (or *ngo om*). This unique "paddy herb" is crunchy and "has a very sharp citrus flavor" (Jackson-Doling et al. 1997: 76). Its distinctive taste and fragrance give the final touch to the Hoianese *canh chua,* as well as to some other local dishes, such as *com ga* (Hoi An-style "chicken rice") or *hot vit lon* (duck embryos). In addition to their sourness, most of these ingredients share other taste and texture qualities: they are usually greenish, crunchy, mostly unripe, and have a somewhat tannin flavor. In Western culinary terms, this soup might be described as "lightly poached fish prepared with unripe fruit and vegetables," as the various ingredients, including the fish, maintain their natural taste, shape, color, and texture, making for an "undercooked" soup.

I was often told that sour soup is "refreshing and cooling and good for the hot summer days." Dang (1997: 35) points out that the reason behind the Vietnamese general preference for sour food stems "perhaps . . . from the hot climate." This "cooling" quality of sourness may be one of the reasons underlying its popularity in Southeast Asia. In addition, as far as my own experience goes, the sour taste somewhat ameliorates the bland and oily taste of freshwater fish. And although very nutritious, sour soup is a light dish, which does not cause fatigue even on very hot days.

A *canh chua* meal, whenever prepared at home, is not served as the liquid element (*canh*) of the five-fold meal discussed earlier. Rather, *canh chua* is usually served with fresh rice vermicelli (*bun*, characteristic of Central and Southern Vietnam), a plate of fresh greens, and a bowl of *nuoc mam cham*. The diners take some *bun* noodles into their bowls, add greens, pour over them a ladleful of the soup broth, and season the whole with the fish sauce dip. The ingredients are then mixed with chopsticks. Slices of tomato and pineapple, as well as bits of the fish, are picked out of the soup bowl with the chopsticks.

Sour soup constitutes a complete meal, encompassing the whole "twofold-turned-fivefold" set of essential ingredients and elements that make for the proper Hoianese meal: a solid basis of rice in the form of noodles, fish, raw and cooked greens, and soupy liquid, mixed together and seasoned with the indispensable fish sauce, lime, chili, sugar, garlic, and black pepper.

A *canh chua* meal comes full circle and allows us to decipher the Hoianese daily, home-eaten meal: based on sound eco-nutritional logic, it features the three essential components (rice, fish, and greens), stands for *am* and *duong* ("rice" and "things to eat"), and accommodates the five elements (earth/rice, water/soup, wood/greens and vegetables, metal/fish, and fire/fish sauce). It then combines all these elements and concepts into a single coherent culinary unit, which is wholesome materially and culturally and which seems to transcend all the different levels of analyses, featuring a complete entity, and making for a very good representation of the harmonious and absolute Tao, the unifying Vietnamese cosmic law.

Finally, it is important to note that though nutritional and ecological considerations and/or universal cosmological principles may appear solid and static, *canh chua* and, in fact, the Hoianese daily home-eaten meal in general, are not merely harmonious and well balanced but also dynamic, flexible, and ever-changing, as the ingredients and cooking styles are hardly rigid and uniform, while the practice of eating itself is vibrant and involves processes of change. As such, the meal is a perfect manifestation of the cosmos and the ways in which it operates. However, it is in the social interaction around food that dynamism, flexibility, and change are expressed most clearly, and these social dimensions are examined in the next chapter.

2 ✺ The Social Dynamics of the Home Meal

In this second chapter on the Hoianese home meal, I expand my analysis in two directions: the first deals with the dynamics of the home-eaten meal, stressing its flexibility, variety, and ability to encompass change; the second sets the ground for the discussion of the interrelations between foodways and other social and cultural practices. I first classify the culinary process into stages, examining how each stage reflects, maintains and, at times, defines intra-family roles, statuses, and hierarchies. Specifically, I examine the conventional view of women as having a lower status, which appears to be in keeping with their identification with the low-status kitchen and cooking. An analysis of the changing roles of Hoianese women with regard to the culinary sphere at home reveals a much more nuanced and dynamic picture, however. The chapter concludes with an analysis of the tensions between the individual and the collective, as they materialize around the Hoianese table, emphasizing elements of social competition and conflict, which are essential though implicit aspects of the Hoianese meal.

PREPARATION, PRESENTATION, AND CONSUMPTION

This discussion of Hoianese foodways is broadly based on Audrey Richards's idea, in her pioneering culinary ethnography of the Bemba of Northern Rhodesia (1939), that all food-related activities could be grouped into either of three categories (or processing stages): "production," "preparation," and "consumption," *all of which reflect and maintain proper social relations.* However, I have made some important adjustments.

First, my work does not include a detailed discussion of the "production" stage, that is, of the entire range of farming, animal husbandry, and fishing, as well as food processing; although these are obviously important, they are beyond the scope of this work (and see Hickey [1964] and Popkin [1979]). Second,

I add another category or stage of culinary process, that of "presentation," which emphasizes aesthetics. This aspect, so central to the experience of eating, has been largely neglected by most food scholars, with the exception of some descriptions of East Asian culinary worlds.[1] Third, I wish to expand upon Richards's perception of culinary practices as reflective of "correct kinship sentiment" (1939: 127) to stress the constructive role of foodways in social interaction.

The "Preparation" Stage: The Kitchen

It was late morning, almost 11 AM, when we got off the ferry at the sandy riverbank of Duy Ngia village across the Thu Bon River. Hieu, our host, insisted that we go straight to the market, as this small village often runs out of fresh merchandise early. Co Dung and Hieu led the shopping and we managed to buy some vegetables, a big mackerel, and a watermelon that looked fresher than the rest of the wilted, fly-ridden produce. Then we pushed our bikes over the sandy paths to Hieu's house.

It was a typical central Vietnamese rural house: one story, tile-roofed, and painted light green, with a tiny front porch. The front yard, of compressed sand, was partly shaded by an apricot tree. The yard also had a small pineapple bed and some flowers. Hieu's younger siblings waited excitedly for the unusual guests near the prickly *thang long* fence ("soaring dragon" or pitaya, a cactus bearing the large pink dragon fruit).

It was getting late, so we all went to prepare lunch. Hieu led us to the side of the house and into a shed where farm tools were scattered. Rice, corn, sesame, and shallots were stored in big sacks under the roof beams. The kitchen was the next structure: a low, square, brick-walled structure, with neither windows nor chimney, thoroughly smoke-blackened and dark. Hieu's teenage sister gave me the fish, a plastic bowl, and a wooden chopping block and led me to the pump. "My father dug the well 10 meters deep in the sand so our water is very cool and clean," she said. I noticed that the pigsty was only a few steps away from the pump and hoped that 10 meters of filtering sand were enough.

As I was gutting the fish, she went back into the kitchen and, a few minutes later, puffs of smoke started billowing out of the slits between the roof and the walls. I rinsed the fish and stepped into the gloomy kitchen. In the dark smoky room, the girl was squatting near the hearth, stir-frying shallots and garlic in a wok, beads of sweat on her forehead. She held her head back, away from the smoke and heat of the fire, as the glare played a game of light and shadow over her face. With her free hand she was shoving pieces of wood deeper into the hearth to maintain the level of the flames and the cooking temperature, while keeping an eye on the rice that was cooking in a sooty pot. Co Dung was squatting by the door, trying to get some light, while crushing lemongrass stalks in a mortar. The brick floor was wet and slippery, the room dark and stuffy, and my eyes quickly filled with tears from the smoke. I stumbled out of the kitchen.

Traditionally, the Vietnamese kitchen or *nha bep* ("house [of the] hearth") was located in a separate building, behind the main structure of the house (Nguyen, K. T. 1993: 42), along with two other buildings: the toilets and the pigsty, an arrangement still common in rural houses such as Hieu's. The building spree that has engulfed Hoi An since 2000 led to the adoption of modern architectural styles in both urban and rural areas. One consequence is that the kitchens in many Hoianese houses were gradually incorporated with the main building. In rural houses, this is commonly done by simply extending the roof to connect the two sections, usually with inferior roofing material (such as asbestos, tin, or coconut palm, rather than the ceramic tiles used for the main building). The ceiling of this extension is also considerably lower than that of the main house. Due to the inferior material and the low ceiling, as well as lack of ventilation, windows, and chimneys, the kitchen is hotter, darker, and stuffier than the rest of the house, even in contemporary homes.

The kitchen floor is always lower than that of the main building, and people use the term "to descend to the kitchen" (*xuong bep*) to describe the act of "entering the kitchen." When I inquired about this, I was told that since water is used in the kitchen it should be lower to prevent leakage into other parts of the house. The floor of the kitchen is also usually paved with cheaper material. Thus, if the house is brick-tiled, as in the poorer houses, the kitchen floor would be made of compressed earth; if the house floor is made of ceramic tiles, as in more modern houses, the kitchen floor would be made of plain concrete, terracotta bricks, or, at least, different colored tiles.

Co Dung's parents' kitchen was a good example. The kitchen and toilets comprised a distinctive unit with common characteristics: a low asbestos roof, concrete floor, and no windows. The walls were sooty from years of cooking and the entire space was substantially less clean than the rest of the house. As this was the only part of the house with running water, the floor was often wet, slippery, and muddy. Only a service door (used to bring in the motorbikes, which were parked inside the kitchen at night) and a weak bulb shed light into this space. A chicken coop was built behind the toilets, beyond the kitchen but under the very same roof.

Another feature of Dung's kitchen was the presence of a pair of wooden slippers at the threshold between the main house and the kitchen and toilet section, to be used by anyone who entered this space, either for cooking or for using the toilets. (Shoes are always removed by the front door when entering a Vietnamese home.) The slippers thus implied that the kitchen and the toilets were not an integral part of the house, but were some kind of polluted/polluting space, where one should not walk barefoot, nor with shoes. These particular slippers, intended neither for the "outside" nor the "inside," hint at the special position of the kitchen as a liminal space "betwixt and between" (and see Bourdieu's [1984: 187] discussion of the role of carpet slippers in distinguishing between social spheres).[2]

In Chi Van's new house,[3] built in 2000 with the proceeds of the sale of her old home to the owners of an expanding hotel, the kitchen was only partly roofed (letting in light and fresh air, but also rain), while the toilets and pigsty were built as an integral part of it. When I asked her why the pigsty was inside the kitchen and not in the yard, as in her old house, she explained that it was easier to feed the pigs this way, as she wouldn't have to carry their cooked fodder too far.

In the modern houses that were first built in the town's new neighborhoods and that have become ever more common in the countryside despite their incongruity,[4] kitchens are an integral part of the house, and are often showy: they include Italianate tiles, electrical appliances, and large sinks and closets. Often, these large Western-style kitchens are hardly used by their owners: a back door leads to a makeshift shed built in the yard behind the house, where the actual cooking takes place.

The "Preparation" Stage: Cooking

The kitchen in Be's parents' house is spacious, and the large windows let in plenty of air and light. The house was planned and built by Be's European husband as a present for his in-laws; thus, its architectural features are somewhat unique.[5] We met Be the previous day in the market and she invited us for lunch to celebrate the last day of the millennium. Upon my request, we agreed to shop and cook together, and now, at approximately 10 AM, we were in the kitchen, preparing the meal.

The planned menu was the following: salad (*goi*) of pickled lotus stems, shredded carrots, and chicken; grilled beef in sesame; fried spring rolls; fish cooked in a tomato and lemongrass sauce. All the ingredients, including oil, sugar, sesame seeds, garlic, and fish sauce were bought that morning ("We have *nouc mam* at home," said Be, "but I bought a better one today.").

Be was running the show, instructing everyone on what to do. Her
niece marinated the beef, which had been thinly sliced at the market,
in *nouc mam,* black pepper, salt, sugar, and sesame. The father (an
ex-ARVN officer) lit some charcoal in a clay grilling-utensil. Irit was
charged with finely slicing the pickled lotus stems and carrots for the
salad. Be placed a wooden chopping block on the floor, rolled some large
wood-ear mushrooms, and chopped them with a cleaver into match-
stick-sized pieces. She quickly mixed them with the softened rice
vermicelli and a handful of the shredded carrots, and told me to
assemble the spring rolls. As Irit and I were unable to squat for long, Be
suggested that we sit on stools and perform our tasks at the kitchen table.

Be and her mother turned to prepare the sauce for the fish. Be
squatted by the wooden mortar and crushed some garlic. I offered my
help and she handed me the pestle, smiling at my attempts to crush the
cloves with strong pestle blows. Pieces of garlic flew out of the mortar
and my back begun to ache. "Go back to the spring rolls," she said,
taking over the pestle, adding the lemongrass stems into the mortar and
crushing them with precise movements.

Sitting near the table again, I started filling the spring rolls under the
watchful eye of Be's mother. I had to be very precise with the amount
and spreading of the filling: too much filling or too much liquid resulted
in a roll that was too fat and soggy; when spread unevenly, the roll didn't
look like a symmetrical cylinder; not enough filling made for a thin,
poor-looking roll. The rolling was tricky too: not only was it hard to
take the rice papers apart and keep them intact, but when rolling, they
often broke and had to be "patched," as a broken shell makes for an oily
spring roll. Irit, sitting beside me high above the frantic activity on the
kitchen floor, was struggling with the cleaver: "How can I cut the
carrots into match-sized pieces with such a big knife? I am sure I will
chop off my finger."

It was 12:00 PM now, quite late for lunch, and everyone was getting
hungry and irritable. A large wok was filled with peanut oil, which was
quickly heated to a smoky hot temperature over a powerful gas flame.
Then half of the spring rolls went in for a quick fry. The rest were fried a
couple of minutes later. The garlic and lemongrass were stir-fried in a
pot and mixed with ground tomatoes, and the fish slices were added for
a short boil. The marinated beef was carefully spread over a metal grid
and grilled over the glowing charcoal, filling the kitchen with a
pleasant, sweet smell. Be's mother took over the cleaver from Irit and
finished slicing the carrots, as the niece shredded the boiled chicken

flesh. The mother swiftly mixed the shredded lotus stems, carrots, and chicken, adding deep-fried shallots, chopped coriander, sesame, peanuts, and some sugar, and squeezed some lime over it, all the while mixing the ingredients gently with her fingers. Be wiped the table and placed the rice bowls and chopsticks on it, and a nephew was sent to the street corner to fetch some beer. By 12:25 PM we were all sitting around the table, ready to eat.

In many Hoianese kitchens, the preparation and actual cooking are performed while squatting on the floor. The kitchen does not have an elevated working space or a table; the floor serves for this purpose. All the taps are knee-high; hence, washing and cleaning are also carried out in a squatting position. The stove (traditionally wood-fed and made of three clay bricks, but nowadays consisting of a metal tripod or a kerosene stove), is also located on the floor. An Australian chef who spent some time in town told me that the amount of energy and effort invested in squatting and standing up when cooking was totally incomprehensible to him. He was even more puzzled by the fact that even some of the professional cooks in the larger restaurants in town adopted the same cooking postures. Indeed, a visit to the kitchen of most local restaurants would offer a similar picture: the kitchens are set lower than the rest of the building, and are generally wet, hot, dark, smoky, and not very clean. Carving, chopping, crushing, and washing, as well as cooking, are often performed squatting, even when hundreds of dishes are prepared daily.[6]

Although Vietnamese cuisine often involves arduous and elaborate preparation, a small number of tools and utensils is used. First and foremost is the cleaver (con dao): a large, heavy cast iron knife. This seemingly crude implement, often weighing more than half a kilogram, is used for everything, from heavy-duty tasks such as chopping firewood or cracking coconuts, to the most delicate ones, such as julienning carrots and papaya. In between, it performs every cutting job necessary: chopping poultry into morsels (horizontally, cutting through the bones), cleaning fish, peeling pineapples, and cutting the ends off bean pods. Since it is made of iron, the knife quickly blunts and rusts, and thus has to be sharpened frequently, usually before each cutting session. Though some kitchens feature a sharpening stone, the bottom edge of a clay bowl is often used. When a thorough sharpening is due, sidewalk stones seem to be popular implements. Smaller, Western-style knives are also common, and are mostly used for minor and secondary cutting jobs.

The second-most-important item is the iron wok (cai noi): deep and hemispherical, it serves a multitude of purposes. Its oval shape makes for an even distribution of heat, and it also conserves oil and energy, as a large frying sur-

FIGURE 2.1. Cooking in a squatting position at a wedding.

face is obtained using only a small amount of oil. The large surface of the wok is essential for stir-frying, allowing for the application of great heat to all the ingredients evenly and quickly, saving expensive fuel and preserving vitamins and other nutrients. Like the cleaver, the wok is used for all kinds of cooking: stir-frying, deep-frying, and boiling, though soups and stews are often cooked in Western-style metal pots (clay pots may also be used for specific dishes). Frying pans are common. Rice is steamed either in electric rice-cookers or in metal pots.

Next comes the mortar and pestle, usually wooden, though some kitchens feature metal or stone utensils. While grinding is an essential Hoianese culinary process, small quantities of ingredients, such as those used for the preparation of *nuoc mam cham,* are often crushed in the serving bowl. Before the development of mechanical mills, rice was pounded by hand in large wooden mortars to remove the chaff. In February 2000, I witnessed the use of such rice mortars at a Ba Na (Bagnar) hill tribe festival in the central highlands in Kon Tum Province. Some dishes, such as *cha ca* (pounded fish [patties]) call for lengthy pounding in a large mortar. On one occasion, the old mortar and pestle were taken out of storage just to show me "how to make proper *cha*." Pounding anything in a mortar, large or small, requires skill as well as strength, as I discovered on several occasions when I failed to obtain an even paste or to keep the food I was pounding from bouncing out onto the floor.

Large chopsticks and a ladle are used for most cooking processes: mixing, stir-frying, turning, and draining. A plastic strainer is a modern addition widely used for cleaning, washing, and draining, along with plastic bowls.

The traditional hearth was fed with wood or coal, which made grilling quite common (Jackson-Doling et al. 1997: 25). The recent popularity of kerosene and gas stoves renders the wood-fed variety much less common in Hoianese kitchens. Grilling is essential for some dishes, so most kitchens have a ceramic charcoal burner. This used to be the actual hearth in many houses and it is still often used for clay-pot cooking in addition to grilling. In stark opposition to the masculine display surrounding the Western barbecue, handling the charcoal burner and grilling are carried out matter-of-factly by women, either inside or just outside the kitchen.

Another noteworthy method is steaming. This technique arrived from cold northern China (Chang 1977) and is not popular in the kitchens of Hoi An. Most Hoianese kitchens do, however, have a bamboo or metal steamer of sorts at hand.

Ovens were not used in traditional Vietnamese cooking, and baking is not common today. The French introduced baguettes (*banh mi,* "flour cake"), along with cakes and croissants, but the former are always baked in professional bakeries (*lo banh mi,* "oven [for] bread") and cakes are prepared in special shops (in fact, many kinds of cakes are not baked, but pan-cooked). Other Western or otherwise modern utensils are rarely used: an industrial dishwasher installed in one of the new restaurants in town was eventually used as a spice cabinet.

The "Preparation" Stage: Hard Work and Cheap Ingredients

One of the most salient characteristics of Vietnamese cuisine is the great amount of hard work invested in the preparation of the dishes, in apparent opposition to the rough tools and utensils, the limited array of ingredients, and the prominence of cheap carbohydrates and vegetables and miniscule amounts of inferior animal protein. Why, then, do Vietnamese cooks invest so much work in what seem to be not only cheap, but low-quality ingredients?

Obviously, there are practical reasons behind the elaborate preparations: the carefully chopped ingredients can be cooked faster, which better preserves the nutritional value and saves energy. Furthermore, cutting the food into small pieces is necessary because chopsticks are used for eating. Beyond practical considerations, however, there are specific culinary explanations that transcend the kitchen.

I often asked why certain cooking methods are used for specific dishes. The answer I received was generally that "this kind of cooking makes for tastier food." "Tastier food" (*ngon hon*) does not refer only to taste, but also to smell, texture, color, shape, and even sound. In one case, Chi told me that "shallots must be fried in the very hot peanut oil before the other ingredients in order to enhance their *thom* [aroma]." In another instance, perspiring and breathing heavily after pounding fish with pestle and mortar for about an hour, I asked why we couldn't buy minced fish in the market. The answer was: "only pounding with pestle and mortar would give the right texture, not as mushy as the stuff you get at the market [where manual mincers are used]."

Another example is the peeling of pineapples, a cheap and abundant fruit, routinely used for cooking or as a snack.[7] Pineapples have one major disadvantage: their prickly external skin is very hard to peel. In canneries, peeling machines cut roughly one centimeter into the circumference of the fruit and also dispose of the fibrous stem, leaving only about 60 percent of the gross material for canning. This would be considered too wasteful by Vietnamese standards, however. Great effort and skill are invested in peeling the fruit with minimal waste: the skin is razed off with a cleaver and the prickly "eyes" are cut out deftly one by one. The fibrous center is left as a "handle" for each piece of fruit. All the while, the cook must be careful not to squash the pineapple's delicate pulp. Indeed, peeling a pineapple properly requires a lot of practice, experience, and hard work.

The hard work and elaborate preparations and cooking methods do not stand in contrast to the poor ingredients, but quite the opposite: they are intended to overcome and make the best of humble ingredients. High-quality ingredients need minimum tampering: a good-quality steak requires little seasoning and minimal cooking. Conversely, humble ingredients necessitate extensive preparation and/or lengthy cooking. The low-quality beef used for Hungarian goulash requires long hours of cooking and the liberal use of onions, garlic, and red paprika. Similarly, in order to prepare the Jewish gefilte fish ("stuffed fish"), the flesh, skin, and bones of the carp, a cheap, oily freshwater fish, are minced, ideally manually, to obtain a rough texture, and mixed with dominant taste agents (dill, onion, garlic, pepper, and sugar). In contrast, fresh lobsters are boiled or grilled very quickly, and steak tartar is not cooked at all (though minced and seasoned), like Japanese sashimi or Peruvian ceviche, both of which require very fresh, high-quality raw fish.

This holds true for Vietnamese cuisine as well: in Hoi An's beach restaurants, fresh prawns and clams are grilled briefly, and served with a squeeze of lime and some chili paste. Fresh good-quality sea fish is cooked very quickly, too. However, as most meals, and certainly most homemade ones, are prepared with humble ingredients, the real art of Vietnamese home cooking lies in the hard work and skill used to produce delicious and multileveled dishes.

The investment of such effort to produce surprisingly elaborate artifacts is not characteristic of Vietnamese cuisine alone, of course. However, this is the culinary expression of a more general Vietnamese tendency to make the most out of meager resources, be it the restricted amount of arable land that nowadays produces enough rice not only to supply the entire population of some 86 million, but also to turn the country into the world's second-largest rice exporter; or simple bamboo stakes, from which the Vietnamese devised implements of war that were used successfully against the superior armies of the Chinese, Mongols, French, and Americans.

The "Preparation" Stage and the Ambivalent Status of Women

Notwithstanding the importance and centrality of food and eating in Hoi An and the variety and elaborateness of the town's cuisine, the "preparation" stage is confined physically and symbolically to the most inferior realm of the house, performed in conditions that are not merely hard but that seem also to be somewhat humiliating. This paradoxical situation calls for some explanation.

It is important to stress that cooking the family meal is the exclusive role of women and that the home kitchen is a feminine sphere, from which men are excluded and consciously abstain. Thus, the location and conditions of cooking should be interpreted as related to the status of women in the family and, for that matter, in society at large. A conventional understanding of the position of women in Vietnamese society vis-à-vis the kitchen would be the following: the low status of the kitchen and the hard work involved in cooking reflect and reproduce the low status of women. Along these lines, K. T. Nguyen (1993: 42), in his analysis of the traditional rural house, points out that "the disposition inside the house reflects the predominance of men. . . . The women's rooms, located at the end of the house, are very dark as they usually have no window. The women stay there only during rest time or confinement, for their place is in the outhouses, kitchen and fields." Thus, the spatial setting of the house simply reflects female inferiority. It could be also argued that the conditions in the kitchen—the lack of ventilation, the fact that it is wet, dirty, polluting, and that cooking is carried out on the floor, in a squatting position, are not merely symbolic representations or reflections of the low status of women, but a concrete and embodied set of practices that create and perpetuate female inferiority.

Such interpretations are not merely trivial but also misleading. For one, it seems that the conservative understanding of gender relations in traditional

Vietnam as being overwhelmingly patriarchal (as in Nguyen's text above) is inaccurate. Second, the social status of contemporary Vietnamese women is complex, ambivalent, and rapidly changing. Following the theoretical premises of this book, the contemporary kitchen should therefore reflect these propensities and actually serve as a sphere in which they are negotiated and changed. An alternative reading of the women-kitchen-status is therefore necessary.

It is important to begin the discussion of this issue while bearing in mind that today, Vietnamese women control, as they did in the past, much of the family finances and economic activities, as well as most of the daily material decisions (Nguyen, T. C. 1993: 69; Taylor 2004: 97–98). Vietnamese women are often presented as "Generals of the Interior" (*noi tuong*), which is "a hidden but real position" (Nguyen, T. C. 1993: 69). Commerce is almost exclusively feminine, with women comprising the bulk of the petty and medium-level traders and an overwhelming majority of the consumers, controlling much of the commerce and the flow of capital.[8]

Challenging the conservative understanding of Vietnamese society as overwhelmingly patriarchal and male-dominated (e.g., Huard and Durand 1998 [1949]: 129 or Huu 1998: 238), contemporary scholars suggest that patriarchal expressions are just one aspect of the *am–duong* equation (Jamieson 1995: 13, 22–24), as matriarchal and matrilocal arrangements, which preceded the male-oriented system imported from China (Taylor 1983: 76–77), existed and continue to exist as powerful *am* undercurrents (Hirschman and Loi 1996: 229).[9] In fact, Taylor (1983: 13, 77) argues that the Vietnamese traditional kinship system was "bilateral," as it accommodated both matriarchal and patriarchal arrangements. Moreover, the social status of Vietnamese women has improved dramatically during the last century, both within the framework of the communist egalitarian ideology and as a consequence of their role in the war (Kleinen 1999: 184; Malarney 2002: 161–64; Werner and Bélanger 2002). Therefore, what the contemporary kitchen reflects is not simply the presumed low social status of Vietnamese women but actually their ambivalent and shifting position, the outcome of "the diverse and heavy responsibilities that women assume in the household division of labor" (P. Taylor 2004: 98).

Here, Sherry Ortner's (1974) influential "Is Female to Male as Nature to Culture?" is illuminating. In her attempt to explain the quasi-universal low social status of women and their practical inferiority and subordination, Ortner claims that this situation does not stem from the identification of "female" with "nature," as suggested by her predecessors, but from the fact that women have an intermediate position on the "nature–culture" axis. Women are associated with the domestic sphere, which is considered closer to "nature" than the masculine public sphere, identified with "culture" (ibid. 80, 83).[10] However, women actually serve as mediators, and their main role is to transform "nature" into "culture": they are universally charged with training children and socializing them into culture (ibid. 78); women are also charged with cooking—the transformation of natural elements into cultural forms (ibid. 80); women are also responsible for keeping "nature" out of the sphere of "culture" as they are universally responsible for cleaning and tidying: returning dirt to nature and keeping cultural artifacts in order to maintain culture and keep away chaos. It is this ambiguity and liminality—the position of women at the edge of "culture," transforming "natural matter" (children, food, cloth, dirt, etc.) into cultural artifacts—that explains their unique status and their universal inferiority.

The Hoianese kitchen is therefore a particular manifestation of Ortner's general scheme: the kitchen, the Vietnamese feminine sphere par excellence, is neither inside nor outside the house; although it is a polluting space, it produces pure (as in "edible") artifacts; one cannot enter it barefooted nor with shoes on, calling for special footwear. The Hoianese kitchen is located between "nature" and "culture," relegating Hoianese women to an ambivalent and liminal space, which not merely reflects and maintains their social status—below men and between nature and culture—but practically defines it.

Moreover, women's status in contemporary Vietnam is changing, and the kitchen clearly reflects this change. Connecting the kitchen and main building with a roof, installing kerosene stoves, purchasing electric rice-cookers, and "staging" modern kitchens in some nouveau riche houses—all these newly adopted practices reflect the changing status of women. While women are still very much identified with an ambivalent position on the "nature–culture" axis and continue to perform transformative tasks in liminal settings, these changes reflect a shift in their position, which seems to locate them closer to the "culture" apex.

In this respect, changes in the kitchen initiate and enhance the shift in women's status. For instance, when an urban family builds a large kitchen and invests money in new kitchen utensils, the act itself changes the status of the kitchen and, with it, the status of the women of the household, as well as their relations with other family members. Thus, when Van's family invested the equivalent of US$70 (or two months of this household's income in 2000) in a new gas stove, an elevated shelf was built for it in the kitchen. Van explained that the shelf was built so that "the expensive stove wouldn't get wet, especially during flooding." But even if the purchase was made for entirely practical reasons (it is quicker and more efficient to cook with gas, and it allowed Van to work longer hours outside and generate more income) or was status-oriented/fashion-motivated (as most of their neighbors had bought new gas stoves), and even if the shelf was built with the intention of protecting the expensive new purchase, the outcome was that Van began to cook standing up (though she continued to squat while cutting, shredding, or washing). If, indeed, squatting while cooking is the symbolic or practical embodiment of feminine subjugation, it is only reasonable to claim that standing up is as meaningful: it expresses the raising status of women. This change in the kitchen configuration, whether practical, symbolic, or otherwise, has an impact on the broader social structure.

It should be noted that the status of kitchens themselves has also improved in contemporary Hoi An due to other social processes that, in turn, further affect the status of women. Restaurants are burgeoning everywhere in Vietnam, and especially in Hoi An, where tourism is the main force underlying the prospering economy. These tourist-oriented restaurants generate economic capital, which is translated in due course into social capital. As most eating venues in Hoi An were originally operated by women, female restaurateurs were among the first Hoianese to become rich, translating their cooking abilities into wealth, which eventually generated social prestige. This process also explains the increasing number of men now entering the restaurant business, implying that the kitchen is no longer so lowly or strictly feminine.[11]

PRESENTATION AND AESTHETICS

As opposed to the diachronic Western meal, in which dishes are served in a sequence prescribed by the dishes' contents, the Hoianese home-eaten meal is synchronic: all the dishes and utensils are displayed on the table before the meal begins, exposing its aesthetic aspects. Here again, *am* and *duong* relations determine the aesthetic features, with the colors and textures making for harmonious "complementary oppositions." Since rice, the basis of the meal, is neutral tasting, colorless, and shapeless, each of the side dishes can be easily accommodated by rice within the *am* and *duong* framework: the crisp green herbs form one kind of harmonious combination with rice, while the pinkish-yellow fish create another. Rice seems to function as a neutral canvas, over which the other dishes are "painted."

The aesthetics of the *mon an* (side dishes) are also formulated along the lines of *am* and *duong*, appearing in contrasting colors: a green dish (leafy greens or fresh herbs) as opposed to a red one (such as boiled shrimps); a yellow dish (for example, fish in turmeric) in contrast to a dark brown one (roasted beef); while the amber-colored fish sauce adds yet another hue to the array of colors on the table.

The dishes themselves are prepared so that color opposition is maintained and enhanced: squid is cooked so that both its white flesh and purple skin are visible (in Western cooking, the purple skin is often removed and only the white flesh is served; moreover, squid is often fried in batter, which conceals its natural colors); beef is grilled with sesame seeds sprinkled on it, so that the purplish-brown meat serves as background for the golden dots of sesame; marinades for grilled meat often contain sugar that darkens the meat and gives it a glaze, which further enhances color polarization; the black skin of the mackerel is not removed, but is juxtaposed over the red (tomato) or yellow (turmeric) sauce in which the fish is cooked.

Dishes are often given a final touch of decoration that further enhances color contrast: grilled beef or fried fish are served on a bed of lettuce; a dash of chopped coriander garnishes the yellowish stir-fried noodles; and a tomato-peel flower is placed on top of the pale green papaya salad. A standard decoration for fried-in-batter "golden" dishes would be a bed of lettuce leaves framed by sliced tomatoes and cucumbers, generating a red-yellow-green combination that, according to Leach (1974) is a universal structure for color opposition, manifested, for example, in traffic lights. The fish-sauce dip also features red chili slices, white flecks of garlic, and black dots of crushed pepper floating over its translucent amber surface.

The shapes and textures of these dishes also generate *am–duong* combinations, both between and within dishes. Thus, for example, papaya salad (*du du tron*) is composed of colorful julienne strips (yellowish unripe papaya, green cucumbers, and orange carrots), mixed with round (light brown) fried peanuts; grilled slices of beef are decorated with dots of sesame. These two dishes are often served together in Hoi An, their shapes and textures (as well as colors), creating yet another *am–duong* combination.

Cooking techniques not only determine the taste and texture of the dishes, but also the way they look and smell, hence adding further dimensions to their aesthetic qualities. The Western idea of meat, potatoes, and vegetables roasted together and served as a meal would be considered a total breach of harmony in Hoi An, as the entire meal would appear "roasted," tilting it toward one side of the *am–duong* equation. A variety of cooking methods is essential for proper presentation: steamed rice, raw greens, and fermented fish sauce are presented along with fried, stir-fried, boiled, and grilled dishes, not only to create a varied taste experience, but also for visual balance.

It is important to stress that harmony rather than tension is the sought-after quality of *am–duong* relations. Thus, the colors of the dishes are often pale and even purposely diminished in order to soften oppositions: the light green of lettuce, the pale pink of shrimps, or the lucid amber of *nouc mam cham* (diluted with water and lime that not only smooth its heavy taste and aroma, but also lighten its brown color), highlight this tendency to avoid extreme colors and to facilitate harmonious combinations.[12] The cooking techniques further "soften" the color oppositions: the dominant color (e.g., the red of tomatoes in stir-fries, or the dark green of morning-glory in soups) somehow "taints" the paler elements (the squid or noodles, or the water) and diminishes the contrast by reducing the "distance" on the color scale.

The elaborate preparations also contribute to the softening of the shapes: dishes are usually served in chopstick-sized, generally curvilinear, pieces. The "sharp" distinctive squares and triangles, characteristic of Western cooking (e.g., pizza or pie slices), do not occur in Hoianese cooking. Therefore, even though a well-balanced meal consists of dishes with opposing shapes and textures, these oppositions are purposely tempered in order to enhance harmony.

Contrasting textures and cooking techniques also shape another aesthetic aspect, which is generally neglected by Western cooks, food experts, and anthropologists: the auditory experience of eating. To the best of my knowledge, Ohnuki-Tierney, in her analysis of the Japanese film *Tampopo* (1990), is the only scholar to discuss the importance of sound as an aspect of eating. As she points out, the sounds created when eating are a recurrent theme in the film. As opposed to Japanese eating, in which sound is an essential element (as in the slurping of noodles), Western eating is depicted in the film as silent (or silenced) and, therefore, sterile and lifeless.

Eating sounds are essential elements of the Hoianese meal. Here again, harmonious opposition is the desired outcome. Thus, the starchy "silent" rice serves as an "acoustic buffer" for crisp and crunchy sounds (lettuce, deep-fried shrimp crackers, peanuts), for the sucking sounds of noodles, for the slurping of soup, and for the chewing of elastic proteins. At the same time, auditory *am–duong* combinations should exist between dishes (e.g., the crackling sound of *banh trang* [rice crackers] that are added to the soft slurping of noodle dishes with which they are served).

Hoianese etiquette does not call for silent chewing with closed mouths, but just the opposite: food is chewed with mouths wide open and eating sounds are clearly stressed and enhanced by the diners. Thus, when eating a spicy dish, air is loudly inhaled through the teeth so as to "cool down" the spiciness, while raking rice into one's mouth is also characterized by the specific sound of slurping.[13]

Finally, in a chapter dedicated to the "dynamics" of the meal, a word is due concerning the apparently static nature of the "presentation" stage. While the principle of "*am* and *duong*" is dynamic by definition, the "presentation" stage requires a momentary halt of movement. *Am* and *duong* make for a round shape that continuously revolves around its axis. When the food is presented on the table, the revolving stops momentarily, so that *am* and *duong* can be clearly observed and appreciated. As the meal begins, movement is restored and *am—*

duong combinations are created and recreated by the diners, who mix the different foodstuffs and eat them. The frozen moment of presentation allows for an appreciation of the aesthetic aspects of the meal, but this moment is transient.

THE CONSUMPTION OF THE FAMILY MEAL

It was almost 5:30 PM and dinner was about to be served at Van's house. Her husband, back from a hard day's work, was stretched over the wooden armchair in front of the ancestor altar, watching TV. When Van called from the kitchen, he stood up and gestured toward the floor. Van brought over a large tin tray (*cai mam*) and laid it on the floor among us. On it were a pot of sour fish soup, a plate of boiled pork slices arranged over lettuce leaves, garnished with some tomato slices, and some ceramic bowls and chopsticks. The rice cooker, plugged into a socket by the kitchen door, was placed on the floor by Van. She filled the rice bowls and handed them over, first to me and Irit, then to her husband, and finally to her two children and a nephew. Cross-legged, we started eating. Van carefully picked a large slice of fish and placed it in her husband's bowl, and he nodded approvingly. Then he picked a nice chunk and placed it in mine. The children, who had carefully chosen their positions, kept a watchful eye over the TV. "Finish your rice," Van whispered sharply to her daughter, and added another spoon of rice to Irit's bowl.

Several of the basic patterns of consumption of the Hoianese home-eaten meal were clearly observable in the meal at Van's house: the senior female sits by the rice pot and dishes it out to the others; the senior male gets his share first and has priority over the side dishes; one should eat some of each and every dish; everyone is encouraged to eat more rice and to finish all the food on the tray (*an het!* "finish the food!"); the diners are expected to demonstrate self-restraint and to avoid gluttony; and finally, guests are always treated with deference and are offered the best part of the meal, although they, too, should eat with restraint.

As one aim of this chapter is to extend Richards's notion that patterns of food consumption reflect and maintain social relationships and "express . . . kinship sentiments toward relatives" (1939: 127), the question that needs to be addressed is which "kinship sentiments" and social arrangements were reflected in the meal at Van's house? To address this question, a short description of the Vietnamese social structure is essential.

The most important social feature of Vietnamese society is its intricate stratification: no two people have equal status in a given situation. This stratification system is based on the Confucian model of the "five human relationships" (*wu lun* in Chinese [Baker 1979: 11], *ngu luan* in Vietnamese [Marr 2000a: 774]). These "five relationships" ("ruler and subject," "father and son," "elder brother and younger brother," "husband and wife," and "friend and friend") are hierarchical, based on notions of superiority and inferiority, and are focused primarily on age and gender categories (Baker 1979: 11). Reciprocity, and not unilateral enforcement of power, is essential to these relationships: the person who is lower in status is expected to be obedient and respectful toward his or her superiors, but equally, the former must prove responsible and caring in order to be worthy of their subordinates' loyalty.[14]

Age and gender hierarchies, along with the principles outlining the "five human relationships," are clearly expressed within the consumption patterns of the Hoianese home-eaten meal, which are "hierarchical but reciprocal": the first bowl to be filled with rice is that of the senior diner (ideally, the eldest male but, in practice, age considerations surpass gender, making it the most elderly diner, male or female); the youngest participant invites his elders to begin eating (see also Vuong 1997: 67) with a polite "please" (*xin moi*); the senior diner is the first to pick up his chopsticks and take some rice from his bowl, with the others following, ideally along age and gender lines, although considerations such as education, wealth, power, or the fact that some of the diners are guests also affect the order of eating.

When picking out the morsels from the common serving dishes, deference is yet again expressed toward those who are senior. The latter might make use of their privilege, or else respond by yielding to lower-status diners by encouraging them to eat. This act asserts their preferred status and also expresses generosity and restraint (which yields further status and respect). A specific gesture of deference is to pick up a morsel of choice and put it in the bowl of another diner. This is usually a "top-bottom" gesture, an act of generosity and care by a senior toward lower-status diners. In any case, the eaters must "look at the tray and the food of others . . . [in order] not to be selfish . . . balance one's consumption of food and ensure its equal distribution" (Vuong 1997: 67).

The fact that the senior female dishes out the rice to the diners is yet another expression of the ambivalent position of women within the social hierarchy. Distributing the rice asserts the position of the mother as the one who nurtures the family. However, the fact that women cook and serve the others and always get the food after men (of the same age) imply their lower status. This ambivalence is also evident in the fact that the mother has the power to outline the social hierarchy of the situation, by determining the order of serving. I have seen men (or senior women) quietly suggesting/demanding changes when they thought that their wives (or daughters-in-law) misinterpreted the situation.

Beyond age and gender hierarchies, the consumption patterns of the family meal reflect other social values, such as respect for food in general and toward rice in particular (rice is served and eaten first and foremost; children are required to finish each and every grain of rice), as well as self-restraint and discipline: diners should be satisfied with whatever is offered, have some of each dish, refrain from expressing preference or dislike toward any of the dishes, and, most importantly, consider the preferences of others and avoid gluttony. In a home-eaten meal, as opposed to more public food events, the food should be finished—implying that it was tasty and that the amount was appropriate. In any case, uneaten food would be kept for the next meal, while leftovers are carefully collected and fed to pigs, dogs, and poultry.

In addition to age and gender hierarchies, generosity, reciprocity, restraint, and frugality, the meal at Van's house exhibited some important complicating features that call for specific attention. These features, yet again, point to the ambivalent and changing nature of the home-eaten meal as a cultural and social event.

The first feature was the location of the "consumption" stage of the home-eaten meal. Traditionally, meals were served on trays and taken on the floor (sometimes one would sit on a mat or on a low-lying wooden bed [and see Huard and Durand 1998: 25]). This is still a common practice in rural Vietnam and in many urban areas, and is still a very common mode of eating at home in Hoi An.[15]

Eating on the floor, just like cooking on the floor, implies that home-eaten meals are lowly, inclined toward the "nature" apex of the "nature–culture" axis. Indeed, eating is not perceived as wild and animal-like behavior, but rather as an ambivalent practice that somehow reveals and exposes the animalistic aspects of human existence. As we shall see, more elaborate meals, served in more complex social events, are always served at tables. Thus, eating the home meal on the floor should be understood in terms of the relations between eating and the animalistic or "natural" aspects of human behavior, as well as a reflection of the lack of complexity of this kind of meal in comparison to more elaborate food events.

The second feature is the shape of the eating tray or table, which hints at the egalitarian and communal nature of the Hoianese family meal. In contrast to the rectangular Western table, which denotes and imposes hierarchy (the person sitting at the "head of the table" is the "head" of the family), the Vietnamese dining tray (and table) is round, allowing for equal access to the food and implying that all the diners are equal. However, this round tray does have "corners" of sorts: the pot of rice is located near the mother, establishing her place as the "launching pad" of the meal. This position is termed *dau noi* ("pot head," Vuong 1997: 65), a term that indicates the importance of both mother and rice. The father is first served and first to eat, and his place, *giua mam* ("middle of the tray," ibid.), serves as the focal point of the meal. Thus, egalitarian, communal, and hierarchic concepts are expressed and accommodated within the harmony-oriented *am* and *duong* setting (reflected in the round shape of the tray), while social stratification is expressed and maintained.

The third feature is the conclusion of home-eaten meals. Though everyone starts eating together, there is no clear concluding moment to the home-eaten meal, and partakers drift away in what seemed to me at first individually and discreetly. While X. T. Voung (1997: 67) claims that the "participants should try to finish [the meal] simultaneously," this rule was not followed during the Hoianese family meals I observed.

While at first I was surprised by the fast pace of the meal (10–15 minutes) and the apparent rudeness of those who just left the table without excusing themselves or thanking anyone,[16] I eventually realized that the conclusion of the home-eaten meal is also carefully orchestrated so as to express social hierarchies: the senior diners (i.e., elderly and male) would be the first to leave the tray/table, while those of lower status would continue eating for a while. Thus, co Dung's father would be the first to leave the dinner table, while she and her mother would continue eating, just as Van's husband did at his home. At the lunches we had with our guesthouse staff, which were a bit more formal and public than home meals, the receptionists, male and female, would leave the table first, followed by the male employees, then the room maids, leaving the laundress and the cook alone at the table. In this case, education took precedence over age and gender hierarchies (along Confucian lines), with the university-educated receptionists holding the higher status and leaving first, followed by the men and the maids, and finally, reflecting the internal structure of the guesthouse, leaving the cook and laundress, who perform the dirtiest, most manual and physically demanding jobs, to clear up. This issue, along with the fact that those who are of highest status are the ones that *eat less,* is further developed later in this chapter as well as in the other chapters that deal with public eating.

Yet, despite the clear expression of social hierarchies, the Hoianese home-eaten meal is actually a dynamic and, in some senses, ambivalent cultural event. Though structured, stratified, and controlled, it contains elements and arrangements that locate it closer to the "natural" and "animalistic" end of the nature–culture apex. The next event further highlights this inclination:

(We return to the meal at Be's parents' house.)

The round plastic table was set at the center of the large kitchen and the dishes were set on it, making for a colorful sight. There were nine of us, sitting on wooden stools: Be, her parents, her husband and baby son, her teenage niece, one of her sisters, Irit, and me.

A fourteen-year-old nephew and his younger brother, each holding a large bowl, approached Be's mother. She filled their bowls with rice and topped them with some side dishes. They took their bowls to the front door, squatted on the stairs, and used their chopsticks to rake rice into their mouths. Cu Pham ("Little Pham"), Be's son, obviously enjoying his preferential status as the son of the family provider (the foreign husband), demanded his own stool and was now scooping rice with his fingers from his big rice bowl.

Though I was surprised to see Be's nephews eating from larger bowls (usually reserved for noodles), squatting on the floor, away from the rest of the family, I did not pay much attention to this observation. I gradually learned that this was a common pattern: pre-teen children eat separately, away from the family tray or table, squatting at some corner, eating from large bowls, especially when guests are present.

Later on, as I reflected on this phenomenon, I recalled another intriguing fact that could shed light on the eating patterns of children: the word for "child" or "children" is con, but con is also the prefix or generic marker for animals.[17] Returning to Ortner's (1974) interpretation of female inferiority as a consequence of the ambivalent and intermediary position of women on the "nature–culture" axis, she points out that in addition to their role in transforming "nature" into "culture" in the kitchen, they are also charged with transforming children, who "are likely to be associated with nature" in many cultures (ibid. 78). Ortner's argument is supported by the Vietnamese use of the same iconic marker for "children" and "animals," as well the practice of children eating from big bowls while squatting in some corner, just like household pets. Thus, children in Vietnam seem to be culturally conceptualized as animals or, at least, as existing in proximity to the natural and animalistic. When eating, their "animalistic" and noncultured nature is exposed, as eating in itself is ambivalent and dangerously close to physiology and to "nature"; therefore, young children are often excluded from family meals.

As with other speculations, I sounded this idea out with some friends. This time, however, I encountered staunch resistance, even from those who tended to agree with many of my ideas, or at least to accept their plausibility. "We don't think that our children are animals!" concluded co Dung angrily after a long debate, and refused to discuss the matter any further. I suspect that, in this case, I was out of line, not because the interpretation was so far-fetched, but because of the implications, which are quite unacceptable when removed from the realm of the "taken for granted" into the spotlight and reflexive sphere of interpretation.

Finally, though I have emphasized the "natural," ambivalent, and lowly dimensions of the family meal, it is important to stress that eating at home should not in any way be interpreted as animalistic, chaotic, anarchistic, or wild. Though featuring ambiguity and liminality, the Hoianese home-eaten meal is definitely a structured and controlled event, which reflects and maintains Vietnamese norms and values and imposes hierarchy, obedience and social order, as the next case clearly demonstrates:

"I eat very little," said *bac* ("older uncle," a term of respect and endearment toward people older than one's parents) Tang, Chi's father. "I am old now and I don't like eating too much. My wife and daughters run the family businesses and often have lunch with the employees in the shop. Sometimes they share dinner with the employees too. But I often eat alone. My son might come home for lunch, but he eats breakfast and dinner with his girlfriend or friends.

My house is right in the market, so I can choose any breakfast that I please and when I please. However, in the mornings I only drink coffee at my regular café. I often eat lunch alone . . . just some rice. I eat dinner earlier than the rest, as they all work till late. Sometimes I eat the leftovers from lunch.

Several people told me that their fathers ate alone, prior to the women and children of the household. The description of the father dining alone, served by the respectful family members, clearly manifests the privileged position of the patriarch. In a way, Tang's individual eating timetable reflects this tradition: as the senior male, he has the privilege of running his own eating schedule. But the meager meals or cold leftovers he subsists on express other important Vietnamese values, such as restraint and the denunciation of gluttony, as well as modesty and gentleness, all of which are valued Vietnamese masculine traits. Once again we encounter the Vietnamese tendency to "soften" contradictions and to counterbalance license with duty in an effort to maintain harmony: those high on the social ladder are entitled to many privileges, but are also constrained and restricted by a set of expectations and social demands that prevent them for abusing their social position.

CONFLICTS AND TENSIONS WITHIN HOME-EATEN MEALS

Though conflicts and tensions are contained and/or camouflaged as much as possible, a close inspection of the Hoianese home-eaten meal often exposes such feelings. The expression of emotions, either positive or negative, is considered socially inappropriate and shameful, and people do their utmost to control their feelings. An acceptable expression of negative feelings, however, would be avoidance and disregard. Anger can be expressed in family meals by avoiding eye contact, by ignoring the other party, or by simply refraining from the generous or friendly gestures described earlier, such as putting a nice morsel in another person's bowl.

A more pronounced way to express anger, criticism, or discontent is by commenting that the food is not tasty, by refusing the food, or by avoiding the meal altogether. I once witnessed an incident in which an angry husband, without uttering a word, refused to eat the food, causing his young wife to burst into tears. In other cases, the angry, offended, or hurt party would sit with the rest of the family, but their silence and long faces would express their feelings. Sometimes, and only after I inquired, I was told that a family member was absent from the table because he was angry and refused to eat with the others. In another family, an elderly woman and her daughter-in-law, living in the mother-in-law's house, were involved in a long and bitter conflict. As a consequence, the mother-in-law stopped eating with her son and daughter-in-law altogether, cooking her own meals and eating alone. I was told that this was an exceptional case and that this family was beyond reconciliation and beyond shame, as the fact that the old woman did not eat with the others was evident to all and there was no attempt to hide the awkward situation.

In 2006, a conflict had emerged among the members of another family, who were rather well off. The conflict was multidimensional, with different factions of the family allying and disengaging over various issues. The first open conflict, however, erupted during the Tet lunch (which I return to in chapter 7), and was recounted to me in detail, stressing the complete breach of eating etiquette: "Can you believe that my brother-in-law was so rude to my parents and to me during the first meal of the year?! . . ." Later on, the siblings and their spouses and children avoided communal meals and, eventually, the elderly parents themselves stopped eating with one another. My friend commented sadly that his family had become prosperous all too quickly and couldn't cope with their unexpected good fortune. "Since we stopped eating together," he said, "we are not a family any more."

The Collective and the Individual around the Table

Another type of tension observable around the table exists between the individual and the family (or collective). As opposed to conflicts between individual family members, however, tensions between the individual and the collective are not personal but structural and cultural, and are therefore expressed and handled within specific cultural frameworks.

It is important to note that the concept of the "individual" emerged only recently in Vietnam: "Since ancient times, there was no individual in Vietnamese society. There was only the collective: the large one being the country, the small one, the family. As for the individual, its unique characteristics were submerged in the family and in the country, like a drop of water in the sea" (Hoai and Hoai 1968, quoted in Marr 2000a: 787). David Marr points out that the concepts of "individual" and "self" appeared in Vietnam only at the beginning of the twentieth century, as a consequence of exposure to Western philosophies and ideologies. Essentially, the "individual" was "merely an irreducible human unit belonging to . . . something more significant [that is, the family, clan, village etc.]," as is apparent in the word *toi*, which today means "I," but was originally used when addressing persons of higher status (ibid. 787). Furthermore, individualism was perceived as selfish, short-sighted and dangerous and, therefore, was contested and denounced (ibid. 788–95). Marr concludes by suggesting that although "The idea of self-cultivation is very much alive in contemporary Vietnam . . . [t]he idea of each individual struggling for his/her place in the sun remains disturbing. Instead, one is expected to seek creative harmony with [the] people surrounding" (ibid. 795). It is important to note that the consequence of this ideology was the practical suppression of the individual throughout much of Vietnamese history and an increasing tension between the collective and the individual in more recent times.

During the family meal, the superiority of the collective over the individual is clearly expressed. As mentioned, the diners should not express a preference toward any dish and are expected to sample all of them equally, hence refraining from expressing individual taste. Furthermore, adjusting the dish to one's personal taste (using salt, pepper, or other condiments) is not acceptable and condiments are not part of the tableware. The fish-sauce dip, the only condiment (lime and chilli are sometimes served for certain dishes such as noodles), is "universal" and does not accommodate personal preferences. Its role resembles that of "gravy" more than of a condiment.

As restraint, frugality, and self-sacrifice are considered the qualities of a "good family member" (Jamieson 1995: 27), diners should not finish all the food and should try to leave some in the communal plates even if the eaters remain hungry. Restraint should be displayed even if the leftovers might go directly to the pigsty. Furthermore, eating all the food (and draining the sauce over some more rice) implies that there was not enough food on the table, which is often the case with poor families. Though family members are usually well aware of the situation, they would do their best to pretend that there was enough food by leaving some, in order to avoid embarrassing the providers and themselves for being so poor. I suppose that the removal of the children from the table is partly intended to avoid situations where individuals who are not yet sufficiently trained in these conventions might breach the rules and embarrass the rest of the family.

Nevertheless, individuality is expressed at the table, albeit in subtle ways. The fish-sauce dip and the aromatic herbs allow for quiet personal expression, with diners unobtrusively modifying the taste of their food. I also mentioned the gesture of placing a choice morsel of food in someone else's bowl. Here sensitivity is crucial and diners try to guess what their fellow diner's dish of choice would be. Housewives try to cook dishes that please their family members, and family members know each other's likes and dislikes quite well. When diners recognize that a certain dish is someone's favorite, they will encourage him or her to have more than his or her share, a gesture that clearly acknowledges individual taste as opposed to the prominence of the collective.[18]

When senior diners offer food to juniors, they express both generosity and restraint, which are essential for maintaining collective well-being. Such gestures often express special care, especially among husbands and wives: while it is the wife who generally yields to her husband, adhering to the social norms, it is an explicit and loving gesture for a husband to put some choice food in his wife's bowl. Such gestures may also lead to tension and conflict, as expressing preference toward someone essentially implies that the rest are less important. I have witnessed children protesting when their siblings were shown such "culinary favoritism"—another example of individuals demanding acknowledgement in the face of the collective.

HOME AND BEYOND

Despite the centrality of the Hoianese home meal, deciphering it is only the first step when trying to make sense of the culinary sphere of Hoi An. The remainder of this book explores meals eaten beyond home, and is mainly concerned with public eating in different communal, ceremonial, and festive contexts. The multidimensional analysis of the daily meal in this chapter continues to serve as the basis of this investigation, as each kind of feast derives much of its meaning from the differences and similarities between private and public eating.

3 ✬ Local Specialties, Local Identity

Whenever asked by a Hoianese what exactly I was doing in Hoi An, I would answer that I was studying the town's eating and drinking culture (*van hoa am thuc Hoi An*). The common response would be: "Ah, have you had *cao lau* yet?" For most Hoianese, researching the food in their town meant exploring their local specialties (*dac san* Hoi An), among which *cao lau,* a unique noodle dish, is the most prominent.

A book about these local specialties, titled *Van Hoa Am Thuc O Pho Co Hoi An* (The Culinary Culture of Ancient Hoi An), was published by Hoi An's municipal research center, stirring some controversy (Tran 2000). Local critics argued that many of the thirty dishes listed were neither unique to Hoi An, nor to Quang Nam Province—and some were not even unique to central Vietnam. There were also debates over dish names, food terms, and even modes of preparation. Yet what I found most intriguing about *The Culinary Culture of Ancient Hoi An* was that a relatively small town could boast more than thirty local specialties. I later realized that some dishes are considered unique not merely to the district or town but to specific villages (e.g., *banh dap Cam Nam* ["Cam Nam broken crackers"] or *mi quang Cam Chau* ["Quang Nam Province noodles in Cam Chau village style"]). Some of the dishes described as unique to Hoi An can in fact be found in other places, where locals are quick to dismiss Hoi An's claim for exclusivity.

Cao lau and *mi quang* noodles, *banh bao banh vac* dumplings, *hoanh thanh* wontons, *com ga* (chicken rice), *banh xeo* sizzling pancakes, "Cam Nam village 'broken crackers,'" "baby-clam salad," and sweet corn soup: these dishes are commonly acknowledged as the most significant Hoianese local specialties. They are popular, widely available, regularly prepared and consumed, and are important for understanding the relationship between food and identity.

FIGURE 3.1. Local specialties advertised at a restaurant:
wonton, *cao lau,* and white rose.

LOCAL FOOD—LOCAL IDENTITY

Local specialties are powerful markers of territories and places. Susanne Freidberg (2003: 3–4) suggests that "Stories about eating something somewhere . . . are really stories about the place and the people there . . . the reading of a food's story reveals, like any good biography or travelogue, a much bigger story—a cultural geography—of particular times and places."

While such assertions might suggest a clear identification of specific locations with particular "local dishes," a closer inspection reveals that the relationship between food and space is much more dynamic and complex. Mintz (1997: 189) has noted that as early as the beginning of the twentieth century, "masses of people everywhere were matter-of-factly eating food, sometimes as often as every day, that had come from (or originated) very far away," while Freidberg reminds us that "it takes only a few seeds or a handful of immigrant chefs to transform a particular locale's agriculture and food culture" (2003: 4).

It would therefore be highly unlikely that Hoi An, with its millennia-long history of immigration and cultural exchange, would feature some pristine, untainted local food, be it Kinh, Cham, Chinese, or any of the other ethnic or cultural groups that have inhabited the area. The culinary sphere, and specifically

the realm of *dac san* Hoi An, are privileged arenas for the production and negotiation of various aspects of the fluid and dynamic identity of the Hoianese. Although the Hoianese local specialties are only likely to be hybrid and unstable,
or perhaps precisely because they are hybrid and unstable, these dishes embed,
express, construct, and negotiate differing aspects of the Hoianese identity.

CAO LAU AND MI QUANG NOODLES AND HOIANESE IDENTITY

It was "my first day in the field" and I was happy and excited, though the
sky was grey and occasional showers kept surprising me whenever I
tried to leave my hotel room. I decided to officially begin fieldwork by
paying a visit to the only people I knew in town: the guides employed by
the local tourism bureau.

To my relief, they warmly welcomed me. Mr. Thau, the senior guide,
remembered me, and I was promptly invited for a cup of tea. After a few
minutes of pleasantries, Mr. Thau asked cautiously, "So, what exactly are
you going to do here?" I explained that I had come to study the local
culinary culture and he enthusiastically replied: "In this case, let me to
tell you about *cao lau,* Hoi An's most important dish." Somewhat
unprepared, I had to ask for some paper and began to take notes.

In careful and precise English, as if dictating, Mr. Thau talked about
cao lau, mentioning ingredients, preparation modes, seasoning, and
places that made the dish properly. He concluded by describing the dish
as a feast to all senses: "The yellow color of the noodles, the red of the chili
and the green of the lettuce, the crunching sound of the fried crackers,
the fragrance of the gravy, the contrast between the soft and crispy
elements, the several levels of taste, all make for a very special dish!"

That afternoon I went home very hopeful, feeling that everything was
working out so well and that I already had some ideas for the first
chapter of my book, a chapter that I would call "*Cao Lau,* Hoi An's Local
Specialty."

In subsequent months I kept pursuing the issue of *cao lau,* and collected
more information about the dish. To my surprise, I gradually discovered that
the Hoianese were not really clear about the origins of this specialty and were
not really sure how long it had been in Hoi An or even precisely how it is prepared. It was generally agreed, however, that this was not a Vietnamese or Kinh
dish. I was offered several, somewhat contradictory, explanations concerning
the origins and the modes of preparation of *cao lau,* which I term the Cham,
Chinese, Japanese, and "local" theories of origin, respectively.

Some people suggested that *cao lau* was originally a Cham dish retained by the local population despite the Vietnamese conquest in the fifteenth century and the cultural assimilation of the area into the Kinh world. The dish became an integral part of the new culture that evolved out of the fusion between the Cham and Vietnamese settlers. This theory is in line with Charles Wheeler's (2006a, 2006b) claim that the Vietnamese did not deport all the Cham to the South.

The "Cham-origins" theory is supported by the fact that some of the key ingredients used for the preparation of the noodles have "Cham connections." Some interviewees claimed that the essential ingredient is "a kind of ash prepared from a tree that grows only on Cu Lao Cham [Cham Island, a small archipelago of five islands some 15 km to the east of Hoi An River estuary][1] that is mixed with the water in which the rice is soaked before cooking and grinding. This ash gives the noodles their typical yellowish color." I later found that the ash is actually made from *rau gien* (amaranth) leaves, "which can be found everywhere on the beach, but grow in large quantities on Cham Island." Yet I was told by one producer that she bought the ash in the market and had no idea of its origin.

The other "Cham" ingredient is the water used for cooking the noodles. Several informants told me that *cao lau* could be made only in Hoi An because the preparation requires the use of water from the "Cham Well," also known as *Ba Le* (Madame Le's) Well, which was built by the Cham more than five hundred years ago: "The water in this well is always cool and the well never dries up. The water in this well has a special quality: whatever is cooked in it becomes hard. So even though the noodles are steamed several times, they do not turn soft and soggy but harder and harder." Here again, although the producer said that her family always used water from the Ba Le well, she herself felt that she could just as well use water from any other source. Another informant suggested that this specific well was used for generations by Hoianese *cao lau* producers because the water is unusually clean: "the water has no secret . . . it is just clean and pure. Nowadays, we can get good water from the factory or from the government, but in the old times, this used to be the most reliable source of water in town. This is why the noodles were always made with the water of this well."

Within the framework of the "Cham-origins" theory, an interesting point of view was conveyed by prominent Vietnamese historian and professor Phan Huy Le, who told me that the term *cao lau* was Malay-Polynesian—that is, Cham. He further pointed out that some researchers believe that *cao lau* came from the Malay Peninsula, where a similar dish exists. Though this link with Malay Peninsula was mentioned by others, I could not find further evidence to support this claim. However, since the ethnic Cham in Vietnam and Cambodia have recently renewed strong links with the Malay-Muslim cultural sphere (Taylor 2007), this could explain the contemporary Hoianese attribution of Malayan origins to the Cham dish, despite the fact that the recent links were established many centuries after the Cham ceased to exist in Hoi An as a distinctive ethnic group.

While the "Cham connections" of *cao lau* are acknowledged by many with whom I talked, the most popular theory concerning the origins of this dish is the "Chinese" one: *cao lau* is a Chinese dish that was brought over to Hoi An by the *Minh huong*, members of southern Chinese clans. The idea that *cao lau* is Chinese seems quite plausible for several reasons. For one, noodles originated in China (Anderson and Anderson 1977: 338; Tannahill 1973: 145) and spread all over Southeast Asia with Chinese colonists, immigrants, and refugees. Moreover, the influence of Chinese cuisine on Vietnamese eating patterns is so important that a Hoianese restaurant owner simply suggested that *cao lau* "is probably a Chinese dish because most of the Vietnamese dishes come from China."

Second, though the special noodles are the salient feature of this dish, the sauce or gravy (*nuoc leo*), which is considered as crucial, is quite clearly Chinese: it is made from a fatty chunk of pork[2] cooked in soy sauce and seasoned with garlic, onion, black pepper, MSG, sugar, and *ngu vi* (Chinese five spice), which deeply influence the taste of the gravy and of the whole dish. The fact that soy sauce and not fish sauce is used for the gravy further indicates that this dish is Chinese and not Vietnamese.

It should be noted, however, that most of the other noodle dishes coming from China still carry Chinese names (*mi, mien, hu-thieu*) or, at least, resemble in one way or another the original Chinese dish (e.g., Vietnamese *hoanh thanh* are virtually identical to Chinese wontons), but as far as I could find out, the unusual name *cao lau*, the specific kind of noodles, and the unique gravy are unknown in China and, for that matter, elsewhere in Southeast Asia. The term *cao lau* itself does support the Chinese-origins theory, however. The first restaurants to appear in Vietnam in the nineteenth century were owned by Chinese immigrants who had settled in Hanoi. These venues were called *cao lau*,[3] which means "a high pavilion" (Nguyen, T. 1997: 130). The name probably derived from the fact that the kitchens of these eating establishments were located on the first floor and the food was served to the diners on the second floor or gallery.[4] I was often told that Chinese immigrants owned the first commercial eating houses in Hoi An, while most ancient Chinese houses in Hoi An have a second floor or attic. It is therefore reasonable to assume that these pioneering culinary venues were also called *cao lau* and that the name was gradually attributed to the special noodle dish that these venues served, though with a semantic change of tone.

The intriguing name led one of my friends to come up with yet another explanation: "*Cao lau* is dry (*kho*) and fat (*beo*) and therefore warming (*nong*) and suitable for winter. In Hoi An, the winter is cold and wet, as several floods hit town. When the houses get flooded, the Hoianese find shelter in their attics [in Vietnamese, *lau* or *cao lau*], where they wait for the water to recede. In order to combat the effects of the cold and wet weather, they eat a fat, 'drying' soup. As they eat it in their attics, it acquired the name 'attic' or '*cao lau*'. . . ." Although this version got the thumbs down from most people I consulted, it has its own appeal and, as we shall see, further contributes to the discussion of *cao lau* as a vessel of local identity.

In an issue dedicated to Hoi An in the periodical *Vietnam Cultural Window* (produced in Hanoi by The Gioi, a state publishing house), I found yet another account of the origins of *cao lau:* a Japanese scholar recognized it as a Japanese dish (Iacomo 1998: 16). I quickly found out that the idea that *cao lau* could be of Japanese origin had quite a few supporters in town: several locals, including a member of a family that has been selling the dish for more than three generations, affirmed that *cao lau* was indeed of Japanese source.

It is important to note that contemporary Japanese researchers have a deep interest in Hoi An and that the Japanese are the most generous and important foreign sponsors and collaborators in researching, restoring, and preserving the ancient quarter. Their interest is often explained by the ample historical and material evidence depicting an extensive early Japanese presence in Hoi An.

This interest could also be nurtured by a political agenda: bearing in mind the extreme violence of the Japanese occupation of Vietnam and other Southeast Asian nations during the Second World War, I suspect that the Japanese are keen to confirm evidence of their more peaceful historical presence in Hoi An and their contribution to its cultural heritage. If *cao lau,* purported to be Hoi An's most well-established culinary specialty, is of Japanese origin, not only is Japanese presence confirmed but the positive nature of the source of one of Hoi An's most unique and intimate artifacts is stressed. It might be the case, then, that a historical and political agenda, and a good measure of wishful thinking, evoke the idea that *cao lau* is a local version of *soba* noodles.[5]

I have asked several Japanese researchers and tourists whether they recognized *cao lau* as Japanese, but all of them said hesitantly that they didn't think so. Some Japanese student residents put an end to this theory when they told me that cinnamon, a component of the "five spice" seasoning, is never added to Japanese savory dishes and is used only for sweets. Therefore, they concluded authoritatively, the noodle broth could not be Japanese.

In order to better understand the origins and meanings of *cao lau,* I wanted to observe the preparation process, just as I had other significant ingredients and dishes. I was told that only three families in Hoi An produced the distinctive noodles themselves, and asked several friends if they could introduce me to one of these families so that I could document the making of the *cao lau* noodles.

To my surprise, I was told that this would be impossible. As I found out soon enough, they were right: none of the families allowed me to witness the making of the noodles. This was highly unusual, as I was generally most welcome whenever I requested to see such culinary processes.

I could not understand this refusal until co Nguyet, one of my Vietnamese teachers, told me: "Making *cao lau* is a family secret and no one except the family members are allowed to learn it. Even the daughters are not allowed to see some of the crucial stages, so that when they get married, they won't pass on the secrets to their new families. That is why they refuse to let you see how they make *cao lau.*"[6]

The various folk theories about the origins of *cao lau* say a lot about the dish and about the people who eat it. What the different theories of origins (Cham, Chinese, "flooding," and Japanese) have in common is the suggestion that, though definitely local, *cao lau* is not a Vietnamese/Kinh dish in its origins. The fact that Hoi An's most prominent local specialty is not Kinh further hints at the foreign origins of the Hoianese themselves, or possibly, at the blending of various ethnic groups, along with their different cultures, with the original dwellers and their culture. This mixed ethnicity is central to Hoianese culture and identity and is clearly celebrated in the town's name: Hoi An, which means "[the] peaceful congregation," of Chinese and Kinh, as well as people of other nationalities who have managed to live together peacefully for centuries. The local guides proudly tell tourists at the gates of the Chinese assembly halls, where the town's name is inscribed in Chinese characters, that "Hoi An was an international center for hundreds of years, a place where people from many cultures met and cooperated, and where foreigners could live among the Vietnamese in peace."

Consequently, the different versions are not contradictory but complementary: the presence of several theories of origin concerning the most important and lauded local dish suggests a special local identity that is multiethnic and hence unique. *Cao lau* allows for multiple ethnic identities to be successfully expressed. This success is embedded in a dish that is unique and, most importantly, tasty. Thus, when the Hoianese eat *cao lau,* they do not commit themselves to any of the ethnic identities that can be singled out as the "original" or "correct" ones, but quite the contrary: they celebrate the unusual achievement of several ethnic groups who manage somehow to live together harmoniously and peacefully, fusing their diverse traditions into a new hybrid culture.

The "local theory," which I found the most dubious, adds yet another very local aspect to the dish and the identity it depicts: this "theory" does not trace the origins of *cao lau* but explains the enigmatic name in local terms, defining yet again that context. In the rest of the country, floods hit during the summer months, but in Hoi An, due to topographical conditions, floods occur during the early winter months—around November and December, when it turns bitterly cold. Eating a warming winter soup in the attic, having been driven upstairs by the floods, can occur only in Hoi An. By contrast, in the rest of the country people would look for "cooling" dishes during the flood season, which takes place at the end of the summer (August–September). When we consider the local water and local ash too, we realize that *cao lau,* no matter what its origins, is clearly grounded in Hoi An.

It seems, then, that *cao lau* deserves its place of local culinary honor, as it carries the essence of Hoianese existence. *Cao lau's* prominence in guidebooks, local food lore, and restaurants reflects its actual importance as a central vessel for Hoianese identity. At least, that was what I thought until the day I had *cao lau* with Chi.

Chi invited me for lunch and asked what I would like to eat. Considering her culinary expertise as one of the town's best chefs, I asked her to take me to eat the best *cao lau* in town, and so we headed for a small restaurant in Cam Chau village, on the road to the beach.

Mrs. Tho, the proprietor, began to prepare our order. She placed a handful of the thick, quadrate, yellowish *cao lau* noodles in a bowl and poured a ladle of boiling water over them, to warm and "refresh" them. While the noodles were soaking, she picked up a big bunch of lettuce leaves and half-filled another ceramic bowl. She used a perforated ladle to dip some bean sprouts in a pot of boiling water simmering over the gas stove and then spread them over the lettuce. She pressed the noodles with her finger to check their consistency and then drained the water and spread the noodles over the lettuce and sprouts. Taking a large chunk of cooked pork, she sliced off three or four thin slivers, placed them over the noodles, and poured a very small amount of the cinnamon and star anise-scented broth (*nuoc leo*) on top of them. A fistful of crunchy, deep-brown croutons (made of the deep-fried sliced ends of the sheets of rice dough from which the noodles are cut) gave the final touch to the dish.

Mrs. Tho's daughter came over to our table holding two bowls. She placed the bowl of *cao lau* in front of me and another bowl in front of Chi. I looked at Chi's bowl and, to my surprise, saw that she was having *mi quang.* "Are you not having *cao lau*?" I asked. "No," she said, "actually, we don't like it so much."

I must say I was really taken aback. *Cao lau* seemed unquestioned by everyone as being important and was available everywhere: on the menu of most restaurants in Hoi An, including several well-patronized specialty restaurants and food stalls in the old quarter. The freshly made thick noodles themselves were sold in the market. More to the point, *cao lau* was always mentioned whenever Hoi An's *dac san* were discussed. But here was Chi saying, "We don't like it so much. . . ."

Trying to understand what she really meant, I first had to formulate the correct question. When asking a Hoianese what he or she likes to eat, the answer would usually be "rice," and when I asked if they liked *cao lau* they would just say "yes" or "of course." Since these questions led me nowhere, I had to ask a comparative question.

Obviously, the correct question was there all along: what I had to do was to determine which noodle dish was popular in Hoi An and then ask my informants to compare it to *cao lau.* Here there was a clear and uniform answer: the most popular noodle dish in Hoi An was not *cao lau* but *mi quang,* the dish that Chi had ordered.

The full name of this dish is *mi Quang Nam* (Quang Nam noodles). The dish is made of broad, fresh rice noodles, usually white but sometimes colored yellow with turmeric (a prominent spice in the local cuisine), fresh lettuce, aromatic herbs, bean sprouts, a couple of hard-boiled quail eggs, a few pork slivers, and a red stock made from tomatoes, shrimps, and pork fat. It is served with a crunchy rice cracker (*banh trang*), fresh chili, and *nuoc mam.* In the past, the broth was made with some kind of seasonal jellyfish; hence, the dish was offered only in season. Nowadays, the jellyfish is hardly used and the dish is served all year round.

Like *cao lau, mi quang* is usually eaten by locals for breakfast or lunch and is hard to find later in the day. It is sold all over the province, as well as in the neighboring city-province of Danang. I have had *mi quang* in Nha Trang (more than 500 km to the south and four provinces away) and even in Ho Chi Minh City (Saigon). The proprietors, both originally from Quang Nam Province, told me that many of their customers were fellow *que huong.*[7] It should be noted, though, that even in neighboring Danang, the broth tastes remarkably different from that sold in Hoi An, a point that is always stressed by the Vietnamese whenever talking about eating their *que huong* dishes away from home (e.g., Nguyen, X. H. 2001: 101–109).

I asked my friends what they liked more: *cao lau* or *mi quang*. The answers were surprisingly uniform: "we prefer *mi quang!*" When I asked why, I was generally given two kinds of answers beside the obvious "*ngon hon!*" (tastier!): "*cao lau* is dry (*kho*) and fat (*beo*) and, therefore, heating (*nong*)" (and thus not appropriate for the hot climate) or "*mi quang* is cheaper."

Cao lau is considered a "dry" dish because it has only a small amount of thick gravy, while the noodles are compressed, heavy, and relatively hard. Many of my friends claimed to feel their throats dry up while consuming the dish. Here I should interject that such observations—people telling me that while eating they felt an immediate impact of the food on their body, such as a change in body temperature when tasting dishes that were "cooling" (*mat*) or "warming" (*nong*)—were not uncommon. I, on the other hand, felt that my body became hot whenever I ate warm and/or spicy dishes on a hot day, whether I was eating *cao lau* or *mi quang*.

Cao lau noodles were twice as expensive (5,000 dong vs. 2,500 dong per kg of *mi quang*) in the year 2000. Nonetheless, the price for a bowl of either dish cost roughly the same: 4,000–5,000 dong (by 2008 prices had doubled). I was told that the similar price was achieved through increasing the amount of greens in relation to noodles and meat in *cao lau*, so that for the same price the customer got fewer noodles and meat. Thus, though the price of a portion of either dish was similar, *mi quang* was more filling and so, in fact, cheaper.

There were other reasons for preferring *mi quang*. One informant said that he prefers *mi quang* because they are made from readily available ingredients found in every home: "Any family can make *mi* noodles at home; it is easy and there are no secrets. The soup is also based on widely available products easily found in any household and that are not as rare and expensive. People here like to eat things from their gardens, and *mi quang* can be prepared from such ingredients."

Yet, if it is true that the Hoianese prefer *mi quang*, who eats all the *cao lau* that is on offer in town? When asked this question, most Hoianese said that the main consumers of Hoi An's special dish are from out of town: foreign tourists, overseas Vietnamese, domestic Vietnamese tourists, and even weekend visitors from neighboring Danang, Tam Ky, or Hue. One acquaintance, the owner of an antique shop, said: "Whenever we have guests from out of town, I order *cao lau* from the next-door restaurant. The owner is Chinese and he makes it very well. He also charges me only 4,000 dong instead of the menu price of 5,000 dong." Another friend said: "Of course I can make *cao lau* at home. Sometimes, when I have guests, I cook it for them. But my family doesn't like it;

they have had so much already and *they want something different*." Sometime later, I tried to challenge this last comment by pointing out that many people eat *mi quang* and *bun* (rice vermicelli) almost daily, but never say that they have had too much of it or that they "want something different." My remark was gently rebuffed with a smile and led me nowhere.

The owner of a vegetarian sidewalk stall serves *mi quang* daily, but on the first and fifteenth days of the lunar month (black and full moon days, which are *ngay ram* or worship days) offers *cao lau*. Here again we see that *cao lau* is recognized as special, yet the locals prefer *mi quang* as their daily fare. I would estimate that among the Hoianese, the consumption ratio of *mi quang* to *cao lau* is roughly 10 to 1.

Returning to the discussion of the relationship between local food and local identity, several questions come to mind: what is the meaning of this practical rejection of a dish that embodies the harmonious local multiethnic identity? Does this suggest that the locals reject it? And what does the de facto dish of choice stand for? And finally, is there an "identity struggle" between *mi quang* and *cao lau*?

The first point that should be reemphasized is that most Hoianese know very little about either dish and, as one of them told me, "don't really care." For them, the question is whether the dish is tasty or not. Though I agree that taste is crucial, my basic theoretical assumption is that taste is culturally constructed and therefore that the preference of a certain dish over the others because of its taste does not "sterilize" the cultural aspects but does just the opposite: it stresses their importance. As for the *mi quang* vs. *cao lau* "identity struggle," two important points have to be further pursued: the first concerns the cultural identity embedded in *mi quang*, and the second regards its relative prominence.

Quang Nam noodles embody a regional identity—that of central Vietnam. Though nowadays Quang Nam Province is officially only one of several central coastal provinces, Quang Nam as a cultural zone stretches over much of the central coast. Hence, "the southern province noodles" suggest a much wider scope of identity than that suggested by *cao lau*, which is limited to the small town of Hoi An. Furthermore, according to Mr. Sung (the owner of one of the oldest restaurants in town and an endless source of information regarding local and culinary history), Quang Nam was also the Chinese name of the province they established in the conquered Red River Delta. When the Chinese were defeated, this term was adopted by the Vietnamese imperial bureaucracy and attributed to the southern border provinces of the Vietnamese kingdom wherever they shifted to during millennia of expansion to the south (*Nam Tien* or "marching south"). A dish typical of Quang Nam is, therefore, an ethnic Kinh dish that is related to the Kinh expansion to, and colonization of, the south.

Mi quang suggests a totally different identity than that implied by *cao lau*: it stands for the ethnic Vietnamese who colonized the central and southern parts of the country. So when the Hoianese declare (in culinary terms), "We don't like *cao lau;* we prefer *mi quang,*" they actually choose to incorporate and embody a Kinh, expansionist, violent, and even nationalistic identity and reject the cosmopolitan, tolerant, foreign, and somewhat strange identity implied by *cao lau*.

It might seem that what we have here is a blatant struggle between the Hoianese multiethnic, tolerant, cosmopolitan micro-identity and the "Quang-namese" Kinh, expansionist, nationalistic macro-identity. In fact, the story seems to be more complicated, as the culinary struggle of identities, so to speak, is far subtler. The local practices and discourses clearly distinguish between the two dishes: one is explicitly celebrated as the most prominent local specialty, worthy of attention and discussion, while the other is treated as normal and ordinary, more a staple than a specialty. From the opposite perspective, it could be argued that the dish that is less popular with the locals has simply better public relations, mainly with relation to its unique "local" characteristics, while the real local favorite, one that embraces a much wider geographical scope and expresses ethnic majority notions, is simply taken for granted.

Chi further supported this idea of a dynamic balance between *cao lau* and *mi quang* when I discussed my findings with her. "You must remember," she pointed out, "that in Vietnam, every saying has two meanings, which are termed 'bright' and 'dark' . . . and we consider the dark aspect to be the important one." *Mi quang* should not be understood as inferior to *cao lau*, but just the opposite: though it is rarely hailed (and therefore should be perceived as the "dark" element), its prominence is expressed in praxis, making it the more important dish.

This, however, was not the end of the story. As I was talking with Chi about the relations between these two dishes, she suddenly said:

> Let me tell you why we don't like cao lau. *The real reason is that no one makes it properly any more. As you already know, the families that make the noodles do not let anyone see the preparation process, but my father was invited by one of the producers to consult him about his garden. At their house, my father saw the rice soaking in water and asked his host about the ash. The man burst into laughter and told my dad that nowadays no one uses the ash anymore. It takes too long and the amount of clear ash water that can be produced efficiently is too small. So they use some kind of chemical. You see, the taste is not like what it used to be in my childhood; it is not right anymore.*

Though I cannot confirm that the special ash has been replaced by modern chemicals when preparing *cao lau,* I did see chemicals mixed in ash water that were used in making special *banh u tro* ("small ash-cakes") for Tet Doan Ngo, the summer festival (discussed in chapter 7). Furthermore, several people pointed out that the noodles do not taste as they used to, and that many special qualities seem to have disappeared. One of my friends responded to my question about the taste of *cao lau* by saying: "In the past, they used to steam the noodles [during the preparation process] seven to nine times, and so they were really hard. But nowadays, [they are steamed] three or four times at most, and the noodles are not hard enough." Though I am not sure if this claim is correct, the point was that modernization has altered the process and led to an inferior product. If this is the case, it was not the cosmopolitan identity that was being rejected but, rather, the contemporary process of commercialization of every realm of life and, specifically, the turning of Hoi An into a tourist attraction.

Tourism has had a deep impact on the production of local artifacts (Cohen 1988, 1992, 1996, 2000; Graburn 1967, 1984) and most researchers agree that although tourism promotes the production of local arts and crafts and can even lead to a renaissance, it almost always pushes for simplified, standardized, and somewhat vulgarized products. The rejection of *cao lau* could also be explained in terms of resistance to the process of commodification that Hoianese cuisine is undergoing, while *mi quang* is perceived as representing the original local cuisine, unhampered by modernity and tourism.

At the end of our conversation, Chi added apocalyptically: "If the producers don't need the precise water nor the special ash to prepare *cao lau* anymore, soon you will be able to find them everywhere, even in your country. . . ." She was pointing directly to the globalization of Vietnamese and Hoianese cuisines, and suggested that it was a negative or, at least, an "unnatural" process. It is interesting to note that she is herself an important agent in this process: owning three of the town's most successful tourist-oriented restaurants, running an international cookery school where she teaches her "family recipes," and traveling abroad quite often to demonstrate her cooking skills, she is one of the principal exporters of Hoi An's culinary culture. Yet even she found it strange that the special dish of her tiny home town could be "globalized" in such a manner.

BANH BAO BANH VAC DUMPLINGS AND THE HOIANESE-CHINESE

The family that makes *banh bao banh vac* ("plump cakes [and] flat cakes") is one of the nicest and friendliest in town. I stumbled upon them when I noticed a small sign reading "White Rose" (in English), pointing into a narrow alley off one of the main streets. I followed the winding alley that ended in a small yard with some small plastic chairs and tables, wedged between several houses, whose dwellers stared at me through their windows.

I entered the house and saw the family members sitting by a low, wide, solid wooden table, preparing the *banh*—hundreds of translucent, white, flower-shaped dumplings that they carefully arranged in large tin steaming trays. The small room had a low ceiling and was quite dark. The table was set by the window, through which some light came in. I said "hello" and they all lifted their heads, looked at me, and smiled.

Mr. Le's great-grandfather came to Hoi An from Beijing over a hundred years ago, settled among the Hoianese-Chinese, married a local woman, and established the business. A large painting of this forefather, wearing a pale blue Chinese tunic, was hanging on the wall by the family altar. Mr. Le, standing in front of his ancestor's painting, proudly patted the shoulder of his own plump thirteen-year-old son and told me: "He will be the fifth generation of *banh bao* makers. . . ." Mr. Le, his wife and two daughters (twenty-one and eighteen years old in 2000), as well as three or four teenage relatives, were working in the family business. The "heir" was still going to secondary school. His older sisters had not attended high school, as they had to join the business.

Their working day would start at 5:00 AM when Mrs. Le would go to the market to purchase a few kilograms of shrimps, as well as spring onions, mushrooms, and bean sprouts for the dumpling filling. Mr. Le would take some three kilos of rice flour, mixed with some water, and pound the mixture in a large stone mortar to make a dough: "The real secret is in the pounding—how to make the dough. No one in Hoi An knows how to make the dough properly except for me, and I learned it from my mother. I always pound the dough early in the morning, inside the kitchen, with the windows closed, and I don't allow in anyone, including our nephews. This is our family secret."[8]

Most of the work and the greatest expertise, however, are invested in the shaping of the dough into dumplings. There are two kinds of dumplings: the flower-shaped *banh bao* and the simpler, shell-shaped *banh vac*. The first is filled with a paste made of shrimp and pork fat, while the second contains shredded shrimp, onion, mushrooms, and bean sprouts. The first stage of shaping is similar in both cases: a ball of dough, about a centimeter in diameter, is flattened with the palm on the working table. Using an index finger dipped in a saucer of oil, the small circle of dough is shaped into a cup. A pinch of the pink shrimp paste serves as the heart of the "rose," and the top of the thin, translucent cup is then bunched together to form the white "petals." The *banh vac* (flat cake) begins similarly with a circle of dough; the shredded vegetable-and-shrimp filling is placed on half the dough before it is folded and the edges are pressed together to form a semi-circular dumpling. Both types of dumpling are steamed in a *lo* ("oven," actually a steamer) for a few minutes.

The family and their employees spend over ten hours daily making roughly a thousand dumplings (and a couple of hundred more when there are special orders for weddings or other special events). Mr. Tran complained that his back hurts from long years of sitting on the hard, narrow bench, a pain that he combats with the occasional sip of Chinese medicinal wine. When I asked why he wouldn't use a more comfortable chair, he said that it disturbs the flow of movements necessary for the production of perfect *banh*.

The expertise and industriousness of the family is admirable. My wife and I tried several times to work the dough into the correct shape, but it always came out uneven, too thick, or torn. We never even came close to the filling stage, not to mention shaping the dough into a flower. Thanh, the oldest daughter, comforted me: "It took me two years to learn how to make them properly. . . ."

Each order consists of ten dumplings: seven *bao* and three *vac*. They are served on a plate, garnished with deep-fried shallots and accompanied by a small plastic bag of *nuoc mam cham*. Though there are always chopsticks around, the correct way to eat "white rose" is with a spoon: the sauce is poured over the dumplings, which are then spooned with the deep-fried shallots. The dough is fine and translucent, the vegetables are lightly steamed, crunchy, and fresh, and the shrimp filling savory. The combination of lime, sugar, salt, chili, and fish in the sauce enhances and "colors" the taste of the dumplings, and the shallots add a dry crispness and a crackling sound when one is chewing.

Unlike with *cao lau,* Hoianese were clear about the origins of this dish: it came from China and is one of the contributions of the Chinese immigrants (*Hoa* or "ethnic Chinese") to the local culinary scene. The poetic name "White Rose," however, is neither traditional nor Chinese: it was coined by a French tourist in the early 1990s who tasted them at one of the first tourist-oriented restaurants and suggested that they looked like white roses. The name was adopted and became the official Western name for the otherwise untranslatable *banh bao banh vac.*

Though similar dumplings may very well be eaten in China, *banh bao banh vac* are unique in several ways: first, the combination of *nuoc mam cham* (fish-sauce dip) and deep-fried shallots is distinctively Vietnamese; second, the unique shape and color combination of these dumplings are prepared and served only in Hoi An. Finally, they are prepared by just a single Chinese-Hoianese family. This dish potentially expresses several aspects or facets of the Hoianese identity: Chinese, Hoianese, and Chinese-Hoianese.

Like *cao lau,* this dish can be found only in Hoi An. The locals emphasize this fact, suggesting that the dish is a vessel for the expression of local identity. Thus, when *banh bao banh vac* were served at a wedding in neighboring Danang in 2001, and the newlyweds were a bride from Hoi An and groom from Danang (both ethnic Vietnamese), the dumplings were brought to the feast by the bride's family and presented to the new relatives from Danang as "Hoianese," clearly standing for the bride's place of origin.

It is important to note that just as with *cao lau,* most of the consumers of the dumplings are out-of-town visitors who eat the dish in the numerous tourist-oriented restaurants that offer them in the "local specialties" section of their menus. For these outsiders, eating *banh bao banh vac* means consuming a dish that can be found in only one place in the world—Hoi An. For them too, this dish is definitely Hoianese, a local specialty (*dac san*) indeed.

Yet when discussing local Hoianese identity, we must return to the questions raised when addressing *cao lau,* and examine what the locals have to say about this dish. Here again, quite a few Hoianese told me that they "don't like it so much" and that it is "too expensive" (5,000 dong per portion in 1999 and up to 12,000–15,000 dong in 2008). Interestingly, while there was no reference by my interviewees to an alternative dish (such as *mi quang* in the case of *cao lau*), there *is* a very common dish or, rather, street snack, bearing the same name (*banh bao*). This is actually a filled savory bun, popular in many parts of the country, and much larger and heartier than the white rose dumplings. The dough is made from fermented wheat (not rice) flour, the stuffing with pork and eggs, and it is sold by street vendors from mobile steaming utensils for a fraction of the price of white rose, although one *bao* is as filling as a whole serving of *banh bao banh vac*. This kind of *banh bao* is also perceived as Chinese, as the name clearly indicates (*bao* is Chinese for "dumpling" or steamed buns).

For most Hoianese, *banh bao banh vac* are Chinese, a clear reminder of the presence and importance of the latter in the history and society of the country. This cultural acknowledgment should not be taken for granted: although the official history boasts the successful and peaceful coexistence of Kinh and Chinese in Vietnam and especially in Hoi An, the relationship between Kinh Vietnamese and Hoa Chinese immigrants was not always peaceful and soured considerably in the first decade after national reunification in 1975. Acknowledging the Chinese cultural impact and presence is a significant culinary statement.

In my opinion, the most important identity aspect expressed by *banh bao* is that of the Hoianese-Chinese. This ethnic group evolved in Hoi An as a consequence of marriages between male immigrants from various regions in China and local women. Though the regional origins of each of the Chinese communities are acknowledged and maintained through membership in one of the five Chinese assembly halls, intermarriage, mutual assimilation, and the gradual adoption of Vietnamese language and culture seem to have overshadowed these specific regional origins, replacing them with a more general Hoianese-Chinese identity.

This new identity is represented, among other things, by Chinese dishes that are not marked as regional Chinese (e.g., "Cantonese," "Fukienese," "Hainanese") and that feature some culinary inflection that makes them both local and unique. A good example is *hoanh thanh chien* (fried wontons), another prominent Hoianese "local specialty." Wontons, the well-known Chinese dumplings, are generally served in soup and found in Chinese restaurants worldwide; in Vietnam, they are available in Hanoi's Old Quarter and Saigon's Cho Lon (the city's Chinatown).

In Hoi An, only two families prepare *hoanh thanh:* one is originally from Fujian (southeastern China) and the other is Vietnamese, yet the father of the Vietnamese family told me that he learned to prepare *hoanh thanh* "from a friend who worked for the Chinese." The point is, however, that in most Hoianese restaurants the wontons are not boiled and served in a soup but rather are deep-fried (*chien*) and served with a sweet-and-sour sauce made with vegetables and shrimp, flavored with fish sauce. Hence, a classic Chinese food item is given a local twist to create a distinctive Hoianese-Chinese dish.

Regardless of their diverse origins, all Vietnamese-Chinese are considered in Vietnam officially and informally as belonging to a single ethnic group, defined in their identity cards as *Hoa*. This identity is ritually and socially expressed in the All-Chinese Community Assembly Hall (Lop Hoa Van Le Ngia), which serves as a common hall for the various Chinese communities, and is also used by the Kinh Hoianese for rituals. Locally, this temple is called The Lady's Temple (Chua Ba), which along with The Lord's Temple (Chua Ong or Quan Kong Temple), can be found in every Vietnamese city as an integral part of the Kinh worship system (Dong V. 1999: 73; Boudarel 2001: 11). Thus, a Chinese temple serves as a locale for indigenous worship, further pointing to the mixing of local culture with the Chinese into an inextricable Hoianese-Chinese entity, expressed in the fried *hoanh thanh* and steamed *banh bao banh vac*.

Finally, it should be noted that for the "white rose" makers, the Le family, as well as for their acquaintances and friends, *banh bao* are a family matter, a point that they keep making. When contemplating or eating a dish of "white roses" at any restaurant, I picture the Le family members sitting around their working table, preparing the little dumplings. This is an extreme case in which a specific dish evokes a single family: few chefs could boast such complete congruence between themselves and their food.

COM GA AND LOST CHINESE QUALITY

It may seem that Chinese food has an overwhelming presence in Hoi An, and that things Chinese overshadow all other facets of Hoianese culture. On the contrary, the perception of the local identity as "Hoianese" is actually quite pronounced; foreign influences in food are dealt with in various ways. Some dishes are considered as "possibly Chinese," as in the case of *cao lau*. Other Chinese dishes (e.g., *banh bao* and *hoanh thanh*) are given some local color and modified into the Hoianese culinary framework with local taste markers such as fish sauce. In some situations, however, a Chinese dish is detached from its cultural and ethnic roots and is conceived of as indigenous. The popular "chicken rice" (*com ga*) offers a clear example of this:

> I went with Trang and her younger sister for dinner. Trang suggested *com ga,* "a very special dish of Hoi An," in one of the places that can be found every evening on the sidewalk along the fence of Hoi An Hotel. Four or five food stalls had been set up side by side, each dimly lit by a single bulb and indicated by the sign *Com Ga.* Trang parked her motorbike by "the best place." There were only a few customers at that relatively late hour for dinner in Hoi An (6:00 PM in January) and the floor was littered with gnawed bones and used paper napkins. A low wooden-framed plastic shed created a secluded space that somewhat separated the customers from passers-by.
>
> Trang ordered three plates of chicken rice. The owner lifted the lid off a very large tin pot, which released a gust of fragrant steam. She dug into the pot with a large spoon and dished up three plates of turmeric-yellow rice. She then turned to a tray upon which a couple of cooked chickens were piled, heads and feet intact, picked up one of the fowls, and placed it on a chopping block. With a large cleaver, she sliced off about a third of the bird and then chopped it up into smaller pieces, her heavy blows cutting through the bones. Then she tore the meat off the bones with her fingernails and spread it over the rice. She took a chunk

of jellied chicken blood, diced it, and added the small purple cubes to the plates. From a plastic basin she scooped up some fresh aromatic *rau ram* herbs and added the leafy stems to the plates.

The owner's husband appeared from some dark corner, yawning loudly. He picked up the empty chairs and started stacking them over a tricycle parked behind the improvised shed. Trang said: "Look at the chickens, see how their necks are twisted backward as if they were looking up. When we see them lying that way we say that 'the chickens look sadly at the moon.'"

Com ga is, indeed, a very popular dish in Hoi An. I would say that it is the third-most-popular one-dish meal in Hoi An, following only *mi quang* noodles and the different kinds of *chao* (rice gruel). *Com ga* is available by late afternoon each day and is eaten mostly for dinner at more than two dozen venues all over town. These places are often adjacent to venues that sell *chao vit* and *chao ga* (duck and chicken congee) and sometimes the same business serves both chicken congee and chicken rice. The clientele consists typically of workers and lower-middle-class townspeople, although even the better-off also treat themselves to *com ga* every now and again. Just like *mi quang,* and in marked contrast to *cao lau, hoanh thanh,* and *banh bao banh vac,* "chicken rice" is a local favorite, and is generally not offered to outsiders in tourist-oriented restaurants. A plate of *com ga,* costing 5,000–7,000 dong in 2000 and at least twice that in 2007, is a relatively cheap and substantial meal.

To prepare *com ga,* the chicken is boiled for some fifteen minutes with monosodium glutamate and garlic and then removed from the pot. Dry rice is sautéed in a little oil for a couple of minutes and then cooked in the chicken broth. Most cooks add turmeric (*nghe*) to the dish, which gives it a distinctive yellow color. It is important to note that rice is never sautéed in fat before steaming for any other rice dish in Hoi An.

The inner organs of the fowl are boiled separately and bits are added to the plate with the cubes of jellied blood. The proprietor does not cut the chicken flesh into chunks, but literally tears it into small bits, so that "the meat would be easier to mix with the rice and greens." This also makes for a mound of chicken that looks larger than just a few chunks. The final touch is given with the distinctly flavored *rau ram* (polygonum) herb, green papaya shreds, and the locally made sweet-and-spicy chili paste (*tuong ot*), another Hoianese specialty.

My Hoianese friends admit that chicken rice is not unique to Hoi An, but argue that the local way to prepare and serve it is unique: "*Com ga* can be found elsewhere in Vietnam, even in Hanoi," said Quynh, "but everywhere it is different." After a telephone call to a friend in Danang. she added, "In Danang and Dien Ban, only the chicken claws are used, and these are always served intact. In Hoi An, the meat is torn into small pieces." Seasoning the dish with turmeric was also pointed to as being unique to Hoi An, where this spice is popular. Hoi An's special chili paste, *tuong ot* (made of red chili peppers, oil, and spices by several families residing in the old quarter, reputedly Chinese, and a favorite souvenir for Vietnamese domestic tourists) and *rau ram* herb, as well as the eating style of mixing all the ingredients within a single bite, are also presented as characteristic of the chicken rice of Hoi An.

There seems to be a general agreement among the Hoianese that this dish is Vietnamese. I was even told: "*Com ga* is 100 percent Vietnamese, sure!" In fact, *The Culinary Culture of Ancient Hoi An* (Tran 2000: 38–41) calls this dish *Com Ga Pho Hoi* or "Hoi An street chicken rice." It seems to me, however, that *com ga* is a variation of the Hainanese chicken rice dish popular in Southern China as well as in most Chinese centers in Southeast Asia (Anderson and Anderson 1977: 357). Hainan Island, to which the dish is attributed, is geographically closer to central Vietnam than any other geographic region (inclusive of mainland China), so this cultural influence is not unexpected. Furthermore, the Hai Nam ("Hai Nan" in Chinese, or "Southern Sea") community is one of the five Chinese communities that settled in Hoi An over two hundred years ago.

When I suggested that this dish was Chinese, my Hoianese acquaintances did not discard the idea, but pointed out the differences. One said that some Chinese families eat a dish called "Canton-style chicken" (*ga quang dong*), which is similar but much greasier, and is usually served with a chicken-and-cabbage soup. Indeed, the Vietnamese generally attribute liberal use of lard and oil, as well as cabbage, to Chinese cooking.

One Hoianese Chinese said that there is a similar dish called "Hainan Chicken," but pointed out that it differs from the Hoianese *com ga* in several respects: the chicken used for the Hainanese dish is always large and plump and is fried before boiling; garlic and turmeric are not used; the meat is not torn into small morsels; chili sauce and *rau ram* herb are not added; and there is no mixing of all the ingredients for each mouthful. As for the color, she said that "the yellow turmeric color is only beautiful when eating small bits of meat, like in Hoi An. The pale yellow color of the Hainan chicken rice, resulting from boiling the rice in the chicken soup, gives a much nicer look to the larger, intact chunks of chicken that are served in the Hainanese dish." All in all, the status of *com ga* as a Hoianese Vietnamese dish was bolstered, not challenged, by its similarity to the Chinese dish: *com ga* is leaner, yellower, not accompanied by cabbage soup, and so on. For these reasons, it was claimed, this dish is both Vietnamese *and* Hoianese and is certainly not Chinese or Hainanese.

Perhaps a dish gains a certain critical mass of popularity and becomes a marker of localness only when its original foreign roots are forgotten and even denied. Here again, I cannot prove a definite evolutionary process. Did *com ga* first become popular and only then become reconstituted as a local dish, or was it first adapted and only then fully embraced or accepted? Nor do I suggest that this was a planned or a conscious process. Clearly, however, a Chinese dish becomes popular in Hoi An when its foreign roots are denied, while dishes that remain singled out as Chinese or foreign are not that genuinely popular with locals.

In a way, I think that the popularity of *com ga* may explain the popularity of *mi quang* and the de facto rejection of *cao lau, hoanh thanh,* and *banh bao banh vac:* the Hoianese make a clear distinction between local and foreign dishes, opting for the local. By doing so, they reject the presentation of Hoi An as an international and/or Chinese town and opt for a Kinh/Central-Vietnamese/Hoianese identity that has a liberal dose of local patriotism. When eating Hoi An chicken rice, the culinary statement made by the diner is: I am a Kinh dweller of Hoi An.

The adaptations necessary in order to localize a Chinese dish are illuminating. I was often told that the Chinese are gluttons and that their cuisine is remarkably oily compared to that of the Vietnamese. The Chinese preference for animal flesh over fish was also highlighted as yet another manifestation of their gluttony and avidity. This is congruent with the historical perspective, within which the Vietnamese perceive their northern neighbor as an ever-hungry giant devouring anything around him. In order to transform a Chinese dish and incorporate it into the Vietnamese cultural framework, its negative gluttonous aspects have to be removed. Hence, the chicken for *com ga* has to be lean and not fried and the large chunks of flesh are torn into smaller bits, making for a modest dish that connotes the Vietnamese virtues of frugality and self-containment. The addition of *rau ram* adds a distinct regional flavor that further removes the dish from the Chinese culinary sphere.

SIZZLING PANCAKES *(BANH XEO)* AND BEING LOCAL

"I am hungry and it is late," said co Dung, "Let's eat *ram cuon ba Le*" (Mrs. Le's spring rolls). We rode our bikes into the alley that leads to *ba Le* well, turned into a narrower alley, and stopped by the "restaurant," in fact just a loose cluster of low plastic tables and chairs in the alleyway. The occasional passing motorbike riders, cyclists, and pedestrians literally rubbed elbows with the customers.[9] A plastic sheet was loosely hung over the alley, providing some kind of roofing and delineating the eating space. The dirt floor was almost entirely covered by hundreds of used paper napkins (actually small squares of coarse paper that hardly absorb anything), torn lettuce leaves, and other left-overs. The table was smeared with oil. Dung, mumbling "*ghe qua . . .*" (so disgusting), turned to wipe it with the napkins, discarding them on the floor, too.

I recognized a few of the diners who nodded or smiled at me, while Dung and her colleague Ti, both schoolteachers, went through a quick, low-voiced gossip session concerning a couple sitting with their backs to us.

Mrs. Le, the owner, came to greet us and to take our order: "Haven't seen you for a while," she remarked. We ordered *banh xeo* (sizzling pancakes), *thit nuong* (grilled meat on skewers), and *ram* (spring rolls). As she was leaving, Ti whispered in my ear: "She amassed a fortune selling *banh xeo,* and now she is rebuilding her house. . . ." I looked in disbelief at the crude setting and the local clientele, but Ti shot me a confirming glance as Mrs. Le returned and set some plates on our table: a large tray of lettuce leaves, herbs, bean sprouts, shredded banana-flower, sliced pineapple, starfruit, and green banana, another plate of semi-circular rice papers, and individual bowls of thick dipping sauce.

I followed Le to the elevated cooking area. Her daughter was sitting amid a battery of small frying pans, sizzling over kerosene stoves. She poured a spoonful of oil into each cast-iron pan and added a shrimp and a piece of fatty pork into the smoking oil. Then she poured over them a ladleful of thin batter made of rice flour, duck eggs, and water, which crusted immediately into a crisp pancake. She added a bunch of bean sprouts, folded the pancake in two, added some more oil, turned it over for some more frying, and placed it over a bamboo grid to drain the excess oil. Another girl was rolling shrimp, meat, and spring onion in rice paper into "three friends spring rolls" (*ram tam huu*), and deep-frying them in a large wok. Yet another girl was grilling meat. The marinated pork was not skewered but clasped between the "arms" of the skewers whose tips were fastened with a string.

I returned to the table where everyone was already rolling their first *cuon.* Half a pancake, torn with the chopsticks, is placed over the semi-circular rice paper. A fried spring roll, some meat, and a few sprigs of greens are added, not forgetting a slice of tannin green banana and a fine slice of tart unripe starfruit. Then the rice paper is tightly rolled (*cuon* means "rolled"), dipped in the thick sauce (a flour-thickened, sweetened fermented bean sauce [*mam*] reminiscent of the Malay/

Indonesian satay sauce). Even great expertise does not prevent the oil from staining one's fingers and dripping all over the table and one's clothes—hence the coarse paper napkins are always in great demand.

The young couple who were the subject of gossip rose to leave. When they saw Dung and Ti, their teachers, they hesitantly approached our table, crossed their hands over their chests, and bowed their heads in a very respectful greeting. The two teachers grunted in approval, mouths full, and watched as their students left, after bidding respectful farewells to the proprietor and some of the other customers.

Eating *cuon* is unique to Vietnam. This eating style is apparently the outcome of the active cultural synthesis (or mediation) between the chopsticks of Eastern Asia and the South and Southeast Asian use of the right hand to bring food into the mouth, and as suggested earlier, the use of mixed green aromatics that allows for an endless variation of taste in each mouthful. The event described here belongs exclusively to the Vietnamese culinary sphere.[10]

Banh xeo is characteristic of Quang Nam Province. Places that serve *banh xeo* in other parts of the country present it as Quang Nam's special food (*dac san* Quang Nam). Nevertheless, variations of this dish can be found in many places in the Center and South. The Hue version, *banh khoi* ("smoking pancake"), is almost identical, although thicker and always has egg in the batter (in Hoi An, the batter usually only has rice flour and is, therefore, cheaper and "not as tasty"). In several places in Cuu Long (Mekong Delta), I had a much larger pancake, made from similar ingredients, which was not eaten rolled in rice paper (*cuon*). Although these may seem to be minor nuances, they are well known to the consumers and thus denote specific locations.

The most important feature of eating *ram cuon* at ba Le's is the fact that the place is considered distinctively Hoianese. The prices are cheap even by local standards (and Hoi An's food is cheap in comparison to Danang and other large cities, in part because the portions are smaller), costing only a few thousand dong for a complete meal. The setting is informal and relaxed. People of all classes and of varying status, young and old, poor and rich, single, married, and accompanied by children frequent the place regularly. Though beer is served and some male customers may get drunk, this is not a *quan nhau* ("rice-alcohol shop," a male drinking joint that features snacks to have with alcohol) and women of all classes (e.g., respectable high-school teachers) do not hesitate to eat there.

The location is also such that it prevents outsiders from stumbling upon it accidentally, making the place exclusively local. Even visitors from neighboring Danang and Tam Ky, who actively search for hidden local specialties, are rarely familiar with this place. Foreign tourists very infrequently wander into these narrow back-alleys; when they do, the rough setting, unfamiliar dishes, and eating mode, as well as the fact that the owners and most of their customers speak only Vietnamese, make a culinary venture into this place rather formidable. I asked the owner several times if she had any foreign clients and she responded that the few who came were usually invited by local hosts. Therefore, when going to eat in *ram cuon ba Le*, one meets one's friends, neighbors, and acquaintances but rarely a stranger. Eating in this place makes for a sense of Hoianeseness that is unparalleled in any other eating venue in town: if you know this place and you eat there, you really are part of the local scene.

Nevertheless, this kind of local identity—not that of a "dweller of an ancient international port town," a "Chinese," or a "Central-Vietnamese," but one that encompasses the idea of *living here,* the most immediate and nonreflexive of identities—is the hardest to pinpoint or describe, and the one that most people refuse to discuss or even acknowledge. When I asked some of my friends, "Why do you go to eat *ram cuon ba Le*?" they found this question most peculiar and impossible to answer. Even the response "because it is tasty!" was rarely offered in this case. One of them said: "Yes, the place is so dirty and the service is very rude, but I like eating there." Another neatly summed up the local attitudes by saying: "We go to eat there because it is *vui*" (an expression reminiscent of the Thai term *sanuk,* connoting fun, good cheer, *joie de vivre).*

In fact, I was invited by local friends to eat at *ram cuon ba Le* more than to any other food venue in town, sometimes by people whom I didn't expect to meet in such a rough-and-ready and unhygienic setting. In a small town sometimes overrun by outsiders, here is a space where locals can feel at ease, and outsiders do not disrupt the local intimacy. As such, it ironically represents the utmost expression of the romantic tourist notion of a "real authentic place where locals eat." At the same time, it manifests the inaccessibility of such places to outsiders: the few foreigners who eat at *ram cuon ba Le* are perceived as "locals" of sorts.

BROKEN RICE CRACKERS, BABY CLAM SALAD, AND SWEET CORN SOUP IN CAM NAM VILLAGE: STRANGERS AT HOME

Going to Cam Nam, we cycled across the large concrete bridge that connects the town with this large, densely inhabited sandbank, deposited by the silting Thu Bon River in the course of the last century. The view from the bridge is always picturesque: looking westward we could see small boats bustling around the fish market, the coconut-lined pier, and some of the riverfront merchant houses of the old town.

In the distance lies odd-looking My Son, the sacred mountain of the
bygone Cham. Eastward, toward the estuary, the fishing boats of Cam
Chau village docked by the green, tree-and-bamboo-lined bank, their
black and white eyes reflecting in the water.[11] Flocks of ducks were
paddling near the sandy banks of the islet and the large lever fishing
nets were hanging loosely in the afternoon wind.

The islet is quite long but narrow, and so we crossed it widthwise
and cycled along its southern bank. The street is lined with riverside
restaurants featuring large terraces perched on stilts just above the
water. The signs all read: *Hen-Tron, Banh-Dap, Che-Bap Cam Nam*
("Baby-Clam Salad," "Broken Rice Crackers," and "Sweet Corn Soup"
of Cam Nam). As we cycled by, the female proprietors leapt up from
whatever they were doing and beckoned us into their restaurants. But
we stopped at our favorite place, "Green Garden," parked our bikes,
and chose a table overlooking the river and the wobbly bamboo bridge
that connects the islet with a smaller shoal, where corn and watermelons are intensively cultivated in the spring and early summer.

It was a sunny March afternoon and dozens of farmers were irrigat-
ing the green corn stalks with tins carried on shoulder poles. At the
adjacent table were some high-school students. The girls, wearing white
ao dai, sipped their drinks shyly, while the boys played cards loudly.
A young couple from Danang was sitting at another table, easily
identifiable by their stylish clothes, sunglasses, and the mobile phone
left nonchalantly yet conspicuously on the table for everyone to see.
Lien, the proprietor, came smiling to our table with a bottle of soda
water and two glasses of ice. We ordered a set: clam salad, broken rice
crackers, and sweet corn soup.

The tiny clams (*hen*) are dug from the riverbed with special pitchforks
and then boiled for a while to open the shells. The morsels of black flesh
are easily extracted from the opened shells, stir-fried in peanut oil, and
garnished with *nuoc mam,* onion, and *rau ram* herb. The dish is further
seasoned with lime juice, deep-fried shallots, fresh mint, and crushed
peanuts. The salad-like dish (*tron,* or "toss," similar to the Thai and Lao
laap) is served in a small saucer with a crunchy rice cracker (*banh trang
day*) and fresh red chili.

The broken cracker is in fact composed of three crackers: a fresh, soft,
steamed rice paper (*banh uoc*) is fastened between two similar rice papers
that have been dried and grilled to become crisp and brown.
The soft rice paper is glutinous and sticky, and so clings to the crunchy
crackers. The dish is brought to the table on a plate, and then "broken" by

the eaters, who press it down with their palms till it cracks. The broken cracker is accompanied by a special, semi-fermented, unfiltered fish sauce (*mam cai*), seasoned with sugar, chili, pineapple slices, and deep-fried sliced shallots. Finally, the sweet corn soup is served: it is made of fresh corn cooked with sugar, young coconut pulp, and a pinch of salt.

The sun slowly descended and the colors were deepening. It was high tide, and the river rose almost to the height of the terrace. In the darkening water, we could see the conical hat of a baby-clam fisherman. Neck-deep in the water, he was shaking the long pole of his pitchfork in the muddy riverbed, sending small ripples in the water around him.

This romantic setting houses yet another complex, multileveled, and labor-intensive set of dishes. Here again we see how a wide variety of inexpensive local ingredients and taste-agents are combined into culinary creations that are surprisingly rich and complex in flavor—indeed, they are delicious. The "broken crackers" further stress the Vietnamese culinary tendency to produce textures and play with them, using the same material in different states in order to juxtapose seemingly contradictory structures that somehow fuse into perfect combinations. This is quite inexpensive, as a dish went for approximately 4,000 dong (roughly US$0.25) in 2000.

Returning to the issue of food and identity, we are concerned here with three special dishes that are not considered *dac san* of Hoi An, but rather of the relatively small village of Cam Nam, which has only 5,000 inhabitants. If every 5,000 Vietnamese make three local specialties, the total number of unique dishes might surpass 50,000! Though many of these dishes are but variations and nuances, Florence and Storey's (1999: 126) suggestion of "500 unique Vietnamese dishes" falls short of the huge array of available "special" and local Vietnamese dishes.

The local nature of these dishes is clearly indicated by the signs stating the name of the location (in this case, Cam Nam) as a marker of their uniqueness. As a matter of fact, all three dishes, but especially the sweet corn soup and the *mam cai* fish sauce, are widely available throughout Vietnam. I was told, however, that "you can find similar dishes but not the same ones. Here they have a special taste that is better than anywhere else." It is important to note that most of my informants, as well as the proprietors of the "Cam Nam special dishes" venues, who excitedly praised their products as superior to similar dishes elsewhere, admitted at the time that they had never gone further than the neighboring provinces and therefore could not really tell if differences existed. In a discussion about local identity, these facts are not really of importance: what does matter are the claims of distinctiveness and excellence.

Another important point concerns Cam Nam's restaurants as a hub for local tourists. Indeed, an afternoon in Cam Nam is popular among Hoi An's urban dwellers: high-school students as well as their teachers and many other middle-class townspeople frequent these rural venues, set amid the refreshing riverscape, enjoying the special snacks and cold drinks; there, they might also meet various "outsiders," mainly from neighboring Danang (and, on weekends, from as far as Tam Ky and even Hue) and, as of late, international tourists who venture further into an area only recently mapped by the *Lonely Planet Vietnam* guidebook (Florence and Storey 1999: 342).

Crossing the bridge, it seems that the Hoianese themselves become tourists and thus willingly consume the local specialties. There, they feel comfortable and even fashionable, as if they were equal to their envied cosmopolitan neighbors from Danang, who look down at the Hoianese as exotic *nha que* (country bumpkins). Thus, the same people who systematically avoid the much lauded specialties of their hometown are more than willing to consume the local specialties of their own subdistrict, as long as these dishes belong to another region.

This tendency seems to turn the idea of a local specialty as a vessel for the expression of local identity into a sociological paradox: as soon as a practice is identified, named, and marked as "local" by outsiders, it becomes a representation of "external identity"—"their identity in the eyes of the world" (Cohen 2000: 28). It then becomes a commodity that is marketed for a profit, yet can hardly represent the internal identity of the locals, that is, the ways in which they perceive themselves. As this vacuum has to be filled, new dishes are chosen so as to maintain the "internal" local identity. These dishes can fulfill their role as long as they stay unmarked. The discovery and exposure of the new dishes and their tagging as "local specialties" again commodifies them and ends their capacity to serve as proper representatives of internal identity and culture.

For outsiders, however, such "local specialties" offer some new and exciting possibilities for the construction of their own identities as nontourists and even, to a certain extent, as locals. In our case, the Hoianese negotiate a sophisticated urban identity through their consumption of Cam Nam dishes, in line with their own rejection of the "ancient town" and "Chinese" facets of identity and their preference for a contemporary Kinh one.

Yet the Hoianese do not consume Cam Nam dishes without reservation: whenever we suggested a visit to Cam Nam or reported a visit there, the immediate response was: *an hen dau buom* ("[when] eating baby clams, [one's] stomach hurts"). Some people insisted that the clams should be consumed only in the morning, when they are still fresh, as they tend to spoil by the afternoon.

Others said that this is all a matter of luck (and good relations with the proprietors): the clams easily go bad and often cause stomachaches. As a matter of fact, we have had the clams quite a few times, with local and foreign friends, and never had any digestive mishaps. Furthermore, all the restaurants now have refrigerators, making spoiling less likely. Nevertheless, the Hoianese attitude toward the potential dangers of eating *hen* is clear: though this reservation probably echoes earlier times, when proper refrigeration did not exist and when poverty may occasionally have pushed the consumption of nonfresh food over the limits, it also reflects deep-rooted suspicions harbored by townspeople toward the countryside and its dwellers. When the Hoianese say that the clams in Cam Nam village give them stomachaches, they are suggesting that the food is potentially spoiled and the kitchens dirty—just like the people who live there and serve it.

Cam Nam dishes are special in another aspect: their connection to the surrounding ecosystem. All the dishes described so far express local identity due to their cultural and historical contexts. Thus, *cao lau* and *mi quang* have been localized through history, depicting a "culinary mythology" that constructs cultural connections between food artifacts past and present, and the same can be said about white rose dumplings and chicken rice. Cam Nam specialties, however, are local in one more respect: the baby clams are harvested in the river, right beneath the restaurants, while the corn is cultivated literally all around. Therefore, the "locality" of these dishes is literal and stems, first and foremost, from their ecological embeddedness.

My informants often pointed to the setting of the Cam Nam restaurants as the key attraction, and praised the products for being "local" in the most immediate way possible: the distance from the source to the plate does not exceed 50 meters. In these venues, the *local* facet of the "local specialties" is stressed: one can find *che bap* in Hoi An as well as in many other places, yet rarely does one eat corn porridge surrounded by the green stalks from which the fresh corn was harvested. The same goes for the clams. The "broken crackers" are also presented as a local invention, though the locals point to the *mam cai* as the principal local component and unique taste agent. This has to do with the fact that many Cam Nam villagers are fishermen; thus, preparing a special fish sauce would be more "local" than preparing rice crackers, soft or crunchy, as crackers belong to the sphere of rice farming and not to riparian or maritime activities. As a matter of fact, crackers are produced nowadays in Hoi An and not in Cam Nam.

Nevertheless, this neatly presented, context-specific "localness" should not be taken for granted either. In the summer of 2001, I took my cousin to eat the local specialties of Cam Nam:

Just before the beginning of the rainy season, the river was extremely shallow and the shoals were actually separated by muddy puddles where children where looking for river snails. A few miserable-looking dry cornstalks were the only remnants of the lush fields of the previous summer. No farmers or clam harvesters were in sight.

I ordered clams and broken crackers. Lien asked if we would like some sweet corn soup too. "Why," I asked, "how can you have the corn soup if there is no corn?" Lien answered that she buys fresh corn in Hoi An's market and that the corn comes from the vegetable-growing center of Dalat (some 750 km away). I inquired about the price of the clams and Lien said that it came to approximately 4,500 dong a kilo. When I asked why they were so expensive, she said that there are no more clams in Hoi An River, so they are harvested in Tam Ky (some 60 km away) and brought to Cam Nam by traders. "How about the *mam cai*?" I asked cautiously. "No problem with that," she said, "*mam cai* can keep for a long time."

This episode raises several questions about the importance of "space" as a marker of local identity: if local products can be so easily replaced by imported ones, what exactly is the importance of local produce? Is this just a process of commercialization, or does it change the attitude of the consumers? Here again we face the same questions raised about local dishes that are no longer consumed by locals: how is their authenticity constructed; by whom; and what exactly do they (these locals specialties) stand for?

Both Lien and Chi were adamant, however, that corn and clams were only seasonally imported from elsewhere. Chi added that this was a modern market-oriented phenomenon: "When I was a child, you could eat corn porridge only in the corn season, in the summer, and clams only when the conditions and the season allowed. But, today, this is big business. People make money and so they must ensure regular supply. Don't worry, next summer you will have the real clams and corn again."

When I mentioned this instance to other Hoianese friends, they found it somewhat amusing but immediately reverted to "when eating clams one's stomach hurts," emphasizing that now, when the clams come from so far and, furthermore, from a dodgy place such as Tam Ky,[12] the danger is even greater. Here again, I can only testify that there were no unfortunate consequences to the meal. The fear of pollution reflected, yet again, the all-too-prevalent suspicion that outsiders and their food are polluted and polluting. In this respect, the modern Hoianese urban middle class distinguishes itself not merely by consuming the food of others, but also by rejecting imported foodstuffs due to the identity of the producers. Here we actually touch upon food avoidances and taboos, which are usually discussed in the context of religious and ceremonial eating (e.g., Douglas 1957, 1966; White 1992). As we are dealing with daily fare, however, the rejection is not total, the explanations not cosmological or theological, and the "punishment" for deviation mild (a possible stomach upset).

Greenfields

In 2007 a new restaurant was opened in town, called Greenfields. The owner, Mr. Vu, is a well-known Hoianese chef who already owned two restaurants: in the early 1990s he opened one of the first backpacker restaurants in town—Sea Star, a small, relatively cheap, and quite popular place that offers some local specialties (*cao lau,* white rose); simplified versions of Vietnamese and Hoianese dishes; and "backpacker cuisine" (pancakes, pastas, sandwiches, salads, and omelets). Sea Star also offered cooking classes, mostly to small tour groups. Ten years later, Vu bought an old merchant house in the ancient quarter and opened what is probably the most exclusive and popular tourist restaurant in town. The Yacht Club is a cosmopolitan place featuring Vietnamese and international dishes, an extensive bar, and a bakery offering cakes, breads, and croissants as well as homemade ice cream and many kinds of imported coffee; the cooking classes were upgraded and moved to a special classroom, and Vu was doing very well professionally and financially.

But Greenfields was a different story: "In this restaurant I'll prepare the local specialties of Hoi An and some of the dishes cooked by my mother," he told me when we were discussing his new idea (which I supported enthusiastically), "but I'll make them just as they should be, with the right ingredients and the right taste. This is going to be my best restaurant." During this conversation he also mentioned that it had become increasingly difficult to satisfy the ever increasing number of Western tourists visiting town, who were not backpackers anymore but full-fledged tourists "who demanded their steak to be just like back home, even through the quality of beef, both local and imported, can never match the meat quality in Australia." Yet Vu was very confident about Greenfields: "When it comes to local food, I can cook the best-ever dishes from the best-ever ingredients."

As far as I was concerned, this was a wonderful project, as one of the best chefs in town was about to set up a living museum for Hoi An's local specialties, a culinary temple in which the best local foods would be cooked just as they should. I closely followed the restoration of yet another mansion in the old quarter and took part in the planning of the menu, which included explanations of each of the dishes, their origins, ingredients, cooking style, and mode of eating.

A few weeks before the opening, Vu invited some "relatives and friends" for a test run. While I thought that the food was excellent, quite a few of the participants, many of whom were Vu's relatives and involved in tourism, were critical and told me later that they didn't find the food special, thought that the menu was strange, and were mostly worried about the price: "Who would pay US$2.5 for *mi quang* when you can have it in any street corner for 50 cents? And besides, tourists never eat *mi quang*."

The opening day was slow, and on the eve of the second day, Vu was upset and worried. Untypically, he seemed quite lost and even told me that this project was the biggest gamble he had ever taken and he was not sure that it was a good idea. On the third evening, however, he was more cheerful: "The Aussie couple that had dinner last night came back for both lunch and dinner and said that they would eat here every single meal, until they try all the dishes . . . they said that they have never had such food anywhere."

Within a week, Greenfields was busy and doing well, and in 2008 it was establishing itself as one of the best places to eat in town. It was not as packed as Vu's other restaurants, but the clients were very happy and many returned time and again. The intriguing point, however, was that the clientele was not exactly what Vu had expected: while most Hoianese restaurants cater to Western tourists, with some specializing also in East Asian tour groups, Greenfields attracts Vietnamese clients and specifically those belonging to three affluent groups of increasing socioeconomic importance: overseas Vietnamese, upper-middle-class Vietnamese tourists (mainly from Hanoi), and members of the new Hoianese elite—business people, government officials, and civil servants.

Vu told me that this was an unexpected development. In 2005, I had begun a research project that focuses on Vietnamese tourists, and in 2006, when he was planning Greenfields, I suggested that he should also consider the Vietnamese market, as increasing numbers of Vietnamese tourists, both overseas and domestic, as well as affluent Hoianese, were eating at the Yacht Club. Vu thought at the time that these clients were essentially imitating Western tourists and did not call for special attention. As it turned out, Greenfields appeals to Vietnamese and Hoianese customers no less (and possibly more) than it does to non-Vietnamese. And in fact, they are willing to pay what seems like extortionate prices so as to eat high-quality local specialties. As one friend enthusiastically said: "Vu's *mi quang* is really the best in town, and even though it is very expensive, it is ok to pay for this quality." She also pointed out that, as a neighbor, she gets a 20 percent discount, so the price is not that high.

Here, the commodification of Hoi An's local specialties takes an unexpected turn: while modernization, industrialization, consumerism, and, especially, tourism undermine the notion of local specialties as unique dishes that the locals produce from indigenous ingredients for their own consumption, it is a modern, tourist-oriented establishment, the epitome of postmodern consumerism, that offers the locals the opportunity to savor their own dishes, prepared from high-quality ingredients according to traditional recipes. While some of the ingredients and cooking methods are modern, Vu insists that his dishes "are made properly and therefore taste as they did in the past," a point confirmed by quite a few Hoianese. Vietnamese and overseas Vietnamese customers, who lack the historical and cultural capital necessary for the evaluation of the Hoianese specialties, suggested that the high quality of ingredients and professional cooking result in very tasty food that reminded them of other dishes they used to eat in the past. For the Vietnamese diners, then, Greenfields was about nostalgia no less than about good taste.

LOCAL FOOD—LOCAL IDENTITY

In this chapter I have discussed the cultural meanings underlying some of the Hoianese special dishes, and stressed their role in the complex processes of production and reproduction of different aspects of the Hoianese identity. Interestingly, researching the Hoianese "local specialties" led me along the various stages of the sociological debate concerning the nature of identity (Cerulo 1997): from a monolithic, essentialist recognition of a single, seemingly arbitrary artifact (such as *cao lau*) as representing the "natural" and primordial essence of a place, I was led by my informants first to understand that identity is actively constructed and reconstructed by different social and cultural agents and arrangements, and then to realize that each version is only one of many culinary narratives competing in the arena of social and cultural production of identities.

The "Hoianese identity," or, more accurately, the identity of each and every Hoianese, is only situational and temporary: an unstable combination of varying degrees of the range of aspects mentioned in this chapter. Different measures of *cao lau* pluralism, *mi quang* nationalism, *banh bao,* and *hoanh thanh* Chineseness, as well as *com ga* and *ram cuon ba Le* localness, are combined by each individual so that he or she might produce an individual identity as a Hoianese. These combinations are temporary, fragile, and easily changeable, constantly reshaped by culinary trends, personal preferences, and changes (such as the inclusion of white rose dumplings in a Kinh wedding).

The analysis of the Hoianese local specialties points to a few issues and tensions that seem to characterize contemporary Hoi An and highlights various facets of contemporary Hoianese identity. The most salient feature is the tension between the explicit (and official) perception of the Hoianese society as pluralistic, tolerant, peaceful, multiethnic, and flexible (reflected by *cao lau*), and the opposing self-perception of the Hoianese as belonging to the national(istic) ethnic-Vietnamese culture (expressed by *mi quang*). The practical rejection of *cao lau,* despite its discursive flagging, suggests that although the contemporary Hoianese acknowledge (and capitalize on) this multiethnic image, they prefer the Vietnamese one.

Another major source of tension exists between the Kinh dwellers of Hoi An and the descendants of the various Chinese communities. Though the Chinese origins of many Hoianese specialties are acknowledged, these dishes are modified to varying degrees in order to represent the Chinese customs in terms that are culturally acceptable to the Kinh. Interestingly, these modifications generate dishes that are considered "Chinese but unique to Hoi An," distancing the dishes and those who prepare and consume them from China. The adaptation of Chinese food into the Hoianese context reaches its climax when a regional Chinese dish such as Hainanese chicken rice is completely severed from its ethnic roots and localized to the point that it is no longer considered Chinese. In this respect, these dishes reflect not only the ambivalent position of the various Chinese communities in town but also hint at the process of assimilation that they have undergone. As we shall see in chapter 6, the Hoianese Chinese seem to be renouncing their regional origins and replacing them with a new identity: that of the Chinese Hoianese as a distinctive local group.

Another tension expressed in culinary terms exists between the Hoianese town dwellers and their rural neighbors. In this case, the cautious consumption of "local specialties" of nearby villages seems to function as a Bourdieuan mechanism of distinction. Yet while Bourdieu discusses broad categories of edibles and dishes (1984: 175–200), here we have a case in which specific dishes are significant diacritic signs that are involved in the process of reproducing class distinction. In fact, the consumption of Cam Nam specialties by the Hoianese is an ambivalent process, as fear of physical and cultural pollution is intermingled with the quest for the intimate, unmediated immersion with the countryside. Interestingly, these apparently authentic and intimate relations are so important that in certain circumstances they are "staged" (Mac-Canell 1973) by the dwellers of Cam Nam in order to attract their Hoianese clients.

A general tension exists between the local and intimate nature of "local specialties" and their commodification and touristification. While this process is often depicted as unidirectional and negative, leading to cultural monotony and flatness as the new consumers have no means to appreciate the quality of local specialties, we have seen how cultural institutions such as Greenfields can change the course of these processes. The point, of course, is that the food at Greenfields is now consumed by foreigners as a marker of authenticity, while locals are attracted by the nostalgia it offers.

The concluding point concerns the role food preferences play in processes of cultural production. One point that this book strives to make is that the culinary sphere is not merely a passive mirror image of existing social and cultural orders, but that in certain instances foodways are actively involved in negotiating and reshaping these arrangements. Though it could be argued that each of the Hoianese culinary specialties merely reflects a facet of local culture, the important point is that the Hoianese have the agency to choose from this repertoire of ideas and arrangements and to actively shape and reshape their respective identities.

Here we are reminded of Swidler's (1986) "culture as toolkit." For Swidler, who developed Daniel's (1983) perception of culture as toolbox, culture is a set of practices from which social actors can choose those they deem fit to deal with given situations. I suggest that the realm of "local specialties" is a specific drawer in Swidler's toolkit, with the various dishes standing for various "tools" used in order to construct and negotiate identities. Though the number of tools, that is, the repertoire of cultural practices and strategies (and, in our case, the number of dishes) is limited, the important point is that each individual can choose the tool/dish she or he deems appropriate in order to handle any given situation. In some instances, the tools/dishes are redesigned (as in the case of the Hoianese chicken rice), invented, or borrowed from elsewhere, and added to the repertoire of possible practices.

While the various dishes might be mere reflections of other cultural arrangements or perceptions, the culinary sphere is shown in this chapter as an arena in which social actors have the agency to use a variety of "culinary tools" so as to produce, negotiate, and reconstruct their identities.

4   Feasting with the Dead and the Living

Though rituals and festivals have always been at the center of anthropological attention, the special food, elaborate preparations, and eating practices characteristic of such events have often been ignored in anthropological writing or, at best, have been treated as anecdotal or trivial.[1] Even Shaun Malarney's (2001) analysis of war-dead commemorations in Vietnam, which includes detailed descriptions of the ritual and its wartime and postwar transformations, has no more than: ". . . and then [the mourners] share a communal meal . . ." (ibid. 68). I argue that the culinary aspects of such ceremonies are at least as meaningful and important as the formal ritual. The analysis of foodways in such events actually sheds light on issues that are often overlooked.

Ancestor-worship ceremonies (*dam gio,* "death anniversary gatherings," sometimes referred to as *cung ong ba,* or literally "worship of grandfather and grandmother") are the most common family rituals held in Hoi An. As every person has two parents and four grandparents (in some cases even more since, prior to 1975, polygamy was legal and there are several polygamous families in town), most Hoianese conduct or participate in several *dam gio* rituals annually. While some families worship more than two generations of ancestors (see also Jamieson 1995: 22), this is quite rare in Hoi An. In practice, most Hoianese worship only those ancestors whom they personally knew, while long-deceased ancestors are usually remembered only in more general ancestor-worship events, such as Tet, if at all. Since extended family members, friends, and neighbors are routinely invited to join these rituals, most people participate in well over a dozen such events each year. Indeed, most other Hoianese rituals and festivals include some aspects of ancestor worship. As one of my informants pointed out: ". . . they say that we are Buddhists or Taoists, but for me, I think that we are ancestor worshipers. This is what we mostly do."

Hoianese ancestor-worship rituals are large, expensive affairs, with a few dozen to more than two hundred participants and costing on average no less than 15,000 dong (about US$1) per guest in 2000, and often three times as much.[2] The rising costs and standard of living, higher salaries, and ever increasing social competition for prestige make it almost impossible to estimate equivalent expenses in 2008, but US$2–5 per guest would be a good estimate. Multiplied by several rituals per year, one realizes the enormous investment in work, time, and money involved. The fact that the bulk of this investment of time, effort, and money is in the preparation of the feast, and that much of the time during the ritual itself is spent consuming the food, underline the centrality of food at ancestor-worship events. Indeed, the guests are literally invited to *an dam gio* or "*eat* [the] ancestor worship," further emphasizing the importance of the culinary dimension of these gatherings.

In this chapter I discuss the feasts at four ancestor-worship ceremonies, beginning with a detailed description of a *dam gio* arranged by a peasant family. The analysis of this event exposes the basic ideas embedded in ancestor worship and serves as a baseline for comparative analysis of similar rituals conducted within other social contexts. I continue with an ancestor worship that took place in the house of an urban, lower-middle-class family. Here, I stress aspects of continuity and change: though many features of the previously discussed event are maintained, there are several meaningful modifications that need to be considered. The third part of this chapter deals with two vegetarian ancestor-worship feasts, in which animal flesh was substituted by mock meat dishes and the Buddhist monks who attended were treated with special deference. These culinary arrangements challenge some common assumptions about Vietnamese cosmology and metaphysics and introduce the controversy over the moral stance of vegetarianism.

My main argument in this chapter is that although ancestor-worship rituals are explicitly concerned with death and the afterlife, the dishes and culinary practices suggest that *dam gio* are equally about the living and their social interaction. Specifically, I show how the feast celebrates proper kin relations and aspires to the well-being and success of the extended family.

ANCESTOR WORSHIP AS "FAMILY-CYCLE" EVENTS

Life-cycle events are rituals that mark specific and nonreversible changes in one's social status (Turner 1967: 93–111). Such rituals mark the shifts between stages in a life: birth, childhood, puberty, adulthood, marriage, parenthood, "seniority" (or retirement), and death. It could be argued, then, that ancestor worship hardly qualifies as a life-cycle event, since the person to whom the ritual is dedicated is actually dead. Such an argument reflects the modern Western notion of a finite set of life-cycle events oriented to an individual that automatically end after a person's death, rather than the Vietnamese longer-term and family-oriented perception of sociality and notions of the afterlife. In fact, the Vietnamese celebrations would be more accurately described as "family-cycle" events: rituals oriented toward the family as a whole over one or more generations with reference to one or more family members. This point merits a brief discussion of the centrality of the Vietnamese extended family as a synchronic entity and of the cosmological theory of the "parallel worlds."

The extended family was the basic social unit in the pre-modern (i.e., pre-French) Vietnamese society (Jamieson 1995: 22–25). Although the supremacy of the Vietnamese family has been challenged in the past 150 years by Western notions of individualism on the one hand and by communist ideology on the other (ibid. 1), Pham Van Bich (1999) concludes that traditional family patterns and concepts have resisted these pressures and still prevail. Indeed, as Pham points out, the improved standard of living and the economic independence stemming from *doi moi* have led to the restrengthening of the Vietnamese family and to "the restoration of many traditional features since 1987" (ibid. 252).

Hoianese are emphatic that their families—especially their parents and children—are the most important thing in their lives. "I don't need anyone," said co Dung. "I could even live without my husband, but never without my children." Another friend with a Westernized lifestyle pointed out that her mother is her best friend and only confidant, and that in fact she had no friends beyond her immediate family members: parents and siblings.

The Vietnamese perceive of the family as a synchronic entity. This is a Chinese-Confucian notion (Taylor 1983: 36; Huard and Durand 1998: 125), whose impact should not be underestimated: "There is an underlying assumption in the Chinese thinking on the family that there is a 'Continuum of Descent' . . . [that is] a unity, a rope, which began somewhere back in the remote past and which stretches on into the infinite future . . ." (Baker 1979: 26–27). For the Vietnamese, "the communitarian character of the family found expression not only in the relationships between the living members, but also in those between the dead, the living and the unborn. . . . The family was understood as a human community stemming from the ancestors, often going back four or five generations or as long as the family could remember . . ." (Pham 1999: 19).

The second element crucial for understanding Vietnamese ancestor worship is the cosmology of parallel worlds: a Sino-Vietnamese belief that maintains that the world of the dead is a mirror image of the world of the living, and, therefore, the living and the dead have similar material and emotional needs. There is one difference between the two worlds, however: while material production is possible only in the world of the living, the dead have control over good luck. Thus, while the dead depend on the living for their material needs, the living depend on the protection and goodwill of ancestors for their own happiness, success, and prosperity. The living and the dead are thus interlocked in a circle of everlasting mutual obligations.

Perhaps it is no coincidence that ancestor rituals resemble Western birthday celebrations, which were as uncommon in pre-modern Vietnam[3] as they are today. As at a birthday party, the deceased person (represented by his photograph) "sits" at the head of the table, which is adorned with gifts and flowers, and is surrounded by relatives and friends who join him for a feast (often featuring his favorite dishes) marking his very own special day.

In sum, we realize that for the Hoianese, the dead continue to exist in one form or another. Indeed, they hold an extremely powerful position in regard to the fortune and well-being of the living. Most Hoianese take the existence and ability of their ancestors to influence their present well-being for granted. Since the dead continue to exist and to take an active part in family affairs, the rituals marking their death anniversaries are stages/events in the family cycle.

Ancestor Worship of Xuan's Grandmother: Feasting with the Dead

Chi Xuan invited us to participate in the ancestor-worship ceremony for her husband's late grandmother. Her son was waiting for us in her house at 11 AM, and he led us through the maze of narrow sandy alleys that wind their way between the houses and shady yards sprawling between the main road and the river to his grandparents' house.

The grandparents' home was a typical Central Vietnamese rural house: a rectangular brick structure with a low, sturdy tiled roof, painted pale yellow and framed in green and blue, built on an elevated ramp to avoid seasonal floodwaters. The packed sand yard was enclosed with a wire fence and was shaded by a few large sapodilla and jackfruit trees. A yellow-blossomed peach was planted in front of the main door, its young buds sprouting on the bare branches, ready to bloom in the coming New Year Festival (Tet). There were six round tables in the yard, each with ten plastic stools, already set with food for the feast. Electric fans had been placed by the tables, ready to relieve the stifling heat.

The large front doors of the house were wide open. From the yard I could see the preparations taking place inside. The curtains of the ancestors' altar (*ban tho*, or "table for worship"), a robust wooden cupboard located just in front of the central door, were drawn open. A string of small flashing bulbs illuminated the altar. On a shelf above the altar stood an icon of the Buddha. At the top of the altar itself there were several black-and-white photographs of men, women, and one young man in a military uniform. Flowers in a vase, fruit in a bowl, a cluster of smoking incense sticks, and several lit red candles placed in a can of uncooked rice were arranged in front of the pictures. There were also a bottle of rice spirit (*ruou gao*) and a plate of *trau cau* (betel quid: a mildly narcotic mix of betel leaves, areca nuts, and lime). Two elderly men who had just finished placing a paper with Chinese characters on the altar then turned to beat a shiny bronze gong.

To the left of the main altar was a smaller one, with a photograph of an old woman surrounded by white funeral flags embroidered with black Chinese characters. A similar array of offerings was set on this altar, though on a smaller scale. I asked Xuan why there were two altars; she explained that the central one was for the ancestors, whose photographs, she pointed out, were displayed. Then she led me to the smaller altar and said: "This is my grandmother. She died two years ago when she was eighty-six." I asked why she wasn't being worshiped at the central altar, to which Xuan explained that only after the third anniversary of her death would the mourning period be over and "grandmother will move to the main altar."

In front of both altars were rectangular wooden tables—with chairs—heaped with dishes. The bowls at these tables were full of rice. The head of a boiled pig, covered by its lacy caul resembling an embroidered veil, was placed on the table in front of the main altar. Near the head was a ceramic utensil holding some burning candles and smoking incense sticks.

One of the elderly men picked up a bundle of colored papers from the table, lit them with the flame of the candles, and took the burning pile to the gate, where he laid it on the ground and watched the colorful papers turn black and swirl up in the hot air.[4]

I went to the back of the house where women were cooking and arranging food on serving plates. There was a lively and cheerful atmosphere in the cooking area, where squatting women were grilling meat, filling bowls with rice, and arranging meat slices on plates garnished with lettuce leaves and flowers carved out of carrots. I recognized some of the women as neighbors, but on that occasion most of them were introduced as relatives.

More guests arrived and filled the yard. The older men, wearing old-fashioned European suits and ties, formed a line by the front porch, each kowtowing on a straw mat in front of the main altar and lighting an incense stick. Some of them beat the gong. The elderly women, most of whom were dressed in *ao dai*,[5] turned to sit by the wooden tea-table that had been moved from its permanent position in front of the ancestor altar into the yard. The younger guests, especially the women, went to help in the kitchen.

By 11:30 AM, Xuan's father-in-law had invited the older men to sit by the table in the yard in front of the main door of the house and the altar. The elderly women took their places at the next table. As soon as a table filled up, the guests would begin eating. Younger guests, still pouring into the yard, took their seats around other tables, men and women at separate tables. The men called out to their friends to join them; each table was made up of guests of roughly the same age. Preschool children received large bowls of rice topped with morsels from the side dishes, and went to a corner of the yard where they ate with their spoons.

Each table, heaped with about a dozen dishes, was a mosaic of colors and textures: spring rolls stuffed with pork, mushrooms, and rice vermicelli (*ram*); boiled pork (*thit heo luoc*); rice vermicelli sautéed with green beans (*bun xao dau tay*); sticky rice soup with curdled pig's blood (*canh nep lay huyet heo*); pork and potato curry (*canh cary khoai tay gio heo*); mixed fresh aromatic greens (*rau song*); beef steak (*thit bo bit tet*); roast pork (*thit heo nuong*); mixed fried green beans (*dau tay xao thap cam*); and boiled pig's innards (*long bau tu gan heo luoc*). Each guest had a full bowl of steamed rice (*com*). A saucer of fish sauce dip was on each table. No drinks were present except rice spirit.

The atmosphere was gay and friendly. Everyone was eating, many of the men drinking alcohol, and lively conversations were sparked as the younger guests talked loudly across the tables. As more guests arrived, two additional tables were brought in and set up in the yard. The plates of food from the two rectangular tables set in front of the altars inside the house were removed and served to the late arrivals. "Why don't they sit inside, by the set tables?" I asked Van, Xuan's sister-in-law. "Those are the tables for the ancestors," she replied. "Now they have finished eating [*"an roi"*] and the food that was left is for the others." Some of the women walked between the tables, adding rice to bowls or topping up the other dishes.

By that stage, some of the guests were leaving, first stopping to drink a small cup of tea from a large kettle on the fence just by the gate. Van, a teacher, excused herself and left for the afternoon school shift, along with some pupils. Soon most of the guests had gone, with their motorbikes roaring away. Piles of half-consumed dishes still remained on the tables. It seemed to me that most of the food was left uneaten.

At that stage, one of the elderly men reached for a notebook that was kept inside the ancestor altar and handed it to a younger woman. The guests who had not left, mostly older people, formed a line in front of the altar. Each approached the altar and after a short discussion with the man in charge, handed over some money, stating aloud their full name and the sum they had given. The young woman carefully noted down each name and the sum donated.

Ancestor worship is explicitly dedicated to the dead and in some respects to their relations with the living. From the perspective of the dead, the ritual is clearly intended to supply various needs in the afterworld: they are provided with material as well as aesthetic goods (money, clothing, flowers, and incense), their well-being is ensured (as the paper figures will take over their punishments), the entire extended family is gathered to pay them respects, and an elaborate feast is served to them.

From the perspective of the living, worshiping one's ancestors is necessary to win their favor to ensure good luck and success. Indeed, when I asked what exactly is said when praying to the ancestors, I was told that the worshiper states her name (and, sometimes, address)[6] and asks the deceased for help in personal matters such as health, success at school or in business, a safe journey, matters of the heart, or child-bearing.

From a cosmological perspective, the fact that the dead require a constant supply of material goods, and that they can control some aspects of the world of the living, means that death does not entail the complete secession of being but rather some kind of different existence, which has unmistakable material (as opposed to transcendental) features. The feast clearly supports this notion, as the food is served first and foremost to the dead. Only when they have eaten ("*an roi*," technically, when the incense sticks lit on the altar have burned halfway out) are the living invited to join the meal and consume the leftovers. When talking about this issue, one of my informants boldly claimed that the ancestors eat some of the food and that, due to this mode of consumption, "the dishes from the altar, when served later to the guests, taste different than the rest of the food." While she herself suggested that long exposure to incense smoke, heat, and dust on the altar might have something to do with the altered taste, she insisted that the transformation was mainly due to the dead consuming some part of it.

What is unique about the feast, however, is that while the ritual is composed of a set of abstract and symbolic acts and artifacts—the prayer, the sound of gongs, the aroma of incense, and the candlelight, as well as a set of paper offerings—the food served is by no means abstract or symbolic: it is real. Thus, food

FIGURE 4.1. Food offered to the ancestors at an ancestor-
worship feast; altar in the background.

FIGURE 4.2. Tray with food offerings for ancestor worship; clockwise
from the top next to the vase of chrysanthemums: rice wine, *im,*
mineral water bottle, glasses of green tea, rice, soup of bitter gourd
stuffed with minced pork, fatty roast pork, stir fried greens with beef
and congealed blood, steamed chicken, fried noodles with green beans
and carrots, fried spring rolls with omelet wedges, fish-sauce dip,
whole fried fish, rice crackers, and sponge cakes.

is the only element that concretizes the existence of the dead, forming a link
between the world of the living and the afterworld and overcoming the concep-
tual gap between the diachronic existence of the living family and the synchronic notion of a "continuum of descent." Indeed, if not fed, the dead spirits
may turn into hungry ghosts who roam the world in search of food. These
ghosts are extremely dangerous and are therefore fed in almost all rituals.[7] The
important point is that my informants explained that spirits might become
hungry ghosts when not *fed,* while the other offerings were never mentioned,
stressing again the central role of food in concretizing otherwise abstract and
symbolic beings and relations.

FIGURE 4.3. Men's table at an ancestor-worship feast.

The offering of food and, more so, ceasing to feed those who died long ago, seem to have another very important role in the cosmological order: if feeding the dead ensures their continual existence, ceasing to feed them leads to their final evanescence. This is extremely important, as otherwise the world would be chockful of an ever-increasing number of souls. Such a world would be completely immobile and stagnant and, therefore, dead. Indeed, Hugh Baker (1979: 88), in his discussion of Chinese ancestor worship, points out that "the soul, if not worshipped, might eventually just melt away and cease to exist. . . ." Thus, while feeding is the act that materializes the dead and ensures their continuous existence, it is the cessation of feeding that leads to their final departure.

Feasting with the Living

While ancestor-worship rituals are explicitly dedicated to the dead, these gatherings serve as arenas of social interaction that go well beyond the dead and are concerned mainly with the living family members and the interactions among them. First and foremost, ancestor-worship rituals are the most frequent occasions at which the boundaries of inclusion of the extended family are manifested and where belonging to a specific social group is expressed, maintained, and intensified. Thus, participating in these rituals should be perceived as a kind of "membership card" in the extended family.

The shared meal clearly enhances these feelings of belonging: just as a shared pot of rice represents the communal character of the Hoianese family, and as the division of food among the family members is the utmost expression of mutual dependence and responsibility, so are ancestor-worship feasts instances in which these principles are expanded to include entire extended families. Thus, those who share such meals make the following culinary statement: "We are one family; we are responsible for one another; we share our food and our fate."

The eating arrangements in these feasts reflect some basic organizing principles of Vietnamese society, most prominent of which is the precedence of the elderly over the young, with the older guests sitting in the most respected place, as close as possible to the ancestral altar. As at other meals, the elders are served first; often they finish eating even before the younger guests have even started. This arrangement includes the dead ancestors: as they are the oldest members of the (synchronic) family, they have the most respectable seats (right at the altar), eating before anyone else and concluding their meal before the living begin to eat.

The second feature concerns the priority of male over female family members: women are charged with cooking the food and serving it to the rest of the family, mainly to the men. Here again, the cooking is done on the floor, outside the house, near the toilet and the pigsty, so that the ambivalent position of women (as those who transform nature into culture) is reenacted. A third feature is the ambivalent position of young children, who are relegated to the margins of the cultural sphere.

As mutual responsibility is a key issue, the meal at Xuan's in-laws' house was concluded with a bill: it was a clear expectation that the family would share the expenses of the ancestral feast. Here we meet a traditional custom in a modern guise, that of "incense and fire land" (*dat huong lua*): a special category of land, owned by the extended family, whose crops were devoted to subsidize ancestor worship (Jamieson 1995: 24). In the contemporary setting, when the recently allocated land is in fact private again in all but name, but where communal family or village fields, such as that of "incense and fire," do not exist any more, the extended family members have to contribute money to share the expenses. What I found most striking was the explicit and open manner in which the money was collected. As I was accustomed to "taking care of the bill" in more discreet ways back home, I felt embarrassed at first upon witnessing these blunt declarations and their careful documentation. I will return to the subject of the public sharing of expenses in my discussion of weddings in the next chapter.

THE FOOD

The feast at Xuan's ancestor worship was different from daily domestic meals in three essential respects: there was far more food, a greater variety of dishes, and the emphasis was on meat. The basic components of the home meal had almost disappeared: steamed rice (*com*) was considerably less central and fish was not served at all (except as fish sauce). Furthermore, there was a clear inclination toward dishes of foreign origin. In line with my theoretical framework, I will first address the nutritional qualities of the food and only then turn to its sociocultural aspects.

The most salient nutritional feature of the feast at Xuan's was the huge amount of food offered. While the quantity of food in daily home-eaten meals is limited (if not frugal) and while meals eaten out are often small (at least, by Israeli and Western standards), ancestor-worship feasts routinely feature huge amounts of food. Though the guests eat much more than they would normally have at home, and are constantly encouraged by their hosts and fellow diners to continue eating, there is such an excess of food that approximately 40–50 percent is left on the tables.[8]

Even so, the huge amount consumed during such events serves essentially as a "calorie filling-station." In traditional Vietnamese society where people spent much of their lives on the brink of hunger, feasts were always events that combated chronic nutritional deficiency. Today, while the local markets have abundant food and most Hoianese do not go hungry, it is still quite difficult to find an overweight adult in Hoi An.[9] Bearing in mind that most Hoianese still make their living from hard physical labor, and hence need the extra calories, this seemingly excessive amount of food still serves as an important periodic source of additional calories for many Hoianese.

The same holds true for both the great variety of dishes and the emphasis on animal protein. The meager daily diet of rice, fish, and greens is complemented in feasts by a large variety of much-needed nutrients such as animal and vegetal proteins, vitamins A, B, and D (from animal flesh, internal organs, and eggs, as well as vegetables such as carrots and beans [Guggenheim 1985: 150, 158]), and lipids (from animal and vegetal fats). Again, bearing in mind that most Hoianese do not have access to a properly balanced diet, and are therefore slim and short,[10] the festive meal allows for a partial replenishing of such deficiencies and ensures a more wholesome diet. Nutritionally speaking, we could conclude that a feast is an event where unusually large amounts of calories and nutrients are consumed in order to compensate for chronic deficiencies.

Nutrition, however, hardly explains why and how people share their food and why specific ingredients are combined into certain dishes. It does not explain why certain ingredients are transformed culturally in specific directions. These are sociocultural arrangements and can only be explained as such.

The most salient gastro-social phenomenon that took place at Xuan's ancestor worship was the public redistribution of accumulated wealth among the members of the extended family. Those who are better off contribute to a meal in which the poorer members of the family and those of lower social status have better access to more nutritious (and more expensive) food. Therefore, the festive meal is an act of solidarity and generosity among extended family members and their friends: every now and again, the rich share some of the capital they have accumulated, converted into nutritional currency as it were, with their poorer relatives.

There seems to be more than pure sentiment and generosity to this redistribution of wealth. Several elements cannot be explained merely by generosity: the excessive food, the insistent urging by the hosts to continue eating, the systematic refusal of the guests, especially the older ones, to eat more than just a few bites, and the public contribution to the expenses. These suggest that other social considerations also play a part in the nature and dimensions of the feast.

The excess of food and, crucially, the excess of expensive food (especially animal protein) displays the wealth and power of the hosts. The culinary statement here is: "We can offer so much good food because we are rich!" This also explains why the hosts insist that their guests eat more, often placing choice morsels in the guests' bowls: this not only expresses hospitality but is also a clear demand to physically incorporate this generosity.

The guests, however, are generally reluctant to consume all the food offered, and gradually turn from verbal refusal to body language in order to express their unwillingness to eat more, under the growing pressure of their hosts. Iris Kalka (1991), studying the Israeli culinary event of "coffee and cake," also noted this tension between the hosts' insistence that the guests should eat and the guests' refusal. Kalka claims that in the Israeli case, the hosts offer expensive, calorific, often homemade (that is, labor-intensive on the part of the host) cakes to their guests, many of whom are overweight and actually on diets. The hosts clearly expect their guests to give up their health and aesthetic considerations to accept and incorporate these tokens of hospitality; refusal is a breach of etiquette, taken as an insult.

There is, of course, a clear difference between these cases: Kalka's upper-middle-class Israelis have practically unlimited access to food and overeating is detrimental to their health, while most Hoianese are certainly not overweight, or may even be undernourished, so that the expensive, rich food probably could contribute positively to their diet. Nonetheless, the major transaction in both cases is social and not nutritional: the Israelis eat the cakes in order not to offend their hosts, while the Vietnamese restrain themselves in order to save face. When guests only nibble on the festive dishes, they are making a public statement about themselves: they are well fed, satiated, and, hence, well-to-do. Just as in the Israeli case, however, rejecting the food altogether is offensive and should be avoided.

Interestingly, the Israelis, like the Vietnamese, make a point that eating to excess is a vulgar practice of the less affluent (ibid. 120) and therefore avoid such behavior. A similar point is made by Susan Rasmussen (1996: 79), who shows how among the Tuareg of Northern Niger, the ability to show restraint while eating and the resulting slim figure are esteemed qualities among men of the upper strata. All these cases seem to be local modifications of the general principle of restraint as characteristic of the higher social strata, outlined by Bourdieu in his discussion of the habitus (1984). In sum, we can see that in Hoi An, as elsewhere, negotiations over festive tables are also about prestige and social status.

The public process of sharing the hosting expenses for such a feast further supports this claim: if offering a festive meal were a pure act of generosity by the better-off members of each family, there would not be such public declarations. The fact that the amount paid by each contributor is declared aloud suggests that this is not merely an act of generosity, but a token in the social economy of "face" and honor (alternatively, this could be a mechanism that ensures generosity, as the demand to publicly state the amount of money donated obliges larger sums; most probably, this mechanism works both ways: allowing public demonstration of one's generosity while demanding it).

Jamieson (1995: 30) claims that festive culinary interactions were key elements in what he terms the "prestige economy" of the traditional Vietnamese village, one that used to determine the status hierarchy in pre-modern rural society. Thus, the better-off periodically shared their wealth with the poor, expressing solidarity and demanding the upholding of their social status in return, while the poor enjoyed, every now and again, spells of better nutrition and tastier food. However, they had to pay with their own prestige: the more they ate, the lower they descended in status. Jamieson (ibid. 33) neatly summarizes the basic principal of food and prestige as such: "from each according to his desire for face, to each according to his willingness to lose face."

A point of reservation is warranted here: though many Hoianese hardly earn a living and are to some extent undernourished, the increasing prosperity of the past few decades has resulted both in improved nutrition and even in overeating among certain sectors of society. Generally speaking, the younger generation is now taller and heavier: schoolchildren and young people in Hoi An are physically larger than their parents, younger siblings are larger than their elders, children from rich families are larger than those from poor ones, and urban children are larger than those from the countryside. Beyond quantitative data supplied by Tu and Le (2002) in this regard, a glance at any family album of photographs taken at festive events over the years will offer much visual evidence of these changes.

One outcome of this prosperity and better nutrition is the appearance of "fat" people (*map*),[11] mainly townspeople who live a sedentary life but maintain the cultural eating logic and practice of subsistence rice farmers ("always eat as much as you can because you never know what tomorrow will bring") and, therefore, tend to overeat (according to Tu and Le [2002], in 1990 some 17 percent of the Vietnamese consumed more than 2,400 kcal per day, an amount that could lead to being overweight, and their numbers must have risen substantially within two decades of relative prosperity). While most of these persons would hardly be described as fat by Western standards, and definitely not as obese, small bellies and plump figures are more visible these days in Hoi An, especially among the businessmen and public servants who belong to the emerging middle class. These are mostly educated men and women, who are well aware of the dangers of being overweight. They are also aware of the demands of contemporary beauty ideals, as well as of the traditional expectation to prove strength of character through restraint (physically expressed in slim figures). They often express anxiety about their weight, and try to limit their food intake, especially at festive events in which the dishes are exceptionally rich and excessive, explaining their avoidance for health and beauty reasons. Thus, modern strictures on food consumption, stemming from excess, are infiltrating the traditional arrangements, which were the outcome of perennial food scarcities. Nevertheless, as the custom is still for the host to exhort and for the guest to refuse, there is no change in praxis, only in underlying motives.

Prosperity and the expression of wealth, power, prestige, and cultural capital are reflected not only in the amount of food offered, but also in the composition of the ingredients, the cooking techniques, the structure of the meal, and the style and origins of the dishes. Here we touch directly upon the symbolic aspects of food: not only on the "how" of eating, but also on the "what."

I pointed out earlier that the centrality of steamed rice is diminished in festive meals. We will see later that in more sophisticated contexts, steamed rice is replaced by more elaborate rice dishes, while its quantity is sharply diminished. Fish, the other key element in daily Hoianese meals, is not served at festive meals (with the exception of fish sauce). This was true of every Hoianese feast in which I participated. When I asked why fish was not served at festive meals, I was told that fish is cheap. I insisted that there were expensive fish that cost roughly the same as pork or chicken (about 30,000 to 60,000 dong [US$2–3] per kg in 2000) and definitely more than duck. At that, point the explanation became, "We don't eat fish in feasts because we eat fish every day." Hence, it seems that it was not only quality and price that determine the prestige of a specific food, but also the entire category to which it belonged and the frequency and contexts in which items from this category were consumed. Here we encounter Durkheim's notion that food classifications express distinctions between the sacred and the profane (Mennell, Murcott, and Otterloo 1992: 2).

If fish and rice lose their importance and even disappear from festive meals entirely because of their ordinary and profane nature, it is necessary to explain the continuous presence of fish sauce, both as a condiment (when cooking) and as a side dish (the fish-sauce dip). Here we realize the centrality of *nuoc mam* as a taste agent or, more precisely, as the essential taste marker of Vietnamese food. *Nuoc mam* remains on the festive table because without it the dishes simply would not taste "right." Fish sauce is, therefore, not only a nutrient and definitely not merely a fish dish or a fish extract. Fish sauce is *the* taste agent that defines Vietnamese cuisine and, as such, must accompany a festive meal just as it defines all other meals as Vietnamese.

The flesh that substitutes fish at festive events is that of domesticated animals: pigs and chickens as well as cows and ducks. These replace fish for two reasons. First, these animals belong to the sphere of "culture" and their flesh is therefore appropriate for the celebration of events that are relegated to the "culture" apex on the nature–culture axis. This is probably why the flesh of wild "jungle animals" (*thit rung*) such as snakes, lizards and boars, or semi-human animals (ambivalent or inter-categorial in Mary Douglas's terms), such as dogs or cats, is never served at ritual feasts despite being expensive and prestigious.

The second reason for the prominence of flesh of domestic animals is in the context of farming: these animals are part of the Vietnamese rural setting, and as such, represent it. The countryside is symbolically and materially celebrated and consumed at rural festive meals, as the diners emphasize their relationship with their environment. Thus, in an ancestor worship that took place in Dien Ban (a neighboring rural district), the menu was almost identical, except for an extra dish of silkworms steamed with pineapple (*tam hap trai thom*). The host encouraged me to have some and proudly explained that Dien Ban is famous for its silk production. The silkworms were central to local farming and, therefore, are added to the festive menu. An alternative reading of the eating of silkworms would be in terms of poverty and protein deficiency, but if this were the case, why would my host have made a point about the silk production?

Festive cooking techniques are also important and meaningful. The Vietnamese home-eaten meal consists of mostly boiled or steamed dishes. The rice is steamed and the fish often boiled with vegetables into *canh,* which can best be translated as soup.[12] Protein items are sometimes cooked in a pan, but water and condiments are usually added to create a sauce that is often served in a bowl as a side dish, to be poured over the rice. Home cooking seldom involves stir-frying, while deep frying, which is rare, is usually followed by an addition of some kind of sauce (e.g., *ca xot ca chua*, or "fish in tomato sauce": the fish is first fried and then braised in tomato sauce). Roasting and grilling are hardly ever used to produce daily meals. Returning to Xuan's ancestor-worship meal, we realize that grilling, deep-frying, and stir-frying were dominant cooking techniques. Rice was obviously steamed, though, as noted earlier, its centrality was very much diminished. Pork was boiled, but the resulting stock was not used for secondary cooking (for soup or gravy). Though two kinds of *canh* were served—"sticky rice with curdled pig's blood soup" and "pork and potato curry"—both dishes were thick stews that did not resemble the everyday watery *canh*. All in all, the festive meal is much less diluted than the regular meal and the dishes tend to be drier (*kho*), thicker, and more substantial.

Lévi-Strauss (1966b: 938) noted that "boiling [as opposed to roasting] takes place without loss of substance." This makes boiling the most economical cooking mode: the raw ingredients are transformed by cooking without any loss and the water itself is "charged" with nutritional value and becomes edible as soup or gravy. It is therefore easy to understand why the Vietnamese home-eaten meal is mostly boiled or steamed: this cooking method preserves the nutrients to the optimal degree and expands the volume of the meal with an easily accessible and virtually free ingredient: water.

However, as the festive meal is intentionally wasteful and showy, the cooking techniques also serve this end. Roasting, grilling, and frying—the "dry" cooking techniques—are chosen precisely because they are wasteful. They denote filial piety and devotion to the ancestors as well as generosity and prosperity: not only are the ancestors and guests offered a slew of expensive dishes, but these are cooked in a extravagant manner.

The last important difference between daily and festive meals concerns the origin of the dishes. Examining the menu at Xuan's ceremony, we realize that almost half of the dishes were of declared foreign origin: two had foreign names: *ca ri* or curry and *bit tet,* from the French *bifteck* /English beef steak (Krowolski and Nguyen 1997: 180); two featured French beans (*dau tay,* literally "Western legumes"); and another featured potatoes (*khoai tay* or "Western tuber").

Why are foreign dishes and ingredients served and stressed in Hoianese ancestor-worship feasts? After all, it seems more reasonable to expect traditional or "authentic" dishes to be perceived as more appropriate for such events than dishes that are clearly marked as foreign. When I raised this question, many of my interviewees were adamant that these dishes are not foreign and rejected my assumptions about foreign names or origins, claiming that these dishes were Vietnamese and that the suffix *tay* "is just a name." Among these informants there was agreement that these are traditional dishes that have "always been served in such events." Others acknowledged the foreign connection implied by the names of the dishes and ingredients, but could not explain why these dishes are regularly served in festive meals. Here, I will further develop my argument concerning the meaning of foodways at such ceremonies as public manifestations of social and cultural capital and suggest that serving foreign food, and especially French food, stands for modernity and sophistication.

Foreign dishes are served precisely in order to add a French ambience and style to the event. Indeed, consuming foreign food as a token of refinement and sophistication has been a social practice throughout recorded history. It was not only the ancient Roman (Strong 2002: 36–39) and Chinese elite (Chang 1977) who indulged in expensive and rare foreign delicacies. New York Jews, for example, used Chinese food to construct a modern, cosmopolitan identity in the postwar era (Tuchman and Levine 1993). Hence, the stress on the foreign in the Hoianese feasts is yet another way to garner prestige. As Chi pointed out: "Of course we eat French food in such events. In fact, everything we do in public is influenced by the French."

THE URBAN FEAST

I now turn to describe an ancestor worship that took place in a different context. The family in this case was urban (though not very well-to-do), as were most of the guests. As a counterpoint to the previous example, the following case offers an insight into elements of conflict and change, which were hardly visible in the previous case.

> Cu asked Ti to tell me that I was invited to the worship ceremony of his late father. I wanted to get there early to see the preparations, and Tanh, Ti's boyfriend, dropped me off at Cu's house and returned to work. At 10 AM, only some of the close relatives, mainly women, were there, busy preparing the food. Cu's mother was squatting by a kerosene stove outside the newly built house, frying pieces of chicken. "Food will be very tasty," she told me. "We cooked everything that he liked to eat."
> Cu's twenty-year-old sister and her (Cu's sister) boyfriend were setting up an altar in the front yard: "This is for the spirits that are outside, that have no family to take care of them. We must give them food so they

won't be hungry and disturb us," she explained. On the altar they placed
two bowls of uncooked rice and coarse salt, with a candle stuck in each,
five glasses of rice-alcohol, some fruit, flowers, incense sticks, and a set
of paper goods for the dead.

Inside the house, just in front of the main doors, the family's ancestral
altar was ready for the ceremony: the late father's photograph was
displayed in the center; fresh flowers, a large bowl of fruit, and some
candles were added to the daily offerings of incense, tea, and cigarettes.
A small table was erected in front of the altar. The wooden tea-table and
armchairs that are set in most Hoianese houses right in front of the
ancestral altar were removed to make room for the approximately thirty
guests invited for the ceremony and feast.

Dishes began to be brought out from the back of the house. A plate of
each dish was carefully placed on the small table set in front of the
ancestral altar and on the altar erected in the front yard. By 11:15 AM, all
the dishes were ready, completely covering the surface of both altars.
During the next hour, guests kept arriving, the women and the younger
men turning immediately to help with the preparations. The older men
arrived some twenty–thirty minutes before the appointed hour (12:00
noon) and were promptly invited to light incense. They also took their
places on the floor, in front of the altar.

Cu, the deceased's only son, started worshiping at the altar outside: he
lit the candles and three incense sticks, which he lifted toward his
forehead, and bowed three times. Then he planted the incense sticks in
the incense burner, cast the uncooked rice and salt in five directions
(north, south, east, west, and center) and burned the paper offerings.
After this was done there was a pause, as Cu watched the incense sticks
attentively. As soon as they had burned halfway (after some twelve to
fifteen minutes), he poured out the rice wine from the cups on the
ground and refilled them with tea. Later he told me: "the ancestors eat
for half an incense stick." Hence his substitution of tea for the alcohol,
as tea is always served at the end of the meal.

Ti whispered in my ear: "We are waiting for Cu's uncle. Cu's mother's
relations with him are not so good and now everyone gets upset because
he is late and the food is ready." At last the uncle came, wearing shorts
and slippers, and the guests were invited to take their places on the
floor. There was a careful but discreet arrangement of the seating, with
the older and more senior sitting closer to the altar. Women took their
places to the right of the altar (facing the door), while men sat to the left,
according to the directions of *am* and *duong*. There was a moment of

hesitation when my place was to be determined; I was Cu's guest, but ten years older than him. Moreover, I was a foreign guest. Cu suggested that I sit among the senior men but I insisted, using my camera as a pretext, on sitting among my friends, who took their places at the "lower" end of the room, ready to help and serve the food.

The starters were set on the floor before the guests were invited to eat, along with individual bowls, spoons, chopsticks, paper napkins, saucers of *nuoc mam cham* (fish-sauce dip), and bottles of beer and soft drinks. There was a plate with two kinds of sliced meatloaf (*cha* and *nem*) and deep-fried spring rolls (*ram*), arranged over lettuce leaves, along with a saucer of *nuoc mam cham*. Then came whole steamed chickens (*ga hap chanh*), cut up into chopstick-size morsels, and served with a dip made with lemon juice, salt, and pepper. The portions had been carefully reassembled into a whole bird, with head, wings, and claws in their usual position. The third dish was a lotus-stem salad (*goi sen*), made of shredded, lightly pickled lotus stems mixed with boiled shrimp, pork, peanuts, fried shallots, coriander, *rau ram* (polygonum herb), and onion, seasoned with lime, sugar, and fish sauce, served with a roasted rice cracker (*banh trang nuong*). As it was an extremely hot and humid day, iced tea was served in large beer glasses. Bottles of the Vietnamese La Rue beer, Coca-Cola, and Sprite were opened and everyone was encouraged to eat and drink. I was struggling with a gummy piece of chicken, not entirely cooked by my standards, when Cu's mother placed another morsel in my bowl saying, "Eat some chicken leg, it is better than the breast that you are eating."

A few minutes later, large bowls of *sup ga xa* (chicken and lemongrass soup, with snow mushrooms, carrots, and cabbage) were brought in by Cu's mother and sister, with the aid of some younger female guests. The soup was poured into the same bowls that had been used for the starters. Sliced fresh baguette (*banh mi*) was served with the soup and some of the diners dipped their slices in their soup.

The next set of dishes was then served: roast chicken (*ga ro ti*), chopped into chopstick-size morsels and served over lettuce leaves, fried noodles (*mi xau*) topped with the shredded chicken innards, and large plates of fresh aromatic greens (*rau song*). The guests dipped the chicken into a spicy fish-sauce dip and gnawed the tough meat off the bones. Finally, small sponge cakes and *banh it la gai* (glutinous rice cakes with a sweetened green bean paste filling, a local specialty) were served.

By now, no more than twenty or twenty-five minutes since the meal had begun, Cu's uncle, who had hardly touched his food, left, followed by some of the older guests, who had eaten. The floor was littered with dirty dishes, used napkins, gnawed bones, and half-empty bottles. The atmosphere now turned gay and tipsy at the younger end of the table, with the now more relaxed guests still eating and drinking. I whispered in Ti's ear: "Isn't it supposed to be a sad event?" and Ti answered: "Why should they be sad? He died six years ago. Then, they were very sad. But now they have already forgotten."

There were many similarities to the meal we had seen conducted in Xuan's house (beyond the prominence of age and sex hierarchies): the abundance of food, the emphasis on the flesh of domesticated animals, the diminished position of rice, the absence of fish, and the rather extravagant cooking modes. However, there were some fundamental differences that might further contribute to our understanding of the agency of foodways during feasts. Some differences, such as the amount and types of meat, are only expansions of ideas discussed previously in relation to prestige and class. Others, such as the different structure of the meal and the addition of certain dishes, suggest new culinary ideas. Yet other differences, such as the composition of the guest list or the relations between those invited, point to changes that are taking place in contemporary Hoianese society.

First, attention is due to the socio-psychological component of the ancestor-worship feasts, which defines them as emotional safe havens for the family members. An important aspect of ancestor worship is the psychological comfort offered to the immediate family by their guests, which is clearly augmented by the festive meal. On the day on which the memory of the dead is conjured up, relatives and friends gather to share the grief (*chia bun,* or "divide the sadness"). The culinary context, however, turns the event into a merry feast. Where I had expected solemnity and nostalgic sadness, I encountered a cheerful party that, as mentioned earlier, reminded me of a Western birthday celebration. Thus, the feelings of sorrow and loss were substituted by the light-hearted sense of a friendly gathering, supported and enhanced by the good food and alcohol.

Serving the favorite dishes of the dead ancestor, a common practice at such commemorations, is clearly intended to apply the ability of food to comfort. When eating the favorite dishes of the deceased, the diners remember him in the comforting context of home cooking, thus reestablishing a close and warm emotional bond with the dead person, as well as among the living. Here we see how food invokes deep psychological and emotional feelings that influence and define given social situations. Furthermore, serving the favorite dishes of the deceased implies that he is still accessible, as his preferences are those that

FIGURE 4.4. Women's table at an ancestor-worship feast.

define the content of the meal. Indeed, *dam gio* is celebrated a day prior to the actual death anniversary, "when he [the deceased] was still alive and could still eat."

Another psychological element has to do with the seating arrangements—the older a guest is, the closer the placement to the altar. When I realized that this was the organizing principle, I was deeply moved: it must be very hard to sit at the table knowing that soon enough one would be "on the altar," as it were. I gradually realized how comforting and reassuring this setting is: yes, I may be dead soon, but I would still be at home, surrounded by friends and relatives, feasting on my favorite dishes. The food and eating arrangements are a reassurance that death does not entail the end of social life.

The Culinary Refinements of Social Competition

Chicken was the highlight in most of the dishes served at Cu's ancestor worship, while Xuan's family mainly used pork. Indeed, Xuan's family slaughtered a large pig for the feast, whereas Cu's mother slaughtered a dozen chickens. Before discussing the different cultural meanings attributed to the flesh of these animals, I would like to stress the similarities between them. When I asked Trang why pork and poultry are always served at ritual meals, she went to ask her grandmother and returned with the following answers: "Pig brings the money to the house. The pig only eats leftovers but we can eat every part of the pig [see chapter 7]. Rich people roast entire pigs, just like in the Hoi An Hotel, because the pig helps them get the money." As for chicken, Trang said that "chicken eat mostly rice. Rice in Vietnam is like money and so, when the chicken eat the rice, they keep your money, like a bank." Chickens and pigs, then, symbolize thrift and efficiency, Vietnamese virtues essential for economic success and prosperity. Thus, consuming pork and poultry is a culinary statement of commitment to the values of thrift and, hence, the wish for economic prosperity.

While Cu's mother said that chicken was her late husband's favorite meat, which explains the emphasis on poultry in this event, social prestige is also a factor here, as poultry is twice as expensive as pork. Pigs are larger than chickens, multiply quickly, and are fed on leftovers and organic garbage, while chickens are more vulnerable and require some grain as well as leftovers.

Moreover, pork denotes "the countryside": pigs need a large sty and large amounts of food, mainly leftovers mixed with farming residues, such as rice bran (cam), chopped banana trunks, or corncobs. Pigs also produce large amount of smelly excrement, and thus their pens require proper ventilation and drainage. Pigs can be found in almost every rural house around Hoi An, but rarely within the city limits or in urban homes, where conditions do not permit their rearing.[13] Chickens, on the other hand, are smaller, require less space and less food, are less polluting and, therefore, are routinely raised in cages in the kitchens and small yards in the town of Hoi An itself. Pork, then, evokes the countryside, while chicken implies an urban setting. Thus, when serving chicken, it is urban dwelling and sophistication, as well as generosity and wealth, that are implied, along with devotion to one's ancestors, while pork hints at the countryside and is suggestive of fewer material and cultural resources.

In fact, Cu's family did offer pork, in the form of cha and nem cold cuts and sausages. Serving such pork dishes is, yet again, an expression of affluence and sophistication: these two types of meatloaf are made of pounded marinated pork that is seasoned, boiled, steamed, or left to ferment. Though basically a technique of meat preservation, serving plates laden with cha denotes, yet again, prosperity, as these sliced charcuterie are composed almost solely of pork meat and fat and, therefore, are both highly nutritious and expensive.

The chicken at Cu's house was chopped and served according to the Vietnamese custom: morsels cut perpendicular to the bone. The mounds of beautifully roasted chicken pieces, burnished reddish-gold with the spices that had been rubbed into the skin, were composed of bone and only a little meat, however. Here, *appearance* is the key factor denoting prosperity. Hence, in the social game of expense and prestige, the costly meat is served in small amounts that are enhanced through manipulative presentation.

The cooking techniques as well as the names of the dishes encompass, yet again, foreign influence: *ga ro ti* is "roast chicken" (actually, fried in fat, as ovens are not used in Vietnam). The soup was termed *sup* (though lemongrass, which is the dominant taste, is clearly local). Here again, foreign dishes and cooking methods suggest sophistication and cultural capital.

The display of foreignness and prestige continues with the soft drinks: when eating at home or when eating out every day, the only drink on offer is a cup of tea at the end of the meal. In rural feasts, such as the one at Xuan's in-laws, rice wine (*ruou gao*) is usually offered, also in teacups. However, at Cu's house, iced tea, bottled soft drinks, and beer accompanied the meal. The diners had individual glasses, and ice was plentiful. Soft drinks and beer are certainly more expensive than tea and rice wine, thus further adding to the cost of the meal. Moreover, drinking water and soft drinks during the meal is a Western custom and the drinks are clearly of foreign origin: Coca-Cola is probably the foremost American icon, and beer (*bia*) was introduced to Vietnam by the French (Krowolski and Nguyen 1997: 177). In this case, the beer also had a French brand name (La Rue). Sometimes, canned soft drinks and beer are served instead of bottled drinks. As cans are two or three times more expensive than bottles, they too are tokens in the culinary prestige-economy.[14]

On the subjects of mild intoxicants, it should be noted that in Xuan's rural feast, a plate of betel leaves and areca nuts (*trau cau*) was offered on the altar, while Cu's family offered cigarettes. The habit of chewing the intoxicating mixture of areca nuts, betel leaves, and lime is on the decline in Vietnam, and today is considered appropriate only for old women. Smoking is, however, a ubiquitous habit, especially among men, who are practically obliged to smoke at social events, whether they like to or not. Here again, a foreign (though very popular) practice that is linked to the culinary realm (a substance taken orally and influencing the body and mind) gradually substitutes traditional practices and ritual arrangements. Moreover, expensive and/or imported cigarettes imply further refinement and wealth.

Another foreign culinary arrangement was the serving of sweets or "dessert" to conclude a meal. Though one of the desserts was the very local sticky-rice cake (*banh it la gai*), the other was a sponge cake, which is clearly foreign. Moreover, desserts as such are rarely served in daily home meals, as the sweet taste is usually an integral part of some of the dishes (as in sweet-and-sour dishes or the fish-sauce dip), which is always counterbalanced by other tastes so as to provide a balanced *am–duong* combination. Sweetmeats (*che*) are consumed independently as snacks, and are never eaten at the end of the daily meal. Western-style baked cakes are rarely eaten and are never made at home.[15] They are bought in special bakeries and are quite expensive. Thus, the sponge cake at Cu's meal embodies two foreign concepts: that of a cake, and that of a dessert.

Serving a dessert at the end of the meal points to yet another nonindigenous custom that fundamentally changes the structure of the meal. As pointed out in the first chapter, the daily home-eaten Vietnamese meal is synchronic—served all at once. In order to fully appreciate a Vietnamese meal, all the dishes should be present simultaneously on the table so that the diners can not only sample the taste and beauty of each dish, but also experience the meal as a gestalt phenomenon. The colors, textures, smells, and tastes of all the dishes in a meal are the key to the appreciation of its balance and harmony. In Cu's house, however, the meal was diachronic—that is, divided into stages. The sequence of the meal was quite similar to the Western culinary temporal arrangements: starters (cold dish and/or salad), soup, main course, and dessert. Thus, the structure of the meal and the temporal arrangements also designate an extraordinary situation, implying foreign ideas that, in turn, denote sophistication and wealth.

It is important to note that the incorporation of Western arrangements is not wholesale. A good example is the fact that all the food was eaten with chopsticks from rice bowls and that these eating utensils were not changed during the meal: the cold starters, soups, main dishes, rice, and even the desserts were consumed in the same single bowl and managed with the same pair of chopsticks. Though metal forks and spoons are widely available, they are rarely offered at festive events.

Concluding the comparison of an urban feast to one in the countryside, we observe two main differences: urban dwellers use more expensive ingredients, thus expressing their wealth, and tend to rely more heavily than their rural counterparts on foreign culinary dishes and arrangements in order to demonstrate their cultural capital. These differences stand for the refinement and higher status and prestige of urbanites. Refinement and status, of course, come at a price: further expense and harder work.

Conflict and Change around the Table

It should be clear by now that some measure of social rivalry is a central aspect of festive meals in Hoi An, and that this is at least as important as the functional aspects of reactivation and reaffirmation of the existing social order or the integration of the extended family. Therefore, it is only reasonable to expect that conflicts might be exposed or erupt under such circumstances. Furthermore, as foreign and modern practices (and the ideas they carry) seem to be valuable tokens in this prestige-oriented social economy, modern and controversial ideas might be expressed in the culinary arena. However, as rituals tend to be conservative, the introduction of new practices could raise objections and lead to conflict.

Yet, in the harmony-seeking Vietnamese society, where one's "face" is one's most important asset, competition, conflict, and struggle are subtle. The public expression of emotions, especially negative ones, embarrasses all those present and may cause grave loss of face to the person who expresses them; I, for one, have very rarely witnessed such instances. Stress, anger, and conflict exist, of course, but such emotions are manifested subtly. Yet low key as they may be, Vietnamese can (and do) exchange insults during feasts that are, yet again, expressed and responded to in subtle ways.[16]

Cu's uncle very publicly announced that tensions exist between Cu's nuclear family (*nha Cu* or "Cu's house") and himself. He expressed his feelings in several ways, none of them verbal. For one, he arrived late, forcing a delay that embarrassed everyone and especially the hosts. This intentional delay created an unwanted gap between the conclusion of cooking and the serving of the food, which could have resulted in overcooking, cooling down, or prolonged exposure of the food to heat, dust, and flies. He also arrived in shorts and slippers, demonstrating sartorial contempt toward his hosts and disrespect toward his late brother, as no male over fourteen would wear shorts at a formal event, while shoes are the proper footwear for such events (even if taken off at the door as is customary). The tension was further exposed by the fact that his wife did not come with him, another clear breach of etiquette. Finally, he was the first to leave, hardly touching the food or talking to anyone. Though this is generally acceptable for elderly guests, neither his age nor his relation to the deceased permitted such behavior. I did not see him contributing to the expenses either, and this action further stressed his disengagement, which is unusual and improper for an older brother.

Though the uncle was clearly out of line, everyone kept a poker face, pretending that nothing unusual had happened. I had to let go of this subject as my questions were abruptly hushed by Ti; therefore, I cannot provide detailed information as to the nature of the problem. It is a good example, however, of the ways by which the Hoianese express anger publicly, using the context of a festive meal and their knowledge about proper and improper conduct to make a point. It is important to note that the tension was contained and managed so that emotions were expressed without people losing too much face or causing too much embarrassment.

Two of the guests who took part in the preparations would probably not have been invited to this ceremony had it been conducted some ten or fifteen years earlier: Ti and Cu's sister's boyfriend. Both belong to the modern categories of boyfriend/girlfriend. It is not that such a status did not exist ten years ago. Both academic and literary works on the Vietnamese family and society in the nineteenth and twentieth centuries suggest the opposite: love affairs between young men and women were common and the concept of arranged marriage, though hailed as the proper way, was not the only possible option. However, the public declaration that two young people are bonded by romantic love, and the public recognition and legitimacy of such relations are new. Here, nineteen-year-old Ti and Cu's twenty-year-old sister were allowed to publicly express their relations with their boyfriends in the very event that stresses family relations. Indeed, when the sister's boyfriend helped to set up the altar, he behaved in the manner of a son-in-law, even though he was not yet a son-in-law and might indeed never be one.

However, both guests were very much aware of their awkward position and, therefore, were eager to help with serving the meal. Neither is a close family member and the boyfriend is, in fact, an adult male. If they were standard guests, the boyfriend would either sit among the young men and be served or, if he married Cu's sister, would take part in the ceremony as a son-in-law. Ti would probably offer to help, but her help would be minimal, as she is not a relative. Yet their help was accepted and their position was camouflaged: they assumed the role of young relatives, ignored their relations with their partners (who held a "legitimate" position in the event), and avoided attention and criticism.

This was further manifested by their allocated seats. The age and sex hierarchy that is prevalent at the "higher" end of the table tends to disintegrate at the "lower," younger end, away from the altar, where the young men and women mix into a dynamic mass that is constantly in flux. Young children add to the confusion in this section of the table, where unmarried couples can sit together under the more flexible arrangements. In fact, there is a carnivalesque tone to the "lower end" of the table: excessive consumption of food and drink and, specifically, meat and alcohol, both associated with carnal lust, loosening of social control, and illicit sex. The lower end is always merrier and noisier.

The legitimizing of romantic relations among young people in the context of a family-oriented meal sheds light on yet another tension characteristic of contemporary Hoianese society: the tension between the individual and the family. Allowing young people to choose their partners and to experience some degree of premarital relations, or merely accepting such behavior by ignoring it, is new and controversial in contemporary Vietnam. In this case, we see again how individualism slowly expands into an ever-increasing number of spheres, gaining legitimacy in practice, if not in word. The context of the extended family meal seems to be convenient for such encroachment, as the social statement is easily camouflaged by the fervent atmosphere. Here, among neighbors, friends, and kin, the public consequences are not so threatening, both because the matter can be still considered an internal family affair and because the festive atmosphere induced by the good food blunts the sharp edges of the situation.

In summing up the subject of conflict and change as manifested in ancestor-worship feasts, two points are important. The first is that conflicts and processes of change are usually subtle and delicately expressed. The tendency to maintain harmony and avoid disagreement and blatant struggle seems to cool down, restrain, and contain anger. This does not make for a conflict-free society but for the repression of such feelings: steam is released through narrow "cracks" in the social situations: subtle breaches of the proper conduct, which people seem to be highly skilled at detecting.

The second point is that precisely because of the delicate nature of such stressful situations, the arena of public eating seems to be an appropriate sphere for the controlled release of such tensions. The mere presence of extended family members calls for proper conduct even when problems arise. When Cu's uncle insulted his hosts, he did it gently and the reaction was poker faces all round and the containment of the insult. Tones were maintained at normal level and everyone made believe that "everything was all right." Of course, Cu's uncle publicly made a statement that could not be ignored either. All the members of the extended family, as well as neighbors and friends, could not help but witness his behavior and so the point was nevertheless clearly made. The same went for the presence of the young unwed couples. They were kept in the background and behaved accordingly, yet their presence was quietly noticed and their relationship acknowledged and, in fact, endorsed.

Finally, a word is due regarding another important change: since 2004, two dishes have been added to the ancestor-worship feasts: steamed cuttlefish (*muc hap*) and grilled (or fried) prawns (*tom nuong*), which are served at the beginning of the feast. When I inquired about this new custom, the responses were unanimously forthright: "we offer *muc* and *tom* because we can." Thus, Hoang, who invited me to his father's *dam gio* in 2000 and again in 2005, commented on my question regarding the addition of cuttlefish and prawns: "Once we were poor, but now we are not poor anymore [*het ngeo roi*]." While squid and prawns are aquatic creatures, they are expensive, especially when it comes to the larger species (such as tiger prawns and large cuttlefish). Moreover, they are extremely popular among the tourists visiting Hoi An. Consuming these dishes is, therefore, linked to tourism and evokes further prestige. I return to this addition of expensive seafood to festive menus in the next chapter, dedicated to wedding feasts.

THE VEGETARIAN ANCESTOR-WORSHIP FEAST

Though the consumption of animal flesh in ancestor-worship feasts has been presented so far as being both emphasized and meaningful, I have participated in several ancestor-worship feasts in which the food was vegetarian. This is worthy of special attention as it raises questions about several points that I have made regarding the meaning of meat as a marker of social prestige and rural cosmology.

The following and concluding section address two vegetarian ancestor-worship feasts. I show how, to varying extents, they represent an attempt to "have your cake and eat it too," as the ideas presented so far concerning hierarchies, the prestige economy, and moral values are maintained, while new religious and cosmological notions are also expressed through the consumption of mock meat dishes.

Mai met me in the market and invited me to her grandmother's ancestor worship in Dien Ban (a neighboring town). The next morning, Duyen, Mai's neighbor, picked me up on her motorbike and we rode to Dien Ban. The ceremony took place in the house of the late mother, where her eldest son now lived. When we arrived, the house was already packed with guests, mostly from Hoi An and Danang. Five tables had been set in the front room, where the son was preparing the altar.

The usual frantic activity characteristic of such events was taking place at the back of the house. Several women were arranging food on dozens of serving plates. Others were grilling slices of beef over a smoky charcoal stove, frying chicken pieces, washing vegetables, or sorting greens. Mai was cooking vegetables in two large tin pans placed over powerful gas burners. She told Duyen what kind of help was needed. Duyen, wearing tight blue jeans and a shiny yellow blouse, went into the backyard, squatted by a large wok, and began deep-frying what I thought were pieces of squid.

I tasted one of the deep-fried chunks and asked, "What is this?" Duyen answered: "This is vegetarian squid (*muc chay*). It is made of flour. It tastes almost the same, doesn't it?" I agreed with her as the taste and, particularly, the gummy texture, were highly reminiscent of squid. "You know," she continued, "all the dishes today will be *chay* [vegetar-

ian]." I asked why and Duyen reminded me that this was the first day
of the lunar month[17] so the food "must be vegetarian." I carefully
examined the dishes: the large plates of what looked like *cha* (charcuterie), grilled beef encrusted with sesame seeds, and fried mackerel.
Everything looked exactly as it did at any feast I had attended. So did
the preparations, such as the slicing of baguettes for the thick *la gu*
(beef ragout) or the preparation of the fish sauce dip.

Mai asked me to take the food to the altar: "Four plates of each dish."
I asked why four and she explained that in her family they worship four
generations back and a dish is served to each generation.

Transferring the dishes, I had more time to examine them: spring
rolls (*ram*); batter-fried squid and crabs (*tom cua fit bot*); lotus-stem
salad (*ngo sen tron*); grilled beef with sesame seeds (*thit bo nuong me*);
roasted goose (*ngong ro ti*); fried chicken in fish sauce (*ga chien mam*);
liver sautéed with mushrooms and Dalat (a famous vegetable-growing
center) leeks (*gan nam xao he Da Lat*); mutton ragout (*la gu thit cuu*);
pork meatloaf (*cha*); fried mackerel (*ca thu chien*); salad dressed with
mayonnaise (*dau tay ca rot cu den tron bo* or "West[ern] beans, carrots,
and black beets mixed in butter"). The "meat" dishes looked exactly as if
they were made of real animal flesh.

Mai and Duyen repeatedly assured me that all the dishes were "100
per cent vegetarian." Some of the flesh substitutes (such as the squid and
crab) were made at home from different kinds of flour (mainly wheat,
mung bean, and soy bean). Others, like the charcuterie and the fish, had
been bought from a vegetarian restaurant. The fish not only had a dark
skin made of seaweed, but also a fishlike texture, and looked exactly like
the real thing. Other vegetarian ingredients were imported from Korea;
the "beef," for example, was one such item. It was a dry, industrial
product that had to be soaked in water and then handled as if it were real
beef: marinated, seasoned, and then chargrilled. It had the correct color
and texture, and the caramel and sesame seasoning camouflaged it even
more. "You will see," said Mai, "all the dishes will taste exactly like they
should."

Mai's family prepared a vegetarian feast because the worship day was a vegetarian day. On the first and fifteenth days of each lunar month, many Hoianese
eat only vegetarian food, both at home and outside. The *dau hu* (tofu) stands in
the market are very busy, while many of the noodle and rice stalls around town,
as well as those providing takeaway cooked food, offer vegetarian versions of
their daily fare. The four vegetarian restaurants in Hoi An are packed with din-

ers, and several other venues are set up only on these days to sell cooked vegetarian food.[18]

Mung mot and *ngay ram,* black and full moon days/nights, collectively
termed *nhi trai,* are related to Buddhism (Huu 1998: 212; Seneviratne 1992: 187)
and were even termed by some of my informants as "Buddha days" (in English). Observing a vegetarian diet on the first and the fifteenth days of each
lunar month is a minimal requirement of Vietnamese Buddhism, expanded by
the adherents to several days per month, several months a year, or even complete abstinence from all animal products (Huu 1998: 207).

The Vietnamese Buddhist leader Thich Thien Hoa (1992, quoted in Huu
1997: 90) offers three reasons for Buddhist vegetarianism: compassion, karma,
and hygiene. Compassion stems from the Buddhist belief that all living souls
are equal as "they all carry a bit of Buddhiety" (ibid.). This essential equality
creates a sense of compassion toward all other beings, leading to nonviolence
and vegetarianism. Karma is the dogma according to which the destiny of a
living being is determined by the totality of his past actions: "All living beings
. . . devour each other and suffer the punishment . . . of births and rebirths"
(ibid. 91), and vegetarianism is one way of avoiding the sinful act of murder so
as to improve one's karma. Vegetarian hygiene can superficially be understood as the avoidance of edibles that spoil easily and cause disease. It could
also be understood as ritual purification and spiritual hygiene, however.[19]

Huu (1998: 206–207) claims that the Vietnamese term *an chay* ("to eat veg-
etarian/plain") does not stem from the Chinese word *tsai,* or "vegetables"
(Chang 1977), but from the *nom* (Sino-Vietnamese) character *trai,* which means
"pure," as in *trai gioi:* the ritual purification of the body and mind before the
great imperial sacrifices in the Chinese and Vietnamese courts. This process
included bathing, wearing clean clothes, and abstaining from music, coarse
language, alcohol, sex, eating animal products (meat, eggs, and milk) and
stimulating spices (*ngu vi tan:* onion, garlic, leek, shallot, and *hung cu* or asa-
foetida). Thus, the vegetarian diet is intended to purify the body and mind
through reflexive abstinence.

Thich Thien Hoa further recommends that Buddhist practitioners of a
vegetarian diet abjure a sense of pride in their observance. This includes "refraining from feeling superior to those eating meat, avoiding praise for en-
during long periods of abstinence, avoiding asceticism and *avoiding making
fake dishes from vegetable ingredients*" (1992; quoted in Huu 1997: 92, my emphasis).[20]

Cohen (2001) in his study of the Vegetarian Festival in Phuket points to a
similar paradox: the cleansing, purifying act of austerity has turned in recent
years into public feasts of conspicuous consumption of vegetarian dishes. Five-

star hotels offer expensive nine-course feasts of "mock meat" dishes. Cohen quotes a Sino-Thai food critic who, though praising the culinary art of the chefs who produce these "counterfeit dishes," comments on "the tenuous morality of using vegetable products to forge illusory meats for those who have forsworn consumption of the real thing" (ibid. 64).

Huu (1997: 100) also notices this paradox, and explains that Vietnamese Buddhism is a "corrupted" version of the original teaching of the Buddha. Describing the historical process of the blending of the pure Buddhist doctrine with Confucian and Taoist elements, he stresses the influence of the "triple sacrifice" (*Tam Sinh*) of ox, pig, and goat and claims that "as it was forbidden for Buddhists to kill living beings . . . they sought up [*sic*] vegetarian dishes as offerings." He claims that the popularity of Buddhism among the royal families further encouraged the tradition of vegetarian mock meat cuisine, as only such elaborate dishes were deemed proper for the royal table, even when prepared by Buddhist monks from vegetarian ingredients. Spending some time with Cohen at the Phuket Vegetarian Festival and discussing this apparent paradox with several Vietnamese informants, I found that both in Hoi An and Phuket, most of those consuming vegetarian mock meat dishes did not perceive this practice as paradoxical or as embodying an internal contradiction. Their experience was coherent and the moral question did not concern most of them.

Relying on the previous analysis of ancestor-worship feasts, a number of points can be made concerning the organizing principles of such vegetarian feasts. The feast in Mai's house was shaped by two cultural demands: the first was to offer a "proper meal," and the second was to adhere to a vegetarian diet that is the custom of that specific day. The first level includes all the practices and ideas described so far about nutritional demands, social structure, and the prestige economy. Indeed, all the characteristics of a common, that is, meat-oriented feast, were there: large amounts of nutritious, special, expensive and labor-intensive food were cooked by the women and the young and served to the elderly and the men. As at any other feast, many ingredients and dishes were of foreign origin and hence evoked a measure of prestige. As for processes of social change, Duyen and many of the younger women were wearing Western-style clothing and mingling freely with the younger men, thus expressing modern concepts of women's emancipation and equality, as well as a sexuality that, as I suggested earlier, has to do with the carnivalesque aspects of the event. Yet all of these were expressed without the use of real meat. Thus, serving a lavish mock meat feast allows the participants to "have their cake and eat it too," adhering to the moral demand of avoiding animal flesh while feasting on it.

BUDDHIST ANCESTOR WORSHIP

Dep invited us to the worship ceremony for her mother-in-law. She insisted that Irit had to come because "Irit is a vegetarian[21] and the feast will be vegetarian, so she can eat many tasty dishes." This was the third anniversary of Dep's mother-in-law's death, which concludes the mourning period, when the deceased is "removed" from the temporary side-altar to the main ancestral altar.

Dep's husband, his younger brother, and three-year-old son were all dressed in the white mourning outfit when we arrived. The old, worn-out funeral wreaths and flags were set around the small altar with the photograph of the deceased on top. To my surprise, Dep's husband told me that we had to wait for the monks, whom I had never seen participating in ancestor-worship rituals. Eventually three Buddhist monks arrived, slim and ageless, dressed in brown gowns, their heads shaved. They began to chant from their prayer book, every now and again beating a bronze gong and a wooden, fish-shaped drum that produces sharp, hollow sounds.

As is usually the case in such ceremonies, the kowtowing, lighting of candles and incense, the casting of raw rice grains, and the burning of the paper offerings were performed, as guests kept entering the tiny house, filling the small front yard and eventually blocking the narrow alley. All the while, the monks kept chanting. After some time, the oldest monk approached each of the white-clad mourners in turn, removing the cloth covers from their heads and dropping them on the floor. Then he led Dep's husband, the elder son, to the small altar and instructed him to take the photograph of the dead mother and place it on the main altar.

Now the guests took their seats. Food was served and the event took on a happier tone. The monks were led to the best table, the only one erected within the front room, as close as possible to the altar. I was invited to join them. "Why won't you sit with us?" I asked Dep's husband. "Oh no," he replied, waving his hand and looking embarrassed, "We are too small (*nho*) to sit with the *thay* ("teachers," and also Buddhist monks).

The food was considerably less colorful and impressive than what I was used to at such events: spring rolls, pumpkin soup (*canh bi*), stir-fried eggplants, banana flower salad, and a dish of tofu with vegetables. The dishes were bland, cold, and somewhat sweet. The only contrasting condiment was a bowl of fermented soybean sauce (*mam*) spiced with some red chili. The monks ate very slowly, hardly touching the food at all. "We eat three times a day," the oldest monk told me. "We are not Hinayana monks who beg for food. We work very hard in the garden and so we must eat to have energy. But we eat very little."

When the meal concluded, the monks reached into their pockets for cigarettes. The old monk said: "It is OK, we don't drink alcohol or have sex, but Buddha never forbade smoking." Seizing the moment, I asked: "How come you participate in ancestor worship? Didn't Buddha say that all souls reincarnate?" The monk smiled and said: "They believe that the ancestors are here. Of course, they are wrong. . . . But we came here to help them remember their relatives."

Dep approached our table and said: "You should have been here yesterday too. Yesterday, mother was still alive and so we cooked everything that she liked so that she could eat it. You know, she was very Buddhist and ate only vegetarian food."

The common practice of eating vegetarian food on the first and fifteen days of the lunar month notwithstanding, vegetarianism in Hoi An is usually practiced by the adherents of either Buddhism or the Cao Dai religion.[22] Indeed, the event at Dep's house was arranged along Buddhist lines: the lavish, conspicuous feast was modified into a humble meal. Though the amount of food was larger than in usual home-eaten meals, the structure was almost identical: rice, soup, a dry dish, fresh greens, and sauce (although there were several dry dishes that were deep-fried and stir-fried). Culinary excellence, displayed in layered tastes, complex structures, and remarkable aesthetics was not manifested in this meal, nor was there a Western, prestige-invoking influence. In fact, the tastes and textures were somewhat below the standard of even a home-eaten meal. Thus, beyond the limited role of the festive meal as a "caloric-filling station," the notions of prestige and social competition were not expressed at all. This was a genuinely humble meal, consisting of bland, simple, cheap, and none-too-tasty food, reflecting the Buddhist ideals of humility and of the pre-eminence of the spiritual over the material.

The most important culinary modification along Buddhist lines was the total exclusion of animal flesh, real or fake. Though the meal included vegetal proteins (tofu and fermented soybean sauce), they were not shaped or flavored to resemble animal flesh. Thus, the Buddhist principles of compassion and nonviolence, which lead to vegetarianism, were not merely adhered to materially (as in the previous feast at Mai's house), but observed on the moral level too. Furthermore, by avoiding mock meat dishes, the "corrupting" ideas of the feast as sacrifice, suggested earlier by Huu, were rejected and the Buddhist values were embodied in a purer fashion.

The seating arrangements suggest a modification in the social hierarchy too, as age and sex become secondary to the clergy. The monks were not classified according to their relative age but were grouped in a single category that was perceived as superior to any other social category present at the event. Thus, it was the monks, and not the elderly men, who had the best table, as close as possible to the family altar. From this perspective, the Buddhist seating arrangements challenge the common social hierarchies. However, while "eating above" and "seating before" (Jamieson 1995: 31), the monks complied with the ideals of restraint and self-imposed frugality and even pushed them further, as they hardly ate at all. Just as in other food events, those who had privileged access to the food were expected to enjoy it the least.

Age hierarchy did play a role amongst the monks themselves, however. The younger monks clearly yielded to their elder, served his food, and did not eat until he did. The other guests simply observed the common age hierarchy, treating the monks collectively as if they were the oldest guests. Indeed, the monks were the first to finish eating and the first to leave.

It might be the case, then, that the normal eating arrangements and the social hierarchy they reflect were not fundamentally challenged in the Buddhist context, but only expanded to include another social category, that of the religious clergy. Interestingly, the word *thay,* which is used to denote "monk," also means "teacher" (and clairvoyant). Teachers are also highly respected in contemporary Hoianese society and are often seated at places of honor, regardless of their age. Thus, the Confucian respect for teachers, as well as the Buddhist reverence for monks, are both accommodated within the existing social hierarchy, perceived as privileged categories treated as if they belonged to the category of elders.

Another issue brought up during this event relates to the notion of the favorite food of the deceased that should be offered on the day preceding his or her death anniversary. Though this culinary arrangement is common at ancestor-worship feasts, it essentially contradicts Buddhist doctrine and, therefore, requires some elaboration. I pointed out earlier that offering food to the dead implies that death does not mean the end of existence or the cessation of material needs. When preparing the deceased's favorite dishes, a point is made about their continual presence and accessibility. As for the feast held on the day prior to the death anniversary, this event exposes the perception of time in the realm of the dead. It seems that the dead exist within an annual cycle, in which their life and death are repeatedly experienced. This is reflected in a set of ceremonial meals in which the deceased is alive on the first day (one day prior to his death anniversary) and dead (again) on the next.

Such notions of life and death are completely incompatible with the Buddhist doctrine of karma and reincarnation. The principle of karma maintains that the soul is born and reborn in an endless number of reincarnations and that the belief in a stable singular soul is not only wrong but, in fact, the source of human suffering. The dead do not exist in any form and a Buddhist ancestor worship, vegetarian as it may be, is oxymoronic and impossible as far as Buddhism goes (for a similar discussion of Buddhism and ancestor worship, see Baker 1979: 98–100).[23]

From the religious and philosophical perspective, we could accept Huu's (1997: 100) claim that Vietnamese Buddhism is amalgamated with (and "corrupted" by) Confucian and Taoist beliefs and practices. This amalgamation is known as the "Vietnamese Triple Religion" (*Tam Giao dong Nguyen* or "the three religions having the same source"). Thus, the ancestor-worship ceremonies led by Buddhist monks and followed by a vegetarian feast reflect the syncretic nature of the everyday, lived Vietnamese religion. However, such scholarly explanations do not clarify how this paradox is resolved in practice.

Here, the role of the feast as a multilevel social arena, where contradictions are softened and internal tensions and paradoxes accommodated, should be highlighted once again. Earlier in this chapter I suggested that social conflicts are contained and accommodated within the safe, convivial, and intimate context of the festive meal. It seems that the same principle applies when it comes to religious and philosophical paradoxes, such as the one described above. The feast helps reconcile opposing ideologies by creating a comfortable and comforting context that softens the edges of the contradictions. Sharing food induces an intimate, familial ambience and the various social categories are accommodated into the family system. As soon as the monks assume the role of "elders," they acknowledge the basic hierarchy that defines the Vietnamese family and society and do not challenge it. The vegetarian food and, especially, the plainness of the fare that was served at Dep's home, represent the Buddhist ideals of compassion and humility. Thus, seemingly contradictory ideologies are adhered to at different levels of the very same feast: while the social structure and the perception of life and the afterlife are maintained by the eating arrangements, Buddhist compassion and humility are expressed in the food itself. Here again we realize that the culinary sphere is so flexible that it allows those partaking of the feast to "have their cake and eat it too."

5 ✒ Wedding Feasts

FROM CULINARY SCENARIOS TO GASTRO-ANOMIE

Weddings are the single most important event in Hoianese lives. Complex affairs lasting several days, they involve a huge expenditure of time, effort, and
money, in a series of ceremonies that fundamentally alter the social positions
of the bride and groom as well as their extended families. Food has an extremely important role and each and every ceremonial stage of a Hoianese
marriage is marked by some kind of feast—indeed, guests are literally invited
to "eat the wedding" (*an cuoi*).

Following a brief discussion of "traditional" Vietnamese weddings, this
chapter is organized according to the chronological stages of a contemporary
Hoianese wedding, but the ceremonies and feasts described belong to separate
weddings in different social contexts. Thus, while the sequence in which wedding ceremonies develop from one stage to the next is maintained, there are
intra-stage comparisons that stress the prominence of the Hoianese culinary
scenario, while modifications that were made to this culinary script under particular social circumstances are singled out for discussion.

The last part of the chapter is dedicated to a wedding feast in which the culinary scenario was challenged by another festive formula—modern and external. Though this feast was on the verge of collapsing into what Fischler (1979)
has termed "gastro-anomie," it was successfully contained and skillfully handled by the members of the different social groups at the wedding. This event
allows for the discussion of culinary innovation as launching social change or,
rather, for foodways as models.

TRADITIONAL AND CONTEMPORARY WEDDINGS

Weddings in Vietnam have been the subject of much debate, criticism, and
even political controversy during the turbulent past two centuries. Traditional

Vietnamese weddings[1] were long and complex affairs, encompassing several rituals and incurring great expense.

Four big ceremonies made up the traditional wedding. The first was *le*[2] *xem mat* ("the ceremony of seeing the faces"), which was conducted after the matchmaker reached an agreement with both parties concerning the wedding (Huu 1998: 228–30). On this occasion, the extended family members had a chance to meet each other and to scrutinize the prospective bride and groom. Next came the engagement (*dam hoi*, literally: "asking for marriage," also termed *an hoi* or "eating [and] asking [for marriage]"). This was sometimes followed by a period of *lam re* ("working groom"), when the prospective groom was required to live and work for his future in-laws as part of the dowry agreement (Pham 1999: 28). The third ceremony was *le cuoi*, in which the bride's family would set the terms of the wedding (*tach cuoi*). Finally came the wedding itself (*dam cuoi*), a celebration that would last for several days and consisted, yet again, of a set of ceremonies. The wedding procession of the groom's family to the bride's house was followed by the "offering of the red string" (*te to hong*) in the bride's house. Then came *ruoc dau:* the "escorting-the-daughter-in-law" procession (the term for "bride," *dau,* means "to please," the kind of behavior expected from brides). Following the procession, the two families would celebrate in a joint feast, marking the new union between the parties by sharing a table. In the evening, the bride would prostrate herself before the groom and then together they would kowtow in front of his ancestral altar, thus concluding the incorporation of a new wife/daughter-in-law into the groom's family. A postnuptial ceremony reaffirmed the consummation of the marriage. Each and every stage and ritual involved food offerings and food gifts, as well as some kind of festive eating. Some of these feasts were offered to hundreds of guests: extended families and even entire villages.

Under the Communist regime the traditional arrangements were reformed. The official reasons for the reform were that the traditional wedding was a feudal, undemocratic, and wasteful social institution that, moreover, denigrated women to the level of merchandise, bankrupted families, and abused communal property (Huu 1998: 231; see also Malarney 2002: 148–51). The regime also had a less explicit agenda: ideologues wanted the Communist Party of Vietnam to replace the family as the core of society and as the sole source of social legitimacy. Therefore, a "New Life Wedding" was created and imposed throughout Vietnam, wherein a much smaller number of family members and friends were joined by "representatives of the offices, factories and cooperatives where the bride and groom worked . . . [who] would exhort the couple not to forget their duties towards the Motherland and their new-found happiness" (Huu 1998: 231). Ambivalent Huu admits that these events, though accompanied by music, "became monotonous and unattractive . . . and after the return of peace, [many people turned to] a more lively form [of wedding] by drawing from both the traditional and the foreign" (ibid.).

Contemporary Hoianese weddings contain many traditional elements, but are compressed into a quicker sequence of ceremonies. There are usually only two phases: the engagement (*dam hoi* or *le dinh hon*) and the wedding (*dam cuoi*). The engagement ceremony is a short affair lasting from late morning until lunchtime (though sometimes preceded by another meeting between the parents, termed *tham nha* or "visiting the house"), while most Hoianese weddings last for two days. The first day is dedicated to *hoi than* ("intimate/friendly gathering"), in which the parents of the bride and groom offer separate feasts to their respective extended families and friends. The next morning, the groom and his close relatives arrive in procession to the bride's house, where a short ceremony is held. Then comes *ruoc dau:* the bride is taken to the groom's house, where another *hoi than* is held, this time for both families. That same afternoon, friends and relatives of both parties are invited once again to an event that includes a feast and a karaoke session. This event is termed *dai ban* ("inviting friends"), and is clearly a modern addition. Though these arrangements are common, contemporary Hoianese weddings are rather flexible, so that certain elements may be omitted or compressed, while others are expanded or added.

Wedding dates are set after consulting a fortuneteller (*thay boi*) and/or a geomancer (*thay dia*), who determine the optimal time for the wedding according to astrological charts and/or the principles of *phong-thuy* (the Chinese *feng shui*).[3] These ritual experts determine the most auspicious date for the wedding so as to enhance the chances of success, good luck, and happiness. I was told that a good fortuneteller or geomancer can overcome problems and even compensate for cases when the bride and groom had incompatible birth dates by determining the proper times for the various rituals.[4]

Though the birth dates of the bride and groom are crucial for determining the proper timing, there are seasons and dates that are generally considered to be fortunate and auspicious, such as the ninth, eighteenth, and twenty-seventh days of the lunar month[5] or the month right before Tet. A modern inclination is toward weekends (Saturday and Sunday) when many people are free. Thus, it is often the case that dozens of weddings are held on the very same day, as a certain date is considered exceptionally auspicious (and/or convenient).

COOKING FOR AN ENGAGEMENT CEREMONY

Chi Xuan sounded very excited on the phone: "My neighbors have an engagement ceremony (*dam hoi*) at their house tomorrow and they have asked me to cook. You can come and watch."

The next morning I walked to Xuan's house at around 7:30 AM. It was easy to know which was the place of the ceremony, as people were coming and going out of the house, and a strong scent of burning firewood came from the backyard. I followed the voices to the tin-roofed kitchen behind the house, where I saw Xuan squatting by the hearth, her face streaked with soot. At her feet was a blood-soaked sack, quivering every now and again. "We have just slaughtered the chickens and ducks," she said, pointing to the sack.

Xuan placed a large tin cauldron over the hearth and filled it with water. Then she handed me a pot of boiled quail eggs and told me to peel them. As soon as the water was hot, she took one of the bird carcasses from the sack, dipped it briefly in the boiling water, and quickly plucked its feathers. She used a small knife to slit its posterior, and inserted her hand into the body cavity, gently extricating the inner organs. She disentangled the guts and used the knife to dismember the heart, lungs, and liver, carefully removing the gall bladder. "You could be a surgeon," I exclaimed. Xuan answered seriously: "I am very quick, and a good cook as well, so all my neighbors ask me to help in their feasts." I asked if they paid her and she replied that she had to help (*can giup*) them when they asked, and that they would do the same for her. Sometimes she is asked to cook for people who are not neighbors or relatives and in those cases they would pay her daily wages (some 25,000 dong, about US$1.70 in 2000).

While frying the chicken that had been rubbed with turmeric ("for a beautiful gold color"), Xuan told me how to stuff the ducks with a mixture of green beans, dried plums, and the shredded internal organs, and then to tightly sew up the body cavity with a needle and string before cooking.

As lunchtime (11:00 AM) was approaching, more women arrived into the kitchen and the atmosphere became frantic: the stuffed ducks were boiled in sauce and the chickens were steamed, then chopped into morsels with a heavy cleaver. Pork marinated in lemongrass was grilled and arranged on plates, along with vegetables pickled in fish sauce. Slices of *cha* were arranged on serving plates and bread was sliced for the snow mushroom, peas, and pork soup. It turned out that one of the guests was a vegetarian, so a young man was dispatched to *quan chay ba Dam* ("Mrs. Dam's vegetarian restaurant"), where he purchased several mock meat dishes: imitation roast pork, steamed chicken in lemon sauce, meat and mushroom soup, *cha*, and even roasted duck, all made of flour, soy products, and vegetables.

A convoy of cars, their front windscreens decorated with red "double-happiness" Chinese characters, approached the house. Some of the women in the kitchen hastened to welcome the guests who formed a line by the front gate, holding the large red trays with wedding gifts in preparation to march into the house. Xuan gave me the final instructions: she would take the ducks out of the pot and place them in soup bowls. I was to arrange the quail eggs around each duck and pour the sauce over them.

The meat of farm animals is an essential component of the Hoianese festive meal, and the quantity served rises dramatically in proportion to the importance of the event. The nutritional importance of animal protein notwithstanding, the prominence of meat in festive meals is symbolic and meaningful. Fiddes (1991), in his book dedicated to meat as a "natural symbol," suggests that eating the flesh of other animals is the supreme act of human domination over all other creatures: "Killing, cooking and eating other animals' flesh provides perhaps the ultimate authentication of human superiority over the rest of nature. . . . Thus, for individuals and societies to whom environmental control is an important value, meat consumption is typically a key symbol" (ibid. 65). Veal, then, "enjoyed high prestige [in Britain] for many years . . . *because* of the extreme subjugation of the creatures intrinsic to its production" (ibid. 44, original emphasis). Similarly, by slaughtering and consuming the flesh of farm animals at public feasts, the Hoianese are making an explicit culinary statement regarding their dominance over other living beings, and of culture over nature in general.

Furthermore, as in many other cultures (see, for example, Sahlins 1976: 171), it is believed in Vietnam that when consuming animal flesh, and specifically its muscles (in the form of red meat, rich in blood), the strength and vitality of the animal is incorporated into the body of the eater. Thus, the flesh of powerful animals, such as cows, or catfish—which are exceptionally muscular and/or feisty—is considered nourishing and strengthening. The meat of wild or undomesticated animals is considered overpowerful, however, a possibly dangerous substance that should be consumed in moderation and with caution.[6] Hence, only the flesh of domesticated animals is eaten at feasts—the flesh of wild animals is never served on such occasions.

The Hoianese prefer their meat as fresh as possible. Thus, in most festive events chickens, quails, ducks, and even pigs are slaughtered just before cooking. Often, these are home-reared animals fattened up especially for the occasion.[7] In other cases, the birds are bought alive from a supplier or at the market and are slaughtered at home. The only kind of meat that is generally bought at the market for festive occasions is beef, probably because cows are too large to be butchered at home or to be consumed at a single feast.

The preference for freshly killed meat probably originates from traditional hygiene and health precautions, as prior to the arrival of electricity and modern refrigeration (round-the-clock electricity reached Hoi An only in the early 1980s, and affordable refrigerators from China only in the late 1990s), meat "on the hoof" was the best guarantee of quality and freshness. However, the taste, smell, color, and texture of the flesh of freshly slaughtered animals is remarkably different from that of chilled or frozen meat, and the Hoianese, accustomed to the taste of fresh meat, frown upon frozen or pre-slaughtered flesh.

Freshness is essential for yet another sought-after quality of meat: the vitality and energy of the living animal, which gradually fades after its death: "The fresher the meat," I have often been told, "the more energy it has." From the nutritional perspective, the Hoianese are right: several nutrients, and especially vitamins, begin to disintegrate as soon as the animal dies and further degenerate during storage and cooking (Zilber-Rosenberg 1996: 92).

The idea that fresh meat contains the vital essence of the animal also explains the preference for tough flesh that is hard to chew off the bone. This chewy texture results not only from what in the West would be seen as undercooking but also from the livestock and animal husbandry techniques. Most livestock in Vietnam (except pigs) are, by and large, free-ranging and develop strong muscles and lean frames. Chickens, for example, are categorized into *ga ta* ("our chicken") and *ga tay* ("Western chicken"). The latter is usually of European stock and raised in Western-style poultry farms. Its flesh is considerably more tender than that of "our chicken," the locally bred free-range muscular bird. But Hoianese definitely prefer the local, muscular fowl and willingly pay as much as double for it.

Slaughtering the animals just before the feast is therefore the outcome of several nutritional and cosmological considerations: it guarantees the freshness and hygiene of the meat and the maximal preservation of its vital nutritional components, as well as the essential power attributed to it. On-the-spot slaughtering enhances the quality of the meat and with it, the quality of the meal and the social prestige involved. The common practice of slaughtering and processing the meat at home in situ, instead of buying it from the market, also means a lot of additional work. Here again, painstaking efforts contribute to the prestige accrued in the production of the feast: the more work is invested in preparing the fare, the greater the prestige acquired by the hosts.

In addition, the long, arduous, and complicated preparations require the help of kin and friends; therefore, there is enhanced family and social integration. Just as in the North American potlatch, intragroup reciprocal arrangements are devised in order to achieve common goals. As Xuan pointed out, however, those who are not close relatives are not included in the reciprocal system and have to be paid for their help.[8] The outcome is that intragroup integration is intensified, while social distance is expressed toward those considered "outsiders." Thus, the preparations of the festive meal make for a social mechanism that creates and maintains the borders of inclusion of the extended family.

The last point I wish to make about this event concerns the symbolism embedded in the presentation of certain dishes. In the previous chapter, I pointed out that in Hoi An, pork has rural connotations, whereas chicken dishes are considered urban, refined, and sophisticated. However, the mode of presentation of the dish is also meaningful: Xuan pointed out that the duck should be surrounded by eggs. This reminded me of what another friend told me about a dish called "perched phoenix" (*phuong hoang sao*), composed of a steamed chicken served whole over a bed of deep-fried crisp yellow noodles surrounded by tiny quail eggs. This dish, he said, represents proper family values and good motherhood because a hen is "a good mother that takes care of her children and provides for their safety." He also pointed out that chicken and duck are usually served at weddings and other family feasts along with eggs or lotus seeds, "which look like eggs." Thus, it is not only the ingredients and cooking modes that are laden with social symbolism, but also the ways in which certain key dishes are presented.

Bac and Trung's Engagement Feast

We left our room at 8:30 AM and walked in the pouring rain to Trung's parents' home, right inside the market. The front doors of this relatively modern concrete shop-house were wide open, and the front room had been cleared of merchandise. By the ancestral altar, a long table had been erected in the center of the room and covered in white and crimson silk tablecloths. It was set with Western-style white porcelain teapots and cups (on loan from the family's tourist-oriented restaurant) and had several packs of expensive 555 cigarettes (Trung's father's and, reputedly, Ho Chi Minh's, favorite brand). Arranged on the altar were a large brass burner (empty, as "it is too expensive to burn so much sandalwood"), a vase of flowers to its left and a bowl of fruit to its right, three huge incense sticks, and two red candles decorated with a dragon and a phoenix respectively. There were also two small trays, one with ready-to-chew betel quid (*trau cau*) and the other with a fine porcelain pot of *ruou gao* (rice wine) and some half-filled cups. Colorful paper-cut letters were pasted on the wall behind the altar, reading: *Le Dinh Hon 4.11.99 9.11 Ky Mao* (Engagement 4.11.99, the 4th day of the 11th month of [the year of the] Fire Cat).

Everyone was waiting for the groom's family. The atmosphere was tense and solemn. Hung, the bride's father, suffocating in his dark suit and smoking nervously, consulted an elderly man, who, as I later found out, was the bride's family representative in the ceremony (a friend of the family who was asked to officiate because of his "high position in society before 1975: he worked with the Americans, but not any more").[9] The kitchen area at the back of the house was livelier, but there was an efficient and busy air. Trung, the bride, was sitting in one of the small backrooms, wearing a beautiful blue silk *ao dai* and matching *khan* (turban), putting on her makeup. She seemed more relaxed than the rest.

Suddenly, a girl came running into the house shouting: "They are coming. . . ." The guests stood up and formed a line by the door. The bride's family representative stood by the threshold, followed by Trung's father and mother, and then the rest of the family members, in descending age order. Trung herself did not come out to welcome the guests.

The groom's family was led by his uncle, who officiated as the family representative. He was followed by Bac's mother (Bac's father was no longer alive), his brothers, and the other guests. Bac, dressed in a black suit, was last in the line. The younger guests stood in pairs, carrying round, red, gift-laden wedding trays decorated with Chinese double-happiness characters. Bac's twin nephews, dressed in tartan kilts and red berets with pink pompoms, resembled live double-happiness characters.

The two family representatives exchanged brief greetings by the door and then introduced the guests to the hosts. The men, dressed in suits and ties, shook hands, and the women, wearing winter brocade *ao dai,* bowed. No one talked and smiles were tense. Those carrying the gifts went to the altar and set down the trays (two of each) laden with areca nuts, rice wine, tea, sandalwood, cakes, and *cha* loaves. Trung's father, the host, kowtowed and worshiped in front of his ancestral altar. The groom's representative requested the host's permission and kowtowed too, while the host lit the candles and some sandalwood.

The bride's family representative led the guests to seats on the left side of the table (the *duong* or male side), while the hosts took their places on the right side. The older the person, the closer to the head of the table and the ancestral altar he or she was seated. The bride's ninety-four-year-old grandmother, the family elder, was seated right by the altar.

Husbands and wives were seated next to each other. The younger members of both families (mostly teenagers) had a table in one of the back rooms. The groom had disappeared.

There were two sets of mutually welcoming speeches by the representatives ("now that we are going to be one family, we must help each other . . .") and only then were the bride and groom invited to come out from the interior of the house to be presented to the guests. They did not speak or worship. Trung was led to her future mother-in-law, who placed two golden rings on her finger. At that stage, the photographer took some portraits of the bride and groom with several family members. When the photography session was over, the young couple left the room and were not present for the rest of the event. Once they had left, tea was offered to the guests and only then did everyone loosen up and start chatting, and the men began smoking. A few minutes later, the porcelain teapots and cups were cleared and canned soft drinks and beer were placed on the table.

Hue, Trung's eldest sister, told me that the dishes for the engagement meal had been chosen by Trung herself and prepared by her mother's cousin, a cook in a restaurant. The guests wiped their chopsticks and bowls with paper napkins and filled their glasses as the first dish was served. It was *cha con con:* three kinds of *cha* (meat loaf) slices, served with sweet-and-sour pickles, arranged in the shape of a dancing bird, with a carrot head and feathers and a chili beak. Trung told me later that "in Saigon, this dish is much more beautiful, it really looks like a live, dancing bird." The dish was served with crisp deep-fried shrimp crackers (*banh tom*).

Other dishes soon followed: lotus-stem salad; a clear chicken consommé with snow mushrooms, pork, and quail eggs; and a whole chicken steamed with Chinese medicinal herbs and lotus seeds. There was also a dish of steamed shitake mushrooms served on a bed of Chinese snow mushrooms, garnished with dashes of ketchup and mayonnaise. Hue explained that the last dish was created especially for the occasion by one of the bride's sisters, a chef who owns a successful tourist-oriented restaurant.

Finally, trays of profiteroles and triangular slices of spongy white ("American") bread and butter were served. Small cups of Vietnamese coffee were brought from outside: black coffee (*ca phe den*) for the men and coffee with milk (*ca phe sua*) for the women. Hue whispered in my ear: "Now even women can drink coffee, but always with milk." Vietnamese green tea was served along with the coffee.

FIGURE 5.1. Cha pork charcuterie and lotus stem salad.

At that stage, the groom's family rose to leave. Again, there were short mutual speeches, and the guests paraded out. Bac, the groom, left the house, walking last in the row again, but then said something to his elder brother and returned into the house.

Only then did everyone fully relax. The cameraman arranged some more photographs, Hung smoked, and everyone talked cheerfully. The table was cleared and a feast of leftovers was laid out for those who had cooked and served the meal. Trung now returned to the room wearing a sweatshirt, her hair all messed up, and joined the meal, which included heaping servings of each of the earlier feast dishes, placed casually on serving trays. Interestingly, a dish that had not been served at the formal feast was added: a colorful rice dish garnished with vegetables and lotus seeds, called *kim ngoc man duong* ("house full of jade and gold"). Beer and soft-drink bottles were opened and toasts were made to the bride and groom. There was a palpable sense of relief and of "mission accomplished."

Sociologists and anthropologists have long noted the socioeconomic function of weddings as an agreement between two families intended to enhance their shared wealth and social status and to ensure their continual existence through procreation (Ember and Ember 1990: 179; see also Harris 1991: 123, 125; Davis and Harrell 1993: 21).This pragmatic aspect of marriages is actively camouflaged in contemporary Western weddings, which tend to stress individual choice and romantic love, as well as sexual exclusivity (Adrian 2003: 66).[10]

The socioeconomic nature of contemporary Vietnamese marriages is explicit. Bac and Trung's engagement ceremony clearly reflected the marginality of the bride and groom, downplayed the importance of their feelings for each other (though this was definitely a love match), and stressed the priority of the families, as well as the socioeconomic nature of the newly established relationships between the parties, with the eating arrangements clearly serving this purpose, both in etiquette and in content.

The marginality of the couple who were getting engaged was clearly demonstrated by the fact that they were not even present at the main meal. If participation in a festive meal demarcates the borders of inclusion, Bac and Trung seemed to be outsiders at their own engagement ceremony (or, put differently, the engagement was not between them but between both their families, as represented by their elders). In fact, they spent much of their engagement sitting with the children in the back room, and even there, they did not eat. They were briefly displayed to the guests as if they were merchandise (and, indeed, Trung was purchased and marked, as it were, by her future mother-in-law). Only when the guests left did Trung eat, sharing her meal with the family employees who had cooked and served the food during the feast. Moreover, Trung did not share the meal with her future husband, who, as far as I could see, did not eat at all.

Beyond the exclusion of the future bride and groom from the ceremony, the function of the feast as creating and enhancing companionship between the two families was obvious. The engagement ceremony included a series of drinking and eating events that expressed the diminishing social distance between the parties, and was planned so as to gradually enhance intimacy. Thus, Vietnamese green tea was offered at the first stage of the ceremony, implying formal politeness but also distance and reservation, as tea is the formal drink served to any guest who enters a Vietnamese house. Canned soft drinks and beer followed. These drinks stand for closer social relations, as they are less formal than tea (they also imply prestige, because of their foreign origins and the fact that they were canned and, thus, more expensive than bottled drinks). Beer also acts as a social lubricant: along with other oral stimulants (such as tobacco, betel quid, and coffee) the alcoholic beverage fills in the embarrassing empty spaces with ritualistic activity (of preparation and consumption), and, more importantly, blurs the senses of the consumers to a certain extent, softening their social and personal inhibitions. Thus, drinking beer together does not merely reflect the deepening relations, but facilitates and enhances them.

Finally, the meal itself was aimed at inducing friendly and intimate relations at this first stage of the marriage process. As Douglas (1975: 256) puts it: "The meal expresses close friendship. Those we only know at drinks we know less intimately." The meal does not only "express close friendship," as she suggests, but also sets the proper ambience for the creation of such relations. As at ancestor-worship feasts—intended to both console the family and promote friendship and intimacy among its members—the lavish feasts in engagement and wedding ceremonies generate a pleasant atmosphere that enhances intimacy and mutual positive regard between the parties.[11]

Interestingly, the deepest intimacy was expressed in the post-ceremony feast, when all the "outsiders" had left the house and only those with long-standing close relations shared the meal. Here, much of the etiquette and "front-stage" (Goffman 1959) behavior that characterized the previous part of the event was replaced by a free-spirited, happy mood, which was further expressed in the unstructured presentation of the dishes and the large amounts of food consumed by the diners. Thus, despite the culinary attempt at getting the parties together, it was still the household that had the most intimate relations.

Betel Quid, Tobacco, and Alcohol

A traditional culinary element of the Vietnamese wedding is *trau cau* or betel quid: betel leaf rolled around a sliver of areca nut with a dash of lime paste. Chewing the mix causes the ingredients to react, releasing a mild intoxicant. The chemical process induced by the saliva changes the green color of the components into red. Regular chewing of betel quid stains the gums and tongue red, as can often be observed among elderly Hoianese women.[12]

Although a degree of intoxication, rather than the satisfaction of nutritional needs or desires, is the expected outcome of chewing betel, I consider it to belong to the culinary sphere because it is a culturally manipulated substance taken orally in order to influence the psychophysical state of the consumer (for a similar analysis of the role of the taste of betel quid in social interaction, see Kuipers 1991). Despite its diminishing popularity in Vietnam and the perception that chewing betel is an outdated, unhygienic, and unaesthetic habit, hardly appropriate even for old women, betel quid is still very much the icon of the Vietnamese wedding (Huu 1998: 668)[13] and its importance in the contemporary Hoianese wedding is clear: I was told that "there is no wedding without *trau cau*."

FIGURE 5.2. Wedding cake, betel quid, and rice wine at a wedding.

I can think of two reasons for the prominence of the betel quid as a key symbol of weddings, both related to the red color of the chewed mixture. The first reason is modified along the lines of the explanation suggested by anthropologist Harvey Goldberg (personal communication), concerning the use of henna in Middle Eastern engagement ceremonies, where the green leaves of this plant are pounded into a red paste and then applied in intricate designs to hands, face, and feet. Goldberg suggests that the mere act of color transformation reflects the deep change that takes place in the bride's life. Moreover, red is the color of blood, thus symbolizing the loss of virginity, which is so central to the wedding and to fertility (and see also Leach 1974: 22, Solomon 1993: 123–27). Thus, red substances, such as henna or betel quid, most probably stand for the consummation of the marriage.

The second explanation is more culture-specific. In Vietnam, as well as in the rest of East, Southeast, and South Asia, red is the color of the Polar Star and therefore of the entire cosmos, as well as of fire, energy, power, and money (hence the expression "red envelope") and altogether, of good luck. The decorations, invitation cards, money-envelopes given as presents, and, most importantly, the bride's wedding dress itself, were red in pre-modern Vietnam and are still very much so today. The red color of the chewed betel quid symbolizes all these desired traits and outcomes.

Tobacco has now taken over the practical aspects of the betel quid as a habitual social lubricant, as betel quid is rarely chewed, especially among the young. Tobacco belongs to the culinary sphere for the same reasons that define betel quid as food: it is a substance taken orally in order to influence the psychophysical condition of the consumer (used at times to overcome hunger or promote bowel movements). However, tobacco does not change its color (definitely not into red) and therefore cannot serve as a key symbol for weddings. For this reason, the traditional and the modern substances were both present in the ceremony, one intended for its practical aspect and the other for the ritual and symbolic domains. The *trau cau* were left untouched, while the cigarettes were widely smoked through various stages of the ceremony.[14]

Alcohol was hardly drunk during this feast: the rice wine was left untouched and very few cans of beer were opened. This was probably because Hung (the bride's father) is strictly opposed to alcohol and rarely drinks. Avoiding alcohol also demonstrates social refinement, since drinking is popular in Vietnam and alcohol abuse is endemic ("80 percent of retired Vietnamese men are alcoholics," said my friend Kim, when I realized that his father had a serious drinking problem). I was often told that many men squander their family income on alcohol and that domestic violence is a common outcome; the gravest concern of several of our female friends was their husbands' excessive drinking. Thus, avoiding alcohol and rejecting drunkenness is definitely in vogue in Hoi An, especially among those of higher status. In any case, showing restraint with alcohol, just as with food, is deemed respectable and a sign of moral superiority. At Bac and Trung's engagement feast, the benefits of social lubrication offered by the alcoholic drinks were perceived only secondary to the expression of proper class behavior, and alcohol was discarded (or, more accurately, left for more informal settings, such as the feast of leftovers that followed the main meal).

CULINARY INNOVATION AND SOCIAL RISK

In the previous chapter I suggested that foreign ingredients and dishes, which are expensive and require substantial cultural capital, imply sophistication and hence serve as tokens of prestige in the social economy. At Bac and Trung's engagement feast, there were numerous foreign culinary elements. Opting for such foreign artifacts involves a certain measure of risk, however, as the attempt to introduce new culinary artifacts could fail—as indeed happened.

As Hue pointed out, a dish had been created specially for this feast. It was a fusion of Vietnamese, Chinese, and Western culinary elements: local mushrooms, imported and expensive Chinese snow mushrooms, and imported industrial ketchup and mayonnaise. The combination did not work out well and the few guests who did try the dish disliked it. As one of the diners told me: "the taste was strange and the texture too slimy." I had to agree that this dish was most unappetizing. The ingredients were slimy and soggy, and the lashings of commercial tomato ketchup and mayonnaise dominated the dish.

Thus, the special new dish failed to add prestige despite its foreign-inspired culinary innovation. Obviously, the failure was not merely culinary, but also social. The guests left this dish uneaten and even the bride's family members discussing it during the meal concluded that it was "not tasty" (*khong ngon*). Serving food that is "not tasty," either foreign or local, is problematic and involves a considerable loss of face. After all, the guests' refusal to eat the dish, however expensive and modern it was, meant that the hosts had not taken proper care of their guests.

I hesitantly asked the chef-sister who had devised the dish why the guests disliked it. She just waved her hand dismissively and said that people in Hoi An are too provincial (*nha que*) and conservative and that there was nothing wrong with the dish. When explaining the rejection of the dish in such terms, she removed the issue from the culinary sphere into the social one, or from her cooking abilities to the guests' level of sophistication, blaming the rejection on their limited cultural resources. Another jarring note in the use of Western ingredients was related to one of the dessert items. It should be noted that desserts are not ordinarily components of the Vietnamese meal, but a borrowed French element. As with other Western food items, desserts are served during a Vietnamese meal as a mark of cultural refinement. The choice of desserts items during the feast were rather inappropriate: French profiteroles[15] and the incongruous buttered white bread slices. While cream puffs could be considered a proper dessert according to Western culinary standards, bread-and-butter is definitely not. Indeed, it is unimaginable that bread-and-butter would be served as a festive dish, and even less so, as a dessert.

Looking at bread-and-butter from the Hoianese perspective, however, it seems that this dish does adhere to the Western definition of a proper dessert as an extraordinary, luxurious, and rare item whose essential taste and texture differ considerably from that of the other dishes. In a reversal of the norm in the West, spongy sliced bread is rather a rare and expensive delicacy in Hoi An. The local bakeries produce only crusty baguettes, while soft pre-sliced sandwich bread can be bought only in expensive delicatessens in the neighboring metropolis of Danang. Butter, too is an expensive import from New Zealand, Australia, or France. Bearing in mind that sweetness is an integral element in most Vietnamese dishes, we realize the culinary logic behind the choice of bread-and-butter as dessert: the bland, pale, spongy and fatty dish is completely different from the complex tastes and textures of the other dishes on the festive menu. Thus, although bread-and-butter is incongruent with the Western definition of "a festive dish" and/or "dessert," the Vietnamese context renders it appropriate for these culinary definitions.

While the invented mushroom dish was a failed culinary innovation and the bread-and-butter was a problematic implementation of a Western culinary idea into the Vietnamese context, the coffee served at the end of the meal should be considered as a successful story of culinary integration. Introduced by the French as part of their colonial efforts (Pilleboue and Weissberg 1997: 48), coffee drinking and the institution of the café became essential elements of the Vietnamese culinary world and contemporary culture. It should be noted, however, that serving coffee at an *engagement* feast was not only a modern convention, but was even subversive. Beyond the modernity and refinement expressed by serving coffee at the end of the meal (in Vietnam coffee is rarely drunk at home and definitely not at the conclusion of a meal), the subversive act was to publicly serve coffee to women in such a formal and public setting.

Coffee is considered in Vietnam a masculine (*duong*) substance, and coffee drinking belongs to the realm of men. Respectable women do not drink coffee and certainly refrain from doing so in public. However, at Bac and Trung's engagement festivity, coffee was blatantly served to, and consumed by, both men and women. The culinary statement made here was that of women's liberation and equality: women were not only allowed but even actively encouraged to publicly consume what is considered a clear masculine substance. In order to soften the culinary manifesto, and for the sake of balance and harmony, when served to women, the male essence had to be diluted, as it were, with condensed sweetened milk, a very feminine substance. Thus, when Hue said, "Now even the women can drink coffee, but always with milk," she was referring to women's equality, but also to the cultural edict of avoiding extreme and/or explicit challenges of the social order.

DUC'S WEDDING

Chi Tam spotted me in front of her house and called me over. She said that her youngest brother, Duc, was getting married in a few days' time and that I was invited to the wedding. Excited, Tam said: "All my family will come from Vinh (a city in North-Central Vietnam), and I will introduce them to you." Tam handed me a pink, heart-shaped invitation, marked with a red double-happiness character, for the wedding lunch at the Hoi An Hotel. "Would you like to come to the ceremony in the morning too?" she asked. When I enthusiastically accepted her invitation, she told me to be at her house at 8 AM to join the procession to the bride's house.

At 8:30 AM, we left in a convoy of some seven cars and vans, front windscreens decorated with red paper-cut double-happiness characters. We drove to the bride's house, about one kilometer away, just on the outskirts of town. There, we got out of the cars and the groom's family representative, "the young brother of the mother, who is an ex-military teacher and VC [Viet Cong] from Vinh," arranged everyone in line according to their seniority and handed out the round red gift trays bearing rice-spirit bottles, *banh phu te* ("wife and husband cakes"), and bunches of areca nuts to the young relatives. The first in line was Tam's mother, as her father was too frail to come all the way from Vinh.

We walked past the gate, which was decorated with arched coconut palms and a large red paper lantern, through the front yard where a large shed had been erected for the wedding (it had also been used for the bride's family banquet the previous day) and into the house. The senior guests were invited to sit to the left (the *duong,* male side) of the table in front of the altar. The table was not large enough for the fifty people present and the younger guests were led to a side table.

Both tables were set with teapots and cups, cigarettes, betel quid, rice wine, and red watermelon seeds (*hat dua*), but no one touched the refreshments. In fact, all those present were solemn and quiet (though not really nervous, as at Bac and Trung's engagement ceremony described previously). The bride, wearing a fancy Western-style wedding dress (in crimson) and groom (in a dark suit) were invited to come up from the back of the house to stand by the altar, as the family representatives presented each and every person by their name and position in the family (I was the only one who was not a family member and was introduced as "a friend of the family and a researcher in the university"). After mutual speeches concerning the new relations between the the two families "that are becoming one," the mother-in-law put a gold ring on the bride's finger. Only now did everyone relax, tea was poured into the cups, cigarettes lit, and people began to crack open the watermelon seeds between their teeth.

I was sitting at the side table and Tam's younger sisters interrogated me and encouraged me to have some rice wine, as the mood became increasingly cheerful. At that stage, the refreshments were cleared and cups of coffee were served (milk coffee for the women), along with individual slices of *banh kem* ("cream cake," a sponge cake decorated with colored margarine flowers). Seriousness was then restored, and another set of mutually welcoming speeches followed. Now the guests rose to leave. The bride left with the guests and took her place in the groom's car.

The convoy headed for the Hoi An Hotel. When I asked Tam why she did not hold the banquet in her house, she replied that her house was too small and, besides, it wasn't her father's house but her own, and thus "it was not necessary to do it there."

While we were waiting for the other guests to arrive at the hotel, the bride (who, by then, had changed into another wedding dress, this time of brown silk) and groom were walking around the garden with the photographer, who choreographed them in romantic poses. A few minutes later, the bride's family members arrived. I was told that the bride "must always leave before her parents so that she wouldn't cry."[16]

It was already 10:30 AM and the guests were ushered into the hotel's air-conditioned dining room, where they took their seats by round tables without refreshments. The bride and groom stood on the small stage in front of the crowd. A middle-aged man (I later learned that he was the karaoke DJ) led the next ceremony: couple by couple, the guests were invited to the stage, where the women put golden rings on all the bride's fingers (on both her hands), while the men straight-forwardly declared the amount of money that was placed in the envelopes they handed to the groom. Every move was photographed and videotaped. The guests were then asked to wait outside for the tables to be set up.

By 11:30 AM the guests were once again invited into the dining hall. The older guests took their seats at the front, by the stage and DJ station, in sex-segregated tables. The younger guests took the rear tables, sitting with their spouses and children. More guests were pouring in, many of them neighbors and friends who had not taken part in the previous ceremonies. The guests did not look for the newlyweds nor their parents, but went straight to find their places at the tables.

The menu was presented in a transparent plastic stand on each table: *dong xuan ruc ro* ("splendid eastern spring": cold cuts, spring rolls, and pickles); *sup bap tom cua* (corn, shrimp, and crab soup); *goi rau cau + banh phong tom* ("fresh vegetable poem": lotus stem salad plus puffed shrimp crackers); *ga hap hanh* (steamed chicken with onion); *cary banh mi* (curry served with baguette); *trai cay* (seasonal "mixed fruit": *long an* [longan] and *chom chom* [rambutan]). On each table were saucers of soy sauce, chili paste, and lemon with salt and pepper, as well as bottles of Coca-Cola, Fanta, and La Rue beer.

The meal began. Loud conversation filled the large hall. The DJ led the karaoke singing, took orders for songs, and invited guests to come to the stage and perform. The younger relatives and friends came on stage and sang theatrically, loudly cheered by the others. Waitresses were walking between the tables, adding chunks of ice to the glasses and pouring drinks.

Drinking was big at my table. Several young cousins from Vinh were encouraged by Tam's seductive younger sister to compete for *tram phan tram* ("hundred for hundred" or "100 percent"): a drinking game in which those toasting have to finish all the drinks in their glasses. The groom and bride (this time in a white wedding dress) arrived at our table and the tipsy sister insisted that they empty their glasses too. Her young brother gulped down his glass, while the bride took a sip and then discreetly tried to spill the rest of the beer on the floor. Tam, a little drunk herself, whispered in my ear: "Be careful of my sister. She sells coffee in Buon Ma Thuot,[17] a real *dan toc* ("ethnic minority") woman." The sister filled my glass with beer and said, "Don't forget to come at 4 PM for the *dai ban* (friends' party); we will have much more singing and drinking."

The solemn ceremony and the cheerful festive meal that followed were very similar to those described previously, yet the setting of the feast differed remarkably: the meal was not prepared and served at home, but was catered by a professional culinary establishment: a hotel restaurant. Tam offered both functional and ritual explanations for not offering the feast in her own house. For one, her house was "too small," and second, her family's ancestral altar was in her parents' house in Vinh. Therefore, "it was not necessary" to offer the feast in her house. However, I think that there was another reason for the decision to have the banquet at Hoi An Hotel, one that involves, yet again, social prestige.

Tam, who lives away from her family and hometown, had done very well economically and was running a successful transport and tourism operation. In fact, her young brother (the groom), had left Vinh and come to work with her in Hoi An, where he met his Hoianese bride. On the occasion of his wedding, Tam had the unique opportunity to demonstrate her economic success and cultural sophistication to her entire social world: the Hoianese (her husband's family members, her own friends and business partners, and the bride's family members), as well as her own relatives, on the rare occasion of their visit to town. Inviting everyone to Hoi An Hotel for two meals (as another meal was served that afternoon, and for an even larger number of guests) served this purpose.

Economic success was demonstrated the unusually large sum of money spent on the banquets. I was told that the price of the meal was 32,000 dong (slightly more than US$2) per guest and that the price of the two feasts exceeded US$1,000. A similar meal prepared at home would have cost roughly US$100–200.[18] However, Hoianese homes lack air-conditioning, and there are no chefs or waitresses (in European uniforms!) and the hard job of cooking and serving has to be carried out by the hosts themselves. Thus, Tam's culinary and social statement was: "I can spend all this money in order to feed my guests and to relieve myself of the duty of preparing the food for them, because I am so successful."

Beyond displaying wealth, however, the choice of location implied sophistication, modernity, and cosmopolitanism. Indeed, the three-star Hoi An Hotel was the best and most expensive hotel in town at the time, and most Hoianese would not dream of entering its gates and strolling in the garden, not to mention have a meal in the restaurant. This had to do both with the high prices charged for the hotel services (US$40–50 per room), as well as with the fact that the clientele was mostly foreign. When inviting her relatives and friends to a banquet at the Hoi An Hotel, Tam was also demonstrating her access to a privileged space, where she and her guests were suddenly accepted as legitimate customers.

Moreover, when inviting her relatives and friends to a meal in the Hoi An
Hotel, Tam was not the only beneficiary of prestige. With her money, she purchased access for everyone into this lucrative and modern extension of the outside world. Though this access was limited both in time and space (a few hours
in the garden and the restaurant), it empowered all the participants. I noticed
this feeling of pride in the guests' deportment, their clothes, body language,
and conduct, which were markedly different than in the more common home-
arranged feasts. Indeed, I was told that "people like to be invited to weddings at
Hoi An Hotel," implying that the special context contributes to the self-esteem
of those invited for such events. To be honest, I too had the same feeling: "Wow,
I am invited to a meal at the Hoi An Hotel!" and dressed with care and was on
my best behavior.

Ceremonial Wedding Dishes and Symbolic Presentation

While most of the dishes discussed so far were intended for actual consumption in the various food events, another category of dishes exists, whose role is
clearly ceremonial and symbolic: those carried by the groom's family members
to the bride's parents' house on the morning of the wedding, where they are
displayed on the ancestral altar. These dishes are carried in special round trays,
marked with a red double-happiness sign. Usually there are two trays (again, in
relation to double happiness) of each of the following items: areca nuts and
betel leaves, bottles of rice spirit wrapped in red cellophane, *cha* loaves and
"wife and husband" cakes.

Basically, these items represent the traditional bride's wealth, which included much larger amounts of rice cakes, meat, alcohol, and betel quid as
minimal requirements (Papin 1997: 8–14). In traditional Vietnam, these dishes
made up the bulk of food for the wedding feast itself. In contemporary Hoi An,
they seem to be only a tribute to the traditional custom as, with the exception
of the "wife and husband" cakes that are commonly served at the end of the
meal and are often taken home by the guests, these food offerings are not eaten
during the feast. A few words are due concerning "wife and husband cakes"
and two other dishes that were carried in Bac and Trung's wedding procession:
these consisted of a whole roast pig and a tray bearing a dish of red sticky rice.

"Wife and husband cakes" are a version of the more ordinary *banh su se:*
steamed cakes made of tapioca flour dough stuffed with green beans and coconut shreds. While ordinary steamed cakes are wrapped in leaves, these cakes
are served enclosed in a specially woven coconut-leaf box with a lid. At one
engagement party where these cakes were served, the groom's parents told me
that the box represents the marrying couple, with the base standing for the
wife and the lid for the husband; the two parts combined make up a family.

They also said that the base and the lid stand for *am* and *duong* respectively, as these cosmic elements are also models for the expected relations between husbands and wives. Thus, in the case of these cakes, it is the structure of the ceremonial vessel in which the festive dish is offered, and not the dish itself, which expresses the proper relations between husbands and wives. Hence, food symbolism is not necessarily expressed only in the ingredients or the preparation modes, but also in other aspects, such as the utensils and vessels in which they are offered (indeed, the round trays, marked with a double-happiness sign and offered in pairs, are in themselves meaningful).

Xoi is a dish of steamed glutinous rice, usually mixed with beans or sweet potato, garnished with sesame seeds or coconut shreds. It is a popular breakfast dish, especially in the countryside, as it is very filling and "gives enough energy to the farmers." Bac's family offered Trung's parents a special glutinous rice dish: *xoi gac*. The pulp of the orange, prickly, papaya-like *momordica* fruit was cooked with sticky rice, coloring the dish red, and dotting it with large, star-shaped brown seeds.

Xoi gac is an iconic Northern wedding dish, without which no wedding is complete (Huu 1998: 187). Here again, it is red that makes it a dish fit for symbolizing the marriage ceremony. This was the only time I saw *xoi gac* served in a Hoianese wedding, however. Hue (the bride's sister) explained that as her father's family had originally come from the North (her grandmother moved to Hoi An in the late 1930s), it was agreed that a typical Northern wedding dish would be part of the ritual offering. Thus, the regional roots and identity of the bride's family were manifested and reaffirmed in a local context. Like Italian food served at Italian American weddings in the United States or Moroccan dishes offered at weddings of Moroccan Jews who have immigrated to Israel, a tribute is made to the family's origins and past. Nevertheless, such public culinary manifestations should not be taken for granted. In many cases, they are intended to make a point within public contexts. Trung's family specifically asked for *xoi gac,* clearly intending to remind all those present that they came from the North. As in the case of Hoianese local specialties, we realize that food is often used as a vessel for specific aspects of identity and localness.

The other dish that was carried ceremonially in Bac and Trung's wedding procession was a whole roast pig, its head covered with a white caul that was reminiscent of a bridal veil. But the reason for the covering was not to do with modesty or some reference to the bride. When I asked Hung, the bride's father, why the head of the pig was covered, he explained that its eyes and ears are shaded so that "it won't be able to see or hear bad rumors about the bride and report them to the ancestors, to whom it is offered." He also pointed out that if the pig's ears were cut off, this would imply that the groom's family "heard bad things about the bride and were trying to conceal them from the pig by cutting his ears off." Hung added: "If they had offered me such a pig [that is, with the ears cut off], I wouldn't accept it and I would have to cancel the wedding because this means that they think badly of my daughter."

The veiled pig was carried in a procession, just like the other presents offered to the bride's family, from Bac's to Trung's parents' house, where it was placed on the ancestral altar. The crimson-glazed creature, carried by four people on a wooden stretcher, represented the virtues of the bride. For one, the large amount of meat was a culinary statement made by the groom's family: they thought highly of the bride and were willing to offer such a large pig for her. Nonetheless, no matter how precious the bride was, a measure of precaution was taken by veiling the pig's head. The culinary statement was thus: the bride (and her family) might not be so perfect and, therefore, it would be better to cover the pig's ears as a precaution, so as to prevent it from overhearing possibly ugly gossip.

As Hung pointed out, the publicly carried pig could also be used to express outright criticism: if the members of groom's family had heard negative things about the bride, they would cut the pig's ears off. While the ritual explanation is that the pig might hear the rumors and report them to the ancestors, the actual consequences are that everyone in town would see the mutilated ears during the procession and would realize what the groom's family thought of the bride. Such public culinary criticism would probably lead to the cancelation of the wedding.

THE HOIANESE FESTIVE CULINARY SCENARIO

The similarity between the ancestor worship and wedding feasts in terms of structure, sequence, and content is striking: Hoianese feasts seem to follow a single formula. This uniformity is unexpected for two reasons: first, the feasts were offered in very different ritual contexts: death memorials as opposed to weddings; second, they were prepared by people of considerably different socioeconomic backgrounds. Thus, what we have here is a general formula that arranges all Hoianese feasts, transcending ceremonial and social categories. Following Ortner (1973, 1990), I suggest terming this general formula "the Hoianese festive culinary scenario."

Ortner defines cultural scenarios as "pre-organized schemes of action, symbolic programs for the staging and playing out of standard social interactions in a particular culture." Thus, "every culture contains not just bundles of symbols . . . [or] ideologies but also organized schemas for enacting (culturally typical) relations and situations" (1990: 60). Cultural scenarios are general operative

FIGURE 5.3. Men's table at a wedding.

schemes that social actors implement in practice and, by doing so, imbue their actions with meaning. Ortner claims that such scenarios include "not only for-mal . . . named events, but also all those cultural sequences of action which we can observe enacted and reenacted according to unarticulated formulae in the normal course of daily life" (1973: 1341). In the next pages I will discuss the Hoianese general formula for festive meals as a "culinary scenario."

The Hoianese festive meal is composed of four stages, which can be roughly termed (borrowing from Western culinary terminology) starters, main courses, soups, and desserts. The starters include sliced *cha* (pork meatloaves), spring rolls, and some kind of *goi* ("salad"), served with deep-fried shrimp crackers (*banh tom*). The several main courses are made of the flesh of domestic animals (pork, chicken, and beef) or from vegetarian mock meat. Two kinds of "soups" are served at feasts: a bird-and-egg soup, which is actually one of the hot dishes, and a stew made with potatoes, onions, and carrots called *cary* or *lagu*, which is served with baguette slices. Finally, there are desserts, usually some kind of "cake": either Western-style cakes or some local steamed *banh* (a sticky rice and beans sweetmeat). Seasonal fruit is sometimes served too.

Seats are allocated according to the guests' age and sex. The guests sit at round tables, use bowls and chopsticks, pick morsels of food from the commu-nal platters on the table, and encourage each other to eat and drink. They also

FIGURE 5.4. Bird-and-egg dish.

monitor one another discreetly, as restraint and consideration are expected and appreciated. Extra food is served to entire tables and not to specific individuals. Those sharing a table are of approximately the same age and sex. They are usually engaged in conversation, which is a crucial component of the meal as a social event. In this respect, the eating etiquette serves to maintain and enhance the stability and harmony of a strictly stratified and hierarchic society.

The structure of the feast, its sequence, and the dishes themselves are imbued with cultural and social meaning. I will begin with the prominence of animal flesh: meat represents human superiority over nature and is charged with the physical power of the animals, which the diners consume. Because meat is expensive and nutritious, its abundance stands for prosperity, wealth, power, and generosity. Specifically, both pork and chicken represent the virtue of thrift, as well as the desire for prosperity (as these animals eat leftovers and transform them into meat, fat, and eggs and thus "bring money into the house." See also Huu and Cohen [1997: 27]). Pork has a more rural connotation, while chicken, at least in Hoi An, denotes urban sophistication.

Bird-and-egg dishes stand for proper family relations and proper parenthood, as a nesting bird symbolizes the self-sacrificing parent. Interestingly, this dish is often abstracted: while the large chicken eggs are substituted by smaller quail eggs, they can be further substituted by lotus seeds and even by litchis, due to their similar shape and color. In some cases, the eggs are not served intact, but are simply mixed in the soup, coagulating into poached egg-drops. Moreover, while chicken and duck are commonly used, they are sometimes substituted by pork and even other kinds of flesh. Thus, a soup of pork and crab with egg drops is probably a highly abstract form of the bird-and-egg family-oriented dish. It is important to note that this dish is served along with the main courses, while *la gu* is served only after these dishes have been eaten.

La gu (or *ra gu*), or the very similar *ca ri*, are always served at Hoianese feasts. These beef stews are served with sliced fresh baguette. In fact, they are exotic versions of French *ragout* and Indian beef curry (and see Narayan's [1997] discussion of "Indian curries" as invented British colonial items): the ingredients (beef, onion, carrot, potato, and baguette) were introduced to Vietnam by the French (Krowolski and Nguyen 1997: 178–80), while the seasoning is Indian: star-anise, cinnamon, black pepper, clove, and ginger. Whether French, Indian, or both, these dishes are clearly foreign and are therefore considered cosmopolitan and prestigious. The same is true for other foreign ingredients and dishes often served in feasts, such as string beans, which are called *dau tay* or "West[ern] beans," or green peas, called *dau Ha Lan* ("Holland peas").

Serving the festive meal diachronically is also a French culinary arrangement,[19] while the rare descriptions of feasts in traditional Vietnam (Papin 1997:

5–24; Jamieson 1995: 31) do not mention such sequencing of festive meals. In this sense, the extraordinary and prestigious nature of the feast is enhanced not only by foreign dishes, but also by the adoption of foreign etiquette. The introduction of desserts could also be understood along these lines.

However, the foreign dishes and the meal sequence have been modified and manipulated to such an extent that they can hardly be recognized as French or foreign any longer. Indeed, many of my informants claimed that these were traditional Vietnamese wedding dishes served in the traditional sequence, thus eroding, as it were, the innovative, cosmopolitan, and prestige-invoking nature of the adopted foreign arrangements.

Finally, it should be stressed again that the entire festive operation is aimed at two goals: from one perspective, the feast creates, expresses, and enhances family integration, with the lavish food and abundant social lubricants facilitating this process; from the other perspective, feasts seem to serve as arenas for fierce social competition for prestige.

All factors considered, the general formula of the Hoianese feasts stresses three main issues: proper kin relations, prosperity, and prestige. These three concepts are all related to one central theme: the centrality and omnipresence of the family. Thus, feasts served in the different life-cycle events, whether in ancestor-worship rituals, marriage ceremonies or, as we shall see in the coming chapters, in other public events, are essentially oriented toward the family as the core unit of Vietnamese society. In this respect, the "festive culinary scenario" is but a specific representation of the general Vietnamese cultural scenario, which defines the family as the key social institution.

It is important to note that such cultural scenarios are not all-powerful and rigid impositions that deterministically control our lives. While they may be thought of as superstructures that define our modes of action, they have a certain measure of built-in flexibility that allows adjustment of the general scheme to specific contexts, allowing some agency to the social actors. Indeed, as Ben-Ari (2000: 53) points out, "such models . . . rarely appear in the empirical world as ordered representations or systematic categorizations. . . . Rather, they usually appear as complicated (and often confused) sketches . . . about 'what we are' and 'what we do.' . . ."

Moreover, as was evident in the discussion of the ceremonial dishes (roast pork and red sticky rice) offered to Trung's parents, dishes with specific symbolic meanings are added to the scenario in certain circumstances. "Wife and husband cakes" are served at wedding feasts but not at ancestor worship feasts, and the same goes for roast pork. The red sticky-rice dish (*xoi gac*) was even more specific: it was not only its red color that made it appropriate as a wedding dish in Hoi An, but had the bride's family not arrived from the North, it would not have been served at that wedding. Along the same lines, I was told that stir-fried noodle dishes, routinely served in ancestor-worship feasts, stand for longevity "because the noodles are long" (and see also Tan 1998: 12), longevity being a most important concern in these rituals.[20] Thus, such "ceremony-specific" dishes obscure the general nature of the culinary scenario by stressing the specific over the general.

Finally, at any given period, there may be various cultural scenarios competing for hegemony. In Swidler's (1986: 280) terms, during "unsettled" periods (as opposed to "settled" ones, in which cultural schemes are "loose," flexible, and accommodating), new schemes or "strategies of action" (ibid. 279) challenge the old ones. In such periods, "differences in ritual, practice or doctrine become highly charged . . . [and] fraught with significance" (ibid.). However, if cultural scenarios are "loose" in certain periods or contexts, and if they compete with other formulae in socially unstable periods, two conclusions should be drawn concerning the nature of the "culinary scenario."

The first is that the culinary scenario is only a *model for* the proper festive meal while, in practice, most feasts contain elements of the scenario (in one form or another), but not necessarily all of them. Thus, as I suggested earlier, the scenario is routinely manipulated and/or fine-tuned to a certain extent, so as to adhere to specific contexts.

Second, though the culinary scenario depicted above represented the prominent scheme for Hoianese feasts and was perceived by most locals as the natural order of things (Swidler 1986: 280), there were attempts to outline new scenarios. The last part of this chapter is dedicated to exploring an event in which the Hoianese festive culinary scenario was challenged by an alternative scheme.

BAC AND TRUNG'S "INVITING FRIENDS" FEAST: A CASE OF "GASTRO-ANOMIE"

The day after Bac and Trung's wedding, I saw Trung and her sister threading pieces of fruit on long bamboo skewers. Trung explained that she was preparing fruit kebabs for her *dai ban* ("inviting friends") party, planned for that afternoon. Her sister said: "It is going to be a very special and very wonderful meal. There has never been such a meal in Hoi An before!" When I inquired about it, she smiled promisingly and told me to wait and see.

That afternoon we walked in the pouring rain to the All-Chinese Community Temple (Chua Ngu Bang, or "five communities temple"). The bride's younger brother Minh and a few of his friends were trying to hang a large plastic sheet over the temple's courtyard to shelter it from the heavy rain. Chi, the sister and a professional chef, was wearing her uniform (white trousers and vest), arranging large trays of food on tables on one of the daises. Two of her restaurant employees were setting up a gas stove and preparing large woks and other utensils. I was surprised to note the absence of tables and chairs for the diners. Chi explained: "This will be a buffet meal, like in the big hotels in Saigon. The guests will take whatever they like on their plates and then they can walk around."

Hung, the bride's father, anxious and smoking nervously, asked me to help him carry crates of beer in from the car parked outside. I asked him why he was so nervous, as the wedding was practically over and all that was left was this informal party. Hung sighed and answered: "I don't know why my children must always do things differently. No one has their weddings in temples, and I am really worried about the food. Trung and Chi chose the dishes and this way of serving food, but I don't know. . . ."

The karaoke team overcame the routine electricity problems. Loud music filled the temple yard. Guests were pouring in, taking off their raincoats or shaking their umbrellas and hats. They looked puzzled as they looked for tables and chairs and realized there were none. Eventually, most of them just stood by the buffet, chatting and watching the preparations.

There were well over two hundred people when the bride and groom finally arrived. Trailed by a photographer, they walked through the parted crowd straight to the low stage set in the central hall, and stood by the multi-tiered cream cake topped with Western-looking bride-and-groom dolls. Bac's university professor (who had come all the way from Saigon) was invited to give a speech and was followed by Trung's professor. Someone handed them a large knife and the couple ceremonially sliced the cake, holding the knife together. Bac pulled up a bottle of champagne, shook it vigorously, and struggled for a while with the cork, until the bubbling liquid pushed it out in a loud pop. The guests cheered and applauded as he poured a glass, took a sip, and handed it over to Trung. Loud music filled the air and everyone turned to the buffet.

The wide buffet tables were laden: sandwiches made from spongy bread, deep-fried shrimp wontons, some cooked meat dishes, shredded fresh vegetables, Western-style sausages, *cha* cold cuts, sliced baguettes, and a colorful rice dish. There were bottles of chili and soy sauce and ketchup; beer bottles and soft-drink cans; and napkins, glasses, plates, knives, and forks. At one end of the buffet stood a large pineapple that resembled a giant porcupine, bristling with hundreds of fruit kebabs. Chi was working hard at the other end of the table, frying wontons and stir-frying meat and vegetables, sending around sizzling sounds, steam, and appetizing aromas.

As two hundred guests were trying to get to a table that was only a few meters long, the situation became chaotic. Those who arrived first were trying to figure out what was on offer and how they were supposed to eat it. Chi and her employees tried to explain what was going on to the puzzled guests, but could hardly be heard over the noise and music.

Most of the guests had never eaten at a buffet before and didn't know how to approach the food. First they had to figure out where the plates were—at one end of the table—and then head toward them. Meanwhile, other guests were approaching the table from all directions. The "fruit porcupine" and the cooking station, located at opposite ends of the buffet, further disturbed the flow of people along the buffet. As there were more and more people trying to reach the food, it was very hard for those already holding food-laden plates to back away from the buffet and make room for the others.

The guests further required extra time in order to understand what kind of food was offered, as several dishes were new to them. When they finally did figure things out, it was difficult to decide what to eat, how to eat it, and in what sequence. Finally, when they had made their choices, taken some food onto their plates, added the appropriate sauces, picked up some cutlery, and managed to back out of the crowded buffet area, they faced another problem: where were they supposed to eat? There were no tables and people just walked around, plates in hand, trying to use their forks (as there were no chopsticks and no one would eat with their hands). Many of them wanted to drink beer, but in order to do that they needed a third hand.

Nevertheless, chaotic as the situation was, it was still a Vietnamese chaos. There was no pushing, or complaining, or impatient outbursts. Those who were stuck around the buffet table, unable to move and obviously embarrassed, wore frozen smiles, bowing their heads and mumbling apologies. Those further away, as soon as they realized that there was a problem, moved to the dance area or turned to chat with their friends and with the bride and groom. A friend of the bride took the microphone and began to sing, and the younger guests began to dance. In a few minutes, most of those who crowded around the buffet had dispersed and the attention shifted to the singers and the dancing couples, while those carrying plates in hand managed to rest them on the wide wooden banisters and the scarce temple furniture. Other guests were approaching the now less crowded buffet.

The elderly guests, mainly relatives and friends of the bride's parents, were obviously at a loss, their body language expressing their sense of being offended as well as criticism. Suddenly I saw Thuy, the bride's mother, setting a couple of tables that had somehow popped up at the other side of the temple yard. Hung, the bride's father, wearing an apologetic expression, rallied these guests and led them to the tables. Thuy hurried to the buffet, filled plates with food, and rushed back through the rain-swept yard to set them on the tables. Within a couple of minutes, the tables were covered with food, drinks, crockery, and cutlery, and the elderly guests took their seats and started eating, with the bride's parents waiting on them.

As most of the guests managed to eat and drink in one way or another, the cheerful mood was soon restored. One of Hung's old friends went on stage and sang pre-1975 songs with great skill and enthusiasm, with the crowd clapping and cheering. Hung, holding a bottle of beer (it was the only time I ever saw him drinking alcohol), whispered in my ear: "He is very good, isn't he? When we were young, he would win all the singing contests." I raised my beer bottle and said: "What a great party!" Hung gulped down the rest of his beer, looked at me and said: "You know what, it really is a great party."

Bac and Trung's "inviting friends" feast was a clear case of "gastro-anomie," a term coined by Fischler (1979, 1980) to describe situations in which changes in the eating habits occur so quickly and profoundly that the diners can barely adjust or cope with them. In our case, the Hoianese festive culinary scenario was replaced by a new cultural scheme that was radically different and unfamiliar to the point that the guests were at a loss initially. Despite the inevitable chaos, however, both guests and hosts employed various strategies in order to salvage the event, which ended rather successfully.

Instead of the familiar four-staged feast served to the tables, Trung and Chi decided to offer their guests a buffet meal. When I talked to them later about the event, Chi told me that she had wanted the feast to look like those "in the hotels in Saigon." Buffets are not merely structurally different from more formal "sit-down" meals, but stress different social ideas and ideals, require different abilities, and fundamentally alter the interrelations between hosts and guests. First, a buffet requires guests/diners to actively pursue the food and thus stresses self-initiative, motivation, and dynamism. Second, buffets are devised to offer a wide range of possibilities, and usually feature a large number of dishes. Buffets are designed to accommodate personal preferences, and thus support and enhance individualism.

From the perspective of the social group, it should be noted that the diners at a buffet are not required to be considerate of the others, as even those sharing a table do not eat from common utensils (as food is served in large platters on the buffet table itself, which are constantly refilled and intended for everyone).[21] Moreover, buffet meals totally ignore social hierarchies and status, as proper etiquette requires only that the guests patiently queue for their turn. In this sense, a buffet is a democratic and egalitarian mode of dining. Finally, the role of the hosts in buffet meals is sharply diminished, as the guests have to take care of themselves. Here again, it is individualism and egalitarianism that are sought after and appreciated. Altogether, it could be argued that buffet meals stress self-initiative, dynamism, personal freedom, variety, equality, and, most importantly, individualism.[22]

It should be recalled that the Hoianese festive culinary scenario stresses precisely the opposite ideals and behavior. Hoianese feasts are aimed at enhancing social integration and stability, as the guests are carefully monitored and mutually restrained by their co-diners, while age and sex hierarchies are strictly enacted. As family integration and prestige are highlighted, individuals are expected (and forced to) give up personal preferences to support the common goal of harmony. In this respect, serving a feast buffet-style was not merely innovative but actively subversive.

Undoubtedly, Trung and Chi's limited experience with the new cultural scheme they were trying to imitate and introduce further added to the confusion that characterized the first part of the event. In fact, I think that they mixed up the culinary arrangement of a cocktail party with that of a buffet meal.

A cocktail party is a drinking event that involves the serving of cold and hot appetizers and finger foods. The guests do not sit but walk around, a glass of (alcoholic) beverage in hand, and nibble the food. The stress is on mingling, light conversation, and movement, which are both reflected in and facilitated by the tiny snacks. More than anything, a cocktail party is intended to familiarize strangers, with the aid of alcohol (Douglas 1975: 254–55).

A buffet meal is a different affair altogether. First and foremost, it is a proper meal, featuring the same kind of food that would be served at tables at a formal meal, though, as pointed out earlier, in greater variety and differently presented and consumed. Moreover, buffet meals require tables, chairs, and eating utensils. Looking back at Bac and Trung's feast, we realize that these remarkably different eating arrangements were confused and mixed into one eating event, in which buffet food was supposed to be consumed as if the dishes were appetizers.

The hosts' inexperience with the novel meal format led to other difficulties. The buffet table itself had to accommodate a steady stream of guests without overcrowding and jams. To do this, a buffet should also have a clear "departure point" (where the plates are located) and the food should be arranged such that a unidirectional and free-flowing movement of diners is assured. Cooking stations, considering their performative aspects, should be set apart so as not to disturb the flow of diners serving themselves from the buffet. Sauces and condiments are either set on the dining tables or offered in personal utensils, and the same goes for the drinks.

As there was only one buffet table for over two hundred guests at Bac and Trung's feast, the area was far too crowded. The free flow of diners was hampered by the fact that there was no clear departure point or logistical planning (say from appetizers to main courses to desserts). Moreover, the cooking station and the "fruit porcupine" at both ends of the table blocked any possibility of flow in either direction. As sauces and condiments were offered in large, commercial-sized bottles, diners further held up others when attempting to decant some onto their plates. Finally, the drinks were not served at a bar or at the tables (as there were no tables), but on the very same buffet, and carrying them with the plates, utensils, and napkins required considerable skill.

The comparison between the festive culinary scenario and the meal at Bac and Trung's party shows that the menu was quite different as well. In fact, none of the usual repertoire of dishes that make for the festive culinary scenario was served at this feast. As far as content goes, however, it seems that some of the basic culinary principles, as well as the sociocultural ideas they imply, were maintained. First, there were extravagant servings of costly food items, especially meat, indicating the generosity, wealth, and power of the hosts. Second, foreign culinary influences were prominent, implying cultural sophistication and refinement, aimed at enhancing the hosts' prestige. Third, local identity was expressed in the *hoanh thanh* (the local wontons). Moreover, the rice dish was a variation on the theme of the festive *kim ngoc man duong* ("house full of gold and jade"), with its notions of prosperity and longevity. Even the shredded vegetables could be read as a version of the *goi* (salads). Thus, though the entire range of dishes was radically substituted, the change did not necessarily mean a total rejection of the ideas implied by the traditional menu. In fact, it may be read as a sophisticated case of reproduction, as most of the old logic was expressed in a new guise.

Here again, a certain lack of knowledge concerning Western culinary concepts, which this event had striven to imitate and replicate, led to what seemed (to me) to be bizarre culinary choices. Hotdogs and bland bread-and-butter sandwiches are not considered appropriate for Western wedding feasts, while both the ceremonial slicing of the wedding cake and the popping open of the bottle of champagne are perhaps outdated clichés, and also performed incorrectly, at the wrong moment of the feast: together, and before the meal.

More unusually, cooking, which is always done offstage, as it were, in the kitchen, was brought to center stage with Chi, the chef, as the star performer. Here, a public individualistic statement was made by Chi herself concerning the profession of cooking as a performing art, suggesting that the act of cooking is in itself aesthetic and worthy of admiration. Moreover, bringing cooking to the forefront in this way challenged common gender concepts: given the lowly status of cooking in Hoi An, Chi was boldly claiming that women and feminine practices are as appropriate for the public sphere as men and male activities.

Altogether, Trung and Chi launched a powerful culinary attack on the prevailing social order. It was not merely about culinary innovation and the introduction of new dishes and eating modes. By imposing a buffet meal on their guests, by offering new dishes, and by putting the spotlight on cooking, the sisters were rejecting the acceptable social norms and ideals of stability, hierarchy, restraint, and order, stressing instead dynamism, self-initiative, and self-fulfillment. Most importantly, this feast featured the notion that the individual, and not the family, should be at the center of attention (indeed, one symbolic dish was notably absent: the bird-and-egg dish, which represents proper family relations).

Coping with Gastro-Anomie

Though Bac and Trung's feast was clearly a case of gastro-anomie, the participants managed to reorient themselves, modify their behavior, and were thus able to contain the event, which ended rather successfully.

Generally speaking, two distinctive strategies were employed by the guests in order to cope with the awkwardness of the buffet. I term these "passive avoidance," and "selective adaptation."[23] These strategies were not randomly opted for, but selected from the Vietnamese repertoire of cultural scripts according to the social status of the actors. The elderly guests (the friends of the parents and the most respected guests) opted for avoidance, while the younger guests (the friends of the bride and groom) preferred to adapt selectively.

Passive avoidance meant refusing to participate in the game. By doing so, the elderly guests were making a clear statement: they refused to accept the kind of hospitality that was being extended to them. These guests were reluctant for two reasons: being older, they were probably more conservative, less open-minded, less flexible, and less receptive to changes; second, the elderly guests had the most to lose from the new arrangements, as it was their privileged position that was being challenged: they were expected to give up their front tables, their priority when eating and attentive service, as well as their role as public monitors and critics of the behavior of the other guests. Obviously, they were reluctant to do so.

Here we should note that alternative reactions were possible; for instance, they could have opted for more active strategies: they could have advanced to the buffet and demanded priority or could have left the event altogether. Such active strategies would have only aggravated the situation, however, and would have caused further loss of face for everyone. Therefore, they just gathered at one corner, where everyone could notice them, and by merely standing there, imposed a restoration of the customary order.

The process of restoration was intended to rectify the situation. Therefore, the bride's parents themselves, and not the young family members, had to go through the public humiliation of setting up the tables during the feast and personally waiting on their guests. When the older guests' loss of face resulting from being ignored was restored, the social score was settled and they could join the event wholeheartedly.

The younger guests opted for a strategy of flexible and selective adaptation. At first, they all tried to approach the food at once, as they would have done at a conventional seated feast. As soon as they realized that this was physically impossible, those further away left the buffet area and moved to the dance floor. These guests returned to eat only later, when things settled down. By doing so, they expressed patience, respect for the others, and restraint.

Those trapped around the crowded buffet table also did their utmost to behave properly according to the Vietnamese standards: they avoided physical contact or pushing, were patient, and wore frozen smiles to hide their embarrassment. Those who did manage to get some food carefully retreated from the table. When they realized that there was no proper place to sit and eat, they simply ate standing, or over improvised tables, concluding their eating as fast as they could before joining the chatting, singing, and dancing.

The interesting point is that in order to deal with the new and unfamiliar setting, the guests turned to traditional values and common scripts of behavior: the younger guests adhered to the ideals of restraint, patience, respect for the others, and the demand to remain calm and avoid emotive behavior, while the elderly resorted to the rules of proper hosting. Indeed, these traditional values and common scripts of behavior were the only cultural tools available for the guests to make sense of the situation in which they were trapped.

Here again, Swidler's (1986) conceptualization of culture as a "tool kit" (based on Daniel's [1983] perception of culture as a "tool-box") seems to explain the mixed strategies employed by the guests. Swidler suggests that "[a] culture is not a unified system that pushes action in a consistent direction. Rather, it is more like a "tool kit" or a repertoire . . . from which actors select differing pieces for constructing lines of action" (1986: 277). When a social group is faced with innovation or change, the actors turn to their tool kit and look for the most appropriate means with which to deal with the new circumstances.

This is exactly what happened in Bac and Trung's "inviting friends" party: the guests were faced with a new culinary arrangement with which they were unfamiliar. At first, they were paralyzed. After a short while, however, they reached into their cultural tool kit and found appropriate ways to handle the situation. Obviously, as there were guests from different echelons, different cultural tools were deemed appropriate. Essentially, it was age, that most important Vietnamese social attribute, that defined the proper strategy or tool opted for: while the elderly chose passive avoidance, the young opted for selective adaptation. By implementing both strategies (or cultural tools), the guests were able to successfully contain the threatening state of gastro-anomie.

HEINEKEN AND CRAB

In 2006, Ty, one of my Hoianese friends asked me: "Have you heard about *Heineken va cua* (Heineken and crab) weddings?" When I replied that I had not, he elaborated, "As of recently, more and more *Viet Kieu* (overseas Vietnamese) come to Hoi An to find wives."[24] They often have their weddings in the Hoi An Hotel or in the new big restaurants. We call these weddings *Heineken va cua* because they offer Heineken and crab."

As mentioned in chapter 4, two dishes were added in recent years to the Hoianese feast menu: squid and prawns. These dishes are expensive and popular with tourists and, as such, their inclusion in festive meals confers added prestige upon the hosts. Adding Heineken and crab to the menu is yet another (big) step up the status ladder: Heineken is the most expensive beer manufactured in Vietnam (imported beers are even more costly) while crab has always been a luxury; in recent years, the combination of ever growing demand and scarcity from overharvesting have made crab ever more costly.

After confirming my observations regarding price and prestige, Ty added, "You know, the invitations for *Heineken va cua* weddings often say 'please don't bring any present.' . . ." He gazed at me steadily, and when I smiled in response, changed the subject of conversation.

Ty's subtly conveyed last point is an extremely important one: hosts who throw Heineken-and-crab weddings are not satisfied with offering food and drink that are well beyond the means of most Hoianese but are making another statement: "We are so rich that we can offer you the most expensive food and drink at our wedding and we don't need or want your contribution, as we can easily handle these great expenses on our own."

Though for most *Viet Kieu* grooms the prices of wedding feasts in Hoi An are ridiculously cheap (US$2–3 per head for a home-cooked feast, US$5–8 in an up-market hotel, and US$10–12 for a Heineken-and-crab feast in 2007), asking the guests to refrain from giving presents is not merely an act of generosity or a statement of wealth but actually an outrageously rude breach of etiquette in clear violation of the rules that arrange the exchange of presents (Mauss 1990) and of the whole notion of commensality: instead of a celebration of a common pot of rice and common destiny, attending a Heineken-and-crab wedding and refraining from giving a present means admitting the utmost superiority of the host, the extreme inferiority of the guest, and, as a consequence, an unbridgeable socioeconomic gap within the extended family.

Although Hoianese feasts are intended to maintain and enhance extended family cohesion and contain competition for prestige, festive food becomes at times a means to challenge acceptable norms, define new kinds of relationships, and hence, serve as a *model for* a new social order.

6 ㏿ Food and Identity in Community Festivals

Community festivals in Hoi An are celebrated by social groups larger than the household (*nha*) or the extended family (*gia dinh*), but the actual number of the participants does not exceed several hundred. Participants in community festivals know each other personally, at least to a certain extent.

I have opted to present four feasts that represent the wide range of communities in town: the meal served at the Tran clan ancestor worship ceremony, the Protestant church's Christmas picnic, the Cao Dai annual communal feast, and the banquet prepared for the Phuoc Kien Chinese community festival. Just as in life-cycle events, community festivals consist of two parts: a formal, ritual stage and a feast. Here too, much of the preparation, effort, cost, and time are invested in the festive meal.

While the eating arrangements at community festivals are remarkably similar to those defined by the family-oriented "festive culinary scenario," the dishes and menus are diverse, with each communal meal featuring a specific set of dishes that distinguishes it from the others and imbues it with particular meanings. The menus and dishes mainly concern the collective identity of each community, or, rather, the complex, multileveled and often contradictory identity of each group, as well as their positioning within Hoi An, the nation, and beyond.

THE TRAN CLAN ANCESTOR WORSHIP

On the third day of Tet, I was invited to Li's house to participate in the Tran clan[1] worship. As I crossed the gate into the walled courtyard of the compound,[2] I saw that the doors of the ancestral hall were wide open. Some elderly men were busy at the altar, which was covered with a red cloth. While I chatted with Li, more guests arrived, mostly men but also some women and children. I could tell by their way of dressing that they were not from Hoi An. Li confirmed my observation and said that most of the guests had come from Danang. He added that clan members who live in Ho Chi Minh City did not come as "it is too far." Altogether, some forty men, ten women, and seven children were present.

The worship consisted of incense and votive-paper burning, reading the names of the living clan members (the list was burned as soon as the reading ended), and the kowtowing of representatives of the various generations in front of the altar. All the worshipers, except for a single elderly woman, were male. The rest of the women went straight to the kitchen to help with the food.

Worship completed, everyone turned to the long table set in front of the altar. Seating was according to generations: the more senior the generation, the higher (closer to the altar) the location. The elderly woman who had participated in the ritual was sitting first to the right (the *am,* female side). The other women served the food and joined the table only later, taking the lower-status seats away from the altar.

Only three dishes were served: lotus-stem salad (*goi*) with beef, which was served with rice crackers (*banh da*); pork and snow-mushroom soup with quail eggs; and Hoianese chicken-rice (see chapter 3). Both salad and soup were decanted from large bowls into smaller individual ones. The chicken rice, consisting of yellow turmeric rice, shredded chicken, and sliced green papaya, was served on individual plates. The elongated table did not allow for conversations to develop as they would have if the people had been dining at round tables, so the meal was unusually quiet. Though beer was served, no toasts were made. The eating was soon over, and the guests left the table and dispersed into the yard. I approached Li, who was talking to two men. He introduced them as his cousins and said, "We meet very rarely, and now is our chance to catch up."

The traditional Vietnamese village often consisted of several families belonging to a single clan (Nguyen, V. H. 1995: 22; Huard and Durand 1998: 126). The ever-increasing size of villages, as well as urbanization, internal and external migration, and government resettlement policies (see Hardy 2005) deeply eroded the status of the clan. Thus, in contemporary Hoi An, clan activities in general and clan worship in particular are conducted by only a few families, most of them of Chinese ancestry.[3]

Like ancestor-worship ceremonies, clan worship features two levels of social interaction focused on food and eating: the replenishing of food for the ancestors and the reaffirmation of kin relations through a shared meal. Thus, just as in ancestor-worship feasts, the sharing of food in clan rituals is intended to create intimacy and closeness among those who rarely meet. Concomitantly, the age and sex hierarchies and eating etiquette characteristic of family feasts are maintained at clan feasts. Thus, the culinary statement expressed in clan feasts is: "We eat like a family because we are a family."

While "eating like a family" is characteristic of Hoianese community feasts, the composition of diners in the Tran clan worship differed from family feasts in general; the menu deviated substantially from that outlined by the Hoianese festive culinary script, in terms of both magnitude and content. At extended family feasts, the proportions of men and women guests are usually similar; there are people from different age groups, and always quite a few children running around. In contrast, at the Tran clan worship feast, most of the guests were middle-aged men, and only a few women and children were present. When I asked Li about the preponderance of men, he explained that most guests had to drive all the way from Danang and this was "too difficult for women and children." Though his explanation was reasonable, women and children often come to ancestor worship ceremonies or weddings from Danang and even from further away. The point, then, was not about geographic distance but social distance: it seems that people are less enthusiastic about and less committed to clan ceremonies. As men are formally the family heads and blood descendants of the clan, they are obliged to make the effort, while their wives and children are excused. Yet even among the men, the effort was expected to be "reasonable," and hence clan members who lived in Saigon were not expected to attend.

The presence of so many elderly men made this event unusually formal, solemn, and reserved. It became clear, then, that although men are prominent participants at family feasts, it is women and children who bring warmth, intimacy, and conviviality. Thus, even despite playing subordinate (secondary and tertiary) roles, women and children are the actual markers of "a family" at such public events.

The difference between family and clan feasts is also evident in their respective menus. While the festive culinary scenario requires at least nine courses, served in four stages, only three dishes were prepared for this two-stage meal. Moreover, it was a much diminished meal: while meat featured in all three dishes, it was boiled and shredded (in the salad), not grilled or fried (the more luxurious cooking modes). Last but not least, Hoi An chicken rice is a commercial dish and not a feature of the festive culinary sphere.

Altogether, both the composition of the guests and the menu suggest that this clan worship ceremony was perceived as less important than family rituals and feasts. Thus, though the Tran clan still conducts the ritual and distant relatives do congregate to share a meal that reaffirms their kin relations, the meal's diminished dimensions suggests that these relations are weaker and less demanding than proper family relations. A more accurate interpretation of the culinary statement embedded in this meal would therefore be: "Yes, we are relatives, and we do share our food occasionally, but we are not that close."

The degree of clan cohesion was not the only message implied by the food, as the dishes themselves were meaningful. Two of the dishes belong to the Hoianese festive culinary scenario: lotus-stem salad with beef and pork-and-snow-mushroom soup with quail eggs, while a third dish belongs to the commercial culinary sphere and is a local specialty (*dac san*). I will now turn to the meanings of these dishes as markers/components of the Tran clan identity.

The *goi* ("salad"), a combination of raw and cooked ingredients, is uniquely Vietnamese. Though similar salads are common in Southeast Asian cuisines (e.g., the Thai and Lao *laap*), the use of pickled lotus stems is unique to Vietnamese cuisine. This dish therefore has a Vietnamese identity (with a hint of Francophone influence, implied by the beef).

The pork-and-quail egg soup was discussed in the previous chapter as representing proper parenthood and proper family relations. I also pointed out that this dish might be "abstracted," as the bird and eggs could be replaced by other kinds of meat and egg-like ingredients, which are generally local. In the Tran clan feast, the abstraction assumed a Chinese direction—pork and snow mushrooms—and hence celebrated its ethnic ancestry.

The most unusual dish served at this feast, however, was the chicken rice. This, in fact, was the only time I saw this dish served at a festive event. Chicken rice belongs to the sphere of commercial street dining and is hardly considered suitable for a feast. Moreover, a dish of chicken rice is a meal in itself (nutritionally and culturally satisfying, self-contained, independent), whereas festive dishes are never independent of each other and are always served alongside other dishes that, together, make for a coherent meal. Serving chicken rice for a clan feast therefore merits an explanation.

I asked Li why *com ga* was served at his clan worship, pointing out that I had never seen it served at any other feast. He explained that *com ga* was "easier to make," implying that the clan feast was not important enough for the participants to make more of an effort. Chicken rice was opted for as a culinary shortcut.[4] Thus, bearing in mind that special food is a key element in distinguishing between the "sacred" and "profane" (Durkheim and Mauss 1963: 13), serving this dish seems like an easy way of inducing a festive atmosphere with minimal effort and expense. Obviously, opting for such shortcuts points yet again to relatively weak clan cohesion.

Saving labor and expenses while keeping a measure of social distance was not the only notion implied by *com ga pho Hoi,* however. During the meal, I noticed that the guests were rather excited about the dish. One of them told me, "In Danang, *com ga* is not so good." Here, he was pointing to the local nature of this dish and, when describing it as "better," expressed his own local patriotism and his pride about being a native of Hoi An. When discussing the Hoianese local specialties in chapter 3, I suggested that while this dish is probably of Chinese origin, the Hoianese consider it completely local and point to modifications such as the shredding of chicken flesh or the addition of the local chili paste (*tuong ot*) as markers of authenticity and uniqueness. Thus, serving this dish to the geographically scattered descendants of a Hoianese clan serves to reconstitute their Hoianese identity. Though there are several local specialties that might serve this purpose, chicken rice, with its built-in Hoianese identity, yet possible Chinese inflections and low cost, was probably the most appropriate dish for the Tran clan feast.

One further point about chicken rice concerns its stand-alone nature: as each diner receives an individual plate, there is no direct food sharing. Serving such a dish substitutes individual for communal eating, yet again points to the relative looseness of relations among the clan members. Altogether, it is easy to see the sense in serving the apparently unsuitable *com ga pho Hoi* as the perfect vessel to express the entire sociocultural meaning of this clan feast: it marks the event as celebratory but not too festive, expresses measured and limited kin relations, stands for Hoianese identity, and hints at Chinese origins.

At this stage, we may consider the entire food event so as to decipher its meaning: distant relatives are gathered to celebrate a formal event that marks their common ancestry; as at most Vietnamese ceremonies, the event revolves around a communal meal; the menu reflects the festive nature of the event, the cultural roots of the participants, and other specific aspects of their identity; and it also makes for a reminder of a certain degree of social distance between them. Thus, proper kin relations, Hoianese, Chinese, and Vietnamese aspects of identity, and a measure of prestige are expressed in this feast, along with the notion that this event is not too important and that those participating in the ceremony and sharing food are not very close.

This last point is very important. In the previous chapters, I suggested that eating practices and food sharing demarcate the borders of inclusion among kin and construct the idea of a "family" as a coherent social unit. The present case suggests that much finer culinary nuances allow for the subtle expressions of different degrees of proximity and distance. Thus, "drinking with strangers vs. eating with friends" (Douglas 1975: 256) or routinely sharing rice with first-degree relatives as compared to the consumption of festive food with extended family members are oversimplified categories and distinctions. Analyzing the what and how of eating (that is, the dishes and modes of consumption) allows for much finer distinctions and a better understanding of the complex structure and internal relations of a given social situation.

THE PROTESTANT CHURCH'S CHRISTMAS DAY PICNIC

It was Christmas morning, and we walked to the small Protestant church. Thuy told us that every year there is a "picnic" (she used the English term) in the churchyard on Christmas Day. She invited us to join the service and the meal.

The small church was decorated with Christmas ornaments: garlands of flickering lights, a Christmas tree, a shining red star over the door, and a large poster of the three kings entering the barn by the altar. The church was packed with men in suits and ties, women in winter *ao dai,* and children in coats and knitted hats. A choir of young girls in white *ao dai* sang beautifully and the pastor preached. Then the pastor was joined by Santa Claus; both handed presents to the best students in the Sunday school. When the ceremony was over, everyone moved to the backyard for the picnic.

There were more than thirty round tables in the shaded courtyard, set with colorful plastic bowls, spoons, and wooden chopsticks. Each table had a plate of thinly sliced *thit bo tai* (rare roast beef), a bowl of pungent *mam nem* (fermented fish sauce dip),[5] a few *banh da* (rice crackers), and a plate of *rau song* (fresh aromatic greens) mixed with slices of unripe starfruit and green banana. Two women in conical hats were cooking something in a huge iron barrel over a wood fire in a makeshift kitchen in a corner of the yard. Loud Christmas carols ("Jingle Bells" in Vietnamese) filled the yard.

The community members took their seats: the elderly men sat by the tables closer to the church wall, paralleled by the elderly women. The others went to the tables further away in the yard, same-sex tables gradually turning into mixed ones as husbands and wives, as well as younger men and women, took seats together. A separate table was erected for the schoolchildren. When everyone was seated, the music stopped and the pastor used the microphone to say the blessing, with the others clenching their fists and bowing their heads in silence.

As soon as the prayer ended, eating began. Chopsticks were used to pick up the chewy pieces of meat, dip them in the pungent sauce, place them on a torn piece of rice cracker, and top them with herbs. I asked my co-diners why this specific beef dish was eaten on Christmas Day. Xon, a student at Danang University, said: "Maybe because the Maccabees[6] refused to eat pork. . . ." His friend Thuong added: "On Christmas we don't like pork!" Thuy told me later: "I don't know why, but since I was a child, we always eat *bo tai* in the church on Christmas Day."

The dish being cooked in the barrel was *ca ri bo* (beef curry). Several young men served it from large soup tureens, along with freshly sliced baguettes. Each diner ladled the thick curry into his or her own bowl, ate it with spoons, and used the baguette slices to mop up the remaining gravy.

Not much more than five minutes after the blessing, the first elderly men rose to leave. They walked past an ice-tea container by the door, had a sip of green tea, bade farewell to the pastor standing by the gate, and left. The others followed suit and in a few minutes there were only some young men clearing the dishes and several women washing up.

Once a year, the small Protestant congregation (Dao Tin Lanh: "Religion of the Good News") of Hoi An[7] celebrates its festival and shares a meal. The social setting is, yet again, devised along the lines of a family feast: sex and age hier-archies determine the seating arrangements, yet gender distinction blurs among the younger diners. The women and young people cook and serve the food to the elderly and the males. Children too old to be fed by their mothers, but too young to sit at the tables as full community members, eat separately. Just as at family feasts, young males are the ones in charge of carrying the food from the kitchen to the tables, thus marking the public sphere as masculine and restricting the women to the kitchen area. When I mentioned that these are family-feast eating arrangements, Thuy said, "The Protestants in Hoi An are one family so we eat like a family."

An immediate question arises concerning the nature of this "family." It would be reasonable to expect that the Hoianese Protestants would eat like a Christian family, Western style, with husbands and wives and their children sitting together. However, the seating arrangements were clearly Kinh-Viet-namese. Thus, the Hoianese Protestants eat as if they were *a Kinh family,* and this should be understood as a fundamental culinary statement about their self-definition: "We eat like a Kinh family because, though Protestants, we are Kinh."

Nevertheless, though it aspires to the project of eating "like a family," the structure of the meal and the dishes are not congruent with the Hoianese fes-tive culinary scenario. There were only two dishes, both of foreign origins, both stressing beef and the non-Vietnamese culinary concept of meat and bread. As we shall see, these unique culinary features encapsulate some ideas about the event itself and about the notion of being a Hoianese Protestant.

There were, in fact, only two dishes in this meal, as the beef, crackers, fish sauce, and greens are the components of a single dish, "undercooked beef," while the beef stew and bread are the essential components of "beef curry." Both belong to the sphere of public eating, are sold in specialty stalls or restaurants, and constitute meals in themselves. Indeed, although *ca ri* is also a regular component of the festive Hoianese culinary scenario, this was the only time that I saw undercooked beef served at a feast. Just as in the Tran clan feast, the small number of dishes, as well as the fact that one of them is a commercial dish, suggests that the event is special, but probably not too important, reflecting the level of cohesion of this community. The dishes served at the Christmas picnic were very different from those served in the clan feast, however, and so were their cultural meaning.

Both dishes have external origins. The *ca ri*, as its name implies, has Indian roots and is mildly spicy. *Bo,* beef in Vietnamese (from the French *boeuf*), was probably introduced to Vietnam by the French,[8] along with baguettes. This dish combines French and Indian ingredients, as well as cooking methods (long simmering). Undercooked beef is a local specialty of Dien Ban, a town on Highway 1, some 10 km from Hoi An. About a dozen restaurants located right along the highway display whole roasted calves to attract passing vehicles and serve the chewy meat with a fish sauce dip, rice crackers, and greens. The beef and other ingredients for the Christmas picnic were bought at one of these restaurants. Hence, this dish is "twice foreign": not only does it stress beef, but it is the local specialty of another place.[9]

There are several plausible reasons for choosing these specific dishes for the Protestant Christmas meal. Both feature expensive and foreign beef and therefore are luxurious and special enough for a feast. Moreover, both beef and Christianity were introduced to Vietnam by the French and, hence, it is only appropriate that food of French origin be served at a feast celebrating a religion brought by them. Christianity is further implied by the fact that both dishes are structured along the Judeo-Christian concept of "bread and meat," while rice appears only in the form of a cracker. Finally, creating a feast with a dish from another town stresses the foreign roots and even the alienation of this community.

Although these points may explain why a Christian community might choose such dishes, they do not fully explain the Protestant element embedded in this feast. Here I suggest that beyond the notion of being a minority, which is probably experienced by all Vietnamese Christians, the Hoianese Protestants see themselves as a minority within a minority, and this aspect of their communal identity is also represented by their festive fare.

My informants pointed out that beef was chosen not only because it was foreign, but also in defiance of the ubiquitous pork. They ate beef either because they "don't like pork at Christmas" or because "the Maccabees refused to eat pork." Although Christians, including the Hoianese Protestants, do not consider pork to be unclean as Jews do, this meat is rejected on the congregation's most important day. This shunning points to the distinct religious identity of the Protestants in Hoi An: they consider themselves to be different and, in a sense, superior to the other Hoianese, including the Catholics.

Thus, for example, a Protestant informant told me with a disapproving look on his face, "We don't worship our ancestors . . . we don't believe in such things," while another pointed out that "even the Catholics have altars in their houses."[10] This purist self-identification leads to a feeling of being a minority within a minority (they are not just Christians among heathens, but also Protestants among Catholics). As this identity is negotiated mainly in opposition to the Catholic community, the choice of beef requires an intra-religious explanation: like the Maccabees, they reject pork and thus distinguish themselves from Catholics, defining themselves as purer and more devout.[11]

The Christmas eating customs of the Hoianese Catholics further highlighted the Protestant singularity. The Catholic community had no communal feast (a fact that implies a relatively low level of cohesion), and each family had its festive dinner at home, after the Christmas Eve Mass. I was told that the traditional dish for this festive family meal is *ca ri ga:* chicken curry eaten with sliced baguette. Serving only one dish for the Christmas feast further hints at the relatively low status of this event among the Hoianese Catholics. Moreover, this dish can hardly be described as festive fare, as it is commonly consumed for breakfast in commercial food venues around town. Nevertheless, the spices and French ingredients (onions, carrots, potatoes, and baguette), as well as expensive chicken, make it costly and special enough for a festive meal.

I was invited for a Christmas meal at the house of a Catholic family who operates a tourist-oriented restaurant. For some reason, the formal meal itself did not materialize and family members kept coming and going, each person grabbing his own portion. Eventually, I was invited to sit with the grandfather, and a dish of *xoi dau xanh* (sticky rice with mung beans) was served to each of us in a small saucer. I asked the old man why this dish was served for the Christmas meal and he replied, "Every year, we eat *ca ri ga* (chicken curry), but someone told me two weeks ago, why should you eat *ca ri ga* for Christmas? You should eat *xoi dau xanh;* this is a Gregorian dish. So I told my daughters to cook it tonight!"

I have suggested that serving only chicken curry for the Christmas feast reflects the relative unimportance of this event for the Hoianese Catholics. My hosts, in fact, further "downplayed" this meal by serving sticky rice. *Xoi dau xanh* is cheap peasant breakfast fare, hardly appropriate for a feast.[12] However, the grandfather's claim that this was a Gregorian dish (whether he meant "French" or a favorite of Pope Gregory was unclear) invested *xoi dau xanh* with a new prestigious meaning, distancing it from the local sphere. By doing so, he upgraded the dish and, with it, the entire event. In either interpretation, Christmas culinary customs among the Hoianese Catholics are far less elaborate than those of the Protestants.

Thus, while a Christmas feast distinguishes the Hoianese Christians from their fellow townspeople, the respective festive culinary arrangements of the Catholics and Protestants highlight the differences between these two congregations. Moreover, these culinary customs stand for two divergent communal identities: the familial, intimate, purist, and "minority within minority" Protestant identity; and the less crystalized and less devout, more-local-than-foreign Catholic one.

THE CAO DAI NEW YEAR FESTIVAL

The tiny Cao Dai[13] community gathered at the colorful temple to celebrate the annual festival on the fifteenth day of the first lunar month. Mr. Xanh, a prominent community member who had invited me to the event, told me, "This is an ancestor worship for everyone in Hoi An." By 11:30 AM, the elderly members had gathered and changed into white *ao dai* with red, yellow, or azure ribbons.[14] At 12:00 sharp, they walked into the temple, worshiped, and chanted. The younger community members who arrived during the ceremony watched in silence.

About a dozen round tables had been set in the large front porch of the temple. When the prayers ended, the congregants took their seats, strictly according to their age and sex. There were four dishes on the tables: *ram chay* (vegetarian spring rolls), sliced *banh Tet* (New Year cake, a boiled rice cake stuffed with mung beans), vegetarian *banh nep*,[15] and *canh chay* (mushroom and tofu soup). There were also communal saucers of *tuong* (thick fermented soy bean sauce), into which the diners added slices of red chili. Halfway through the meal, one more dish was served: *bun chay* (vegetarian rice vermicelli). Each diner received a bowl of fresh rice noodles, added some aromatic greens, and ladled over this some thin, clear broth from a communal tureen. There were no drinks on the tables, but on their way out, most diners had a sip of green tea from large kettles.

Like the Protestants, the Hoianese Cao Dai community members eat like a Kinh family, probably because they consider themselves a family-like community and Kinh. As opposed to the Hoianese-Protestant notion of a minority within a minority, however, the Cao Dai adherents conceive of themselves as representatives of the entire population of the town, as suggested by Mr. Xanh, who said that the worship was done "for everyone." This all-encompassing self-perception is embedded in the syncretic nature of Caodaism, which amalgamates Buddhism, Taoism, Confucianism, animism, heroes cult, and ancestor worship, as well as Christianity, Judaism, and Islam (Gobron 1950; Marr 1981: 90).

The food served at this meal, however, was hardly syncretic, nor did it manifest the all-encompassing confidence that might be expected from a religion of such broad scope. In fact, the meal was humble and the dishes were bland, lukewarm, and rather flavorless. I remember thinking that this was one of the least exciting festive meals I had attended in Hoi An. Indeed, the gap between the all-encompassing ideology of Caodaism and the meager meal is the key to understanding this culinary event, as well as to obtaining a better understanding of Caodaism in general.

The most prominent feature of the meal was the fact that it was arranged along Buddhist guidelines: the food was strictly vegetarian and very plain. Considering that Confucianism, Taoism, animism, and the monotheistic religions do not preach vegetarianism and, in fact, often require animal flesh in rituals, it seems that Buddhist foodways have the deepest influence on the eating practices of the Cao Dai adherents. Given the theoretical assumption in this book concerning the interrelations between food and culture, it may be concluded that despite Caodaism's proclaimed syncretism, Buddhism is its main source, as is suggested by Gobron (1950), who terms Caodaism "Reformed Buddhism."

Vegetarianism as means of purification is also common in Taoist rituals (Schipper 1993; Cohen 2001). Cohen points out that at the vegetarian festival in Phuket, Thailand, which is defined as a Chinese festival, vegetarianism as a means of purification is accompanied by the wearing of white cloths and abstention from alcohol and sex. White garments and abstention from alcohol are among the basic requirements of Caodaism (Gobron 1950: 44), and abstention from sex is expected from the high dignitaries (ibid. 34). It seems that Cao Dai vegetarianism, and Caodaism in general, can also be explained in terms of the Taoist scheme of physical purification.

The next step is to determine what kind of purity is pursued by the Caodaists: the Buddhist spiritual purification or the Taoist physical one. Cohen (2001: 67) reconciles these somewhat ambiguous attitudes and suggests that "[Vegetarianism] is religiously considered as an act of contrition for the sins incurred by the killing and consumption of animals in the course of the past year. . . . Magically, it is conceived as a cleansing of the body from dangerous physical impurities. Eating *che* [vegetarian] food is thus an act of merit in the Buddhist sense, as well as a means to attain good health [in the Taoist sense]." Undoubtedly, both aspects of purification are relevant in our case, yet the food at the Cao Dai feast suggests that there is another type of purification going on here: the purging of polluting foreign influences from Vietnamese cuisine.

While the festive culinary scenario features foreign ingredients and dishes, aimed at enhancing the prestige of the hosts, and while Hoianese Christians rely on foreign dishes to express and stress the foreign sources of their spiritual world, the Cao Dai feast included only Kinh dishes. Consequently, the New Year cakes, spring rolls, sticky-rice cakes, vegetable soup, and rice vermicelli stand for Vietnamese cuisine, and the fact that these are vegetarian versions stresses the sought-after purity. Thus, while Caodaism is explicitly an all-encompassing, eclectic, and flexible doctrine, the food at the most important festival of this community hints at the opposite, emphasizing Vietnamese culture and identity.

Indeed, though Tran Quan Vinh (commander-in-chief of the Caodaist troops and South Vietnam's minister of defense in the late 1940s) pointed out that Caodaism strove to become a spiritual force not only in Vietnam, "but also and especially for the nations of Europe and America" (Gobron 1950: 161), the notion of national purification was prominent on the Caodaist agenda. Its leaders thought of Caodaism as the "national religion" and the "state religion" of Vietnam (ibid. 159) and as a vehicle for national unification and independence. They competed for political and military hegemony in the South so as to build "a free and independent Vietnam . . . controlled by itself [that is, by the Cao Dai leaders] . . . and structured in its own idological image" (Jamieson 1995: 180).

This tension between nationalism and universalism lies at the core of the Cao Dai religion, which emerged in the context of the deep frustration experienced by the Vietnamese regarding their failure to resist French colonialism (Marr 1981: 303). Like other religious sects that developed at the time, it preached for the adoption of specific Western ideas in order to overcome the shortcomings of traditional Vietnamese culture so as to combat colonial rule with the best of both worlds. Such ambivalence is hardly tenable in the long run, and the festive menu points to the direction this religion took: the goal is not only national independence, but also cultural purification. Hence, the main idea expressed in this meal, the rejection of anything foreign, hints at the undercurrents in the Caodaist agenda.

Aspiring for purification explains both the vegetarianism and the exclusion of foreign dishes in the Cao Dai feast, and indeed calls for a humble feast.[16] It cannot fully explain why two of the dishes (the sticky-rice cakes and the rice noodles) were so cheap and common. Here again, in line with the analysis suggested for the Tran clan and the Christmas feasts, serving such dishes should be understood as reflecting the secondary nature of the event for the participants. Indeed, serving common and cheap commercial dishes at a feast (similar to serving hot dogs or fish and chips at a Western feast) reflects the relative unimportance of the event and erodes its magnitude.

The attitude of the participants supports this assumption: there was a matter-of-fact air to this event, with participants wearing none-too-clean and rather ragged white garments and performing the ritual in a way that looked to me rather off-handed. I could feel none of the pomp, color, and magic of the daily ceremonies in the Cao Dai Holy See in Tay Ninh.[17] I thought that I had perhaps stumbled upon a minor event, but the participants told me that this was the largest annual event celebrated by their community. Moreover, regular checks on both this and the smaller Cao Dai temples in Hoi An confirmed this: although the buildings and grounds were well tended, I never saw any other activity taking place in them.

Here I would like to suggest that the poor quality and the plainness of the food reflected not only the relative unimportance of the event itself for the partakers, but also pointed to the insignificance of the Hoianese Cao Dai community in general. While Caodaism is regaining some of its pre-1975 popularity in the Mekong Delta,[18] in Hoi An it seems to be fading away. The two temples were obviously intended to accommodate larger congregations, yet except for the event described here, I have never seen them open; moreover, other Hoianese said they did not know much about the Cao Dai community.[19]

All in all, it seems to me that Caodaism is fading away in central Vietnam and that the subdued feast I observed reflected this process. Though the humble nature of the event could be explained by the moral and spiritual demands of Caodaism, serving ordinary, cheap street food is also a statement about the fading self-confidence of the community members, as well as their minimal desire for prestige. Though they did perform the ceremony and arrange the feast, their none-too-festive feast reflects the weak (or weakening) solidarity and self-esteem of the Hoianese Cao Dai community.

THE PHUOC KIEN TEMPLE FESTIVAL:
PREPARATIONS AND DISHES

It was the sixteenth day of the second lunar month, when the Phuoc Kien community celebrates its yearly festival. "Today we worship *Luc Tanh Vuong Gia* (The Six Princes), the ancestors of our community,"[20]

I was told by Mr. Do, the president of the Hoianese Phuoc Kien community, a tall and impressive man who looked very elegant in his smart suit with a red silk flower in the lapel. I asked about the flower, and he explained that each participant in the feast had to book a seat for the meal and that the flowers served as entry tickets. The flowers came in three colors: red for the community leaders, azure for the Hoianese community members, and pink for out-of-town guests. Each flower was marked with a number that corresponded to the guest's table.

Inside the temple, several young Fukienese-Hoianese women were busy setting the places at more than fifty round tables with red tablecloths, bowls, chopsticks, and glasses. The tables completely filled the inner yard of the temple. More and more people kept pouring into the temple, many holding flower offerings. They crossed the yard and entered the inner sanctuary, where they offered flowers, lit incense, and kowtowed in front of the several deities worshiped in this temple.[21] Many worshipers turned to draw divination chips.[22]

The tables in front of the altars were set with flowers and fruits, but the most prominent offerings were whole, golden-glazed roasted pigs. There were seven pigs by the main altar (of Thien Hau) and three more by the community ancestors' altar. Each pig was covered with a green banana leaf and had a yellow banner with Chinese characters on its back. One of the banners was written in Vietnamese and read *Nguyen Phung Lien, Da Nang* (which, as I found out, was the name and address of the donor of the pig). A small knife with a red ribbon tied around the handle was placed in a bowl of salt next to each pig. There were also trays of *xoi dao xanh* (sticky rice cooked with mung beans) by each altar. As I was watching, more food offerings were brought to the main altar: two boiled ducks, their innards and curdled blood tied with a string and placed on their backs; two whole fried fish; two boiled pork legs; and a plate with two cooked red crabs in their shells and three hard-boiled chicken eggs.

In the backyard, more than fifty men and women were preparing the food. Most of the men belonged to the staff of the caterer, *Hoang Ngoc* (Jade Emperor), a Chinese restaurant in Danang. The women were all local members of the community. The chef, a tall man with long, silver hair tied in a ponytail, told me that his restaurant was famous for Chinese banquets and often catered such events. He showed me around the cooking area and explained the preparations: that morning they had slaughtered one hundred chickens, one hundred ducks, and ten pigs for the estimated 550 diners, and now they were cooking the food. Most of the men were handling the meat: frying, broiling, and carving the chicken, ducks, and pork, and slicing the *cha*. The women were washing and sorting greens and cleaning seafood.

One of the roasted pigs was brought into the kitchen. A male cook severed the head, placed it on a plate, and sent it back to the altar. The rest of the pig was chopped up into morsels with a heavy cleaver. The chef told me that the roasted pigs were offered by rich community members. Some of the roasted meat would be served to the tables during the feast and the rest would be divided among the community members who could not attend the festival. The leftovers would be donated to the poor.

He showed me the menu: *Khai Vi* ("open the stomach/taste" or "starters"), a colorful plate of six kinds of *cha* (meatloaf) served with pickled vegetables; crab and bamboo-shoot soup (*sup mang cua*); chicken cooked in milk (*ga sot sua*); pork dumplings (*heo quay banh bao*); duck in medicinal herbs (*vit bat thao*); Fujian-style rice vermicelli fried with pork, crab, and shrimp (*bun gao Phuoc Kien*); and *trang mieng* (literally "rinse the mouth" or "dessert") of fruits. I asked whether the food was Fukienese, and he answered that "the vermicelli are from Fukien, but the rest of the dishes are Chinese." His own family came from Quang Dong (Canton/Guan Dong Province in China) and he said that he generally cooks South Chinese food.

Before we turn to the culinary aspects of this event, a few comments should be made about its nature. This festival is celebrated on the sixteenth day of the second lunar month, which, according to the Chinese calendar, is the worshiping day of Thien Hau (Anderson and Anderson 1977: 379),[23] the central deity of the temple. However, the festival is locally named Le Luc Tanh Vuong Gia Cong ("the festival [of the] Six Princes") and is dedicated to the six founders of the local Fukienese community. In fact, Anderson and Anderson (380) point out that "in communities that have other patrons, she [Thien Hau] does not get the big sacrifice: the local patron does." Thus, this event should be understood as an extended version of ancestor worship, with the entire community worshiping its ancestors and celebrating its own foundation.[24]

The culinary setting supports the idea that this is an ancestor-worship event, but some culinary differences hint at other cosmological and social ideas. One feature is the sublime and semi-camouflaged notion of a sacrifice, along with the special role of men as its performers. Another is the way in which the feast constructs the different identities of the various types of community members who take part in the event. "Fukienese" would be far too in-accurate to describe the various identities that were negotiated around the ta-bles in this feast.

FESTIVE FOOD AS SACRIFICE

Kenneth Dean, in his work on the popular cults of Fujian (Fukien), suggests that the culinary activities in temple festivals are "sacrifices" (Dean 1995: 131, 133, 138, 154). Other writers (e.g., Anderson and Anderson 1977: 367, 377; and Tan 1998: 14) also use this term when discussing Chinese rituals that include feasts. None of these writers explains the difference between an offering and a sacrifice, though these obviously involve different arrangements. I would like to suggest that it is the way the animals are presented on the altar that distin-guishes between offerings and sacrifices.

In all the feasts described so far, portions of the very same dishes that were prepared for the feast were presented on the altar. Thus, the food prepared for the living and the dead was identical. At the Phuoc Kien festival, however, whole animals were prominently featured on the altars, while the other dishes, intended for consumption during the feast, though presented on the altars, were secondary both in terms of the quantity served and their placement.

The animals presented on the altar shared three unique qualities: natural shape, complete form, and purity. The natural shape of the animals was care-fully preserved throughout their preparation and presentation: the pigs, ducks, fish, and crabs looked almost alive. The second quality was that of wholeness: the animals were presented intact on the altar and the ducks even had their in-nards and curdled blood displayed as proof that each and every bit of their bodies was offered and that nothing had been removed.[25] The third quality was that of purity: although these animals were cooked, they were not mixed, sea-soned, or stuffed with other ingredients, but simply boiled or roasted. Beyond these shared properties, it is important to note that these animals were not consumed by the diners during the feast (except for the pig).

In order to make sense of this mode of presentation, I suggest distinguish-ing between offerings, which are dishes that are cooked and served simultane-ously to the living and the dead, and sacrificial animals, which retain their natural shape, wholeness, and purity when presented on the altar and which are intended mostly for ritual consumption (though they would eventually be consumed, too). Indeed, it could be argued that such events can hardly qualify as sacrifices because the act of killing is not performed publicly or ritually and is not executed by ordained clergy or men of high stature.[26] Quite the contrary, the slaughtering was done rather casually in the temple backyard, where the cooking took place. There were public acts of symbolic slaughtering, however, when those offering the pigs stabbed the small knives with the red ribbons into the roasted pigs' necks. Moreover, only after this symbolic slaughter were the banana leaves covering the pigs removed and the yellow flags marking owner-ship stuck into their backs. At this stage, I was told that the signs were intended to make sure that no-one "would steal the pigs" (that is, to prevent anyone but the owners from claiming to have offered them). Thus, only after the ritual slaughtering were the pigs activated (and hence they had to be named only at that time).

The other sacrificial aspect of this event had to do with the range of the of-ferings, that is, the array of animals presented on the altar. Tan (1998: 13–14), in the only detailed culinary account I have found of contemporary overseas Chi-nese ancestor worship (the Baba Chinese of Malaysia), describes a set consist-ing of a pig's leg, a duck, and a chicken, called *sam seng* (*san shang* in Manda-rin, or "triple sacrifice"). According to Tan, the triple sacrifice is essential in important worship rituals and is "the most significant offering in a grand wor-ship" (ibid. 14). Huu (1998: 212) mentions the "triple sacrifice" (*tam sinh* in Chi-nese-Vietnamese) in the Vietnamese context, but suggests that it was com-posed of ox, pig, and goat. The differences probably stem from the fact that Huu discusses royal rituals, in which the emperor himself sacrificed the large and expensive animals, and Tan describes a ritual that was conducted at home, while the event at the Fukien temple was performed by a prosperous, yet small, minority group. It seems that at smaller-scale events, the ox, pig, and goat are diminished, so to speak, into pigs and birds, while in home-conducted events, a pig's leg with a single chicken and a single duck replace the full-fledged triple sacrifice.

Returning to the combination of offerings, we realize that the entire range of edible animals—mammals, birds, fish, and seafood—consumed by the wor-shipers was represented on the altar. Consequently, the entire edible cosmos is offered.

An unusual offering in this event was that of a plate of crabs and hard-boiled eggs, which are not part of the "triple sacrifice." However, if the sacrifice is in-tended to encompass the entire edible cosmos, then crabs and eggs stand for categories of edibles that are not represented by the triple sacrifice's compo-nents. When I inquired about this offering, I was given two explanations. The first was that crabs and eggs are the favorites of *Ong Dia,* the God of Earth, and are usually offered at "new-house" ceremonies (*cung nha moi*) so as "to receive the permission of the God of Earth to occupy a new piece of land and also to appease the local spirits and ghosts." The second explanation was that, together with pork, these are the offerings for *San Lao* ("Three Old Men"), *Phuoc* ("happiness"), *Loc* ("prosperity"), and *Tho* ("longevity"). These Chinese deities, whose statues can be found in many Hoianese houses, are depicted as three old men: one of them accompanied by a group of boys ("boys bring happiness to the family"), another holding a gold or jade wand (representing "power and prosperity"), and the third holding a pink peach (symbolizing longevity "because the Chinese words 'longevity' [*tho*] and 'peach' [*tao*] are similar"). In our case, I was told that the eggs represent children and happiness; pork stands for prosperity; and crab, due to its red color, means peaches and longevity. Moreover, all round fruits, including the peach, are marked by the precursor *qua*, while a crab is *cua* (uttered in different tones); thus, the crab stands for round fruits and, hence, for peaches, which represent longevity. Here again we observe the wide scope of this event: the intention is to worship as many transcendent beings as possible in the most elaborate mode. Thus, community ancestors, as well as deities and gods that function in different spheres, are all worshiped with a great variety of sacrificial animals.

Nevertheless, appeasing the spirits and gods was not the sole concern of the festival organizers, nor of those who offered the pigs. The signs stuck onto the pigs' backs were not intended only for the eyes of the deities and ancestors, but also (and possibly particularly) to ensure the proper social point-scoring. Anderson and Anderson (1977: 377) point out that among Malaysian Chinese, expensive roasted pigs are rented during similar festivals for a few hours by different families, so that a single pig may be presented on more than twenty altars in a single day. Obviously, showing off one's wealth to the living members of the family or community (or saving face by offering what is beyond one's means) is the reason behind this custom of pig rentals. Returning to the Hoianese feast, it was not only the community that was manifesting its wealth, generosity, and power in exchange for prestige and respect, but also individuals, who seized the opportunity to do the same. Indeed, offering a pig was not an exceptional act of a few prestige-seeking individuals, but an integral part of the event. Thus, through culinary practices, the community manages and contains social competition among its members, streaming it into activities that would benefit not only the individual but also the entire community.

SACRIFICE AND PROFESSIONAL MASCULINE COOKING

Cooking in Vietnam is considered a feminine activity, but ritual and sacrifice are the realm of men. Contracting the feast to a group of male professionals instead of trusting the preparations to the female community members adds a measure of formality and importance to the event, and further emphasizes the notion of sacrifice. Indeed, only the professional men handled the meat and took care of the sacrificial animals, presenting and redistributing them.

The prominence of men in the preparation of this feast also points to the difference between cooking as a domestic female practice and being a cook/ chef as a male profession. Routine cooking is clearly reserved for women in Hoi An, and is conceptualized as an unsuitable activity for men. In fact, women always prepare domestic meals, even in families in which the men are professional cooks, while men enter the kitchen only to prepare special dishes or under special circumstances: either on festive occasions or when other kinds of special food need to be cooked. At festive events, men often handle the meat. They do most of the slaughtering and the major part of the carving but rarely do any actual cooking. The younger men are often involved in presenting the cooked food, while the older men always place the food on the altar (that is, make the actual ritual offering).

Many of my male Hoianese friends, however, are good cooks, and on the rare occasions when they do enter the kitchen, they demonstrate talent and savvy. They would enter the kitchen to prepare specific male dishes, such as coffee or jungle food (I was invited to a few meals in which snakes and lizards were killed, cooked, and eaten by men), or when they wanted to lavish special attention on someone. Indeed, it is a clear term of endearment and intimacy when a man cooks for his wife or friends. Moreover, men are always the ones brewing tea and offering alcohol to guests, stressing their position as hosts.

The important point is that Hoianese men rarely cook daily but are traditionally involved with the public aspects of the preparation of festive food. This fact might explain the paradox of male prominence as professional cooks/chefs as opposed to their abstention from home cooking: the cultural principle of distinction between female domestic cooking and male public and/or ritual cooking has paved the way for the integration and increasing prominence of men in the sphere of professional cooking in Hoi An, especially when public and performative cooking is involved. Thus, if contemporary masculinity is constructed through "participation and achievement in the public sphere and the labor market" (Sasson-Levy 2000: 181, 187), professional cooking is masculine by definition. Yet the long-established link between men and public/ceremonial cooking has probably facilitated the transformation of a strictly female practice into an acceptable and even respectable male occupation.

THE CULINARY CONSTRUCTION OF THE FUKIENESE IDENTITY

There are two additional questions concerning the food that was prepared for the feast: why was the Jade Emperor restaurant contracted as the caterer for the event, and what did the menu and different dishes represent in terms of communal identity? If, as Fischler (1988: 275) claims, eating is "central to our sense of identity . . . in that any given human individual is constructed biologically, psychologically, and socially by the food he/she chooses to incorporate," then the food that is shared by the members of a community on their most important feast day is an essential marker of their collective identity.

As this festival celebrates the foundation of the Phuoc Kien community in Hoi An, it would have been only reasonable for the festival to feature both Fukienese and Hoianese dishes, and perhaps even fused Fukienese-Hoianese items. However, the dishes prepared for the Fukienese feast were neither.

The Jade Emperor restaurant and the food it serves are emphatically "Chinese," as pointed out by the restaurant's chef, who is an ethnic Chinese himself. Opting for this specific caterer implies, then, a general pan-Chinese scope. Indeed, the array of dishes further supports this notion. While only one dish was clearly marked as Fukienese (the vermicelli), the other dishes represented different regions of China: pork dumplings are a typical northern Chinese fare; crab soup is southeast-coastal Chinese; and duck in medicinal herbs and cold cuts is regularly served in most regions of China. But the chicken cooked in milk could hardly be Chinese, as up until recently, milk was not consumed at all in China. In fact, cooking in milk is most probably a culinary innovation introduced by the French.

Altogether, the cultural identity suggested by the various dishes served at the Fukienese feast can be described as all Chinese, with a slight southeastern Chinese inclination and touches of Fukienese and Vietnamese-French cooking styles. No local specialties were served, and the Hoianese character of the event was ignored.

Opting for an all-Chinese menu instead of a provincial one was characteristic of the other Hoianese-Chinese festive meals. I asked one member of the Hai Nam (Hainan) community if he knew any Hai Nam dishes. He replied that he knew several Hainanese dishes and named *bun tom kho muc kho thit nac* ("vermicelli with dried shrimp, dried squid, and lean meat"). When I mentioned *com ga Hai Nam* ("Hainan chicken rice," and see Anderson and Anderson [1977: 357]), he agreed that this was also a Hainan dish. When I pointed out that none of the dishes in the Hai Nam temple festival (which we were attending at the time) was from Hai Nam,[27] he explained that "it is too difficult to prepare these dishes." However, he pointed out that "all the dishes here are Chinese." Looking once more at the array of dishes served at both the Fukienese and Hainamese feasts, and taking into account this last statement, it seems that the menu at these events was not aimed at producing a distinguished Fukienese or Hainanese identity, nor a Hoianese-Fukienese or Hoianese-Hainamese one, but, rather, a general pan-Chinese identity.

This pan-Chinese identity was further stressed by the prominence of the glazed pigs. Tan (1998: 14) points out that "the pig is ritually significant for the

FIGURE 6.1. The gate of the Phuoc Kien Temple.

Chinese," claiming that pork dishes and sacrificial roasted pigs distinguish the Baba Chinese from their Muslim Malay neighbors (for whom pork is taboo). Anderson and Anderson (1977: 378) also claim that the highest class of sacrifice in China involves the offering of a pig "roasted whole with sugar glaze that makes it scarlet-gold." It should be also noted that the Kinh Hoianese claim that pork is Chinese fare.[28]

THE PHUOC KIEN TEMPLE FESTIVAL: THE MEAL

The air inside the sanctuary was thick with incense smoke and Chinese liturgical music. I decided to go out for a short walk and some fresh air. The area outside the temple was very crowded as a small market was gathered by the temple gate with people peddling lottery tickets, religious paraphernalia, and clay figurines from Cam Ha village. The main merchandise, however, was local produce and snacks: fresh corn from Cam Nam village, *banh it la gai Cu Lao Cham* (small cakes wrapped in ramie leaves from Cham Island), *banh cua* (deep-fried bread with crab pate), and *banh dau xanh* (mung bean biscuits). The noodle shops selling *cao lau* were packed.

When I returned to the temple, speeches had just begun. The elderly male leaders of the community spoke in Mandarin to the hundreds of guests sitting by the tables and then named the best students in the temple's Chinese school. The young students were applauded and given gifts. Then the leaders gave a toast and the meal began. Young girls dressed in *ao dai* and wearing azure silk flowers served the food to the tables. I suddenly realized that all the diners wore pink flowers. I approached one of the girls waiting on the tables whose face was familiar and asked what was going on. She explained that the temple was too small and so there would be two shifts: "The leaders [red flowers] and guests from out of town [pink flowers] will eat first. We [that is, the Hoianese, wearing azure flowers] will eat later this afternoon."

Although the menu at this feast was all Chinese, rather than Hoianese-Fukienese, the manner in which the feast was conducted to accommodate the various kinds of clan members underlined their specific social entity. Beyond the fact that this community celebrated its own festival and shared a meal, thus distinguishing itself from the other Hoianese (Chinese and Kinh alike), the silk-flower system and the way in which the meal was divided into stages served to distinguish the Hoianese-Fukienese from the other Vietnamese-Fukienese participants attending the festival.

I have suggested that "eating like a family" is a central characteristic of such community festivals. When an event is too large, with too many participants, most of whom do not know each other, the ability to behave like a family is impaired. The internal hierarchies that pattern "proper behavior" during family feasts depend upon intimate and detailed knowledge of the participants and reflect much more than mere age distinctions, as branches and sub-branches within each family are ranked differently for diverse reasons (e.g., by the position and age of the branch's ancestor; the generation and often the socioeconomic position and/or social status of the participant or his close relatives; or their contribution to the family in other realms). When the participants are strangers, it is practically impossible to "eat like a family."

The silk-flower system was devised in order to solve this problem. The explicit purpose was to help the out-of-town guests (wearing pink flowers) to find their assigned tables and to be able to distinguish the community leaders (wearing red flowers). The locals were marked by azure flowers as hosts and attendants. The flowers were intended to stabilize the fluidity of the event by imposing some kind of hierarchy and order on a potentially chaotic social gathering.

Wearing an azure flower also stood for something else, however: it marked those wearing it as locals, thus reintroducing the borders of exclusion that may have been blurred by the sharing of the festive meal with all those present. Though it was true that the temple yard was too small to accommodate all the participants at once, were this event a proper "family-like" feast, the shifts would have been arranged along the lines of age, with the elders eating first and the younger, both locals and guests, serving the elders and eating later. The fact that the guests from out of town ate first and the locals ate later suggests that the true nature of this event was more of entertaining guests than a family affair.

The Fukienese-Hoianese community festival (just like those conducted by the other Chinese communities in town) was arranged by Hoianese-Chinese and took place in Hoi An. Though the speeches were in Mandarin, the common language was Vietnamese (as most of the participants hardly spoke either Mandarin or Hokkien). Returning to the Hai Nam festival mentioned previously, the friend I was talking to said that the cook at that feast was a "Hoianese-Chinese chef." When I asked him how he would define himself, he answered, "Despite all the difficulties, we consider ourselves Hoianese [*nguoi Hoi An* or "people of Hoian"] and not Chinese. We would like to visit Hai Nam Island, but only as tourists."

The Hoianese character of the event was not completely ignored, however. Those who did not reserve seats for the feast (mainly Fukienese from Danang and Hue, but also Kinh visitors) predominantly ate in local food venues. When I asked such participants why they had not reserved a seat for the feast, I was told that they had not been informed about the possibility of pre-booking, could not afford it, or were not interested in attending. These guests overwhelmingly opted for a lunch of *cao lau*. Many of the out-of-town visitors purchased local specialties such as mung-bean biscuits, *banh it la gai,* or fresh corn cobs from Cam Nam islet. By opting for these dishes, they confirmed the local nature of the event: they had come to participate in a Hoianese festival and, therefore, opted for Hoianese food, in disregard of the explicit Fukienese context of the event.

Altogether it could be argued that though the explicit motive for celebrating the Phouc Kien festival had to do with the founding of the Fukienese community as a distinctive social entity, the food and eating arrangements suggest alternative interpretations. First, instead of a specific Fukienese collective identity, the caterer and the dishes prepared suggested a general pan-Chinese identity, while ignoring the Fukienese context. Second, while the festival was dedicated to the Fukienese patron goddess (Thien Hau) and was celebrated on the very same date by the mainland Fukienese and the members of all the other overseas Fukienese communities, the eating arrangements clearly demarcated the Hoianese-Fukienese community, excluding not only the Kinh Hoianese but also the members of other Fukienese-Vietnamese communities. Finally, those participants who did not share the feast opted for local fare, thus defining the event as distinctively Hoianese, in complete disregard of both the Fukienese and/or the Chinese contexts.

COMMUNITY FEASTS COMPARED

Though the festivals discussed in this chapter differed markedly, the food consumption patterns were quite similar and generally followed those outlined in the family-oriented festive culinary scenario. The function of community feasts is to expand the scope of family feasts in order to enhance intragroup integration and cohesion among community members. Community feasts, like family feasts, are occasions during which some of the accumulated resources of the entire community are redistributed, once again stressing intragroup solidarity and mutual responsibility.

Nevertheless, such redistribution is not only an act of generosity or a statement about mutual responsibility. Community feasts are also spheres in which individual community members can manifest their wealth and power publicly. The Hoianese community feasts can be arenas for fierce social competition for prestige, as witnessed by the names of donors prominently displayed on their sponsored pig.

Despite the tendency to "eat like a family," the eating arrangements in community feasts may sometimes stress differences rather than integration. Thus, the Fukienese festival had two levels of inclusion. In relation to the other Hoianese, the Hoianese-Fukienese expressed their affinity to descendants of Phuoc Kien at large, and the shared feast demarcated these out-of-town people as closer than the non-Fukienese locals. From the intragroup perspective, the silk-flower system and the two-stage feast marked inner divisions and singled out two categories of membership: the local-internal group (the Hoianese Fukienese) and the external one (Fukienese from other places), and the two groups did not share food "like a family."

Feasts at community festivals do not merely map the borders of the group, but also express its collective wealth, power, integration, and sophistication within the system of a prestige economy. Here, adherence to or deviation from the festive culinary scenario serves as an indicator of the relative effort invested by the group: each community offers varying kinds and numbers of dishes at its respective feast, representing different levels of economic and sociocultural involvement. Thus, the magnitude of the feast reflects the relative importance that each community attributes to itself as a social entity within Hoi An.

Moreover, community feasts stand for the relative social position of each of the different communities within a given social system. The lavish Fukienese feast ranked this group high above all other Hoianese communities, while the humble Cao Dai meal reflected the relative weakness of this congregation. Other culinary nuances, such as the number of participants, the proportion of men to women and children, the kind and number of the dishes, and even the meat from which certain dishes were prepared, were all cues hinting at each community's relative social position. The large number of participants at the Protestant Christmas Day picnic, balanced in terms of age and gender and featuring beef, ranked this group above the Tran clan and Cao Dai community in terms of social status in the Hoianese cultural sphere.

The most intriguing culinary aspect of community festivals, however, concerns the role of the festive dishes in the production and reproduction of each community's collective identity, or rather, of facets of each communal identity. While the consumption patterns of all the community feasts were similar, stressing the notion that communities are "like families," the dishes at each event were considerably different. In fact, each feast featured a particular set of dishes that encompassed its unique nature and specific meaning. Thus, the menus that were served at the Tran clan meal stressed its regional-Hoianese roots, while those at the Protestant picnic clearly invoked the foreign origins of this community and were suggestive of their self-perception as "a minority within a minority." The dishes served at these feasts, then, reflected and enhanced the main message or theme of the festival.

In some cases, the food at community festivals challenged the proclaimed character of the event and suggested alternative meanings. Despite the all-encompassing nature of Caodaism and despite the ambitious scope of the ceremony ("an ancestor worship for everyone"), the humble and plain vegetarian meal and small number of participants suggested a much narrower scope, diminished ambitions, and societal weakness. Along the same lines, while the Fukienese festival celebrated this specific, regionally marked community, the menu stressed the pan-Chinese affiliations of this community and ignored its specific regional identity. In this, the food has widened, as it were, the horizons of the event and, as a consequence, the scope of the community and its members: while the festival celebrated the founding of a specific community under very different political circumstances (a few families from a rebellious southeastern province in Imperial China), the food implied a much wider scope of identity, that of China and, possibly, the "transnational Chinese" ecumene

(Ong and Nonini 1997; see also Souchou 2002) as a whole. Thus, the irrelevant Fujianese identity celebrated in the ritual was replaced by the highly relevant, influential, and powerful Chinese identity, composed of the People's Republic of China, Taiwan, and Singapore, as well as other overseas Chinese communities, conjuring up a putative contemporary empire.

We realize, then, that the analysis of the food and eating that takes place in community festivals is crucial for a comprehensive understanding of such events. While the explicit meanings of such festivals are outlined by their ritual and formal stages, understanding the ways in which the food is prepared and consumed and the messages implied by specific dishes allows for a more detailed, more complex, possibly less coherent but clearly more comprehensive understanding of the meanings of these events.

7 ✎ Rice Cakes and Candied Oranges

CULINARY SYMBOLISM IN THE BIG
VIETNAMESE FESTIVALS

This chapter analyzes the special dishes prepared for the three most prominent festivals in Hoi An: Tet Nguyen Dan (Vietnamese New Year, henceforth, Tet), Tet Doan Ngo (Summer Festival), and Tet Trung Thu (Mid-Autumn Festival).[1] The difference between the festive dishes examined so far and the ones I present below lies in the fact that the latter are consumed simultaneously by huge numbers of people—sometimes by most of the nearly one hundred million people in the country and beyond who consider themselves Vietnamese. Thus, the meanings of these festive dishes concern not only the Hoianese but, in some instances, the entire Vietnamese nation, within and beyond the country's borders. These iconic dishes are Vietnamese "key symbols" (Ortner 1973) that are "the most important means by which the members of a group represent themselves to themselves . . ." (Solomon 1993: 117).

The dishes discussed in this chapter are key symbols also because they appear in multiple cultural contexts: their origins are the stuff of legends; they are prepared for domestic and commercial consumption; they are presented as offerings as well as eaten at various food events; and last but not least, they are often mentioned by the Hoianese. Following Solomon's analysis of key symbols (1993: 120), these iconic dishes are not mere representations of the main features of being Hoianese/Vietnamese. They also offer nuanced insights into the meanings that the Hoianese/Vietnamese attribute to themselves, and delineate differentiation as much as solidarity. Indeed, these iconic culinary artifacts express localized and contemporary ideas that go well beyond their explicit depiction of the Grand National Narrative.

The major Vietnamese festivals also have another often overlooked quality: they are celebrated during the uncertain transition from one season to the next. The word *Tet,* which denotes a "festival," originates from the Chinese-

Vietnamese term *tiet*, literally, "the knotty projection between two sections of a bamboo stem" (Huu and Cohen 1997: 6). *Tet*, then, means "an internode . . . a transitional phase between seasons or time periods" (ibid.). The characteristic unpredictability of interseasonal weather threatens stored crops and future harvests, as well as general health and well-being. As we shall see, the analysis of the special festive dishes exposes some of the collective fear and anxiety that underlies the major festivals.

TET, THE VIETNAMESE NEW YEAR

Tet, the festival of "the original sunlight" or "the arrival of dawn" (Huu and Cohen 1997: 6), is the most important sociocultural event in Vietnam: "It is difficult for Americans to grasp how important *Tet* was, and is, to [the] Vietnamese. *Tet* is Christmas, Easter, New Year's Eve, Thanksgiving and Fourth of July all rolled into one celebration. Celebrating *Tet* with one's family was an essential part of what it meant to be Vietnamese, to be a complete human being (Jamieson 1995: 28)."[2] Though there are several Tet in a year, when the Vietnamese talk about Tet they unmistakably refer to the New Year Tet, also known as *Tet ca* (the main festival).

My Hoianese friends were discussing Tet, planning it, and eagerly awaiting its arrival from the moment I arrived in town in 1999, four months before the holiday; they frequently reminisced about the Tet festivities that year until the Mid-Autumn Festival, some eight months after the new year, when preparations for the coming Tet began. "Will you come for Tet?" is the question most often asked by my Vietnamese friends in e-mails and phone calls.

Tet is celebrated on the first day of the first lunar month of the Vietnamese luni-solar calendar,[3] when the sky appears to be at its darkest, somewhere between January 19 and February 20, halfway between the winter solstice and the summer equinox. Considered the first day of spring (Huu and Cohen 1997: 12; Huard and Durand 1998: 108), it is celebrated in between the autumn rice harvest and the spring rice planting, "when the granaries are at the year's fullest" and when agricultural activity is postponed until the beginning of the planting season (Huu and Cohen 1997: 12; see also Hickey 1967: 130). Thus, Tet is neither a harvest nor a planting festival, but marks an "in-between" period.[4]

Although officially celebrated in Vietnam only for the first three days of the New Year, Tet activities last much longer. Planning and preparations begin well before the twelfth month, while the actual rituals begin on the fifteenth day of the twelfth month (the last full moon worship of the year) and the festive air prevails until at least the fifteenth of the first month of the new year. On the twenty-third day of the twelfth month, Ong Tao, the Kitchen God, who "observes the daily activities of the family" from his position in the kitchen (Hickey 1967: 130), ascends to heaven and reports to the Jade Emperor, the supreme heavenly deity. Frantic preparations continue until the last moment of the concluding year, when the ancestors descend from heaven to join their families for the first meal of Tet. The next three days are spent in reciprocal visits to the homes of relatives, teachers, and friends, each visit involving some drinking and eating. Tet ends somewhere between the third and seventh days of the first lunar month, when the ancestors return to heaven.

Traditional Tet customs are summarized in the popular couplet:

Thit mo, dua hanh, cau doi do;
Cay neu, trang phao, banh chung xanh.
Fatty pork, pickled shallots, crimson couplets
New Year pole, strings of crackers, green rice cakes.

In contemporary Hoi An, however, Tet poles (*cay neu*) are hardly erected any longer,[5] "red couplets" in Chinese characters are rarely ordered for Tet, and firecrackers have been banned since 1994 throughout the country. In stark contrast with these fading customs, the dishes prepared for Tet are extremely popular and play a significant role. It could be argued that Tet dishes and meals are the main features of the contemporary holiday, just as they most probably were in the past. Indeed, when people invite each other to visit, they invite them to "eat Tet" (*an Tet*), stressing the inextricable centrality of food and eating in this holiday.

Making Candied Oranges (*Mut Quat*) for Tet

A few weeks before Tet, several new stalls appeared in the market, featuring piles of bright orange kumquats. The huge flood that had hit town in November 1999 had just subsided, but it was drizzling continually and bitterly cold. The female owners of these stalls, clad in woolen hats, scarves, and coats, seemed to be fussing over the little fruits and cooking something over small charcoal stoves. At first I did not pay attention to these stalls, but as they began mushrooming all over town, I asked Giang (the girlfriend of our guesthouse owner's son) what these women were doing. Giang explained that they were making *mut quat* (candied kumquats) for the coming Tet. Then, visibly excited, she suggested that we prepare *mut quat* ourselves.

A couple of days later, Giang, Le (the guesthouse accountant), and I headed for the market. I was surprised to see the large number of kumquat peddlers who had suddenly appeared in the market, selling the little oranges from large woven baskets. Giang and Le browsed around until they found merchandise that they were pleased with and ordered *mot tram quat* (a hundred kumquats). Giang instructed me to pick only bright and hard fruits and to count 120 pieces. When I asked why she said 100 but took 120, she said, "This is how we always buy the *quat* for Tet. . . ." The fruits weighed some 2.5 kg, and for the going price of 1,500 dong per kg, we paid 3,500 dong (about US$0.25 cents in 2000). Giang said we would need one kilogram of sugar.

When we returned to the guesthouse, the other female employees joined us in the kitchen. The men kept popping in, attracted by the excitement and festive air. The first step was razing off a very thin layer of the outer peel, which is "too bitter." The gentle and trained fingers of the Vietnamese girls were quick and efficient with the razor blade, while I kept struggling, scraping off slivers that were too thick and squeezing the fruit too hard. In about thirty minutes, there were some one hundred peeled kumquats and twenty more that I had ruined that had to be thrown away. Le comforted me and said that many people purchase peeled fruits from the street vendors so as to avoid this demanding part of the job. Trang, our next door neighbor, later told me that the going rate for peeling was "2,000 dong (15 cents) for a hundred *quats*" and that she herself contracted the peeling from several neighbors, only to subcontract the actual work to her younger sister for 1,500 dong.

The peeled *quat* were immersed for a couple of hours in lime water "to make them hard" and then boiled in clean water for a short while. The next step was to extract the juice and seeds. Le explained that there were two ways of doing this delicate and time-consuming job: the quick and economic "market-style" squeezing and the labor-intensive home style. In the market, a small knitting needle is inserted into the fruit in order to pierce the inner membranes and squeeze out the juice and seeds. "Sometimes," Le exclaimed critically, "they even remove the inner membranes completely." The market-style fruits are round and hollow and thus cook more quickly, require less sugar, and weigh far less. "Of course," she added, "they are much less tasty." Home-style *quat* require much more work: small cuts are made in the circumference of each fruit and then, with a sewing needle, the seeds and juice are extracted, while the inner membranes are carefully preserved inside. The fruit is then flattened into the shape of a flower.

Obviously, we opted for the home-style, flower-shaped version. As we were working, Giang and Le began arguing about the proper way of cooking the oranges. Le, the thirty-two-year-old accountant, was the oldest woman around, and clearly more experienced and skillful. Therefore, the other girls supported her views. However, eighteen-year-old Giang insisted that things should be done her way. The tension culminated when sugar was melted in hot water to make a syrup and poured over the flower-shaped fruits. Now the pot had to be placed over a coal stove for slow cooking. Le said that the fire was too strong and that the excessive heat would scorch the fruits. Giang insisted angrily that everything was fine and Le left the kitchen in tears. The other girls slipped away and only the two of us stayed in the kitchen, constantly ladling the sugar syrup over the oranges until they gradually became glazed and translucent.

The flame was indeed too high and the bottom layer was burnt and had to be thrown away, but we still ended up with glossy, translucent bright orange little flowers, sweet, bitter, and sour, and much tastier than those sold in the market.

The Kumquat Tree

A dwarf, fruit-laden potted kumquat bush, along with a blossoming peach branch, are both icons of Tet without which no house is really ready for the festival. *Mut quat* are prepared for Tet in Hoi An "because we always have *quat* trees in our houses on Tet." It seems, then, that the candied oranges represent the kumquat tree, which is the essential element of the holiday. Thus, in order to understand the meanings of the candied oranges, we have to first decipher the significance of the tree itself.

I heard various explanations regarding the kumquat. "The *quat* tree has many fruits," explained Hung, "and this is why we bring it into the house during Tet, because we want a lot of everything: a lot of money, a lot of good luck, a lot of food. . . ." Chi, his daughter, added: "The little oranges look like gold coins and in Vietnamese, the word *cam* ["orange" fruit/color] also means "gold." So bringing a tree with many oranges into the house is like bringing in a lot of gold." Thus, the fruit-laden tree stands for prosperity and is intended to symbolize good fortune and/or magically siphon it into the house.

A similar reason was given for the most common Hoianese Tet refreshment: red roasted watermelon seeds (*hat dua*), served with a cup of tea to every guest. One of my friends said that the large bags of red seeds look like "sacks full of money" and that they are "very good gifts for Tet because they bring a lot of good luck." The watermelon seeds are served on a small plate in the center of the table and each guest scoops up a handful and piles it on the table by his cup of tea. Since the seeds represent good fortune, it is as if the host shares some of his wealth with his guests, who are careful to take some, but not too much of it.[6]

Beyond their symbolic role, in recent years kumquat bushes have provided real income for some Hoianese. Many Cam Chau villagers have turned their front yards into nurseries with a huge number of kumquat bushes in concrete pots. The week before Tet, hundreds of truckloads of the dwarf trees are shipped to Danang and other cities, as far away as Ho Chi Minh City. The going price for a potted kumquat was about US$3–5 at wholesale prices in 2000 and so, for these families, the golden fruits were not just metaphors for the desired "house full of gold" (a popular wish for Tet).

Ironically, as it is essential that the fruit should be unblemished and ripened just before Tet, fertilizers, hormones, and insecticides are liberally used. This results in fruit that is so toxic that extra care is taken to ensure that children do not try to eat the appealing yet lethal tiny oranges. Thus, through modernization and consumerism, this desired symbol of prosperity has become beautiful and appealing yet dangerous, almost a metaphor for modernization itself.

In Hoi An, although bushes full of ripe oranges were the most popular, there were alternative notions about their ideal appearance. Co Dung's father, who tends a large bonsai garden,[7] told me that the best *quat* tree does not have only ripe golden fruit, but should also have some green fruit and white flowers. He explained that such trees represent the three generations that ideally live under one roof: the gold grandparents, the green parents, and the flowery children. Along similar lines, Huu and Cohen (1997: 21) suggest that the fruit represents the grandparents, the flowers stand for the parents, the buds for the children, and the leaves for the grandchildren. In any case, the "proper tree" is widely seen as representing a multigenerational family. Thus, the potted kumquat also symbolizes the ideal Vietnamese family.

Huu and Cohen (ibid.) further suggest that the combination of flowers and green and orange fruit stands for continuity and development and aims to ensure an ongoing process in which children and money constantly flow into the house. Here we observe a convergence of the two interpretations: the wealth and happiness of the family depend upon proper kin relations and fertility and vice versa, and the tree stands for both.

Beyond prosperity and kin relations, the fruit-laden kumquat tree, along with the blossoming peach, represent the season, as citrus trees bloom and bear fruit in the winter, while the peach is the first deciduous tree that returns to life after winter, and is the first to bloom. As Tet is considered the first day of spring and is related to nature's annual rebirth and rejuvenation (Huu and Cohen 1997: 15), the peach flowers and ripe oranges represent spring and the rejuvenating processes that characterize it.[8] The combination of kumquat and peach make again for *Phuc Loc Tho* (happiness, prosperity and longevity), the three most desired blessings that find their expression in the festive culinary script.

The Symbolism of Mut Quat

Though my informants suggested that *mut quat* were representations of the kumquat tree and, thus, merely representations of a representation, the candied oranges also have specific meanings related to their taste, their method of preparation, and the fact that they are a form of preserved food—all characteristics of iconic dishes befitting the nation's most important cultural event.

To begin with, the candied kumquats are extremely sweet. Across cultures, sweetness is the most popular taste (Mintz 1986), probably due to the high concentration of available calories in sugar. Opting for a sweet dish in a festive event is only reasonable: while sweetness is always welcome, the dish itself is rich with necessary calories, which the Vietnamese seek to replenish during festive events. In addition, the candied fruit could stand for—as in the case of the Jewish New Year tradition of eating apples dipped in honey—a prayer or wish for "a sweet New Year."

The second salient feature of *mut quat* is the amount of labor invested in its preparation. Here we have an extreme example of a core characteristic of Vietnamese food: cheap ingredients transformed with great effort (five people working about two hours each) to produce a tiny quantity of humble (albeit highly elaborate and tasty) product. In this respect, domestic *mut quat* preparation epitomizes the essence of Vietnamese cuisine and, for that matter, way of life: a huge amount of hard, monotonous, and highly skilled work is invested in extracting the most out of the frugal resources available, be it scarce land, rice seedlings, tiny fish, or kumquats. The results appear to be modest in scale, yet people generally work without complaint, often with enthusiasm and cheerfulness. And my Hoianese friends were clearly pleased with our candying session. Of course the flower-like crystalized kumquats were works of art, pleasing not only to the taste buds but also to the other senses, due to their beauty, texture, and fragrance. Yet, I was wondering whether the small amount obtained justified the effort.[9]

If the hard work involved is a major reason for nominating *mut quat* as a key culinary icon, then contemporary commercialization may seem to work against this argument. Yet although the commercially produced *mut quat* were sold everywhere and highly popular, they were treated with some ambivalence and differentiated from the domestic version. When Le pointed out the difference between the home-made and market-preparation modes, stressing the shortcuts made in the commercial process (less sugar, less cooking, "fake" volume, and substantially less work), she was in fact pointing out that the commercial candied oranges lacked precisely those qualities that make them proper for Tet: if the candied oranges stand for the tendency to work hard in order to transform frugal resources into perfect cultural artifacts, the commercial oranges could hardly represent this disposition.[10]

The last symbolic feature of the candied kumquats concerns their nature as a preserved food served at a time of interseasonal unpredictability. Cooking fruit in sugar is one technique aimed at extending the shelf life of surplus produce and ensuring a constant supply of these nutrients the whole year round. Throughout the holiday, although candied kumquats were a highlight, other preserved fruit—candied or dried pineapple, papaya, coconut, peaches, and apricots—are also served, often in special sweetmeats-trays with many compartments. Hence, the candied kumquats, along with the other preserved fruits, stand precisely for the unsettling aspects of Tet described earlier: the ingredients are processed to overcome the vicissitudes of weather and time, and are ceremonially served at a time when people worry that their food may not last.

Another Hoianese Tet specialty—mulberry syrup (*si ro dao*), along with its by-product, mulberry liqueur (*ruou dao*)—had exactly the same characteristics as the candied kumquats and, as another iconic Tet offering, supports this interpretation.

Mulberry is usually cultivated in silk-producing areas (such as neighboring Dien Ban District), but in Hoi An there is no silkworm farming and mulberry is cultivated specifically for the production of the syrup and liqueur for Tet. The crimson, sour fruit (different from the sweet Mediterranean variety) is boiled with sugar for about an hour into an extremely sweet dark purple syrup, which is served over ice. The boiled fruit is strained out of the syrup and mixed with rice alcohol (*ruou gao*) to make a crimson mulberry liqueur (*ruou dao*). Though commercial mulberry liqueur (along with the similarly prepared *ruou quat* or kumquat liqueur) is widely available, I was proudly offered the homemade drink in several homes.

Like the homemade candied oranges, the mulberry syrup and liqueur are very sweet and require a lot of work. Moreover, just like *mut quat,* mulberry syrup and liqueur represent the importance of food preservation during this potentially hazadous season. Both also encompass the tension between homemade and commercial festive foods. However, while the mulberry syrup and liqueur share these characteristics with the *mut quat,* they have nothing in common with the kumquat tree. Therefore, despite my informants' suggestion that it was the tree that encompassed the symbolic meanings of the candied fruit, it seems that the shared characteristics of the candied kumquats and the mulberry syrup and liqueur are meaningful in themselves in defining these dishes as iconic Tet fare.

Another aspect of the event described above, that is, the conflict between Le and Giang, needs to be explored here. While preparing festive fare together can enhance familial integration, it can also lead to discord. When the female members of an extended family gather to prepare a feast, their close relations are ideally reaffirmed and strengthened. Such warmth and intimacy were clearly observed, for example, among the women sitting together in front of their houses and peeling the kumquats, chatting and laughing. Yet tensions that are usually camouflaged and contained may suddenly be exposed on such occasions, when the culinary sphere turns into a social battleground.

While such conflicts may be reflections of the social structure (e.g., when a downtrodden Vietnamese daughter-in-law expresses resentment toward her oppressive mother-in-law), they might also be attempts at challenging the social order, which is exactly what happened between Giang and Le. Since Le was older and better educated (as well as a better cook and more experienced at making *mut quat*), Giang was clearly out of line when she demanded that her status (as the guesthouse owner's son's girlfriend) be acknowledged. She was not just challenging the accepted hierarchies, but also demanding recognition of the social position of the contemporary category of "girlfriend."

Thus, while the kitchen is ideally the place where the existing social order is reaffirmed and the relations between kin strengthened, it might also become an arena of strife and conflict, where social norms are challenged and negotiated. The next section on the farewell feast for the Kitchen God demonstrates the awareness of the dangerous potential of the culinary sphere, and the symbolic measures taken to contain it.

A Farewell Feast for the Kitchen God

On the twenty-fifth of the twelfth month, Chi invited me to join the worship (*cung*) that would take place in her house at lunchtime. At 11:00 AM, Chi's brother begun worshiping at the altar erected in front of the house. The altar was covered with dishes: spring rolls, fried noodles with beef and shrimps, roasted pork wrapped in fragrant *la lo* (wild betel) leaves, sticky rice cooked with taro (which gave the dish a deep purple color), slices of boiled pork arranged over lettuce leaves, and a bowl of beef curry. Beside these dishes were three bowls of white rice, three cups of tea, and an entire boiled chicken, with its cooked innards arranged on its back.

Beyond the routine set of paper offerings (money, gold, silver, cloth, etc.) there was an elaborate and colorful set of three complete paper

outfits that included boots, clothes, umbrellas, and hats. I asked Chi
what the worship was for and she said that before Tet, it is necessary to
worship "the spirits and ghosts that live outside and also the gods of the
house."

It took me a while to understand that this ceremony was actually the farewell feast for Ong Tao, the Kitchen God, preceding his ascendance to heaven a
week before Tet. One reason for my misunderstanding was that no one had told
me that this was Ong Tao's feast. Moreover, the ceremony was performed on
the "wrong" date, as the appropriate date is the twenty-third and not the
twenty-fifth. By consulting the literature (e.g., Huu and Cohen 1997: 9), I came
to the conclusion that this was Ong Tao's feast, and this was confirmed later by
Chi, who added: "nowadays, we don't worship him so much."

Ong Tao, the god of the hearth, is actually a triadic deity. The legend (Huu
1998: 114–15) tells of a husband and wife who had no children and were, therefore, unhappy. Eventually, the wife left her husband and her village and remar-
ried elsewhere. The lovelorn husband went searching for his wife. On his way,
he lost all his property and became a beggar. One day, he stumbled upon the
door of his former wife's new home. She recognized him and, feeling guilt and
shame, led him into the kitchen and fed him. The beggar, sick and almost blind,
did not recognize his former wife. When he had had his meal, he fell asleep and
the woman, anxious about what her new husband might think, hid him beneath a pile of straw. When her husband returned, he set fire to the straw, intending to use the ash for fertilizing. When the wife saw that her former husband was being incinerated, she jumped into the flames. Her new husband,
seeing that his wife was dead, followed her into the fire. The Emperor of Heaven,
touched by their love and faithfulness, made all three of them household gods.[11]

Huu (ibid.) suggests that the triadic nature of the Kitchen God reflects the
structure of the traditional hearth: three stones or bricks on top of which the
pot was placed. Indeed, this triadic nature was clearly evident in the ritual offerings described above: three elaborate sets of clothing, three bowls of rice,
and three cups of tea.

Ong Tao has an important role in Tet. On the twenty-third of the last month
of the lunar year, he leaves the kitchen and ascends to heaven to report to the
Jade Emperor (Hoang Ngoc, the supreme deity in the Vietnamese pantheon)
about the family doings during the year. On the eve of his departure, each family offers him a lavish farewell feast.

Co Dung was explicit about the nature of the food that should be prepared
for this meal: "We have to cook the best food to make Ong Tao happy, because
then he will give a good report." Huu and Cohen (1997: 18) also argue that

"these gifts [and dishes] certainly aim at influencing the outcome of the report." Another friend pointed out that beyond lavish dishes, it is important to offer *xoi* (a sticky-rice dish) so as "to stick the lips of Ong Tao together and prevent him from telling bad things about the family." Indeed, the feast at Chi's house included both an array of lavish dishes and an exceptional sticky-rice dish. Moreover, while the paper offerings for this ritual should include horses and fish, which are the god's mount on his journey, in some instances he is depicted flying to heaven on the back of a huge bird. Thus, the whole chicken presented on the altar was possibly also offered as the god's mount.[12] All in all, Ong Tao was supposed to leave Chi's farewell feast favorably disposed toward her family: his mount supplied, his palate appeased, and his belly full. Just to be on the safe side, his lips were sealed with sticky rice.

This scenario begs the question as to why the main protector of the house resides in the lowly kitchen. Furthermore, it is intriguing that this problematic and even "ridiculous character" (as suggested by Huu and Cohen 1997: 17), who spends the year confined to the kitchen, is charged with the important role of reporting to the heavens on the eve of the most important event of the year. The answers to these questions once again highlight the ambivalence surrounding the Vietnamese kitchen.

Ong Tao, the divine protector of the house, resides in the kitchen because this is where the well-being of the family is ensured. The female family members, restricted to the kitchen, are actually the ones who maintain the household by tending to the family's physical needs. They are also responsible for the family's prosperity, because women, and not men, were traditionally involved with trade and commerce (Pham 1999: 38–39; Nguyen, T. C. 1993: 69). Thus, the fact that the protector of the house resides by the hearth acknowledges the centrality of women and of cooking in Vietnamese society.

Indeed, the fact that the god of the hearth reports on family affairs to the Jade Emperor reflects the role of the kitchen as the nerve center of the house. The kitchen is where the informal, intimate, and, for that matter, free and honest interactions among family members take place, and where family secrets are revealed. This is the Vietnamese "backstage" (Goffman 1959), where politics, power struggles, love, and hate are exposed and expressed. Ong Tao knows everything about the family precisely because he lives in the kitchen. His feast is also intended to overcome the dangers to the family posed by internal competition and conflict by either "bribing" the god or somehow shutting him up.

Ong Tao's role during the New Year Festival illuminates other issues related to the social position of Vietnamese women. I was told that in the past it was customary to refrain from cooking during the first three days of the new year. The three bricks that made up the hearth were discarded after Ong Tao's departure and replaced with new ones, so that upon his return, the god would find "a new house." Most Hoianese households have modern hearths such as gas stoves, which are, of course, no longer replaced.

While Huu and Cohen (1997: 15) suggest that the cessation of cooking, along with the week-long absence of Ong Tao, represents the death of nature during winter, and his return symbolizes its rebirth, this "kitchen moratorium" serves two additional purposes: it allows for a much needed cleaning of the kitchen, and it imposes a full suspension of female household chores. Consequently, the first function is that of practical cleansing and purification, which are important aspects of Tet, while the other reflects, yet again, the low status of women, as it aims to ensure at least some rest for the overworked Vietnamese woman who, otherwise, would have to serve her family even during Tet.

The fact that this cooking moratorium is no longer practiced raises new questions. It could be argued that contemporary Vietnamese women are not as overworked as their predecessors, and consequently do not need this custom. Alternatively, as elsewhere, improved household technology, the rejection of the traditional power structures (implied by the legend of Ong Tao), and the official ideology and rhetoric of women's equality and liberation in contemporary Vietnam may have actually increased women's responsibilities.[13]

The cessation of the cooking moratorium during Tet is a case in point: while Vietnamese women rested along with everyone else in the past, in contemporary Vietnam women have to cook even during the holiday. In this respect, when Chi said that the worship of Ong Tao was declining, she was also implying that in contemporary Vietnam the kitchen is less central and important than it was, resulting in a further deterioration of the status of women (or, rather, adding further ambivalence to their status).

The First Meal of the New Year

"Will you come to eat Tet ("*an Tet*") with my family?" asked Thuy, a receptionist in the hotel next door. "My parents would like to invite you for lunch on the first day of the new year." When I asked if I could join in the preparations, she said that her parents had fattened a pig for Tet, which would be slaughtered for the feast, and suggested that we come early on the first day of the new year.

When we arrived, the family members were already gathered around the sty, along with the neighbor's daughter-in-law and Mr. Duc, who was hired to do the killing and carving. Thuy's mother told me that she and her neighbors had bought the pig together six months earlier especially for Tet, and that now they would share the meat between the families.

There was a short but fierce struggle between the men and pig, which fought desperately, squealing in an almost human voice. Eventually, it was pinned down, tied tightly, and carried to the kitchen terrace, where it was carefully weighed. Duc asked for a knife and a cup of rice wine. He sharpened the knife on a broken brick and poured some boiling water over its blade and on the pig's chest and neck. Then he gulped down the glass of alcohol and shoved the knife right to the pig's heart. Men, women, and children stood watching in silent admiration, as the blood gushed from the throat of the dying animal into the bowl Duc was holding.

The rest of the process was efficient and unemotional: after draining the blood, Duc shaved the bristles off the pig's skin and put them in a bag ("to make brushes"), poured boiling water on the carcass, and chopped its head off. He carefully disentangled the innards and guts and carved up the pig. The carcass was weighed again and divided between the two families.

As soon as chunks of meat were cut, cooking began. The head, along with pieces of the innards and blood, was boiled in a large pot (Thuy explained that her family got the head because the sty was in their yard). Some meat was boiled in fat and then marinated in fish sauce. The cloven hoofs were boiled into soup, along with the ribs and the other meatless bones. Some meat was chopped for spring rolls. Thuy cleaned the guts ("just like washing socks") and boiled them with the stomach and skin. Some pieces of meat were left uncooked, and she explained that this meat was kept for her married sister, who spent the first day of Tet with her husband's family. Every bit of the pig was processed and used; nothing was discarded.

Beside the several pork dishes, there was beef curry with onions and carrots, *bit tet* (beef steak), and a whole boiled chicken served with *banh da* (rice crackers). There was also a bottle of home-made mulberry liqueur. All the dishes were arranged on plates over lettuce and decorated with tomatoes and carrots. Thuy's father took me to the yard where a large barrel was boiling over a low charcoal fire. He lifted the lid, letting a gust of steam out, and pulled some green, cylindrical *banh Tet* (New Year cakes) from the barrel. "They have been cooking since yesterday," he explained, "and we will have them for lunch."

An altar was set in the front yard. The boiled pig's head was placed at the center, topped with pieces of its internal organs and curdled blood and covered with the lacy white caul. The other dishes were arranged around it, along with a vase of flowers, a plate of fruit (a bunch of bananas and an apple), bowls of uncooked rice mixed with coarse salt, candles, incense, and paper offerings. Thuy's elder brother began worshiping. Thuy whispered in my ear that now he was inviting the ancestors for the feast. As soon as the worship was over, we took our seats and began to eat the first meal of the new year.

All the dishes in the couplet describing Tet as the time for "candied oranges, fatty pork, pickled onions, and green *banh Tet*," were served at Thuy's family feast, with pork being the salient feature. The pig was purchased and fattened up especially for the holiday by the whole family, and their neighbors, who had invested their leftovers, as well as plenty of attention on the animal. Rearing a pig for Tet contributed to familial integration and to neighborly cooperation, while the fattening body of the pig itself was a clear visual manifestation of the Tet feast, contributing to the anticipation of a lavish meal. Yet the careful weighing and division of the meat emphasized the autonomy of the social units within this ad hoc "pig-rearing collective."

The pig is a prime example of the essential Vietnamese values of thrift and efficiency as indispensable prerequisites for prosperity. Though I was aware that pig rearing was highly efficient, witnessing the processing of each and every gram of the animal into food brought home the full usefulness of this animal. After the butchering, the only things that remained were a few drops of blood on the floor and the half-digested food extracted from the pig's guts.

Pigs also stand for fertility. Indeed, chi Luong told me that "pigs easily reproduce and multiply and have many piglets very quickly." This idea is represented not only in the pork dishes, but also in popular traditional Tet woodblock prints that feature a plump pig nursing several young (Huu and Cohen 1997: 27). Thus pork dishes, just like the kumquat tree and candied oranges, express the wish for fertility and prosperity that, together with the wish for longevity, represent the ultimate hopes of the Vietnamese.

Beyond the well-being of the family, Tet pork dishes express other concerns of the holiday and the season. A good example would be the pork cooked in lard and pickled in fish sauce, an exclusive Tet delicacy. Here again, we encounter the notion of food preservation as a key item of Tet fare. Pigs are reared during the rice-growing cycle and their fattening up reaches its climax at harvest time, when they are fed with the chaff. Home-reared pigs are often slaughtered after the harvest and some of the meat is eaten during the holiday. The uncertainties of the season make it necessary to preserve some of the meat, in case of spoiled grain or future crop failure.

Thuy's sister-in-law told me that the pork preserved in lard and *nuoc mam* "can keep for a very long time." The preserved meat was eaten with pickled onions over *banh da* crackers as a single dish. As each of these components is essentially preserved, the complete dish stresses the notion of food preservation, which is so central in the dangerous, in-between season of Tet.

Fruit Offerings for Tet

Fruit offered at Hoianese rituals are seasonal and hence vary. While bananas and pineapples are offered the year round, apples and pears (from China) are prominent during the winter, and durian, rambutans, and longan were popular in summer. The unique combination of fruit offered for Tet expresses social and cultural ideas that transcend the season. The fruit offered at Thuy's feast included a bunch of green bananas and an apple, and the very same fruits were presented on the ancestral altar at Quynh and Nhan's house, which I visited the next morning. As co Dung rightly pointed out, however, both families come from the North and do not follow the local customs. "In Hoi An," she explained, "a specific set of fruits should be offered on the ancestor altar for Tet: custard apple, young coconut, papaya, mango, and watermelon." She showed me that these fruits were offered on her own ancestral altar.

When I asked co Nguyet about this set of fruits, she explained that it was a local custom that had to do with the pronunciation of the names of the fruits in the local dialect: "Custard apple is called *mang cau*. When reversing the order of the words to *cau mong*, it means 'to pray for.' Coconut in Vietnamese is *dua*, but since unstressed *d* is pronounced *y* in the South, it is locally called *yua*. However, the consonant *v* is also pronounced *y* in Hoi An. Thus, the coconut, *dua*, stands for *vua*, which means 'enough.' Papaya is *du du*, and here again the second *du* (with the *hoi* tone) means 'enough.' Mango, *xoai* in Vietnamese, sounds very much like *xai*, which means 'spend.' Sometimes the mango is replaced by pepper, *tieu*, which also means 'spend.' Consequently, the names of the four fruits on the altar: custard apple, coconut, papaya, and mango (or pepper), when pronounced in the local accent, make for the following words: *pray, enough, enough,* and *spend*, which may be construed as the sentence "praying for much[14] to spend. . . ." As for the watermelon, co Dung said that this is also a southern custom "because watermelons are in season in Tet only in the South." Therefore, watermelons represent not merely the beginning of spring, but specifically, the beginning of spring in the South.

Minh, reputedly the best ninth-grade student in Hoi An, consulted her father and repeated co Nguyet's interpretation of the dual meanings of the fruit names in the local dialect. She also suggested that watermelon is red inside and, therefore, "good for Tet." The red color of the watermelon flesh, along with its seeds that are dyed red, stand for prosperity, fertility, and happiness.

Co Nguyet stressed that bananas are never offered for Tet because the word *chuoi* (banana) sounds similar to the word *chui*, which recalls the saying *chui dau, chiu mui* (work hard for nothing) and may bring bad luck. She specifically pointed to the variety locally known as *chuoi lun* (dwarf banana, as the plant is short) as inappropriate for worship "because the large and hard bananas look like the male sexual organ." She disapprovingly pointed out that "the Northerners do use this kind of bananas for worship."

Huu and Cohen (1997: 38) say that in the North, the "five sacred fruits are orange, tangerine, citron, grapefruit and a bunch of green bananas." Though they do not provide any interpretation of the choice of fruits, clearly Tet fruits in the North are different from those in the South, differences that can be explained in several ways. First, the variations are the expected outcome of the different climatic conditions in the North and South, with the set of fruits representing spring in the respective regions. Second, both Hoianese and Northern fruit offerings, though different, seem to express prosperity and fertility: while the citrus is related to the kumquat, an important marker of prosperity, the bananas, with their phallic connotations, could also stand for fertility. Moreover, the banana sub-species that were frowned upon in Hoi An (*chuoi lun*) are exceptional in having plenty of seeds. Thus, just like the watermelon in Hoi An, green bananas in the North could represent prosperity and fertility. Altogether, it might be concluded that the different sets of fruit stand for the same notions: the season of spring, prosperity, and fertility. The choice of distinctive fruits in Hoi An is shaped by local cultural notions, however, and are distinguished from the northern one. In this, the fruit join the blossoming apricot and peach branches, whose colors (yellow or pink respectively) are also clearly marked as northern or southern.[15]

Altogether, we realize how multivocal the Tet fruit are: they represent spring in the different regions and the Vietnamese ideals of prosperity and fertility. Simultaneously, they allow for the expression of cultural and even political inclinations. Such manifestations are tolerated or overlooked: the routine and nonreflexive realm of food seems to be a privileged sphere for symbolic interaction, especially in the context of coercive societies and political systems. After all, the authorities could hardly impose restrictions on the offering of bananas instead of papayas.

Banh Tet: New Year Rice Cakes

While candied kumquats, mulberry syrup, and fatty pork dishes are all important Tet dishes, *banh Tet,* New Year rice cakes, are the pre-eminent Tet culinary icon. I saw the cylindrical, leaf-wrapped, greenish rice loaves offered as the centerpiece on each and every ancestor altar and served at every meal during the holiday and subsequent two weeks. In the first days of the new year, the rice cakes were sliced and served fresh, accompanied by soy sauce with red chili. Later, as the unwrapped rice cakes dry up or became stale, thin slices of *banh Tet* were fried to refresh them.

Banh Tet are not too complicated to make, but require time, labor, equipment, and some know-how. Although the necessary equipment and space are easier to accommodate in suburban and countryside houses like Thuy's, the week before the festival there were large sooty barrels on the sidewalks around town, full of *banh Tet* being boiled. Most families I visited bought them from *banh Tet makers* or in the market.

To prepare *banh Tet,* sticky rice (*nep*) and mung beans (*dau xanh*) are soaked in water overnight. The rice is stuffed with green-bean mash and pork cooked in lard. Bamboo leaves are then folded around the rice and fastened tightly with bamboo splinters. The rice cakes are then boiled overnight in a large iron barrel. The cakes in Hoi An are cylindrical, some 30 cm long and 10 cm in diameter, and weigh about one kg. In order to eat *banh Tet,* the bamboo leaf wrapping is peeled away and the stuffed rice roll is sliced. The outer layer of the cooked rice is tinted a pale green by the bamboo leaf, while the center is yellowish-brown, dotted with chunks of lard. *Banh Tet* are sticky and oily, rather heavy, and definitely filling. There is a vegetarian version (*banh chay*) and a luxurious version with beef. The average price for one *banh Tet* in Hoi An in 2000 was about 10,000 dong (about US$0.70).

Whenever I asked Hoianese why they eat *banh Tet,* they mentioned the story of the *banh chung* (boiled cake) and *banh day* (elastic cake). I asked several of them to tell me the story, their versions being almost unanimous and congruent with the literature (Schultz 1994: 54–62; Huu 1998: 664–65; Nguyen, N. C. and Sachs 2003: 77–85):

> The sixth Hung king had twenty sons and couldn't decide which one should be his heir. One night, a genie appeared in his dream and advised him about choosing a successor. The next morning, the king summoned his sons and told them: "Go everywhere in the world and get me the most wonderful food. The one that brings the tastiest dish will be my successor."
>
> All the sons went off to look for delicacies, except for the sixteenth son: Prince Lang Lieu. Motherless, poor, and lacking political support, he was in great despair. One night he had a dream: a deity appeared and told him that the heavens, knowing his despair, sent him some advice: "Nothing is more precious than rice, man's main food. Take sticky rice, wash and soak it. Shape it into two loaves: one square like the earth and

the other round like the vault of heaven. Use a pestle and mortar to grind some pork meat and fat with some green beans and stuff the square loaf. Wrap the square cake with leaves and boil both kinds for the night. Present the cakes to your father and you'll be chosen as the successor."

Prince Lang Lieu, assisted by his old maid, his wife, and his children, set to work and soon learned how to prepare the rice cakes. When the awaited day arrived, the princes offered their father the most wonderful, exotic and strange dishes, but the king wasn't satisfied: "these dishes are all worthy of curious admiration, but they are strange and too expensive." Then, Lang Lieu presented the rice cakes and told of their divine origin. The king, after tasting the cakes, wasted no time in appointing him heir.

Since that day, it became the custom to prepare *banh chung* and *banh day* (or *giay*, as in Schultz 1994: 55) for Tet. However, the practice of making the round *banh day* has been lost in time and *banh chung*, when prepared for the spring festival, are called *banh Tet*.

At this juncture, I would like to highlight two points regarding the cakes as food items. First, the cakes are nutritionally complete, making for a perfect one-dish meal: they are composed of a firm base of starch, supplemented by vegetal and animal protein, fat, fiber, minerals, and vitamins. The dipping sauce (soy and chili) further contributes salt, vitamins, and minerals. One assumption of my analysis is that understanding the nutritional qualities of culinary artifacts is essential when searching for their meanings. As we shall see, it is their nutritional soundness and wholesomeness that enable *banh Tet* to be the vessel for encompassing extremely complex and varying ideas. The second point has to do with the fact that *banh Tet*, like most other Vietnamese festive dishes, are essentially preserved food items, with their lard, long cooking process, and wrapping. I was told that these rice cakes, when kept wrapped, "can keep for a month and even more."

The most salient symbolic feature of the rice cakes has to do with their shapes: the cakes can be square or circular, and are the shapes of earth and heaven, respectively, according to Sino-Vietnamese cosmology. Preparing sets of round and square cakes for a festival that celebrates the beginning of a new year and the rebirth of nature (Huu and Cohen 1997: 30) is an act symbolizing the creation and recreation of the universe.

Interestingly, neither my informants nor the written sources (Schultz 1994: 54–62; Huu Ngoc 1998: 665) explained why only the square *banh chung* became *banh Tet*, while the round *banh day* are rarely prepared for the festival nowadays.[16] However, taking into account the symbolic meaning of the shapes of the cakes, opting for the square rice cakes stresses the nature of the holiday as oriented toward the earth and toward farming. Indeed, Schultz (1994: 56) suggests that "the square shape is considered a symbol of the thankfulness of the Vietnamese people for the great abundance of the Earth, which has supplied them with nutritious food," while Huu (1998: 665) points out that for the Vietnamese: "*banh Chung* [are a] symbol of their gratitude to the earth which feeds them," and N. C. Nguyen and Sachs suggest that the square cakes "symbolize the Earth, reminding us of the square plots of land from which we grow our crop" (2003: 81). Thus, while the square and round cakes together cosmologically recreate the world, the square cake, which is the festival's iconic dish, stands for the earth and for farming and, hence, for the realm of the Vietnamese people and culture.

The legend is explicit about the centrality of agriculture and, especially, of rice farming in Vietnam: rice, beans, and pork represent the different realms of agricultural production, while the greenish color of the cakes was compared to the color of rice fields by my informants. N. C. Nguyen and Sachs suggest that the cakes are made of rice and salt, "the two essential needs in people's lives, and green beans and pork to symbolize plants and all the creatures of the earth" (ibid.). The cakes, then, venerate farming and rice farming in particular, stressing the age-old nature of the Vietnamese people as rice farmers, and reflecting the nutritional logic of this agragrian culture, which requires complementary vegetable gardening and animal husbandry, while it celebrates the successful harvest, and expresses the wish for bumper crops.

As with the other Tet dishes, hopes for plenty and prosperity are intermingled with real livelihood anxieties, reflecting the unstable nature of the season. Consequently, practical and symbolic measures are taken to ensure the preservation of the stored crops. Due to the extensive boiling, the lard, and the leaf-wrapping, *banh Tet* can keep for a long time (at least a month). In this respect, the preeminent dish in the most important Vietnamese festival is essentially a preserved food item. Here again, this special Tet dish stresses the precariousness of this transitional period while offering some measure of protection against its ill effects.

The legend itself makes two important points concerning the importance of food, and specifically of rice, in Vietnamese culture. First, in Vietnam, one may become a king by winning a food competition. Though it would have been reasonable to expect the Vietnamese to have opted for the best warrior, the shrewdest tactician, or the most moral of the princes as their king, they chose the best cook. Moreover, they could have chosen the most sophisticated, expensive, or exotic dish, but instead they opted for rice. Thus, the utmost importance of cooking, and specifically of rice, is explicitly stressed and reaffirmed by the legend. Rice-cooking competitions are in fact often part of Tet festivities (Huu and Cohen 1997: 12; Do 1995: 46–49).

While certain symbolic meanings of *banh Tet* are explicit, other ideas are more subtle and elusive: I was offered several interpretations of the meaning of *banh Tet* that I found surprising and enlightening. When I asked co Nguyet to explain the moral of the *banh Tet* legend, she stated, "We don't like foreign things!" I was surprised by this line of interpretation, which took me a while to understand and appreciate.

Co Nguyet's patriotic interpretation could be understood as stemming from either of two possible contexts. It could be traced to the three-millennium-old independent spirit of the Vietnamese, who have preferred their homeland and its produce over foreign goods and ideas ever since the semi-mythological era of the Hung kings (Taylor 1983: 3–5), and which persisted throughout the nation's troublesome history of continual struggles for independence. It could also be attributed to the modern patriotic agenda that orients Vietnamese children (and adults) to worship their homeland. As the written sources do not date the legend, it is hard to tell which of the contexts underlay co Nguyet's interpretation. However, the struggles for independence that characterize Vietnamese history suggest that this spirit is neither a modern nor an implanted ideal.

Both the legend and the rice cakes are suggestive of a "pristine" Vietnamese culture.[17] The legend recounts a custom that was established in the era of the Hung kings, long before the arrival of the Chinese conquerors. Thus, the most prominent dish in the most important Vietnamese festival features not only patriotism, but also stands for an independent, pure Vietnamese culture, not yet corrupted, as it were, by Chinese influence.

Nevertheless, the words *banh* and *Tet,* as well as the festival itself, are of clear Chinese origin. The prominence of pork and the use of soy sauce further suggest a Chinese context. Hence, the interpretation of *banh Tet* as a remnant of the original pristine Vietnamese culture interwoven into the contemporary Grand National Narrative actively downplays the impact of millennia of direct and indirect Chinese rule and cultural influence.

These durable, nutritious rice cakes were often carried by Vietnamese soldiers during their endless wars of independence. The cakes are specifically mentioned by the Vietnamese historian Nguyen Khac Vien as provisions for the troops of King Quang Trung (Nguyen Hue) in his victorious campaign against the invading Manchu forces. On the twentieth day of the twelfth lunar month (of December 1788), ten days before Tet, Nguyen Hue rallied his soldiers in Ninh Binh and promised that they would celebrate Tet in liberated Thang

Long (Hanoi) on the seventh day of the first lunar month (Nguyen, K. V. 1993: 104–105). He then rushed "his troops [to the] north, supplied with *banh chung*, which did not require much time to prepare before consuming" (Huu and Cohen 1997: 90). One of my teachers pointed out that in the very same moment, the inhabitants of Thang Long resorted to cooking *banh chung* as a precaution against the anticipated Manchu conquest and pillage. They hid the rice cakes in their wells "as *banh chung* keep very well even in very difficult conditions." Thus, the cakes were used by civilians and soldiers alike as durable and portable iron rations.

Banh Tet (or, probably, their more common version, *banh chung*) were also used as iron rations by Vietnamese troops at the battle of Dien Bien Phu. A French military pilot now living in Israel who flew cargo planes during the Franco-Vietminh war told me that Vietnamese prisoners-of-war captured in the vicinity of Dien Bien Phu in 1953 had "simple but clean clothes and only a bit of rice in some kind of leaf packet as provisions." Indeed, even today, *banh chung* are sold as civilian iron rations in stalls along the exhausting mountainous roads of the Northern Highlands.

As pointed out earlier, *banh Tet* are highly nutritious and sustaining. Moreover, as one-dish meals, they provide an essential feeling of cultural and psychological satisfaction. *Banh Tet,* then, make for perfect iron rations and, indeed, were used as such at various periods of Vietnamese history. Thus, the iconic dish of the most important Vietnamese festival, the one that potentially condenses the essence of being Vietnamese, is actually the food that soldiers take to war.

Here again, understanding *banh Tet* as iron rations can be interpreted in two ways. It can be seen as reflecting the warlike nature of the Vietnamese as people who worship the battlefield and celebrate it on their most important day by feasting on combat rations. Alternatively, the cakes can be perceived as the outcome of a long history of military challenges by external powers, which shaped even the most important Vietnamese festive dish into the form of a sturdy iron ration. It is most plausible that the cakes represent both historical necessity and some sort of pride over such long-term endurance and repeated victories against superior powers.

Whether we choose to perceive *banh Tet* as reflecting the Vietnamese fascination with wars (that is, as aggressors), or as an outcome of a long history of military challenges by outside forces (that is, as victims of violence, courageously resisting aggressors), or as expressing both, the festive rice cakes make a point about the uniqueness of the Vietnamese. These are people hardened by uncountable wars, which they won due to their ability to maximize their scarce resources in order to resist and eventually overwhelm their often stronger enemies. *Banh Tet,* then, are not only about a distinctive Vietnamese culture. They also stand for the spirit that achieved the repeated military triumphs at Bach Dang River, Dien Bien Phu, and in the guerilla warfare that exhausted the U.S. Army.[18]

I mentioned earlier that the Hoianese *banh Tet* are cylindrical, while the cakes in the legend, as well as *banh Tet* made in the North, are square. On this, co Dung suggested an interesting explanation in line with the "patriotic interpretation" referred to above: "When our ancestors moved to the South, they took *banh chung* to eat on their way, because these rice cakes can keep for a long time. However, they made them in a cylindrical shape because in this way they were easier to pack and didn't break and spoil, as the square cakes would have. This is why our *banh Tet* are cylindrical."

Here, not only is a culinary statement made about distinction (we are different and, therefore, our New Year cakes are different), but the reshaping of the cakes is related to an essential cultural difference between the Northerners and the Southerners: while the Northerners stayed behind, in the relative comfort and safety of the Red River Delta, contemporary Southerners are the descendants of those who had the initiative and courage to move to the South and expand Vietnamese culture.

Summing up, *banh Tet* encompass many essential Vietnamese ideals. These humble rice cakes are extremely multivocal and elastic, encompassing a wide range of ideas regarding Vietnamese identity. Hence, *banh Tet* well deserve their status as the most important iconic dish of the New Year and are undoubtedly a Vietnamese key symbol.

TET DOAN NGO (SUMMER FESTIVAL)

A couple of days before the festival, the market became extremely busy. The small poultry alley, where live chickens were usually slaughtered and plucked, was packed with farmers selling thousands of quacking ducks. There was a lot of examining and bargaining and the price of ducks soared. Chicken, an integral part of the Hoianese festive culinary scenario, were hardly sold for this festival. When I asked several of the buyers and sellers why there were suddenly so many ducks, I was offered three lines of explanations: "because we like eating ducks," "because this is the best season for eating ducks," and "because we always eat ducks at *Tet Doan Ngo.*"

There was also an unusually large quantity and variety of fruits: mangoes, custard-apples, pineapples, and bananas, but the most prominent fruits were the large, fragrant *mit* (jackfruit), shipped down the river from Dien Ban district and sold by the market pier. The most sought-after fruits were the red, hairy *chom-chom* (rambutan), brought over in trucks from the Mekong Delta.

Dozens of women were squatting in the sun along the main street of the market, selling different herbs. I saw Xuyen, one of my friends, browsing through the piles of herbs. She told me that these women had come down from the mountains especially to sell medicinal herbs for the festival.

In addition to herbs, some of the women sold minerals and even dried animals such as lizards and snakes. There was general consent concerning the names and uses of the more common herbs, but when it came to rare products, the information became blurred and Xuyen admitted that she wasn't sure about their properties. However, all those involved in selling and buying herbs assured me that it was "the best time to buy medicinal herbs." Xuyen said that her mother-in-law would dry some of the herbs, preserve others in alcohol, and use them over the rest of the year. Co Dung told me later that she used certain medicinal herbs to cook duck for the festive meal.

At the crossroads near the market, the stands that usually sell the local *banh it la gay* (sweet sticky rice cakes stuffed with green beans, wrapped in leaves) offered small pyramidal rice cakes. Some were unwrapped so that the customers could see their yellow-orange color. These were *banh u tro,* the special "ash rice cakes" of the festival.

The Summer Festival is celebrated on the fifth day of the fifth Vietnamese luni-solar month, which is supposedly the longest day of the year and is considered the first day of summer (Schipper 1993: 28; Huard and Durand 1998: 110). Co Nguyet pointed out that there is an aspect of sun worship in this festival: it is the only festival conducted during the day (at noon sharp), and it includes the ritual of "looking several times up to the sun and down to the flowers, seven times for men and nine times for women." She pointed out that it actually looks "as if people were kowtowing to the sun."

This festival occurs in the season of peak growth (Huu and Cohen 1997: 73), when rice and fruit are harvested. Therefore, just like the New Year Festival, this event combines the joyous celebration of a bountiful harvest with an undercurrent of fear that the stored crop could spoil in the granaries. Moreover, this festival marks the beginning of the hot and wet season, a time of disease and pestilence. Thus, this holiday, also known as the Insect Killing Festival (Huu 1998: 127), also expresses fear of disease and epidemics and features several culinary means aimed at preventing disease or combating it.

Fruit and Herbs, the Season and the Prevention of Epidemics

Two fruits were prominent during the festival: jackfruit and rambutan. When I asked about the jackfruit, the response was unanimous: it is the custom to eat jackfruit in Hoi An during the Summer Festival because it is then in season. Thus, jackfruit marks the local season and stands for the beginning of summer in Hoi An and its vicinity. Just like watermelon at Tet, the consumption of jackfruit at this festival contributes to the construction of a local identity bound in time and space.

However, when I inquired about the popularity of rambutan, the responses were not very clear. I was told that though *chom chom* is not a new fruit (according to Vu [1997: 108], it was imported from Indonesia about a century ago), in recent years, there have been new varieties of rambutan: "more beautiful, tastier and cheaper than before," from the Mekong Delta. Thus, the rambutan's popularity is possibly an expression of consumerism: the Hoianese are tempted by the rambutan's enticing look, sweetness, and affordable price as a relative novelty that can be found in the market during the Summer Festival. Moreover, as the proliferation of *chom chom* in recent years is an outcome of the success of *doi moi* (Vietnamese rambutan are primarily exported), these fruit also hint at recent prosperity, advanced farming techniques, improved infrastructure, modernization, and even ideological and political shifts.[19]

Other than jackfruit and rambutans, the fruits served at the Summer Festival should be sour: green mango, unripe starfruit, and pineapple are the basic ingredients of key dishes cooked for the festive meal. The cooling qualities of these sour fruits partly explain their prominence at the festival that celebrates the beginning of summer. I was also told that sour fruits have antiseptic qualities that have to do with the holiday as an "insect killing festival."

The Trang family's festive lunch to which I was invited featured beef hot pot (*lau bo*): thin slices of rare beef dipped in sweet-and-sour soup made of pineapple, tomato, lime juice, and lemongrass. The undercooked beef was rolled in rice paper with fine slices of green banana, sour starfruit, and lettuce leaves. When I asked about these ingredients, Mrs. Trang explained, "We eat sour fruits because they kill the germs." Her husband added that it is very important to have some sticky-rice wine (*ruou nep*), "which also kills germs," a point also made by Huu (1998: 127–28): "This is the occasion to 'kill the insects' in a person's system by eating and drinking . . . anything which is bitter and sour: glutinous rice alcohol, green fruits . . . and other prescribed fruits . . ." so as to combat the malevolent heat and to prevent epidemics.

The next important vegetal element on the festival's culinary agenda was (medicinal) herbs. The dichotomy between "food" and "medicine" does not exist in Vietnam, and every edible item is believed to nourish the body and affect health and well-being (Hoang et al. 1999: 3–8). Therefore, anything edible is essentially or potentially a medicine and vice versa. Indeed, medicinal herbs were used as ingredients for the cooking of some of the festive dishes, such as duck in medicinal herbs. Like the fruit, medicinal herbs were described by the Hoianese as "in season" during *Tet Doan Ngo*. It seems that in the case of such herbs, "in season" signifies the time when their curative properties are strongest. Alternatively, "in season" could refer to this illness-riddled period, when their preventative and curative abilities are extremely important and sought after.

The fruits and herbs consumed during the Summer Festival express two ideas: they represent the summer, which is the fruit harvest season, and specifically the Hoianese summer, when jackfruit ripen; and sour fruits and medicinal herbs are remedies aimed at combating the ill effects of the season. Here again, iconic festive food and ingredients express both the joyous character of the festival and its threatening aspects.

The Legend and the Special Dishes of the Festival

In addition to the fruits and herbs, there were three iconic and unusual dishes in this festival: *banh u tro* (ash rice cakes), roast duck, and *che ke* (sweet sorghum porridge). These dishes have their origins in the Chinese legend about Chu Yuan (332–296 BCE), a loyal Mandarin who fell out of the emperor's favor due to false accusations and, in despair, drowned himself in a river. I heard various versions of this legend that differed from both the Chinese and the Vietnamese written versions (Warner 1984: 152; Huu 1998: 127–28). Hence, I will outline the "master narrative" of the Hoianese legend, presenting in parentheses alternative ideas that are important for our discussion:

> The Chinese Mandarin Phuc Nguyen ("Chu Yuan" in Chinese, also called by my informants Dieu Nguyen or Li Nguyen) was famous for his loyalty to the king and his just conduct with the people. He was loved and admired in his native province. As a result of court intrigues, he fell out of the king's favor. Sad and disappointed, he decided to resign and return to his native province, where he became a benevolent physician and herbalist. On the fifth day of the fifth lunar month, when he was looking for medicinal herbs in the mountains, he disappeared. As there wasn't any trace of him, the people were sure that Phuc Nguyen had accidentally drowned in the river (or, committed suicide by jumping into the river). The people felt sorry for him and feared that fish might devour his corpse. Thus, they prepared small glutinous rice cakes mixed with ash and threw them into the river. The fish immediately gobbled the cakes, but the ash made the cakes taste so bad that the fish lost their

appetite (another version recounts that because of the unusual
pyramidal shape of the cakes, which were pointed in all directions, the
cakes stuck in the gullets of the fish and prevented them from devouring
the corpse of the Mandarin).

From that day on, on the fifth day of the fifth lunar month, people
have worshiped Phuc Nguyen, prepared the special ash rice cakes, and
eaten roast duck, because ducks swim and do not drown (or because
ducks float like the boats that were used to look for his body in the river:
"we eat ducks because they remind us of the boats").[20]

Despite the abundance of versions and nuances, this legend defines a clear
culinary context for the festive fare: the odd pyramidal ash rice cakes are prepared so as to prevent the fish from eating the corpse of Phuc Nguyen; purchasing and cooking medicinal herbs is related to his profession as a herbalist;
ducks are eaten either to commemorate the drowning or as representations of
the boats used to look for him. Underlying the special dishes are two issues not
mentioned explicitly in the legend, however: the dangers of summer and the
Chinese-Hoianese aspect of the festival.

Danger
The special dishes of the Summer Festival depicted by the legend, and especially the unique ash rice cakes, stress the treacherous nature of the region's
summers. For one, both ash and lime, in which the rice is soaked prior to the
boiling of the cakes, and which give the cakes their unique color, taste, and
name, are antiseptics widely used as means of purification. Eating a cake that
requires ash and lime in its preparation stresses the insect-killing and purifying intent of the festival. Thus, these cakes are not merely symbolic, but serve as
practical means of purification.

Moreover, the unique yellow color of the ash rice cakes further denotes
danger: yellow is a natural warning sign and many poisonous animals or pred-
ators (e.g., snakes, wasps, or big cats) are "marked" as dangerous by their yellow color. In Chinese cosmology, yellow is often the color of poison (Warner
1984: 146), while "yellow springs" are the abode of death. The shape of the cakes
also denotes danger: the triangle is a widely used warning shape, as exempli-
fied in road hazard signs.

Likewise, when I spent a day with one of the three Hoianese families that
produce the ash rice cakes, I was offered a local interpretation of the name that,
yet again, had to do with disease. The word *u*, which translates as "brimful" or
"voluminous" and hints at the odd shape of the cakes, is pronounced in the
Hoianese dialect just like the word for the female breast (and not *vu,* as in the

standard pronunciation). Moreover, the name of the wrapping leaves, *la ke* ("*ke* leaves") in a falling (*huyen*) tone, translates, when uttered in a rising (*sac*) tone, into "venereal disease." Thus, the local conception of ash cakes hint at sex and sexually transmitted diseases.

One further important point has to do with the fact that the ash rice cakes, like the New Year cakes, are essentially a form of preserved food, as the leaf wrapping and the long boiling, as well as the antiseptic ash, ensure their long shelf-life. In fact, the cakes are shipped from Hoi An without refrigeration as far as Saigon and even to some towns in the Mekong Delta. Thus, just as with *banh Tet,* the iconic dishes of this festival celebrates the harvest while simultaneously expressing the fear that the stored crops might spoil, or that the next harvest might fail.

While ducks are not mentioned in the written Chinese and Vietnamese versions of the legend, all the oral versions mentioned them. Ducks, then, are most probably a local addition to the legend, either Hoianese or Central/Southern Vietnamese. While most of the people I talked to explained that ducks are eaten because they are "in season,"[21] the oral versions of the legend point to their role in combating danger, either as creatures that can swim (and do not drown) or as a reminder of the boats sent to search for the drowned Mandarin. Ducks, then, are a special festive fare due to their ability to swim and float. Ducks are eaten to ward off the possibility of drowning during the summer flood season. Alternatively, Schipper (1993: 28) points out that the festival is celebrated when ". . . drought threatens. Jousts on dragon-boats . . . are believed to counter the drought." The ducks might also stand for dragon-boats and imply the wish for abundant rains.

Co Nguyet suggested another explanation that relates ducks to danger. She quoted the couplet *dau nam an ga, mung nam an vit* ("eating chicken in the beginning of the year, eating duck in the middle of the year") as the reason for eating roast duck at this festival. She explained that during Tet, "everyone likes to eat chicken but never duck, because duck is slow and wobbly, and eating it would make the entire year slow and wobbly. But on the fifth of the fifth, we eat ducks to wipe away bad luck." Though she could not explain what kind of bad luck is counteracted and how the duck wipes it off (though she suggested that its waddle denotes wiping), she did say that eating ducks is a measure taken in order to combat some sort of threat that characterizes the season.

Whether the danger lies in disease and epidemics, in floods and drowning, in droughts, in the spoiling of the recently harvested crops, or in the failure of the next harvest, the important point is that both rice cakes and ducks express fear, while eating ash rice cakes and roast duck are symbolic or practical measures taken to overcome the threats.

The Chinese Context of the Festival

Beyond the dangers of the season, the iconic Summer Festival dishes stress the Chinese context of the festival. While the legend concerning *banh Tet* is explicitly Vietnamese and could even be understood as anti-Chinese, the legend about the origins of the odd "ash rice cakes" is clearly Chinese: a dish that was invented in China so as to save the corpse of a Chinese Mandarin. Moreover, the two other iconic festive dishes of *Tet Doan Ngo,* the roasted ducks and the sweet sorghum porridge, further stress the Chinese context of the festival.

Co Dung explained that ducks are eaten at the Summer Festival "because duck is a Chinese food." Herbal medicine was also imported from China (Hoang et al. 1999: 1, 3–4). Co Dung herself cooked for the feast what she described as "a Chinese dish": duck in medicinal herbs. *Che ke,* sold in the market and served as a votive offering as well as a snack in most houses I visited during the festival, is known in Hoi An as a Chinese dish. Sorghum was the original staple food of northern China and is still popular nowadays in the rural areas, both as an edible grain and fermented and made into alcohol (Chang 1977). As such, *che ke* further underlines the Chinese context of the festival.

It should be noted that just like most of the other Vietnamese festivals (including New Year), the Summer Festival is essentially a Chinese holiday (Huu and Cohen 1997: 73), which was adopted by the Vietnamese along with the Chinese calendar. However, while the other Tet were transformed and "Vietnamized," as it were, this festival is celebrated nowadays mainly in towns with prominent and active Chinese communities, such as Hoi An. One friend even claimed that "*Tet Doan Ngo* is celebrated properly *only in Hoi An,* because there are so many Chinese in town." As explanations about its key dishes imply, this festival is perceived locally as Chinese.

Here it must be stressed that the open celebration of a Chinese festival in contemporary Vietnam should not be taken for granted as unproblematic. The long national history of struggle against China, as well as the economic and cultural prominence of the local Chinese communities, makes Chinese identity a very fraught political issue in Vietnam. Moreover, the relations between Vietnam and China over the past fifty years have often been strained and ambivalent, with the Chinese-Vietnamese often trapped between a rock and a hard place. A case in point would be the anti-Confucius campaign after reunification, which actually targeted the Hoa and led to their exodus—when they ironically became known around the world as the "Vietnamese boat people." It could be argued that in Hoi An, where Vietnamese and Chinese have cohabited peacefully for the last few centuries (at least, according to the official version), celebrating such a Chinese festival is only natural. Yet the roughly two hundred Chinese (Hoa) families still living in town went through very difficult times between reunification and the practical implementation of *doi moi* in the early 1990s, when their property was confiscated and their civil rights were curbed.

Obviously, the importance of the Summer Festival reflects the deep Chinese impact on Hoianese culture, as well as the diffusion of this culture through intermarriage, since it would be hard to find a family in the ancient quarter even among the Kinh without some Chinese ancestors. Nevertheless, there is also a commercial undercurrent to the celebration of the festival in Hoi An. In fact, Hoi An has provided one of the very few legitimate sources of Chinese culture in contemporary Vietnam, promoted not only by the local authorities but also by the central government, both of which have grasped the economic potential of such an image.

When the Hoianese export *banh u tro* to every corner of the country (or, more accurately, the Center and the South), they directly capitalize on the Chinese identity that is attributed to the whole town. This probably explains the fact that none of the several families that produce the ash cakes is ethnically Chinese: they derive their ethnic authenticity from the image of Hoi An and capitalize on it in a major way.[22]

The fact that a Chinese festive dish is the only cultural artifact to be exported as such to other parts of the country is revealing. While locally produced and invented "Chineseness" is promoted as a means to attract local and foreign tourists, and while the activities of the Chinese communities in Hoi An are tolerated but strictly monitored (as in the case of the Phuc Kien community festival discussed in chapter 6), it has become acceptable to export Chinese food from Hoi An to other parts of the country. Thus, while Hoianese-Chinese cultural autonomy is monitored and restricted, the distribution of Hoianese-Chinese culinary artifacts is not only tolerated but even hailed. The reasons for this tolerance of food, as opposed to the curbing of some other kinds of ethnically inflected displays, are similar to those discussed in the context of politically inflected regional differences in fruits used as offerings.

THE MOON CAKES OF THE MID-AUTUMN FESTIVAL

Finally, I turn to another salient iconic dish prepared for a major festival: the "moon cakes" of Tet Trung Thu, the Mid-Autumn Festival. This festival is celebrated on the fifteenth day of the eighth lunar month, as Hung explained, the night "when the moon is fullest in the year" and therefore, people worship the moon that night.[23] In Vietnamese cosmology, this is the period when the *am* principle takes over *duong* (Huard and Durand 1998: 110; Huu 1998: 408; Cohen 2001), female over male, cold over hot, darkness over light, and winter over summer (Jamieson 1995: 12). The moon, which is a manifestation of the *am* principal, is the focal point of this festival.

Though Tet Trung Thu is termed in China "the lantern festival" (Huu and Cohen 1997: 75), it was usually referred to by my interviewees as "the children's festival," probably because most of its activities are considered to be child-oriented or childish.[24] Besides eating *banh mat trang* ("moon cakes"), the two central "childish" activities of the festival are the unicorn (*con ky lan* or "heavenly unicorn") dance (*mua lan*), and playing with "Chinese" lanterns. Both activities are related to the moon: according to co Dung, the unicorn tries to devour the moon, while the lanterns represent the wish for the return of light when the days become shorter.

The celebration of the Mid-Autumn Festival is second only to the New Year Tet in Hoi An, and is conducted with many activities and much excitement for several days. As I intend to focus only on the moon cakes, I will not describe in great detail the complex nonculinary practices of the festival except for the notable commercialization since 2000 (I was in town during the festival in 2000, 2004, and 2005). Unicorn dance troupes walk the streets and markets and dance in front of every house and shop until they get *hoi lo* ("bribe money"). This is paid to stop the unicorn from devouring the moon (or, according to Trung, the souls of the family ancestors, which are unprotected by the god of the door, Ong Cua, on this specific day). In 2000, there were dozens of such troupes, many of which targeted the central market, whose merchants were increasingly unhappy with the extortion practice. Nonetheless, they all had to pay up and remain calm so as not to "lose face" in public.

While I observed the unicorn dances in the market in the year 2000, many merchants urged me to take over their payments, and suggested the sum of 5,000–10,000 dong. Most of them handed out 200 and 500 dong bills (virtually nothing). These sums disappointed and irritated the dancers, especially the professional troupes, who clearly performed for money. Trung, whom I met in the market, pointed out that when she was a child, "the musicians would play different tunes/beats, and the *con lan* danced differently to each tune. But nowadays, they only want money and know only one tune."

As for the handmade lanterns, decorated with the traditional motives of carps, hares, toads, and "little Bom" (from a popular children's story), which were described by my informants as the "traditional lanterns," were replaced by electrically illuminated plastic figures imported from China. The most popular lantern in 2000 was that of a blond doll that played a terribly out-of-tune version of the Brazilian pop song "Lambada."

This commodification of the festival has continued. Thus, for example, during the festival of 2004, while I was conducting fieldwork in the town again, co

Dung told me that she had asked her students why so many of them perform the unicorn dance, and the unanimous answer was "for the money!" The *Vietnam News* weekly magazine (September 18, 2005, pp. 6–7), in its cover story on the festival, pointed out that though "children and adults still enjoy the holiday, the people who sell moon cakes and toys enjoy it even more, because of their high profits." As we shall see, this commercial air is crucial when analyzing the meanings of moon cakes.

Two kinds of *banh mat trang* are prepared for the festival. The first is the round, white *banh deo* (elastic/flexible cakes), made from pounded sticky rice and stuffed with green beans and coconut shreds. Co Nguyet said that these chewy cakes are always vegetarian and never contain even eggs. The second kind was the brownish *banh nuong* ("roasted cakes," actually baked in ovens), made from wheat flour and stuffed with mashed black beans and lotus seeds, and sometimes preserved eggs and meat. These cakes were usually square. There was another version of *banh nuong,* "popular in South Vietnam" according to Giang, which was stuffed with jackfruit pulp and preserved eggs. The cakes, stamped with a red double-happiness character, are heavy, rich, and sweet.

As opposed to the New Year cakes and the ash cakes, moon cakes were not prepared in Hoi An at all. In 2000, the three cake shops in town were the only places that sold moon cakes for the festival. The owners told me that they bought them in Danang, where "they know how to make them." They were sold in red cardboard boxes with transparent cellophane lids, which typically contained four units (an *am* number): two square cakes and two round cakes. The cakes were expensive, compared to those prepared for the other festivals: a box of four was sold for US$4–6, the equivalent of a schoolteacher's weekly wages.

When I asked why people eat these cakes during Tet Trung Thu, I was told that "the cakes look like the moon" and that "people like to eat *banh mat trang* when they look at the beautiful full moon on the night of the festival." However, the mythological origins of moon cakes seem to be unknown in Hoi An (and the Chinese and other literature on the origins of these cakes is also unclear).

Still, an explicit reading of the meaning of the moon cakes is possible: in a festival that marks the shift from the sunny summer to the cool and dark winter, closest to the autumnal equinox, and from the period of *duong* to that of *am,* people eat moon-shaped cakes because the moon is the icon of *am.* Moreover, as with all the Tet festivals previously described, this festival marks a transition, between the transplanting and the harvest of the autumn rice. Here again, the rice cakes represent both the expectations for a good rice harvest and the fear that something might go awry. Therefore, in order to overcome the psychological anxiety and practical threat, "long-life" rice cakes, stuffed with preserved food items, such as preserved eggs, meat, beans, and coconut, are prepared.

However, the moon cakes have a more implicit meaning: during the Mid-Autumn Festival of 2000, they became an important status symbol in town. As pointed out earlier, the cakes were imported from out of town and were expensive. In Hoi An, where the average income is much lower than in Saigon or Danang, the cakes were sold in only a few places in the wealthier parts of town, and I hardly saw anyone buying them. Moreover, in the few houses in which I did see the cakes, they were displayed on the ancestor altar as offerings, clearly visible to any visitor. In stark contrast to the *banh Tet* and *banh u tro,* the moon cakes were not served to guests, but were kept packed in their fancy boxes on the altar throughout the entire festival and even a few days later: they were exhibited but not eaten. Instead of a festive dish, the cakes were used as a nonedible object, a status symbol expressing wealth and economic success.

This trend seems to have intensified in the following years. The authors of the *Vietnam News* article mentioned above suggest that in Hanoi, moon cakes have turned into objects of conspicuous consumption, with prices of up to US$70. The article quotes "a wife of a company manager" who recounts how her house would fill up with boxed cakes presented by her husband's employees, and points out that "while the cakes are a way to show appreciation, people get carried away in their purchasing." She also claims that as her family members can hardly eat so many cakes, nor can they give so many of them to others, ". . . sometimes the cakes just get moldy and are thrown away" (ibid.). The important point is that moon cakes seem to have become detached from their cosmological meanings and turned into status symbols, encompassing affluence and modernization as well as capitalism and conspicuous consumption, while reflecting the erosion of ideas and ideals concerning cosmology, religion, and national identity.

THE FESTIVE CAKES COMPARED

The three festivals discussed in this chapter are part of a single annual rice-farming cycle, in which the festive rice cakes play two roles. First, the iconic dish of each festival marks it with specific flavor, color, and shape, stressing its unique and extraordinary nature. At the same time, the shift from one kind of rice cake to the next symbolizes the dynamic nature of time and induces a feeling of flow, continuity, and circularity. Second, the rice cakes feature some shared meanings that shed light on the notion of what being a Vietnamese is all about. Table 7.1 summarizes these various perspectives.

TABLE 7.1. Festive Rice Cakes Compared

RICE CAKE	NEW YEAR (BANH TET)	ASH (BANH U TRO)	MOON (BANH MAT TRANG)
Festival	Tet Nguyen Dan New Year (Arrival of Dawn) 1st of the 1st month First day of spring	Tet Doan Ngo High Noon (Insect Killing) 5th of the 5th month First day of Summer	Tet Trung Thu Mid-Autumn ("Moon Festival") 15th of the 8th month Mid-Autumn
Ingredients	Glutinous rice Pork Green beans Bamboo Leaf wrap	Glutinous rice Ash Leaf wrap	Glutinous rice Green/black beans Sugar, coconut, Egg, meat
Shape and Color	Square and Green	Yellow Pyramid	Round and White
Legend	Pre-Chinese Kinh Prince Lang Lieu wins the throne with *banh chung* and *banh day*	Chinese The loyal Mandarin Phuc Nguyen is worshiped with the cakes	Chinese(?) There is no clearly defined legend
Symbolism Color	Green = Rice	Yellow = Sun or Death/Danger	White = Moon
Shape	Square = Earth *Duong*	Pyramid = Danger	*Round = Moon* Am
Ingredients	Farming	Farming Ash = Purification	*Farming*
Meaning	Thanksgiving Harvest protection Nationalism Regionalism	Thanksgiving Harvest protection Danger	Thanksgiving Harvest protection Commercialization Status Seeking

As we can see, the different rice cakes stand for different seasons, legends, ingredients, and events. However, they also combine into a complete annual set that features various shared themes. The most salient notion is that Vietnam is a nation of farmers—more specifically, of rice farmers. Thus, the festivals mark different stages of the rice cycle, while the cakes, as iconic dishes of each festivals, are essentially made of rice.

Rice farming involves much anxiety and stress. Rice farmers are always worried that their harvest might fail or that some calamity will befall the stored grains. In this respect, the rice cakes, as well as various other festive dishes prepared for such Tet transitional periods, are preserved foods that embody these fears and anxieties. Simultaneously, these "long-life" dishes are intended to overcome such psychological and physical threats: if the crops are somehow lost, the preserved rice cakes would last. Thus, the rice cakes can be perceived both as magical charms to ward off bad luck and disaster and/or as practical means aimed at ensuring food provisioning during hard times.

Furthermore, the preserved festive rice cakes, and especially *banh Tet,* are suggestive of the resolute and even warlike nature of the Vietnamese. These rice cakes are compact and concentrated bundles of compressed energy, which last for a long time even under extreme conditions. As such, they are some sort of combat rations that, indeed, were used as such at various periods of Vietnamese history. And when a nation selects combat rations as its primary iconic dish, it is making a strong statement about itself.

From yet another perspective, the transformation of shapes and colors in the rice cakes reflects the complete cycle of nature in Vietnam. The cycle of nature is venerated first by the square *banh Tet,* which is eaten "on the first day of spring" when the (square) earth rejuvenates. The yellow *banh u tro* are eaten on the first day of summer, and their yellow color is that of the sun, the natural element worshiped in this festival. It also stands for the danger of epidemics and floods common during this season. Finally, *banh mat trang* look like the white, round full moon, which is venerated in the Mid-Autumn Festival.

The rice-farming cycle is also represented by the colors of the cakes, which stand for the different stages of rice farming: *banh Tet* are as green as rice seedlings, the yellow *banh u tro* has the color of ripe rice, and the *banh mat trang* are as white as polished rice grains. Thus, when eating the different cakes along the year, the eater goes through the entire cycle of rice farming. Furthermore, as the three natural elements represented by the cakes (earth, sun, and moon), are crucial to rice farming, the two cycles, of nature and of farming, merge into a single rice cycle, represented by the cakes and lying at the heart of Vietnamese culture.

The set of cakes makes for yet another important cultural notion: the distinction between the sacred and the profane (Durkheim and Mauss 1963: 13). The year is composed of long periods of ordinary "profane" time, separated by "sacred" intervals. The iconic dish of profane time is plain white rice, which is shapeless, colorless, and loosely structured. The iconic dishes of sacred time are rice cakes, which have specific colors and shapes and stress the nature of the "sacred" as carefully, meaningfully, and tightly shaped, are wrapped and tied up, that is, solidly structured. Thus, festive periods are marked by the cakes as tightly constructed and meaningful, while normal days are represented by shapeless, "free-floating" plain rice.

The shift from plain rice (*te*) to glutinous rice (*nep*), which is used for preparing the festive rice cakes (as well as festive *xoi* and festive rice alcohol) further enhances the distinction between the profane and the sacred. For one, glutinous rice, even when not shaped into cakes, is "sticky," and the grains tend to "cling" and "hold" to each other much more than plain rice grains. This sticking together reflects the expected social cohesion during festivals, and even enhances it. Moreover, glutinous rice, which was domesticated and cultivated long before the contemporary "ordinary rice" (Huu 1998: 186) is perceived by the Vietnamese as the original and "real" rice (and see Nguyen's 2001 work on the centrality of sticky rice in Vietnamese culture). Hence, when munching on glutinous rice cakes, the diners are transferred to ancient and mythological times and their relations with the communal past and history are reaffirmed and enhanced.

However, it is not only the common roots of the Vietnamese or their shared national characteristics that are expressed by the festive rice cakes. The different cakes also encompass some implicit social ideas, which stress the singularity of Hoi An and highlight contemporary issues. Thus, while *banh Tet* are the single most important iconic Vietnamese festive fare, the local cylindrical version stands for the initiative and energy of the Southerners, who shaped their *banh* as cylinders to better preserve them during the arduous trip to the South. The Hoianese today are making a related point about themselves not only as differing from the Northerners (who make square cakes), but also as having distinctive qualities that single them out as ambitious, brave, having initiative, and, in sum, better.

Along the same lines, the ash cakes stress the Chinese cultural identity of Hoi An and single it out as different and unique. While such an identity is problematic in contemporary Vietnam, it is also a profitable one, and the Hoianese seem happy to embrace and exploit it. As for the moon cakes, instead of a dish, they are perceived in Hoi An as a rare status symbol. In this respect, they express the utmost importance of wealth, prosperity, and prestige in the Socialist Republic of Vietnam.

ICONIC NATIONAL DISHES AND THE CONCRETIZATION OF THE IMAGINED COMMUNITY

While the food discussed in previous chapters was consumed by clearly defined social conventions, this chapter was dedicated to dishes consumed at given festive periods by the millions of persons who make up the "Vietnamese nation," or in Benedict Anderson's (1983) definition, the "imagined community" of Vietnam.

Communities such as the nation are "imagined" because members can only
rely on their imagination in order to encompass the range and boundaries of
their communities. An "imagined community" is actually a "structure of feeling" (Bell and Valentine 1997: 15) more than a concrete entity; each member
"imagines" sharing fundamental ideals, cultural values, customs, and physical
traits with the others. Hence, "imagined communities" are artificial, loosely
structured, and fragile cultural artifacts whose production and maintenance
require complicated mechanisms (ibid. 178), which Anderson identifies as mass
communication and mass literacy, the establishment of "national museums,"
and the obsession with mapping and borders as tools that construct and maintain nations and national identity.

There are more concrete ways by which national identity is produced and
reproduced. Billig (1995) stresses the role of "banal nationalism" as "the ideological habits which enable . . . nations . . . to be reproduced" (6). Banal nationalism "happens all day, everyday and it may often go unnoticed as its seeming
innocuousness does not mark it for special attention (Palmer 1998: 181). However, banal nationalism is always "flagged." This flagging may work at a sub-
conscious level but still serves to constantly remind people of who they are:
"This reminder is so familiar, so continual, that it is not consciously registered
as reminding. The metonymic image of banal nationalism is not a flag which is
being consciously waved with fervent passion; it is a flag hanging unnoticed on
the public building" (Billig 1995: 8).

The special dishes for the major Vietnamese festivals are such "flags" of
identity. Though usually explained by the Hoianese in terms of customs and
tradition, these festive dishes, like national flags, encompass some of the essential explicit and implicit beliefs and ideals of the bearers. The Vietnamese
iconic festive dishes are a means by which the Vietnamese present themselves
to themselves.

Unlike most other flags of banal (and nonbanal) nationalism, which involve
a measure of imagination or abstraction, iconic national dishes are not simply
imagined but are literally incorporated. While flags are still abstractions, festive dishes are edible artifacts that satisfy hunger. Thus, their incorporation
means that the "imagined" nature of the community is transformed and con-
cretized: "I eat; therefore it (the nation) exists."

Iconic national dishes play a critical role as part of a limited group of artifacts that overcome imagination and, hence, "help to communicate and maintain our national identity" (Palmer 1998: 187). "National cuisines" accompanied the formation of nation-states and iconic national dishes were central to
the establishing of imagined communities (Mennell 1985). Indeed, "food and

the nation are so commingled . . . that it is often difficult not to think one through the other" (Bell and Valentine 1997: 168).

Yet, despite the fact that "the history of any nation's diet is the history of the nation itself, with food fashion, fads and fancies mapping episodes of colonialism and migration, trade and exploration, cultural exchange and boundary-making" (ibid.), when we deconstruct iconic dishes or national cuisines, we realize that "there is no essential national food" (ibid.; see also Cusack 2000), but only an amalgam of food ingredients and eating habits brought from elsewhere, and The National Diet is actually a "feast of imagined commensality" (Bell and Valentine 1997: 169). In this respect, Vietnamese iconic festive dishes encompass both perspectives: they represent the nation and concretize it, yet also hint at regional, ethnic, and social identities and entities that transcend the nation.

ᴥ Conclusion

FOOD AND CULTURE—INTERCONNECTIONS

I began my research in Hoi An thinking that the local foodways would merely reflect the existing social order and cultural arrangements, but my fieldwork frequently demonstrated that, on the contrary, the culinary sphere was not a passive mirror image of other social and cultural realms but, rather, an arena of cultural production itself.

A good example of the challenges to my early theoretical assumptions brought about by fieldwork observations would be the various modifications to the script of the Hoianese festive culinary scenario. While this scenario clearly reflects the prevailing social order and cultural conventions, the meaning of significant changes to that script—such as the addition of expensive seafood, or the buffet-style wedding feast—had to be more complex.

To engender a more accurate and sensitive analysis of the culinary events I witnessed in Hoi An, I turned to Handelman's (1998) scheme of "Models, Mirrors and Re-presentations," which better accommodates contradictions and incongruities such as the ones described above.

FOODWAYS AS MIRRORS: SOCIAL RELATIONS AND VALUES

Hoianese eating patterns reflect the prevailing stratification system, governed by age and gender hierarchies. At each and every Hoianese food event in which I participated, older folk were served by, and ate before, younger ones, and men were served by women and had privileged access to food. The sequence of eating was monitored to maintain these hierarchies, which were adhered to under all circumstances in both the private and public spheres.

As age and gender hierarchies essentially overlap (as one can be both an elder and a woman, for example), Hoianese eating etiquette reflects the priority of age over gender. Though public eating events were often segregated in terms

of gender, in most cases the tables were set in parallel lines: the tables of the elderly women paralleled those of the elderly men in spatial relation to the ancestral altar, the central axis of the event, and so forth. Though the elderly men
would be served first, the elderly women would be served immediately after
them, while the younger men's food would arrive only later, to be followed by
that of the younger women and children. At smaller and more private food
events, when eating was only partly segregated, if at all, it was mainly age that
determined the sequence of eating.

The Hoianese eating arrangements, as well as the perception of the kitchen as
an inferior space, reflect the lowly yet ambivalent social position of women,
which results from their role as mediators between "nature" and "culture." The
way in which children are fed further suggests that they are hardly conceptualized as full-fledged human beings, but rather (it seemed to me) as animals. The
culinary sphere does not merely reflect the relatively low status of women and
children but also suggests an explanation: while men belong to the realm of culture, women and children are considered to be closer to nature and, as such, are
inferior and, in some respects, dangerous and in need of constant monitoring.

While age and gender hierarchies are generally adhered to, guests, and especially clergy or other prominent people, are accorded special treatment. In
such instances, age and gender hierarchies are not breached but expanded to
accommodate these people into categories from which their age and gender
would normally exclude them: prominent guests are directed to share a table
with the older men. Here, the existing norms are not challenged but are in fact
reinforced, as age and gender hierarchies are maintained, while the virtues of
hospitality and the customary veneration of spiritual, intellectual, or economic
achievements are properly expressed.

Beyond the social structure, the culinary sphere reflects the Vietnamese
values of diligence, thrift, restraint, and moderation. Vietnamese cooking routinely involves the investment of huge amounts of labor applied to modest and
even frugal ingredients to produce small amounts of humble culinary artifacts.
While many of the resultant dishes are in fact elaborate, complex, and very
tasty, they evoke diligence and express humility. Moreover, restraint and moderation are always expected and even demanded around the table. While each
diner carefully monitors the situation so as not to exceed his or her share and
in order to accommodate the preferences of the others, those who have privileged access to food (the elderly, guests, or VIPs) are actually the ones who eat
the least, as they express self-restraint and moderation.

Finally, the Hoianese culinary sphere reflects two ideals, which combined
make for the cornerstone of Vietnamese culture: hierarchy and harmony.
These ideals, perceived in Western thinking as dichotomous, are interdepen-

dent in Vietnamese philosophy: "when a proper balance was maintained between yin and yang, harmony was maintained . . . [as] proper relations between categories and groups of people produce social harmony" (Jamieson 1995: 11–12; 20–21). Thus, while the *am* and *duong* principle harmonizes the food, social relations are strictly monitored around the table on the same terms so as not to disrupt harmony.

In fact, I have never seen open conflict erupt during a meal, and even when tensions could be sensed, serenity was maintained behind frozen smiles or silence. I have described several events, such as the ancestor worship at Cu's house, in which differences and tensions were evident. However, such tensions were expressed through very slight gestures and nuances, while face was saved and harmony maintained at all costs by adherence to the social norms.

FOODWAYS AS MIRRORS: FOOD SYMBOLISM

Tan (1998), in his study of the foodways of the Baba Chinese of Malaysia, suggests that Chinese food symbolism exhibits four main principles: color symbolism, number symbolism, symbolism by physical appearance (and/or shape), and symbolism by linguistic association (18). He also points to what should be termed "association by value": expensive dishes that reflect wealth and sophistication. While these principles also govern much of Hoianese food symbolism, the Hoianese culinary sphere features two other symbolic principles: symbolism by texture and association by (animal) behavior (and see Nemeroff and Rozin, 1989: 50–51).[1] Table 8.1 demonstrates each of the principles.

While table 8.1 features examples of Hoianese food symbolism, the meanings of the different Hoianese dishes seem to focus on several themes and values, among which the ideal of the "proper" family, its well-being, and its prestige are salient.

The Hoianese festive dishes consistently symbolize proper family relations and fertility. The festive culinary scenario features a variety of "bird-and-egg" dishes (that are sometimes abstracted into "meat-and-egg" dishes, and even into "meat-and-something-white-and-round," such as lotus seeds or litchi), which express proper parenthood, while noodle dishes stand for longevity. Both parenthood and longevity are essential for a multigenerational family, which is also symbolized by the New Year kumquat tree. Along the same lines, food composed of many units (e.g., a plate of watermelon seeds or a fruit-laden kumquat tree) expresses fertility. Pork, too, symbolizes fertility due to the pig's fecundity.

The other essential components of family well-being are prosperity and wealth, with food serving as an important means to convey this message. Thus,

TABLE 8.1. Hoianese Food Symbolism

Color symbolism	The green New Year cakes represent rice; the white Mid-Autumn moon cakes symbolize the moon; the green betel quid becomes red when chewed, standing for the transformation in the bride's life and for her virginity; the bright orange color of the New Year candied kumquats represents gold.
Number symbolism	The five sacred fruits used in the New Year worship stand for the five elements and symbolize the cosmos; the triple offerings for the farewell feast for the Kitchen God represent his triadic nature; the heavily-laden kumquat bush and bags of watermelon seeds represent fertility and prosperity.
Shape symbolism	The square New Year cakes stand for the earth, while the round *banh day* and *banh mat trang* stand for the round vault of heaven and the moon respectively; large bananas symbolize the masculine sex organ and, hence, are rejected as offerings; long noodles represent long life.
Symbolism by linguistic association	The names of the five fruits offered on New Year, when pronounced in the local dialect, are conjured into the sentence "praying for a lot to spend"; the word for "orange"—*cam,* also means "gold," further implying that the New Year oranges sym-symbolize gold; *cao lau* ("higher floor/attic") noodles that should be eaten on the second floor (either of Chinese restaurants or during the flooding season, when the first floor is flooded).
Association by animal behavior	Hens/chickens symbolize good mothering; chickens and pigs symbolize thrift and efficiency; ducks symbolize boats or the ability to float (and not to drown), but their wobbly walk may inflict bad luck during the New Year Festival and wipe it off during Tet Nguyen Dan; beef implies strength, while the flesh of wild animals denotes excessive power, sexual potency, and savagery.
Texture symbolism	Sticky rice symbolizes social cohesion during festive periods; it it also serves to clam up the lips of the God of the Kitchen; roasted meat, with its condensed texture, stands for wealth and power.
Association by value	Plentiful food and a variety of dishes are the utmost expression of wealth; meat in general denotes prestige, while beef in particular is considered luxurious, and chicken denotes urban sophistication, which is lacking in pork; foreign dishes and imported ingredients are prestigious, even when they are industrial and originally cheap; soft drinks and beer also express wealth, while canned drinks are more prestigious than bottled ones.

the candied oranges are related to gold, and bags of watermelon seeds were described as "looking like sacks full of money." Chicken and pork dishes symbolize economic success and efficiency because they embody the transformation of waste and residues into meat. The names of festive dishes such as the wedding rice dish, *kim ngoc man duong* ("house full of jade and gold"), or the set of fruits (which may be parsed as "praying for a lot to spend") offered on the ancestral altar for *Tet,* express the desire for wealth.

The well-being of the Hoianese family is also reflected in the culinary sphere in terms of power and prestige, expressed by generosity and sophistication. While meat is the main symbol of power and wealth, serving large amounts of elaborate and expensive food expresses the hosts' wealth and generosity. Incorporating imported ingredients and/or serving foreign or innovative dishes stand not only for economic capital but also for cultural capital, which further enhances family prestige. Specifically, serving international brands of beverages such as Coca-Cola or Heineken beer reflects cosmopolitanism and worldliness. By the same token, however, avoiding foreign foods—as long as they are identified as such—is also a meaningful declaration about conservatism, patriotism, and the rejection of foreign influence.

Altogether, the Hoianese festive dishes reflect the three essential wishes: *Phuc–Loc–Tho* (happiness, prosperity, longevity), expressed in almost every Vietnamese house by the icons of the three old men (or gods): *Phuc,* surrounded by male children (implying that happiness is to be found in fertility and sons); *Loc,* holding a jade wand, who stands for both power and wealth; and *Tho,* holding a peach—*tao* in Chinese-Vietnamese, which by linguistic association is the symbol of longevity.

Beyond the well-being of the family, Hoianese festive food also expresses the threat, danger, and "bad luck" that characterize farming, with certain festive dishes reflecting specific seasonal threats, most prominent of which is the fear that the stored harvest could spoil or that future crops could fail. Thus, the New Year and Mid-Autumn festivals, which are celebrated right after the rice harvest, both feature "long-life" rice cakes, while the Mid-Summer Festival features a long-life rice cake along with a set of dishes that symbolize the threat of epidemics and the danger of floods that typify this warm, wet season.

The dishes prepared for these events explicitly celebrate a successful harvest and reflect the bountiful and prosperous nature of the season, with harvest food (rice and fruits of the season) as the highlight, yet these very same dishes hint at the dangerous aspects of these liminal periods. In fact, the iconic dishes of these events are the only manifestations of the darker aspects of Vietnamese festivals, which would otherwise remain hidden behind the merry façade.

Importantly, these iconic dishes can hardly be described as mere reflections or as symbolic of seasonal threats. They should be also understood as practical and magical means aimed at combating and overcoming such threats. Long-life rice cakes that can last for a few months might very well serve as iron rations in case the stored crops spoil or the future harvest fails, while people eat ducks during Tet Doan Ngo "because ducks do not drown," thus ensuring protection from this seasonal threat. Such festive dishes are not merely "mirrors," but also play the role of "models," as they are intended to influence and even transform the lived-in world. Handelman was correct in pointing that when it comes to the lived-in world, models and mirrors are not mutually exclusive: the very same dishes reflecting the lived-in world are simultaneously intended to influence and transform it.

FOODWAYS AS MODELS

I have taken part in only a few cases in which specific culinary events were clearly intended to serve as models—that is, were devised so as to transform and replace the existing order of things. Most prominent among these events was Bac and Trung's "inviting friends" party, which was discussed as an event of gastro-anomie, but which will be reanalyzed here as an event-that-models.

In Bac and Trung's party, the eating arrangements radically shifted the scope from the family/collective to the individual, from the past to the future, and from Vietnam to the West. Instead of well-defined age and gender segregated units (of those sharing a table) that are served a set of traditional dishes standing, first and foremost, for the integration and well-being of the family, the buffet meal stressed individualism, self-initiative, and innovation. In terms of consumption modes, the Hoianese demand for proper behavior that includes self-restraint and accommodation of the wishes of others was radically replaced by a setting that requires neither and, on the contrary, required personal initiative. The usual host–guest relations were overturned, as it were, and guests were expected to take care of themselves. Instead of common utensils that require sharing, the food was served in personal units (hotdogs and sliced bread instead of whole chicken) out of large trays, so that calculation of how much each person should have was impossible. Furthermore, many of the dishes and condiments on offer were foreign, as were the crockery and cutlery.

This event was also aimed at transforming the inferior status of cooking and, potentially, of women at large. Thus, beyond the bold disregard for traditional gender hierarchy, the chef was the bride's sister—a successful professional restaurateur in her own right—who located herself center-stage as a (female) performing artist, whose skills were worthy of appreciation and admiration. When cooking becomes a performing art, women, as those responsible for cooking, can be reconstituted as celebrities or culture heroes.

Recall that this food event was on the verge of disintegration when it was rescued by rearranging the event along traditional lines. It could be argued that this model failed to achieve its goals of transforming the lived-in world, but it was clearly an attempt to reshape it—and as such, it was an event-that-models.

Food-events-that-model also evolve in less dramatic circumstances, for instance when it comes to the complex processes by which identities are handled within the culinary sphere. Here again, it would be only fair to say that the culinary sphere routinely reflects the identity of the diners or, more precisely, different aspects of this complex and multifaceted sociocultural construct (Cerulo 1997; Eisenstadt and Geisen 1995: 78; Hall 1996: 6). Yet when choosing to incorporate specific dishes within specific circumstances, people can (and do) turn to food and eating as a means of self-transformation: if change is the sought-after outcome, one can hardly find a better means for personal transformation than through the incorporation of culturally marked edible matter.

FOODWAYS AS RE-PRESENTATIONS

Yet when it comes to identity, my data suggest that the culinary sphere is often an arena of negotiation and experimentation rather than production, as different iconic and marked dishes stress different aspects of identity, which compete for expression and hegemony. In this respect, the category of "re-presentation" seems best to encompass such processes.

While there was some form of contest and challenge in almost all the food events described in this book, three premises were especially prone to culinary re-presentation: the relations between the collective and the individual (which include the subcategories of gender relations and tradition-versus-modernity), competition for prestige, and the negotiation of identities.

The relations between the collective and the individual are high on the agenda of contemporary Vietnamologists (Marr 2000a; Schafer 2000; Malarney 1997; 2002, Pham 1999; and more implicitly in Marr 2000b; Wisensale 2000; Belanger 2000; Charlot 1991; Hy and Diep 1991; Hardy 2005). These relations are usually described as oscillating between the traditional demand for the total submission of the individual to the collective and more modern voices that assert the existence of the individual as a social entity (and see Marr 2000a for the emergence of the individual in contemporary Vietnam), and discuss his or her level of autonomy. While the culinary sphere generally reflects the priority of broader social categories (such as age, gender, status, or education) over individuals, the latter often challenge their submission and try to assert themselves as autonomous social entities in the culinary context.

When Duyen decided to sit with her husband and the other men in an ancestor-worship feast in Dien Ban and not with the other young mothers as dictated by the scenario, she was challenging gender hierarchy and outlining an alternative arrangement in which men and women are equal and in which the spousal relationship is more meaningful than relations between members of the same gender and age. Along similar lines, when Giang demanded that the Tet kumquats should be prepared her way, rejecting the advice of the more experienced Le, she was challenging the privileged position of older people and the educated and demanding that a new social status would be acknowledged: that of a girlfriend.

In fact, Hoianese public food events are quite tolerant about these new categories of boyfriends/girlfriends in family rituals, and also when eating out, as unmarried Hoianese couples often meet in public eating venues that allow them to be "alone together" (Shapira and Navon 1991). During family feasts, such unmarried partners are allowed and even encouraged to participate as a couple. In doing so, these couples challenge the acceptable norms and outline new social perceptions that stress individual choices and romantic love over the traditional family-oriented arranged marriages.

Modernity and innovation as representations of individualism are expressed within the culinary realm not merely in terms of new social categories or different consumption patterns but also in terms of culinary innovation as such. A good example was the new dish (Chinese and Vietnamese mushrooms garnished with ketchup and mayonnaise) especially developed for Bac and Trung's engagement feast. Though the dish was rejected by the diners due to its unappealing texture and taste, the concept of new dishes for such events was not rejected by the participants. Similarly, the growing number of tourist-oriented restaurants in town, and especially "ethnic" ones (Italian, Indian, French) attract ever-increasing numbers of Hoianese, many of whom told me that they want to try new food. It seems that the culinary sphere is an acceptable ground for experimentation with new and foreign ideas, which would be hardly tolerated by either the other Hoianese and the authorities in other cultural contexts. In fact, one of my closest friends told me that he became a chef because in his kitchen he could do whatever he liked: experiment, invent, and turn to Western ideas and ingredients for inspiration; here his family members, and the local political establishment, would not interfere in his cooking in ways that they otherwise would have, had he been taking part in explicit political activities or socially interacting with foreigners.

Another aspect of re-presentation is evident in the position of the culinary sphere as an arena of social competition, with parameters such as the amount of food, the number of dishes, quality of the food, its origins (whether local or exported, from Vietnam or elsewhere), cooking modes, and the effort invested in the presentation of the food as tokens in a social economy of prestige. Though I suggested that the "festive culinary scenario" underlies such meals, with different dishes symbolizing varying degrees of prestige, the point here is that each food event is a re-presentation of the status of the hosts, who make a public statement about their economic and cultural capital: while the festive culinary scenario defines the general framework for such meals, culinary nuances (pork vs. chicken, canned drinks vs. bottles, tea vs. coffee, or boiled vs. roasted meat) determine the social value of the event and the ad hoc re-presentation of the hosts' status.

Of course, such manifestations of prestige call for social "retaliation" and promote competition. While one response to such a challenge is offering ever-more elaborate food events that would shadow previous meals offered by other families, whether along similar lines (with more expensive ingredients, new dishes, and other features) or through contradiction (returning to strict traditional arrangements, to express a dignified conservatism), the other way is to belittle the event by means of restraint. I have detailed several events in which those of higher status refrained from eating, ate very little, or left first. By doing so, they were making a point about their own socioeconomic status: they had enough of everything at home and hardly needed to eat more.

This also explains the exclusion of children from the festive table and their designation to a separate area. Though too old to be fed by their mothers, they are not old enough to behave "properly" and to restrain themselves from gorging on delicacies, expressing enthusiasm that could cast doubt over the image of smug prosperity depicted by their parents' and grandparents' restraint. Hence, children are removed to the margins of the feast, where their behavior cannot embarrass their elders.

The hosts, of course, cannot ignore such a challenge to their re-presented status and encourage their guests to eat—to the point of harassment. While this practice might be explained in terms of being generous and ebullient hosts, it seems that insisting that their guests should eat more is also intended to force the guests, as it were, to acknowledge and embody their hosts' generosity (and see Kalka 1991). As food is always abundant at feasts, tables heaped with leftovers are further manifestations of the lavishness of the feast and the generosity and prosperity of the hosts. Public food events, then, are refined and well-calculated potlatches; as such, they clearly adhere to Handelman's definition of events-that-re-present.

The third important issue constantly being negotiated and experimented within the Hoianese culinary sphere is that of identity, or rather, the various facets of identity and the relations between them. Local specialties reflect different aspects of the Hoianese identity, such as Kinh, Chinese, cosmopolitan, and "local" in terms of space, while local foodways express traditional and/or invented communal identities such as Christian, Protestant, Cao Dai, Fukienese, and pan-Chinese and as well as induces comparisons and differentiation between them. My analysis of the iconic dishes of the big festivals in chapter 7 further highlights the culinary representation of national identity, as well as local and regional aspects.

The re-presentational character of the culinary sphere reaches its climax as specific aspects of one's identity and, for that matter, of entire families and communities are nourished, as it were, by different dishes and, hence, constantly negotiated, renegotiated, and changed. As such, the foodways allow for the expression of identity not merely as a multifaceted construct, but also as a dynamic and multivocal entity. The culinary sphere "raise[s] possibilities, questions, perhaps doubts, about the legitimacy or validity of social forms . . . [and exposes their] hidden or controversial implications" (Handelman 1998: 49). Thus, the Hoianese publicly hail *cao lau* as their iconic dish, which reflects the essential nature of Hoi An as "the peaceful congregation." Yet their actual culinary choices reveal a clear preference for *mi quang,* which indicates regional and even nationalistic inclinations. Crucially, the entire "debate" takes place within the culinary sphere, which serves as a safe arena for oppositional ideas. Yet the conflict is contained within the culinary sphere and does not lead to social change. In fact, the culinary sphere protects the existing social order by allowing the expression of conflict, while containing it.

Another example concerns the kind of identity constructed by the dishes prepared for the different Chinese community festivals. While these festivals explicitly celebrate specific regional identities of Imperial China, such as the Fukienese or the Hainanese, the dishes suggest a new identity, the "Hoianese-Chinese," which disregards regional differences in ancient China and fuses them into a new hybrid entity that also embraces Vietnamese and Hoianese elements. In this context, the culinary sphere challenges the proclaimed intentions of these events and exposes their implicit meanings.

The tensions between national and local identity were also exposed by the analysis of what I term iconic national dishes. New Year rice cakes are discussed as symbols of national unity, expressed in the consumption of a single food item by each and every member of the nation at one and the same time. The cakes, along with candied oranges and pork dishes, define the national character as one of frugality, moderation, efficiency, and endurance. The rice cakes also hint at an inclination toward militarism or, at least, at the centrality of war in Vietnamese history and national identity. Yet the reshaping of the cakes in the Center and South into cylinders is a statement made by the locals about their own nature: they consider themselves independent and courageous and different from their northern counterparts.

Along the same lines, the pyramidal ash cakes of Tet Doan Ngo serve to represent Hoi An as a legitimate source of "Chineseness" while Mid-Autumn moon cakes serve as re-presentations of wealth and sophistication. Here again, other social spheres, most significantly the political one, would have hardly tolerated public expression of such subversive ideas. Within the culinary realm, however, processes of re-presentation are usually tolerated and generally ignored.

Cooking itself is essentially an open-ended process, with personal taste preferences constantly shaping and reshaping the outcome. This explains why Chi begins the first class in her cooking course with the following declaration: "There is no correct way to cook Vietnamese food, there are only family recipes. I can only teach you what my mother taught me and what I like to cook." While the cookbook industry is booming globally, and even in Vietnam, it is still the instruction to "season according to taste" that determines the outcome of a dish. In this respect, cooking is in itself flexible, dynamic, and open-ended and, as such, a practice of re-presentation.

FOOD AND POLITICS

One of the most puzzling aspects of my research is the fact that I am allowed to conduct it at all. The fact that an Israeli anthropologist is permitted to carry out fieldwork in Hoi An for extended periods of time for over a decade should not be taken for granted, considering the political climate, the nation's international policies, and the experience of fellow anthropologists, who report constant surveillance. In fact, I think that I am allowed to go on with my research precisely because of my interest in food: while so many Vietnamese are enthusiastic gourmands who demonstrate something of a "national obsession" when it comes to matters of food and the pleasures of eating, they rarely reflect on the social and cultural meanings of what they cook and eat, and certainly not on its political implications. This is probably why my research was never perceived as threatening or subversive, and I was generally ignored and allowed to do whatever I liked, so long as I confined myself to the realm of food and eating.

It should be noted that due to the taken-for-granted and loosely organized nature of the culinary sphere, even scholars explicitly researching the culinary sphere are sometimes reluctant to acknowledge the importance, immediacy, and magnitude of food and eating. Alan Warde (1997), for example, in his discussion of the relationship between food and identity, claims that many people eat and watch others eat without any judgment. Thus, though people do care about sufficient, affordable, and familiar food, they "are not preoccupied with visual signs of fashion or categorization." Warde also argues that "most people would not be able to decipher codes related to food, nor would they care to" (199–200). Similarly, Stein (2008), in her analysis of the politics of food in the Palestinian-Israeli village, writes about Palestinian restaurants in Israel as political spaces and highlights spatial settings that define political dispositions. Yet, despite her attention to "edibility" as a political construction, she hardly mentions the food itself and does not highlight the messages it conveys.

However, as Scholliers (2001: 9–10) points out: "social demarcation and identification are present in 'simple', 'self-evident' and 'unconscious' matters . . . [and] so called evident consumption of food is relevant to people's identity even if they themselves pay little attention to it." My data indicate that sensitive political issues such as the expression of individualism or the assertion of identities that run counter to the official narrative materialize in the culinary sphere as they do in no other cultural realm. In fact, it seems that the contemporary Hoianese culinary sphere is one of the most critical and subversive cultural arenas. The reason for this unexpected freedom of expression has to do, yet again, with the taken-for-granted and nonreflexive nature of the culinary sphere: the loose structure and permeable borders that allow for criticism and challenge are precisely the qualities that render it unimportant, unworthy of attention, and, therefore, uncensored and unmonitored.

We should also bear in mind that culinary re-presentations mostly materialize within the context of public events and rituals (such as life-cycle events and community festivals), which are composed of a formal stage and a feast. While the formal stage in such events is carefully structured and strictly monitored, either by the participants (as in Bac and Trung's engagement, for example), or by the authorities (as in the divination at the Fukien community festival, which was stopped by the chief of police), the feast is the stage in which tensions ease and the participants relax. And it is precisely at this stage that culinary re-presentations evolve.

Thus, in feasts that follow life-cycle events young women sit beside their husbands and drink coffee and alcohol, unmarried lovers sit together, some guests get drunk, flirtatious, and/or rude, and the meal itself becomes an arena for intense social competition. Along the same lines, specific religious, ethnic, and regional identities and ideas that are never expressed during the formal stages of the festivals are celebrated by the whole nation, and are materialized and expressed in the festive fare.

The point is that when the formal and performative stages of public events are re-presentational, their dangerous and subversive aspects are clearly evident and they become subversive political manifests. Such events are either discontinued (as in the case of the Schembart Carnival discussed by Handelman 1998) or curbed (as was the Carnival in Rio, and see DaMatta 1977). However, when re-presentations feature in the informal, relaxed, and taken-for-granted stage of the event, during the meal, the participants may as well ignore them, as suggested by Warde (1997: 199–200). Nevertheless, my data supports Schollier's (2001: 9–10) argument that such taken-for-granted, unconscious foodways are relevant and meaningful, even if those who eat pay only little attention to what they are doing in social and cultural terms.

An intriguing phenomenon drew my attention in the course of my fieldwork in Hoi An but only now begins to make sense. I refer to the fact that each and every Hoianese social event involves a measure of eating and drinking, except for contemporary state ceremonies. Liberation Day (April 30th, and note the Gregorian dates of such events), International Workers' Day (May 1st), Ho Chi Minh's Birthday, and National [Independence] Day (September 2nd) were celebrated in Hoi An by neighborhood and workplace gatherings, school ceremonies and street parades, with speeches, national flags, slogans, and anthems, but never included any sort of festive eating. Why, then, is there no culinary facet to such contemporary state ceremonies?

Here again, it seems that the loosely structured and permeable nature of the culinary sphere and its open-ended and flexible nature explain why food and eating are not included in the repertoire of practices that comprise contemporary Vietnamese official events. State ceremonies are clearly intended to be "mirrors" and nothing but "mirrors." "It is clear," Handelman argues, "that many of the most pressing dilemmas—of allocation and use of power, of relationship among social strata or the historical validity of a society—are not treated transformatively in the events of the modern state . . . for the 'solutions' to these and other issues are assumed to be built in to the systemic operations of social order" (1998: 81). Hence, in state ceremonies nothing that is loosely structured or permeable is permitted because such elements might encompass criticism and embody a challenge to the existing order. While some expressions of criticism are tolerated or even enhanced as a safety valve in other contexts, food and eating are completely excluded from official Vietnamese state ceremonies because the potential threat to the social order is simply too large.

≈ Epilogue

It is not easy to define and distinguish contemporary anthropology as a discipline today, as postmodernism challenges, blurs, and enhances the transgression of disciplinary boundaries. The problem is further complicated by the fact that anthropology since Geertz has very much given up on Grand Theories and redefined itself as an interpretative science, while quite a few of the most commonly used theories in contemporary anthropology were compiled by scholars from other disciplines (for instance, Anderson's "imagined communities," Said's "Orientalism," and Hobsbawm's "invention of tradition").

It seems to me, however, that for many contemporary anthropologists the discipline is not defined necessarily by a coherent theoretical body but rather by our unique methodology: fieldwork-based participant observation. It is not only the theoretical frameworks that we apply to analyze our data that define our discipline, but also (and perhaps more so) our mode of collecting it.

Yet, defining anthropology as based on participant observation invites yet another array of complications, which begin with the fact that even the term participant observation itself is internally contradicting and, as such, virtually impossible to implement. Moreover, highlighting participant observation as the essential marker of anthropology further blurs the distinction between the anthropologist as "researcher" and as "research tool," defying (or at least challenging) essential scientific concepts such as objectivity, reliability, and validity. How do we deal with this paradox?

For me, participant observation is a praxis or skill, the work of an artisan reminiscent of the craft of a painter or a carpenter. Participant observation can only be learned through practice and is based on the accumulated experience of the anthropologist himself or herself (and if lucky enough, on the ability of teachers and advisers to convey something of what they have learned, mainly through apprenticeship, mentoring, and practical training).

Participant observation contains a set of procedures that each anthropologist devises, applies, and fine-tunes in the field. As such, it is an extremely personal and volatile research tool, dynamic and fluid, in constant need of monitoring and reflection while in the field, and requires transparency in the resulting anthropological text.

In the final pages of this book I turn to describing how I did what I did in Hoi An. This, of course, is a very personal description of many private moments. But it is also a scientific account of the methods I used for my study. While some readers might find such subjectivity disturbing, unscientific, and even damaging, my goal, in the spirit of science, is to describe as accurately as I can the research tools and procedures, so as to allow the reader to critically evaluate my findings. This is yet another paradox that emerges from the centrality of methodology in anthropology: approaching participant observation in scientific terms both weakens and strengthens the ethnographic work. Therefore, in the last section of this chapter, I return to the questions of validity and reliability in anthropology.

GAINING ACCESS

On August 1998, I came to Hoi An for a preliminary visit. Though my research proposal had been approved, I still had no idea how I would get permission to conduct my research, though it seemed obvious that under the prevailing political circumstances, I absolutely needed such permission. As I was acquainted with the staff of the local tourism bureau and knew that they were friendly and spoke English, I first went to them for advice. The guides introduced me to their division head, who was sympathetic toward my project and arranged for me to meet the manager of the department of culture in the People's Committee (the Vietnamese equivalent of a municipality).

I arrived at this meeting wearing shorts, a grave sartorial offense that could have ended disastrously, but luckily my gaffe was kindly overlooked. After being thoroughly interviewed by the official with the help of an interpreter, he told me in English: "OK, I understand. I am willing to help you. If you are able to get the sponsorship of Professor Pham Van Duong[1] from Hanoi, you will be allowed to do your research." Upon my return to Israel, I contacted the Israeli consul in Hanoi who, like me, had arrived in Vietnam as a backpacker in the early nineties and had fallen in love with the country. The consul wrote an official letter to Duong, who kindly agreed to sponsor my project and arrange for my student visa. It later turned out that Duong's sponsorship was my shield and one of my most valuable assets, as the prominent scholar is well known in Hoi An and elsewhere, and mentioning his name was proof of legitimacy.

My next mistake was that I did not formally approach the People's Committee upon my arrival in town in October 1999. Here again, it was only Professor Duong's prompt intervention on my behalf that saved the day when one of my Vietnamese-language teachers was reproached for contacting me without a proper license. Eventually, after providing an "introduction letter" (*gioi thieu*) from Duong, I was summoned to the People's Committee Secretariat, where I was told that I could conduct my research freely: "Talk to anyone and ask anything. . . ."

FROM THE DOOR OF MY TENT

During my preliminary visit in 1998, there were only two foreigners living in Hoi An: a French couple who owned the first tourist-oriented bar in town, a trendy and expensive place (and still popular in 2010). They had been living in Hoi An for three years and were critical and cynical about everything (a common phenomenon among expatriates; see Arieli 2001). Among other things, I asked them about long-term residence in Hoi An. They told me that foreigners were only allowed to stay in hotels, and even though they rented a huge house in the ancient town for their bar, they themselves had had to live for years in a small room at the Hoi An Hotel.

I was rather disappointed about the prospects of having to stay in a hotel or a guesthouse and not with a family as I had originally intended. Thus, when Irit and I finally arrived in Hoi An in October 1999, I decided to check my options again. I inquired in some backpacker-restaurants about the prospects of renting a house; eventually, a restaurant owner whom I knew from previous visits took me to a friend of his who wanted to rent part of his house to foreigners, and had even put up a big sign in English. However, both told me that I would have to go to the public security bureau (the police), to fill out plenty of forms and wait some three months for approval. They also said that the rental fee would be determined by the authorities, who would transfer only some of it to the actual landlord. Wishing to keep a low profile, we decided to give up renting a house and turned to find a place in one of the family-run guesthouses that had sprung up in town.

After inspecting each of the existing sixteen guesthouses, I decided that a small but well-tended guesthouse of twelve rooms on the outskirts of town was the nicest. The receptionist told me that her older sister, Chi, owned the place and arranged for us to meet that evening in the sister's restaurant. It turned out that the sister's family had established one of the first tourist-oriented restaurants in town, pioneered in other tourist businesses, and shortly before we met, had bought the small hotel. The food we had for dinner was so good that the few doubts I had were gone, and my wife and I decided to stay at Chi's place.

Chi and her family became very close friends and my most valuable informants. Chi was keenly interested in my research, which converged with her own professional interests. Her father turned out to be not only an extremely nice and friendly person, but also an endless source of knowledge on almost any aspect of Vietnamese culture. He has a sharp and inquisitive mind, and I was initially surprised at how much he knew about the internal affairs of the town. Chi's brothers and sisters, as well as their spouses, also became close friends. Indeed, several meals and other food events to which they invited us are described and analyzed in this book.

The guesthouse was run by Chi and her family and had a staff of eight: cleaners, a laundress, a gardener, guards, and a cook. The staff, who worked seven days a week throughout the year, had their lunch together, prepared daily by the cook. After a while, we were invited to join them, and we ate with them quite often. Thus, though we did not stay with a family, I had daily access to these meals, which were structured and handled as if they were family meals (indeed, most of the employees were relatives). The staff also made a habit of inviting us to their own family events, here again allowing me to participate in varied food events in different social settings. They also became close friends with whom we often socialized.

The guesthouse and the other family businesses have prospered. Chi gradually expanded and refurbished the guesthouse, adding a new wing and later a small swimming pool and a lovely garden. More staff was taken on and quite a few of the original workers left for other jobs. However, the guesthouse is still small and maintains a friendly familial ambience, and we are treated as relatives rather than guests. Our summer stays have become a part of the guesthouse rhythm, as we spend a couple of months yearly in town, now with our children, for whom these summer visits to Hoi An are a normal part of life.

THE LANGUAGE

As there were no Vietnamese studies of any sort in Israel, I was rather worried about my language skills. In 1998, I found a Vietnamese tutor: one of the several hundred "boat people" who were found at sea by an Israeli merchant ship and granted political asylum. However, as he had fled Vietnam when he was only fourteen and had never had proper schooling, he was not really qualified for the job and these classes were hardly sufficient even for the basics.

When I visited Professor Duong in Hanoi on my way to Hoi An in October 1999, he suggested that I stay in Hanoi for some six months in order to study the language. But I could hardly have given up half a year of fieldwork and, considering my budget and plans, was unable to add an extra six months to my stay. Duong also pointed out that the Hoianese dialect is so different from standard Vietnamese (that is, the Hanoi dialect) that it would probably take a few more months to readjust. When I informed him that I would try to find a language teacher in Hoi An, he was rather doubtful and wondered if this would be possible.

He was right: finding a local language teacher turned out to be complicated. Chi suggested that it would be best to approach one of the local English teachers, with whom we could interact in English at first, and who were experienced in teaching a foreign language. The three teachers I approached turned me down, as did one of the tour guides to whom I turned in my despair. While the teachers never explained why they declined, the guide said: "I dare not try and teach you Vietnamese."

Only after a month did one of my most valued friends—seventeen-year-old Trang (whose parents run a small tourist-oriented restaurant just by our guesthouse, and who was smart, friendly, had a sense of humor, spoke good English and, most importantly, displayed a tendency to speak her mind)—suggested that we contacted her own English teacher: co (miss/teacher) Nguyet, who became one of our dearest friends and one of my most important sources of knowledge.

After discussing a timetable and some sort of curriculum with our newly found teacher, I asked co Nguyet how much she would be charging us. She replied: "I will not take any money from you. . . . For one, this is the first time in many years that foreigners come to study Vietnamese in Hoi An, and I couldn't take money for that. Moreover, the world is round. One day, my children will need help, just like you do now, and someone will take care of them." We were sitting in the tiny classroom, where co Nguyet taught some eight private classes of English daily so as to supplement her meager salary (which came roughly to the equivalent of US$25 a month at the time), struck by her generosity and finding it hard to respond. This was only the first of many instances in which Hoianese demonstrated incredible generosity, which we will never be able to repay.

As co Nguyet could teach us only twice a week, we kept looking for another teacher. Thus, we were introduced to co Dung. While co Nguyet was actually an English teacher, co Dung had a degree in Vietnamese literature and was more oriented toward Vietnamese language and culture. Moreover, co Dung was born in the North, where her Hoianese father, who had left town in the 1960s to fight for "Uncle Ho," met her Hanoian mother. Thus, she could emphasize the differences between the local dialect and the standard pronunciation, which turned out to be of great importance when we were dealing with issues of local meanings and local identity. Like co Nguyet, co Dung is a dear friend and an extremely important source of knowledge. Moreover, she is an accomplished cook and her parents' kitchen was the site of much culinary exploration.

Altogether, we had four classes per week throughout the year. Considering how difficult Vietnamese is, this was hardly sufficient. Vietnamese is an Austroasiatic language (Taylor 1983: 7–8, 43; Dang et al. 2000: 2), with six tones, eleven vowels, and plenty of diphthongs and triphthongs. Its grammar is similar to that of Thai but approximately one-third of its vocabulary is Chinese. The Vietnamese never devised an original writing system. They first borrowed Chinese characters, then modified them into the demotic *nom,* and finally adopted the Romanized *quoc ngu.* The outcome is a very complex language, extremely hard to master.

Nevertheless, as I was practicing Vietnamese for hours a day, my language skills were sufficient for the kind of research that I was conducting. While my Vietnamese language skills are hardly sufficient for researching contemporary Vietnamese media or literature, when it comes to daily interactions, in which I was primarily interested, I was doing fine.[2] Moreover, the research was conducted in two other languages in which I am more competent: English, which many of my interviewees knew to a certain extent (especially those involved with professional cooking and tourism), and the language of food, whose "local dialect" I was exploring.

FIELDWORK PRACTICES: "THE RULES"

When we arrived in Hoi An, my wife and I decided on two working rules: we would eat each meal in a different place, and we would accept any invitation, from anyone, anywhere, and to any event. While these rules turned out to be excessive and impossible to follow in the long run, following them strictly for the first few months was illuminating, providing a better understanding of the nature of the culinary sphere and the phenomenology of eating.

Having each meal in a different place meant two things. For one, in a very short period of time I accumulated a huge number of "research events": three meals per day, a coffee or two, and a snack or a glass of soy milk, not to mention the increasing number of formal events to which we were invited, accumulated into more than one hundred food events within the first month of fieldwork, and a few hundred by the end of the third.

Second, as each and every meal was taken in a different place, I constantly had to think about what was on offer, how it should be eaten, what the setting was like, who my co-diners were, and what they were doing. After a few days, I realized how tiring it was to be constantly focused and reflective when eating. I understood that mealtimes are periods of rest and relaxation, where one replenishes energy, satisfies one's cravings, pleases the senses, and has time to relax, to interact with friends and relatives, or to contemplate matters that are beyond the dining table.

I had to think constantly about what, where, and how I was eating. This was not easy. I gradually realized how automatic and taken-for-granted eating is. Indeed, the nonreflexive and taken-for-granted nature of eating is shown in this book as one of the main reasons why social and cultural processes of experimentation, challenge, and competition abound within culinary contexts.

Accepting each and every invitation meant two other things. First, the increasing number of invitations (culminating to almost a dozen feasts in the three first days of the New Year Festival, which left us on the verge of physical collapse) further enhanced my recognition of the centrality and prominence of food practices. Second, it meant that I was constantly transgressing social boundaries, entering the most private spheres of people who belonged to different classes and social echelons. While this was chaotic at first, it later turned out to be extremely fruitful, as I could compare food events in different social settings and, thus, distinguish between general principles and specific class features.

In the context of crossing social boundaries, I now mention an instance that I found illuminating:

Only a few weeks after our arrival in Hoi An, a young couple rented a little thatched shed just by our guesthouse. The husband worked as a *xe om* ("hugging wheels/vehicle," or motorbike taxi-driver, whose customers hug to avoid falling off) and his wife served very cheap coffee (1,500 dong per cup, when the going rate was 2,000–2,500 dong in most cafés), mainly to other *xe om* and blue-collar workers. One afternoon, the husband saw me walking by and invited me for a cup of coffee. I had a cup with him and went back to the guesthouse. Chi, the guesthouse owner, called me over to the reception and told me disapprovingly: "Look, you don't know this, but we don't have any contacts with people like him, nor should you."

While this event raises questions about several methodological issues (e.g., the monitoring of the ethnographer by the locals), the point that I want to make here concerns transgression of social boundaries: though I wanted to participate in culinary events that would be as varied as possible in all respects, I was expected by my friends to associate only with specific people—those whom they perceived as "appropriate"—that is, those who belonged to their own social echelon or to higher ones. While in the first stages of fieldwork I could excuse such transgressions by my ignorance, at later stages this became unacceptable. Thus, the moment arrived when I had to confront the demand that I comply with the class conceptions of my friends, a moment to which I return later.

FIELDWORK PRACTICES: DOCUMENTATION

It took me a while to figure out the most convenient modes with which to document the data. Eventually, I had devised a set of strategies that allowed for a systematic organization of what I saw, heard, and thought. At all times I had with me a small notebook (plastic-covered, to protect it from rain, sweat, and humidity), in which I noted down anything that called for precise and immediate documenting: menus, names of dishes and restaurants, proverbs, short descriptions of events, new terms, and so on. I also carried around a pocket dictionary at all times. It should be noted that very rarely did I feel odd about procuring my notebook and setting to write. While at first I used to explain that I was a researcher, with my writing actually supporting this claim, most of my friends got used to me saying "Hold on a second," as I reached for my notebook and set to write. In fact, in several instances I was told: "You should write this down," before someone answered a question or mentioned some issue. The only instances when I felt that it would be inappropriate to write notes had to do with comments made on the war and on local politics. At such moments, I had a feeling that the person with whom I was talking had confided in me, and that this confidence must not be abused.

During the first few weeks, I would sit down almost every evening with my notebook and write "proper" field notes. However, this turned out to be very difficult. For one, things tended to become repetitive: what appeared at first to be salient, different, and strange gradually became normal and routine, especially when it came to daily eating practices. Second, writing everything down turned out to be extremely time- and energy-consuming and, in fact, frustrating and disturbing. Indeed, Agar, in his painfully honest book about ethnographic fieldwork, claims: "In my opinion, field notes are the most overrated things . . . [so much] significance is attached to them . . . because they are all we have . . . it takes much longer to record everything you can remember about what just happened than it did for it to happen. In one field methods book, it is suggested that the ratio of recording time to participant observation time is six to one! . . . Field notes, then, are a problem. In their worst form, they are an attempt to vacuum up everything possible, either interrupting your observation to do so, or distorting the results when retrieving them from long-term memory. Not that you shouldn't keep notes, but they should be more focused in topic, and they eventually should be made obsolete" (Agar 1980: 112–13).

Thus, I gradually turned to write notes about specific events that were more salient and unusual.

Other extremely important sources of information were the informal, open-ended discussions I routinely had with friends and acquaintances. Most prominent were conversations with my Vietnamese teachers, with whom I discussed almost daily things that I saw and questions that I had. Here documentation was easy: my Vietnamese language notebook was open and I simply kept writing. I used to approach other people on specific matters and, here again, I would write down details during the conversation. In some cases, the texts were literally dictated, as for example, when a legend was recounted.

At first, I tried to compile the field notes on my laptop. I quickly realized that a word processor is an inadequate tool for recording these: instead of writing down what I remembered, I found myself immediately editing the material, correcting grammar and spelling mistakes, looking for proper formulations, and rephrasing my sentences. Thus, instead of noting down primary material, I was producing processed texts. I soon turned to writing down the notes in a notebook in noncorrectable ink.

Beyond writing, I used two photographing techniques: I was constantly taking slides with a stills camera, and I used a tiny video camera to record specific events. While writing the book, I often turned to my slides for information that was lacking in the field notes. The dozens of hours of video recording also turned out to be an extremely useful means of documentation: while writing the book, I could return to the videotapes and watch time and again the event I was analyzing, compare my field notes and memories ("mind-notes") to the recording, look for points that I had overlooked or missed, and freeze frames so as to inspect minute details.

Obviously, I am well aware that when choosing what to film, I was making decisions about what would be ignored and overlooked. Moreover, it was obvious that the presence of the tiny camera (my own disturbing presence notwithstanding) was noted and reacted to by those present (I used a tiny "handycam," the size of a cigarette box, which was much less intrusive and observable).

Furthermore, the cameras became a pretext for my presence: many contemporary Vietnamese events and rituals (including funerals) are nowadays meticulously video recorded and photographed, more often than not by professional photographers. My slide and video cameras singled me out as a "photographer" and, hence, made my presence acceptable. On some occasions I was actually invited to participate in family events and rituals as a photographer.

DOING FIELDWORK WITH A SPOUSE

I went to Hoi An with my wife, Irit. This fact turned out to be of great importance and calls for some elaboration. Interestingly, a few years earlier I had had
a chat with anthropologist Michael Ashkenazi, and asked him for his advice
concerning preparations for fieldwork. He responded: "You'd better get married before you go and, preferably, have a kid. . . ." Although at the time I wasn't
sure whether he was joking or serious, it turned out that he had a point.

The Vietnamese stereotype of foreigners residing in their country is that of
wealthy, single, middle-aged men, mainly interested in business, young Vietnamese women, or both. In any case, such expatriates are perceived as oppor-
tunistic and exploitative, of whom one should beware. For these very same reasons, expatriates are generally considered as legitimate targets for exploitation
(see also Higgs 2003: 84). The fact that I was married, and that my spouse had
come with me, was somehow proof that I was different. While this does not
mean that anthropology is not an exploitative discipline, it did single me out as
different from the other foreigners who frequented the town, and helped the
people overcome some of the initial suspicion with which foreigners are met.

Irit's presence was, first and foremost, encouraging. While some ethnographers "spend the first few months in the field hiding in a guesthouse room and
reading everything Agatha Christie ever wrote" (Agar 1980: 39), I was not
alone: during the first few months we went together everywhere. In this respect, it was much easier to confront the new environment and meet new people. Moreover, there was always another pair of eyes and ears that could offer
alternative observations and someone else to talk to and discuss what I saw and
thought.

The fact that I had my spouse with me was also important in terms of my
research interests. The Hoianese culinary sphere is clearly feminine, and men
are hardly involved with cooking (unless they work as professional chefs).
Thus, when I inquired about one of the contributors to a book about Hoianese
food, one of my teachers said with a disapproving facial expression: "He likes
cooking, and goes everyday to the market instead of his wife . . . maybe he is not
a real man." Indeed, the relations between ethnographers and the culinary
sphere are often complex. A good example is Sutton's (1997) short paper on the
problems he faced while doing fieldwork in a Greek island, due to the fact that
he was a vegetarian. Sutton points out that Greek masculinity is intertwined
with meat consumption, and being a vegetarian might have defined him as
"not-masculine" or even as gay, a tagging that would have impaired his ability
to conduct his research. However, the fact that he was married served as proof
of his masculinity and led to the interpretation of his vegetarianism as an expression of his responsibilities as a husband and a good Christian. Similarly, I

believe that Irit's presence was a clear indication that though I was interested in food and eating, and though I spent much of my time in feminine spheres and with female informants, there was "no problem" with my gender and/or my intentions.

Irit's presence removed yet another pressure: that of being single in a family-centered society. A single researcher in her early forties who had spent a few weeks doing research in Hoi An was constantly questioned as to why she was single and why she had no children. At some stage, she was approached by a local lesbian couple and the entire situation became quite stressful for her. Moreover, while the complications resulting from being a single person in the field are thoroughly discussed by Kulick and Willson (1995) in their book focused on sex in the context of anthropological fieldwork, the fact that my wife was with me meant that I could not be targeted as a potential husband and as a "one-way ticket" for some local girl (and her family), a quite common event in contemporary Hoi An.

As we grew used to living in Hoi An, Irit, who had her own interests to pursue, became tired of accompanying me and, apart from her own research project (she conducted participant observation in a kindergarten for her own studies), invested most of her energy into developing friendships. Interestingly, while I did my best to maintain all kinds of social contacts and relations, the fact is that the people that Irit liked became not only our closest friends but also the most valuable contributors to my research.

The fact that Irit is a practicing Jew and keeps the Kashrut dietary laws turned out to be a demanding yet valuable asset: each and every time she had something to eat we had to figure out exactly what the ingredients were. While this might seem like an obvious demand from a food anthropologist, the fact is that fastidiously analyzing each and every bite of food soon becomes frustrating and tiring. However, we had no choice but to keep up this inspection during the entire fieldwork period, constantly collecting more data that would otherwise have been overlooked. Moreover, a partial solution for the demands of Kashrut was opting for vegetarian restaurants, which are numerous in Vietnam in the context of Buddhism. Here again, a whole culinary world was revealed to me, along with its religious and moral implications, which would most probably have remained hidden had not Irit been following the Kashrut restrictions. Finally, it should be noted that Irit's sweet tooth, as opposed to my dislike of sweets, led to encounters with a huge array of Vietnamese sweet snacks, fruit juices and shakes, ice creams, and the various culinary establishments that provide them.

Ashkenazi's suggestion turned out to be extremely important: despite the added challenges (such as the need to pay attention to one's spouse and to ac-

commodate his/her wishes, which may not necessarily be in line with the research goals), the presence of a spouse in the field is not only nice, but potentially very productive.

BODY IMAGES

Irit's presence called my attention to another issue relevant to my field of research, and one that I would have probably ignored: that of body image. After a
few weeks of fieldwork, Irit began complaining that she was becoming too fat. I
insisted that she was looking great, which was the perfect truth according to
Israeli/Western standards. However, I was intrigued by the fact that a good-
looking person who was generally satisfied with her looks would suddenly say
that she feels "big, clumsy, and fat."

It turned out that Irit was constantly comparing her own physique to that of
the Vietnamese women around us. Indeed, when compared to the slender
bodies of the Vietnamese and to their gentle movements, we were large and
somewhat awkward. Add to this our tendency to perspire, the smell of our
sweat, our body hair, and our Israeli manner of filling in empty spaces with
our bodies and "auras," as compared to the Vietnamese tendency to "converge"
in the presence of others, it becomes obvious why she was feeling "big, clumsy
and fat."

While Hall (1995) describes how Asian American women are frustrated by
the Caucasian–American–European beauty ideals, and how they turn to plastic surgery and/or develop eating disorders, we were experiencing a similar
feeling in the opposite context: it was our Caucasian bodies that did not adhere
to the local standards of beauty, and we were developing complexes and devis-
ing strategies to overcome these disturbing feelings.

Psychological stress notwithstanding, the sad fact was that it was I who was
actually gaining weight: surrounded by food all day long and constantly encouraged to eat more, I suddenly realized that I was getting plumper by the day.
Luckily, just as I was idly contemplating the unexpected toll that science was
imposing on my body, one of my Hoianese friends asked me if I would like to
jog with him on the beach. I happily complied and then he said, "So tomorrow
at 4:00 AM by the gate? . . ." Though I was shocked by the early hour, I decided
to comply, and that was how I discovered an entire new aspect of Hoianese
lifestyle: predawn exercising on the beach.

It turned out that thousands of Hoianese head daily to the beach for predawn jogs, exercise, yoga, tai chi, ball games, and a dip in the shallow waters (as
most Hoianese cannot swim and would not dare the deep waters). However, as
soon as the first ray of sun would appear, everyone would rush home, and when

the sun would rise, there would be only a few fishermen and crab hunters left on the beach. A couple of hours later, the first Western tourists would arrive at the beach, a process that is reversed in the afternoon: the sun sets, the tourists leave and the locals arrive. . . .

Obviously, as at any Vietnamese public gathering, there is a whole array of dishes specifically prepared for those early beachgoers: roasted sweet potatoes, char-grilled baguettes, noodles, and soy milk are sold next to the bicycle racks, while *chao ngeo*—clam rice-porridge, is sold right on the beach. I would ride my bike every morning to the beach, where I would jog and swim. Then I would have a warm glass of soy milk that, for 500 dong (in the year 2000), included a review of the morning news offered by the stall owner, with an emphasis on Israeli affairs.

Daily exercise is imperative for food scholars' health, and jogging became an integral part of my life, allowing me to enjoy my research without impairing my health or letting me developing eating disorders. Methodologically, however, I learned that whenever engaging in a new activity, the ethnographer is bound to encounter new cultural and social horizons that are somehow always relevant.

INFORMANTS AND THE THINGS THEY SAY

Throughout the chapters I quote friends, acquaintances, and people whom I met by chance. Contemporary anthropology insists that the voices of those being studied should be heard loudly and clearly along with the ethnography, as authentic local knowledge can only be found in what the locals say. While the assumption that the informants always verbally express what they know is dubious (as some cultures are less verbal than the Judeo-Christian text-oriented interpretative cultures with which contemporary anthropology is often engaged), an important issue that is rarely discussed in this context is the reliability of these voices (see Metcalf's [2002] *They Lie, We Lie*).

Obviously, the locals have their own agendas and interests, as well as social images that they wish to project (and see Bohannan 1999; Rabinaw 1977; Turner 1960). In some instances, things simply get confused and it is extremely hard to understand why someone said whatever was said, and how accurate it was. I will briefly sketch an event that left me perplexed and confused at the time. I have decided to leave it open-ended, so as to allow readers to develop their own sense of it.

Trang was my first "informant." I met her in her parents' restaurant, just a few steps from our guesthouse. Friendly, smart, outspoken, and very fluent in English, she told us that she was twenty-one, studying to be an English teacher at Danang Teachers' College.

One afternoon, after only a few weeks in Hoi An, Irit came home from the market and told me that she was approached by a high-school student called Hanh, who said that she was our neighbor and invited us for a visit.

Hanh was waiting downstairs and we followed her on a sandy path that led to some rural houses right behind our guesthouse. We crossed some patches of sweet potato and passed some large bamboo bushes before entering the small house. This was actually our first visit to a rural house, and we were overwhelmed by its grim plainness: the tiny size, the concrete floor, the old furniture with no upholstery, the greyish walls. Hanh's mother and sisters were surprised to see us, yet very enthusiastic. However, as none of our hosts knew any English (besides "Would you like to come to my house?"), and our Vietnamese was not much better at the time, the conversation was quite awkward.

"What does your father do?" I asked Hanh. After consulting her mother, she told me something in Vietnamese, but I didn't understand. We reached for the dictionary but this didn't help either. "Is he a farmer?" I asked, pointing to the word in the dictionary. After a second of hesitation, Hanh said "Yes, yes, a farmer! . . ." "So where is your *con trau* [water buffalo]?" I wondered. After a short consultation Hanh said: "no *con trau*." "Then how do you till your rice fields?" I asked, using my palms to demonstrate what I meant. After a distressed exchange of looks, our host took us out, pointed to a hoe with a long wooden handle and demonstrated hoeing.

I was shocked. My own agricultural background made it clear that she was talking about plain slavery. I simply couldn't imagine hoeing a rice field.

That evening, as we were walking to town, we saw Hanh talking to Trang. We stopped and told Trang that we had visited Hanh's home. Then I asked Trang to translate, and asked again about hoeing the rice field and the water buffalo. Trang looked puzzled for a while and then turned to talk in Vietnamese with the obviously distressed Hanh. Then she burst in laughter and told me: "You know, the father of this girl works for the government. They told you, but you didn't understand. So when you asked if he was a farmer, they just said "yes," to get it over with, but you asked about the water buffalo and they had to tell you that they were hoeing like that. They are not farmers, and no one hoes rice fields. . . ."

I was surprised and embarrassed. At that moment, Trang's mother came over and asked me how I met Trang's classmate. "Classmate?" I asked, "but Hanh is only fifteen and goes to high school in Hoi An, while Trang is twenty-one and studies in the Teachers' College in Danang!" "Oh no," Trang's mother replied, "Trang is only sixteen and studies here. She is not a college student." At that stage, everyone became silent, and after a couple of awkward minutes, we said that we had to go and we left. While I was trying to figure out what was going on, I suddenly realized that Irit was very upset: "Why did Trang lie to us?" she kept asking, "and why did Hanh ask us to visit her house? Just to have a laugh? . . ."

The next day we saw Trang sitting on the sidewalk in front of her house, wearing "headache stickers" with camphor oil on her temples, her eyes red from crying. When she saw us, she ran to us and burst in tears again. We hugged her and told her that everything was all right, and that we understood that she pretended to be older so that we would stay her friends, and she nodded her head, sobbing. "And yet," Irit said, "you shouldn't have lied to us." Trang nodded her head again, and I asked: "Do people often lie here?" "Yes!" she replied passionately, "people here lie all the time. . . ."

WHO OWNS THE FIELD?

In order to further expose the complex and all-too-often problematic relations between the ethnographer and the locals, I now present another event that at the time seemed borrowed from a introductory textbook in anthropology. I describe this specific event as it deals with questions and reservations raised by my local friends regarding the ownership of knowledge as well as authority to interpret it. Here again, I refrain from offering my own interpretation.

We met Quynh at her parents' vegetarian restaurant not long after our arrival in town. She was very friendly and invited us to her in-laws' house, to meet her husband. Quynh and Irit immediately hit it off, while I was very impressed with Hoang, her husband, who is confined to a wheelchair yet managed to study and to set up a prosperous computer school, a remarkable achievement for a disabled person anywhere, but virtually impossible in Vietnam. The fact that Quynh was not disabled added to my respect and fondness for both of them. Moreover, Hoang was a year older than me while Quynh and Irit were the same age. Like us, they were recently married. Becoming friends was only natural, as they were very similar to us in so many ways.

Several months later and well into fieldwork, I developed an interest in the ways by which gender is produced, reproduced, and negotiated in culinary contexts. I spent some afternoons in the notorious *pho Hong Kong* ("Hong Kong Street"), a cluster of garden cafés by the river, whose tiny flickering lights, when reflecting in the water, were said to look like Hong Kong harbor (a far-fetched comparison). Young Hoianese would gather in these cafés, reputedly because they could find some privacy in the secluded darkness, especially at night, and engage in intimate activities. As opposed to brothel cafés, which are called *cafe om* ("hugging cafés"), these garden cafés are more about love and romance than about sex and, therefore, I suggested terming them *cafe hon* ("kissing cafés").

One afternoon, Hoang called and invited us for lunch the next day. While this was quite a frequent occurrence, he also mentioned that there would be other guests for lunch, and named one of our teachers, as well as the senior tour guide in the Department of Culture.

Lunch over, Hoang turned to me and said in a very formal manner: "Now that you are an important man, as you are going to write a book about Hoi An, we have decided to tell you something. We think that you shouldn't go to cafés and write about things such as *cafe om* or *cafe hon*. You are supposed to study culture (*van hoa*), and not these things. Therefore, we have decided to tell you that from now on you should concentrate on serious matters and talk only to people who know about culture. And if you need to talk to someone, you should talk to us."

After a few seconds of silence, in which I tried to contain my surprise and, to be honest, my laughter, I told them that I love Hoi An and that I would never do anything that might embarrass the Hoianese. However, I tried to explain that the Confucian term *van hoa,* which is used in contemporary Vietnam to denote "culture," actually means "highbrow culture" and does not encompass the culture I was after, which, I tried to point out, was more *binh dan* (popular). Therefore, I explained, there couldn't be any place, subject, or person that does not belong to the sphere of culture. I also tried to explain that I was seeking "real" Vietnam, and not some fake old-fashioned image that nobody cares about.

I do not know if I convinced them or whether, as in so many other instances, they thought that I was strange and even a little stupid, but the subject was not raised again.

RECIPROCITY

While it is by now generally accepted that complete objectivity is an unattainable goal in scientific research and that the researcher's mere presence influences and changes the phenomena under observation, I think that anthropologists, due to their deep personal involvement with their subjects of research, "the locals," have no choice but to take an active role in certain instances of their local friends' lives. While this might seem like a problematic distortion of the social reality that anthropologists are essentially seeking, I think that anthropologists are morally obliged to reciprocate somehow for the hospitality they enjoy and the information they obtain (which eventually leads to their own professional and socioeconomic success). Moreover, when becoming involved with the lives of local friends and acquaintances, and when trying to understand their needs, anthropologists not only become more familiar with the intimate aspects of life in "their field," but also have to face the practicalities and constraints of the lived-in world of the locals, as well as the ways in which they deal with them.

I am not talking here about giving some tobacco in exchange for stories, as Laura Bohannan or Evans-Pritchard did, or about paying, directly or indirectly, for interpretation and guiding services (as Rabinow did, paying Ali in cash and taking him in his car to his relatives' events), nor about lending or giving money to someone in need (which I did several times). What I am talking about is sharing with the locals exclusive knowledge that might help them in the long run. Indeed, I made it clear to my friends that I would be more than willing to be consulted on matters in which I had some experience, specifically in relation to tourism.

Thus, for example, when Chi wanted to redecorate the guesthouse, she first asked me to go with her to the luxurious Furama Resort in Danang, where my out-of-date tour-guide card gained us access and a chance to get a glimpse at an international standard hotel. Then we went together to shop for decorations. While Chi didn't really need me for shopping, as her taste and aesthetic outlook clearly surpassed mine, I was glad that I could help. Chi also invited me several times to her cooking classes, and asked for my advice and suggestions. We would have long discussions about my findings concerning the Vietnamese and Hoianese cooking, which, she told me, helped her develop her own understanding of what she was doing and improved her abilities in introducing Vietnamese cuisine to her clients. Chi's family members, who are pioneering and innovative entrepreneurs, also consulted me occasionally about new business opportunities. Here again, they were more knowledgeable than I was on such matters, yet the fact that they did seek my advice suggests that it did have some value.

I also helped Trang rewrite her restaurant menu. In fact, most tourist-oriented restaurants in Hoi An simply photocopy (practically steal) existing menus from other places, leading to a uniform and dull presentation of the Hoianese cuisine despite the actual variety of local dishes. I suggested that we rewrite the menu, highlighting local specialties and explaining briefly what exactly they were made of. While for me this was some kind of a "laboratory test," as I could observe whether tourists change their food-consumption patterns when they have a better understanding of what is on offer, the new menu turned out to be a commercial success, as the stressed "local specialties," which were actually cheaper and more convenient to prepare, were ordered very frequently. I also taught Trang's mother, upon her request, how to cook backpackers' favorites such as spaghetti with tomato sauce, garlic bread, and lassi.

However, my biggest achievement had to do with Hoang, the disabled friend who ran a computer school. One morning, I saw a job advertised in the English-language newspaper, *Vietnam News:* an American NGO working with local organizations of people with disabilities was looking for a national coordinator. I rushed to Hoang's house and we sat down to write a CV and a cover letter. While Hoang was quite surprised with the way I presented his life and life goals, he was pleased with the outcome and so was the NGO. He was invited with his wife to Hanoi, where he was offered the job.

As Hoang and Quynh wanted to stay with their families in Hoi An and wouldn't give up the computer business, they declined the offer. But, with the help of the NGO, they set up a program for training handicapped Hoianese youngsters as Internet operators. Further support from the People's Committee ensured that many of the trainees found jobs in Internet cafés, while others were hired by various government agencies in town. Later on, Hoang and Quynh set up a souvenir shop that sells handicrafts produced by handicapped people from all over the country. In 2010, they were employing more than two hundred disabled employees in different projects. While this project had nothing to do with my research, this is the contribution about which I feel most happy and proud.

VALIDITY AND RELIABILITY IN ANTHROPOLOGY

One of the most disturbing questions that preoccupied me when I returned from Hoi An at the end of 2000 was "What would have happened had we rented a room elsewhere? . . . in another guesthouse? . . . on another street? . . . how would my ethnography have looked had I not met Trang, Chi, co Dung, co Nguyet, Quynh, and Hoang? . . . or if I wouldn't have participated in Cu's father worship, Bac and Trung's wedding, lunches at the guesthouse? . . ." An apparently serendipitous decision such as a place to stay had a tremendous effect on the data I collected and, therefore, must have affected the outcome of my research.

Another disturbing question was "What would have happened had someone else done exactly what I did? . . . lived in the same guesthouse? . . . asked the same questions? . . . met the same people? . . . would he or she have arrived at the same conclusions? . . ." It is clear to me that another person would have necessarily experienced and understood things differently, even if we shared to a certain extent personal attributes (such as age, gender, ethnicity, nationality, religion, marital status).

It is obvious that another anthropologist, under different circumstances (such as having a different place to stay) would have produced a very different ethnography. This would cast doubt not only on the reliability and validity of my own work, but also on the entire discipline, I, however, had a chance to actually check whether my work was, at least to a certain extent, valid and reliable.

In 2005 I noticed that one of the contributors to the Vietnamese Studies Group Web list had an Israeli name. I was excited to find at last another Israeli scholar interested in Vietnam and immediately e-mailed her, introducing myself and my work. To my surprise, it turned out that she was also an anthropologist, and that she was conducting fieldwork toward her Ph.D. dissertation in Danang, only 30 km from Hoi An.

She wrote that she was interested, among other things, in ancestor worship, so I sent her a draft of chapter 4. Her panicked response was that I described exactly what she wanted to describe and analyzed the ceremonies just as she intended to, and that now, as she realized that there was no novelty in her findings, she was worried about the prospect of writing a good dissertation.

While I assured her that she could peacefully continue with her work, which was not focused on food but on childhood, as she was bound to produce a very different text, I also pointed out that inadvertently we had tested the untestable: when fieldwork is conducted "properly"—that is, rigorously, attentively, and patiently—and when the field notes are accurate and rich, when the ethnography is based on these field notes, and when the ethnographer carefully distinguishes between what he saw and heard and what he thinks about what he saw and heard, the resulting text is valid and reliable.

Glossary

an chay	eat vegetarian
an cuoi	"eat" the wedding
an het	finish the food
an hoi	eating and asking for marriage
an Tet	"eat" *Tet* invitation to visit a family at *Tet*
banh bao banh vac	"white rose" dumpling set
banh beo	small steamed rice cakes topped with shrimp paste
banh chung	boiled cake
banh day	elastic cake; also *banh giay*
banh deo	elastic moon cakes
banh it la gai	sticky rice cake
banh kem	cream cake
banh khoi	smoking pancake (Hue version of *banh xeo*)
banh mat trang	mooncakes
banh mi	bread/baguette
banh nuong	baked moon cake
banh phong tom	puffed shrimp crackers
banh phu te	wife and husband cake
banh Tet	Tet rice cake
banh tom	shrimp crackers
banh trang	rice crackers
banh trang day	a triple-layered rice cracker made of a soft rice paper sandwiched in between two *banh trang*
banh u tro	small ash cakes
banh uoc	soft steamed flat rice noodles
banh xeo	sizzling pancake
beo	fatty (of food)
bit tet	beef steak
bun	rice vermicelli

bun chay	vegetarian rice vermicelli
bun gao Phuoc Kien	Fujian-style rice vermicelli
bun xao dau tay	rice vermicelli sautéed with green beans
ca com	"rice fish"; long-jawed anchovy
ca loc	Snake-headed mullet; catfish
ca phe	coffee
ca phe den	black coffee
ca phe sua	coffee with milk
ca ri	curry, Vietnamese style
ca thu	mackerel
ca thu chien	fried mackerel
ca xot ca chua	fish in tomato sauce
cai mam	round food tray
cai noi	wok
cam	gold
can giup	have to help
canh	soup (Vietnamese-style)
canh bi	pumpkin soup
canh cary khoai gio heo	pork and potato curry
canh chay	vegetarian soup
canh chua	sour (fish) soup
canh nep lay huyet heo	sticky rice soup with curdled pig's blood
canh rau muong	morning glory soup
cao lau	Hoi An's special noodle dish
ca ri	curry; also *cary*
ca ri banh mi	curry served with baguette
cay neu	Tet poles
cha	pork cold cuts; pork meatloaf or terrine
cha con con	*cha* served in the shape of a dancing bird
chao	rice porridge/congee
chao ga	chicken congee
chao vit	duck congee
chay	vegetarian
che	sweets
che ke	sweet sorghum porridge
chia bun	"divide the sadness"; share the grief
cho lang	village market
cho vui	for fun
chom chom	rambutans
chuoi	banana

com	steamed rice
com bui	"dusty rice"; rice meal bought from street vendors
com ga	chicken rice dish
com nep	sticky rice
con dao	large cleaver
cung	worship
cung nha moi	new house ceremony
cuon	rolled, with reference to rice paper or fresh steamed rice wraps
dac san	local specialties
dai ban	friends' party; "inviting friends"; part of wedding celebrations
dam cuoi	wedding; the wedding procession of the groom's family to the bride's house
dam gio	ancestor worship; gathering for death anniversary
dam hoi	asking for marriage, also termed *an hoi*
dan toc	ethnic minority
dat huong lua	incense and fire land
dat nuoc	country, lit., land and water; also *nong nuoc* (mountains and water) or simply *nuoc* (water)
dau hu	tofu
dau noi	"pot head"; the place of the senior female who is in charge of distributing the rice
dau tay ca rot cu den tron bo	West[ern] beans, carrots and black beets mixed in butter
dau tay xao thap cam	mixed fried green beans
dip ca	fish leaf herb
doi moi	renovation; the economic reforms launched in 1986 that marked transition from a centrally planned economy to a market-oriented one
dong xuan ruc ro	"splendid eastern spring" dish
fan	steamed rice (Chinese)
ga	chicken
ga chien mam	fried chicken in fish sauce
ga hap hanh	steamed chicken with onions
ga quang dong	Quang Dong chicken
ga sot sua	chicken cooked in milk
ga ta	"our chicken," lean, free range local variety
ga tay	"Western chicken," industrially farmed chicken
gan nam xao he Da Lat	liver sautéed with mushrooms and Dalat leeks
gao	husked rice
gao nep	glutinous rice

gao te	plain rice
gia dinh	(extended) family
gioi thieu	introduction/to introduce
giua mam	"middle of the tray"; position of the father or senior male at the dining table or area
goi du du	green papaya salad
goi ngo sen	lotus stem salad
hai lo	"bribe money" given to unicorn troupe dancers
hat dua	watermelon seeds roasted as snacks
Heineken va cua	Heineken-and-crab wedding
hen	clams
heo quay banh bao	pork dumplings
ho khau	household registry
hoa dao	(pink) peach blossom
hoa mai	(yellow) apricot blossom
Hoang Ngoc	the Jade Emperor
hoanh thanh	wontons
hoi than	friendly gathering (in weddings)
hot vit lon	half-hatched duck eggs
hu tieu	rice noodle dish
hung cu	asafoetida
huong thom	fragrance
khai vi	starters
khan	traditional Vietnamese turban
kho	"dry," denoting roasted, fried or stir-fried dish
khong ngon	not tasty
kim ngoc man duong	"house full of jade and gold"; a dish
lac	*lach* or canal
la gu	ragout; stew
la gu thit cuu	mutton ragout
lam re	working groom, when the prospective groom was required to live and work for his future in-laws as part of the dowry agreement
la tia to	perilla
le cuoi	third ceremony in wedding sequence, in which the bride's family would set the terms of the wedding
le xem mat	the ceremony of seeing the faces
lo banh mi	oven for baking bread
long an	longan
long bau tu gan heo luoc	boiled pork innards

lua	rice seedlings
Luc Tanh Vuong Gia	the Six Princes/elders of the Phouc Kien Hoianese
mam cai	special, semi-fermented, unfiltered fish sauce used as a dip
mam nem	fermented fish sauce dip
map	fat
mi ga	chicken noodle soup
mi Quang Nam	*mi quang* or Quang Nam Province noodles; noodle specialty of the province
mon an	"things to eat"; dishes
muc chay	vegetarian squid
muc hap	steamed cuttlefish
mung mot	black moon night
mut quat	candied kumquats
Nam Tien	"marching south"; historical migration of Northerners to the South
nem	pork sausage
nep–te	lit., "sticky rice–plain rice"; denotes yoking of opposites
ngay ram	full moon days; worship days
ngo diec	also *ngo om*
ngo om	paddy herb; see also *ngo diec*
ngo sen tron	lotus-stem salad
ngon hon	tastier
ngong ro ti	roast goose
ngu hanh	cosmological theory of the five elements
ngu luan	Confucian model of the "five human relationships"
ngu vi	the five tastes
ngu vi tan	Five stimulating spices (in Buddhism)
nha	house/household
nha nuoc	government; lit., house and water; also country
nha que	countryside
nhi trai	black and full moon nights
nho	small
noi tuong	"general of the interior" (woman)
nom chu nom	obsolete Sino-Vietnamese alphabet
nong	hot; warming food
nuoc leo	gravy
nuoc mam	fish sauce
nuoc mam cham	fish sauce diluted with water and lime juice, seasoned with sugar, ginger, and chilies
nuoc mam nhi	virgin fish sauce

Ong Tao	the Kitchen God
pa te	paté
pho	noodle soup made with beef or chicken
pho co	ancient quarter
phuong hoang sao	"perched phoenix" dish
quan chay	vegetarian restaurant
quan nhau	drinking place (where snacks are served to go along with the alcohol)
que huong	home, place of birth
quoc ngu	romanized Vietnamese alphabet
ragu	ragout; stew
ram	spring rolls filled with pork, mushrooms, and rice vermicelli
ram chay	vegetarian spring roll
ram tam huu	"three friends" spring roll
rau	fresh greens
rau gien	amaranth
rau muong	water morning glory
rau song	mixed fresh greens and herbs
ruoc dau	escorting the daughter-in-law procession
ruou dao	mulberry liqueur
ruou gao	rice alcohol
ruou quat	kumquat liqueur
sam seng	triple sacrifice
San Lao	Chinese for the Three Old Men: Phuoc, Loc, Tho (happiness, prosperity, longevity)
si ro dao	mulberry syrup
sup bap tom cua	corn, shrimp, and crab soup
tach cuoi	terms of the wedding
Tam Giao dong Nguyen	three religions from the same source
tam hap trai thom	silkworms steamed with pineapple
tao	peach
tay	Western; Westerner
te to hong	offering of the red string in the bride's house
Tet	used alone, it signifies the Vietnamese (Lunar) New Year
Tet Doan Ngo	Summer Festival
Tet Nguyen Dan	Vietnamese New Year
Tet Trung Thu	Mid-Autumn Festival
thay	monk, teacher
than pho	city

thang long	soaring dragon or pitaya, the bright pink cactus fruit
thay boi	fortuneteller; geomancer
thit bo nuong me	grilled beef with sesame seeds
thit bo tai	rare roast beef
thit heo luoc	boiled pork
thit heo nuong	roasted pork
thit nuong	grilled meat on skewers
thit rung	jungle meat
tho	longevity
thom	aroma
tom cua fit bot	batter-fried squid and crabs
tom nuong	grilled or fried prawns
trai cay	mixed fruit
trai gioi	ritual purification before imperial sacrifice
trang mien	"rinse the mouth"—dessert
trau cau	betel quid
tron	toss, as in a salad
tsai	side dishes; lit., "vegetables" (Chinese)
tuong	thick fermented bean sauce
tuong ot	sweet and spicy chili paste
vi	taste
Viet Kieu	overseas Vietnamese
vit bat thao	duck in medicinal herbs
vo nho	minor wife
vui	lighthearted fun
xa lach	lettuce
xin moi	please
xoi	steamed glutinous rice garnished with peanuts, sugar, meat, and chili paste
xoi dau xanh	steamed glutinous rice with beans
xuong bep	descend to the kitchen

Notes

INTRODUCTION

1. This restructuring was intended to advance Hoi An's status from "town" (*ti xa*) to "city" (*thanh pho*).

2. Vietnamese citizens must be listed on a household registry (*ho khau*), maintained by the Public Security Bureau.

3. The *que* in the hamlet's name means "cinnamon."

4. See United Nations Educational, Scientific and Cultural Organization (UNESCO), "Decision 23COM VIIIC.1—Hoi An Ancient Town (Viet Nam)," available at http://whc.unesco.org/en/decisions/2637.

5. Fourth-to-first millennia BCE according to K. V. Nguyen (1993: 14); the second millennium BC to the second century CE, according to Wheeler (2006).

6. The Indianized states of Southeast Asia (which includes the Khmer kingdoms) were independent indigenous principalities, heavily influenced by Hindu and Buddhist cosmology, politics, and culture.

7. Co Nguyet (my Vietnamese teacher) suggested that the name Faifo originated from the habit of the merchants navigating the river to ask, "*Co* phai pho *khong*?" ("is this the town yet?"). Wheeler (personal communication) suggests that it is most likely that the term came from another Chinese town such as Hiu'an in Fujian Province or An Hoi in Guangzhou.

8. A variant account describes *quoc ngu* as initially developed by an unknown Spanish missionary or missionaries, probably with the help of local converts, during the late sixteenth century, and adopted and popularized only during the early twentieth century (Jamieson 1995: 67).

9. The bishop of Hoi An at the time of writing had been the personal priest of Ngo Dinh Diem, the first president of the Republic of Vietnam.

10. While Hoi An was relatively safe during the war, two of war's worst atrocities, the Ha My and My Lai massacres, took place in the area (Ha My is only 15 km north of Hoi An and My Lai is 60 km to the south), while major battles were fought in Central Vietnam (Kwon 2006).

11. While anthropological convention applies the term *informants* to those locals who "supply information," a term that enhances the "scientific" seriousness of the text, my methodology is based on long-term personal relations that go far beyond

instrumental gathering of data. I therefore use the terms *friends, acquaintances, people I talked to, Hoianese,* or pseudonyms when referring to those who generously shared their knowledge and ideas with me.

12. The first tourist-oriented clothes shop in Hoi An was opened in the early 1990s. In 1995, the town was already known among backpackers as "the place where you make clothes." In 1999, there were close to one hundred shops. In 2007 I was given any number between four hundred and eight hundred shops. This industry has an overwhelming presence and impact.

13. This term refers to all Westerners, including Israelis.

14. Charles Wheeler (personal communication) suggests that port names in general are advertisements to potential shippers and merchants. Hence "peaceful congregation" had very little to do with self-identification, but was intended to attract and lure potential customers. I further explore this idea in chapter 3, when dealing with Hoi An's local specialties.

1. DECIPHERING THE HOIANESE MEAL

1. The parents of a Hoianese friend were utterly surprised when I told them that dogs in Israel are mostly fed meat and that our dog would not even consider eating rice.

2. The law now requires that all the dead must be buried in communal cemeteries, which are also often located among the rice fields.

3. *Lac* probably derives from the Vietnamese word *lach,* which stands for ditch, canal, or waterway (Taylor 1983: 10). Thus, the early Vietnamese named themselves after the rice irrigation system they had developed, stressing the utmost importance of rice farming in their culture.

4. According to Huard and Durand (1998: 165), there were well over two thousand varieties and subvarieties of rice grown, sold, and consumed in the Vietnam in the late 1940s.

5. Bread was probably as important in the Judeo-Christian world as rice still is in Vietnam, as suggested by the Jewish custom of blessing the food only when bread is present and by the transformation of bread in the sacrament. However, meat lies at the center of the contemporary Western meal, clearly overshadowing bread as the epitome of the meal (see Douglas 1975; Adams 1990; Gvion-Rosenberg 1990; Fiddes 1991).

6. In 2000, local fishermen refused to equip their boats with life jackets because they were worried that it might offend Tien Hau, the goddess of sailors and seafarers. The provincial authorities adroitly overcame this impasse by supplying life jackets imprinted with the image of the goddess.

7. M. Steinglass, "Overfished Vietnam Subsidizes More Fishing Boats," Voice of America News, May 8, 2008, http://www.voanews.com/english/archive/2008-05/2008-05-08-voa15.cfm.

8. This trend toward shrimp aquaculture, encouraged by the central and local governments for its high income and export potential, is already backfiring, according to some foreign environmentalists I met, as these ponds tend to be unhygienic and highly polluting, threatening the quality of riparian and coastal waters.

9. For home consumption, mackerel and other large fish are rarely bought whole. One or two slices or steaks, each weighing about 100 grams, would be bought for a family meal for several adults and children.

10. This is in contrast to Jean, the only foreign restaurant owner in Hoi An in 1998, who said, "I can't trust the local suppliers. In order to maintain the integrity of my menu, I have to buy large quantities of fish whenever they are available and then fillet and freeze them." So despite the fact that his fish restaurant was situated next to one of the largest fish markets in central Vietnam, he regularly served frozen fish.

11. While a comparison of *nuoc mam* to wine is due, "one impassioned Vietnamese [argued that] the comparison is inadequate, since fish sauce is a more sophisticated product than wine: only a tiny number of wines survive longer than fifty years, whereas fish sauce continues to grow in flavor and complexity indefinitely. The wood of the barrels in which it ferments, the quality of the anchovies and the salt from which it is made, the weather and the temperature during the fermentation process—all these factors, he explains with a faraway look in his eyes, affect the flavor of the finished product. 'The producer,' he continues, 'knows that the sauce is ready for bottling when the flies have stopped swarming over the rotting brew'" (*Economist,* December 21, 2002, p. 76).

12. Some of my Hoianese friends were careful to peel apples and pears imported from China because "the Chinese use very strong pesticides to get such beautiful fruits." Thus, a deep sense of pollution, which is cultural in essence, can manifest itself in various guises.

13. In 2006 I was told by some friends that they only buy greens with holes in them: "Nowadays farmers use extremely poisonous pesticides, which make for perfect leaves but poison the eaters. So we prefer pecked-at leaves, as bug-bites suggest that these chemicals were not used. . . ."

2. THE SOCIAL DYNAMICS OF THE HOME MEAL

1. Ashkenazi and Jacob (2000: 139–66) present aesthetics as a central, meaningful element of Japanese cuisine, as do other anthropologists dealing with Japanese foodways (Allison 1991; Noguchi 1994); Cohen and Avieli (2004) stress the importance of aesthetics (or lack thereof) in shaping tourists' attitudes toward "local food" at tourist destinations.

2. Co Dung's kitchen was thoroughly refurbished in 2004, in line with processes of change that will be discussed shortly.

3. Chi Van was one of my most important informants. Her family (husband and two children) belong to the Hoianese newly emerging working class: rice farmers who gradually shift into blue-collar professions. Van kept inviting me to food events at her home, as well as in the houses of her kin and neighbors, thus introducing me to the culinary practices of this specific social echelon.

4. Urban houses in Vietnam were traditionally very long and narrow, as the front of the house facing the street is often used for trading and, thus, is much more expensive. In congested urban areas, houses might measure 3 m in width and 30 m in length. With affluence, these houses become ever higher, with three floors almost the

norm in Hoi An. The outcome is huge houses, of some 300 m², whose higher floors are essentially empty and serve, above all, to show off wealth and sophistication.

5. Admittedly, he made some serious errors, such as reserving the best section of the house (the front room on the second floor) as a bedroom for his parents-in-law. They refused to use that room, as the best place in the house should be reserved for the ancestral altar. Moreover, grandparents are supposed to sleep separately, as a shared bedroom implies an active sex life, which is deemed inappropriate in the elderly (and see Baker 1979: 5 for a similar custom in China). The most serious faux pas was the building of an en-suite toilet. Not only is this an unknown arrangement since toilets are polluting and traditionally built outside or, nowadays, at the back of the house, but it also prevented the parents from turning that room into an ancestor worship area. Eventually, the toilet was locked, the ancestor altar was established in the best place in the house, and the in-laws slept in separate rooms.

6. Hoianese friends who set up a restaurant in 2004 did not heed the advice of an older relative who is an experienced chef and allowed only very limited space for the kitchen, while offering an extensive menu that featured several grilled dishes. The temperature in the tiny kitchen soared to over 40° C and the menu had to be simplified. The point is that the well-being of those working in the kitchen was hardly an issue and only the fact that they were about to collapse made the owners rethink their menu.

7. Fruits such as pineapple or watermelon are often served with salt or a mixture of dry chili and salt. According to Chi, the salt is essential for maintaining *am–duong* to counterbalance the sweetness of fruit.

8. It could be argued, however, that feminine dominance over microeconomic affairs actually represents the low status of commerce in Confucian thought (Nguyen, T. C. 1993: 69). Thus, for example, village markets (*cho lang*) in Northern Vietnam were always located outside the village (that is, beyond the "bamboo hedge"), reflecting the idea that trading and commerce are lowly and hence suitable for women (see also Bich 1999: 97). Indeed, since the late 1990s, with the liberalization of the economy and increasing importance of commerce, men seem to have gradually taken over commerce, now seen as a rational, scientific, and political domain appropriate for men (Taylor 2004: 109–110).

9. These scholars suggest that a bias toward analyzing the Vietnamese culture as a reflection of the Chinese one, along with a tendency to focus on explicit social structures among the precolonial elites, led previous generations of scholars of Vietnam to ignore the implicit matriarchal arrangements.

10. Traditionally, Vietnamese men's middle name was *Van,* which means "literature" and "letters" and denotes "culture" (as in *van hoa*), while women's middle name was *Thi,* which potentially denotes "goodness" and "advantage," but was interpreted by one of my informants as "just a woman."

11. A distinction should, however, be drawn between home cooking, which is universally feminine and of low status, and professional, high-status cooking, which is a male domain (Ortner 1990: 80). In fact, in several male-operated Hoianese restaurants, it is the wives, daughters, or female employees who perform the actual cooking backstage (that is, in the kitchen), while the male "chef" is busy hosting his guests within the public front-stage sphere of the restaurant.

12. While turmeric powder, for example, gives a deep yellow color to many Indian dishes, small quantities of fresh turmeric root are used in Hoianese cooking, resulting in a much milder yellow color.

13. Eating sounds are not class-specific in Hoi An, as people of different backgrounds make similar noises (including burping during meals). The only Vietnamese with whom I am familiar who do eat silently are those who have had intensive contact with Westerners.

14. Does the Vietnamese family really adhere to this Chinese model? I think that treating Vietnamese society as a carbon copy of the Chinese one is problematic, to say the least. As I have pointed out, a "Vietnamese-oriented" approach should not deny Chinese influences, but should acknowledge the influence of autochthonous and Southeast Asian traditions. Thus, though the "classic" approach views the family as modeled along Chinese-Confucian lines, a more "Vietnamese approach" would treat the family as a system of "bilateral kinship" (Taylor 1983: 13, 77, 284), emphasizing the looser, more egalitarian, and more female-oriented patterns. Nevertheless, it would be equally misleading to ignore the fact that the Vietnamese society is very hierarchical, patriarchal, male-oriented, and heavily influenced by the Confucian model of "five human relations."

15. When we were invited for a meal, food was often served on a table. Most probably, this had to do with our presence. Meals at Van's house were always eaten on the floor, however.

16. In contrast with Western etiquette, in Hoi An it is considered unfriendly and impolite to thank a host for a meal. For that matter, thanking is rare, especially among relatives and friends. I was often told: "Don't say thank you, just smile [*chi cuoi*]." Refraining from thanking does not mean that there is no feeling of gratitude or debt among friends and relatives, but just the opposite: within the "five human relation-ships," deep feelings of loyalty and debt exist and generosity is always expected. Therefore, thanking for something that is built into the relationship implies that the act was not genuine and that the relations are artificial.

17. As Vietnamese is a monosyllabic language, the number of possible syllabic combinations (generating words) is quite limited. This limitation is phonetically compensated for by eleven vowels, the extensive use of diphthongs, and six tones, factors that greatly increase the number of syllables/words. Grammatically, the language is enriched by the use of generic markers, a set of prefixes that precede nouns and relate them to specific realms (e.g., the word *ban* with a falling tone has diverse meanings, such as "football goal" or "discussion," but means "a table" when preceded by the prefix *cai* with a rising tone, which is the generic marker for "household utensils").

18. Since co Dung noticed that I liked her stuffed crabs, she went out of her way to make them when we were invited for a meal at her house, and her parents encouraged me to have more of them. Crabs are expensive and are calculated as one per diner. Thus, when encouraged to have another crab, I was supposed to eat someone else's portion. Obviously I had to refuse, but my refusal was bluntly interpreted as if I didn't like the dish, thus offending my hosts. . . . Co Dung's next move was to buy an extra crab so that I could have another portion.

3. LOCAL SPECIALTIES, LOCAL IDENTITY

1. Although Cham Island was only a secondary anchoring and provisioning point related to the Cham port (Cua Dai), that is, present-day Hoi An.

2. Though pork is very popular in Hoi An, it is commonly identified with Chinese cuisine and, at times, serves as a derogatory marker of Chinese identity (see also chapter 4).

3. Without the falling tone *huyen* over the word *lau*.

4. This arrangement is still common in China, where many "local-specialties" restaurants feature a kitchen on the first floor, where the dishes are also served casually. Diners who are having a full meal are led to the second floor, where they pay twice as much for the same dish.

5. A Japanese friend doing anthropological fieldwork in Vietnam told me that she had heard other Japanese suggesting that *cao lau* was a version of the Japanese *soba*. She had never tried *cao lau,* however, and could not confirm or negate this claim.

6. Keeping the secrets of the trade within the family is common in Vietnam. According to X. H. Nguyen (2001: 87), "It is difficult to get the precise information about the preparation procedure [of *com vong,* a glutinous rice sweet]. . . . The truth lies under the so-called *giu nghe to* (to preserve the profession learned from the Trade Genie); in other words, to preserve professional secret. Sometimes the truth is intentionally or accidentally exaggerated and even made mysterious."

7. *Que huong,* "home," or "one's place of birth," is a very important term in modern Vietnam. In a country where millions left the countryside for the cities or for faraway provinces due to war or socioeconomic conditions, this term serves to refer to one's "real place of origin," usually in the countryside, with all the implicit psychological and sentimental meanings. Here, it points to the special bond between people who are far from home and who can assuage their homesickness and nostalgia.

8. "It is very simple to make *banh bao,*" said Chi, "but it takes too much work. Mr. Le sells them cheaply and that is why he is the only producer in town." In the summer of 2001, I heard that Mr. Le's younger brother had established his own *banh bao* business. This resulted in an ugly fight between the sisters-in-law. Most people still prefered Mr. Le "because this family is nicer," and his brother eventually went out of business.

9. Eating venues set up along busy streets are commonplace in Vietnam. This arrangement has earned the poetic name *com buy,* literally "dusty rice," a title that acknowledges the setting and especially the dust scattered over the food by the passing motorbikes (Huu 1998: 190).

10. During a visit to Hoi An in August 2003, Dung, my Vietnamese teacher, who was writing her M.A. thesis at Hue University, told me that Vietnamese scholars think that rice paper and fish sauce, the two most essential and iconic ingredients of the Vietnamese cuisine, are actually of Cham origin. "Thus," she pointed out, "*cuon,* even if unique to Vietnam, is not originally Vietnamese." Since this book has no historical pretensions as such, I can't confirm or reject these claims. However, if this claim is correct, a whole range of questions could be asked about the origins of the Vietnamese culture, challenging, for example, the official presentation of the northern cultural

arrangements as the original, pure sources of Vietnamese culture (see Taylor [1998] and Wheeler [2010] for claims along similar lines).

11. Most sea and river boats in Vietnam are decorated with a pair of eyes at the bow. These serve several purposes: they scare away the sea monsters that mistake the eyed boat to be one of their own kind, and they "allow the boat to see its way." The reflection of the black and white spots in the water just beneath the bow helps the navigator identify treacherous rocks and other obstacles.

12. Tam Ky, some 60 km south of Hoi An, is the recently nominated capital of Quang Nam Province, since Danang, the previous (and obvious) capital, became an independent province-city. "There are only corrupt policemen and prostitutes in Tam Ky," said an informant, reflecting the general Hoianese perception of this town.

4. FEASTING WITH THE DEAD AND THE LIVING

1. See, for example, Baker (1979: 71–105) and Rosaldo (1980: 187); and in the case of Vietnamese rituals: Hickey (1964: 127–29); Popkin (1979: 93–94); Kleinen (1999: 175–76, 182–83); and Malarney (2002: 92, 150–51).

2. Kleinen (1999: 182–83) reports that the costs for death anniversary banquets amounted to US$200–400 in the Northern village where he conducted his fieldwork.

3. Only the fifty-ninth/sixtieth birthday was celebrated, marking the completion of an entire calendar cycle, entitling exemption from tax and *corvee* labor and membership in the village council and, as one of my informants pointed out, "the time from when you get lots of respect but no one would listen to you anymore."

4. This set of paper goods is intended for the use of the dead in heaven and usually includes money (U.S. dollars, Vietnamese imperial bills, and traditional coins printed on paper, but never contemporary money with the icon of Ho Chi Minh), as well as gold and silver, clothes and fabrics, and green, yellow, and red sheets printed with figures or faces that are supposed to stand in for the dead if they had to undergo punishment in hell. More elaborate sets include full traditional outfits, with additions such as boots and umbrellas; there were even models of houses, cars, and other consumer goods. An informant pointed out that paper motorbikes are offered only to those who could drive when they were alive, although bicycles are never offered because "it is too hard to cycle in the sky." All of these paper objects are intended for the daily needs of the dead and are burned during the ceremony so that "they will go up to heaven." Interestingly, the only stalls in the market that leave some of their merchandise unlocked are those selling such paper goods, as "the ancestors will be very angry if you sent them stolen goods."

5. *Ao dai,* or "long dress," is the Vietnamese traditional costume. It consists of a long, tight-fitting tunic with a high Chinese collar and long sleeves, slit at the sides up to the hip, and loose trousers. The contemporary versions of *ao dai* are of considerable sociological interest as they represent regional variations, as well as age and gender arrangements (men rarely wear them nowadays and usually dress in Western-style suits). Contemporary *ao dai* are often transparent, so that underwear is visible. Thus, a seemingly modest and conservative outfit is, in fact, rather daring, reflecting some of the tensions in Vietnamese women's lives.

6. Once, when I asked an informant who had just finished worshiping, "What exactly did you say right now?" an argument evolved, as one of those present claimed that ancestors and gods know exactly who you are and do not need information such as a full name or address, while another insisted that either a full name or an address is necessary.

7. Near our guesthouse there was a little pond where ARVN soldiers had executed three Viet Cong fighters during the war. The family who lives by the pond, that of an ex-ARVN officer, was instructed by the local authorities to take care of the altar and worship the spirits of the dead Viet Cong soldiers. The ex-officer himself told me that if he did not worship these spirits they might haunt his family and, thus, he willingly complied.

8. As is generally the case, the excess food is never thrown away. Uneaten food is kept for eating later while partially eaten leftovers are fed to pigs and other household animals.

9. I was told that the president of Hoi An's People's Committee (the mayor) is so honest and uncorrupt that he and his children are "very thin, because they don't have enough money to buy food." In another case, a teenage girl from a very poor family, who reported to me daily about her family eating patterns, was extremely slim. Upon inquiry, I was told that her family is too poor to buy enough food, a fact confirmed by reports concerning the eating patterns of her family.

10. The median caloric consumption in Vietnam in 2000 was 1,931 kcal/person/day, about 93.2 per cent of the amount recommended by the Vietnamese Institute of Nutrition and roughly 85 percent of the international standard, with urbanites consuming 1,859 kcal and rural-dwellers 1,954 kcal (Le et al. 2002: 70). While the median caloric consumption has not changed much since the late 1980s, the nutritional value of the diet has clearly improved with the protein ratio reaching recommended levels and the fat ratio increasing substantially (Tu and Le 2002). While malnutrition among children has substantially diminished during the last two decades, more than 30 percent of Vietnamese children below the age of five were still underweight and under height (ibid.).

11. Though the term *map* is used today to denote an overweight person, it also means "corpulent," "portly," and even "strongly built" (e.g., a friend looked at Arnold Schwarzenegger's photograph and said that he was *map*). The double meaning stems from the fact that up until a few decades ago, there were no fat (as in overweight) people in Vietnam. Those who were able to put on extra weight could eat more because of their superior position as "strong men" or "big men," in Sahlins's (1982) terms. Indeed, the Vietnamese word for *slim* or *thin—om—*also means "sick," undoubtedly not by coincidence. Once, a friend who had not seen me for a while pointed to my belly and said, "I see that your health has improved." Thus, in a society that lives on the brink, or memory of hunger, an overweight person is "strong" and/or "healthy," while a thin one is "sick."

12. My host boiled a bunch of "water morning glory" (*rau muong*) leaves for a couple of minutes, drained them, and placed them on a plate. Then she poured the greenish boiling water into a bowl, squeezed some lemon juice into it, and told me: "Put the soup (*canh*) and the vegetables on the table."

13. A friend from Hanoi told me that when she was a child, in the early seventies, her parents reared pigs in the small porch of their third-floor city apartment. It seems that in extreme situations, pigs might be reared within urban contexts.

14. See also Friedman (1990: 315) on canned drinks and prestige.

15. In 2008, I brought some dried yeast and baking instructions to one of my wife's friends. She baked bread in a toaster oven and was extremely excited about her culinary breakthrough.

16. I have rarely witnessed violence in Hoi An. This does not mean that violence does not exist but, rather, that it is restrained, restricted, or well hidden. Neighbors usually turn a deaf ear while policemen refuse to interfere in matters such as wife-beating, which they label as private. In the rare instances that violence does erupt in public, it is often extreme. It seems that when the inhibiting mechanisms collapse, all hell breaks loose and people really do try to kill each other. And when men get drunk, they have a social license to express their emotions publicly and, often, violently. However, the ability to cause real harm is limited and the social criticism involved is limited to "they were drunk."

17. On the first and fifteenth of every lunar month (black and full moon nights, *mung mot* and *ngay ram*), many Hoianese eat vegetarian food (denoting a Buddhist context). At nightfall, many families erect small altars in front of their houses and shops, where they worship "homeless" ghosts.

18. The rituals of *ngay ram* involve the setting up of altars in front of the houses and shops, usually after sunset. The offerings include uncooked rice, fruits, incense, candles, paper goods, and water, which are offered to "the ancestors and spirits that have no family." Festive meals are not part of the ritual, and cooked food (vegetarian or nonvegetarian) is not offered. Since 1998, the local government has initiated a tourist-oriented event called Hoi An Nights. On full-moon nights, the old quarter is closed to traffic, "Chinese lanterns" illuminate the streets, temples are opened, and a wide range of "traditional" activities (such as the local poets' society meeting or martial arts performances) are conducted. The locals, many of whom are irritated by the demands of this tourist-oriented event, maintain the custom of setting their altars and worshiping in the streets on these nights.

19. Functional explanations of religious dietary laws and taboos, mainly in terms of health and hygiene, can lead to irreconcilable paradoxes. Many contemporary Israeli Jews claim that the Jewish dietary laws (Kashrut) are health- and hygiene-oriented. Thus, "the pig is filthy" and "mixing of milk and meat causes digestive difficulties." They often quote contemporary scientific findings (usually from daily newspapers) to support their claims. However, such claims are potentially dangerous in religious terms: what would happen if scientific research were to determine that pork is the ultimate health food or that milk helps digest meat? And what about our substantial knowledge concerning the dangers of red meat, even that of "clean" animals such as cows? God is turned into a dietician and, as such, might be wrong and in need of constant update. Thus, such explanations might undermine religious belief to the point of heresy.

20. It should be said that Thich Thien Hoa takes an extreme stand on this matter. I was often told by Hoianese Buddhists that Buddha forbade killing. As long as

"murder" is not committed, there is no moral problem and meat might be consumed by both laymen and monks. Hoianese fishermen who kill large numbers of fish for a living turn to the doctrine of karma to counterbalance their "bad" actions by performing "good" deeds, such as visiting temples, donating money to monks, and avoiding fishing on full moon nights (for a similar attitude among Theravada Buddhist Sri Lankan fishermen, see Seneviratne 1992: 187).

21. Irit, my wife, is not a vegetarian but adheres to the Jewish Kashrut dietary laws and therefore did not eat meat in Vietnam (as even "clean" animals require ritual slaughtering). However, she did eat eggs, milk products, and clean fish (which do not require slaughtering). This system was nicknamed by our friends "Jewish vegetarianism" (*an chay co thai*).

22. As for Buddhism, different levels of vegetarianism exist in Cao Dai (Gobron 1950: 34–35). See further, chapter 6.

23. Buddhist monks also represent an antifamily or, rather, anti- "continuum-of-descent" ideology, since they renounce marriage and parenthood. Bearing in mind that the worst offense against the ancestors is avoiding marriage and refraining from having children, which results in the rupturing of the family continuum, the participation of Buddhist monks in ancestor-worship rituals is paradoxical in itself.

5. WEDDING FEASTS

1. Traditional here refers to the ruling period of the Nguyen dynasty (1802–1945) and serves only as a baseline for comparison to the present situation. This period was one of great social change; hence its traditional nature is only relative. See also Pham (1999: 4).

2. *Le* literally means to kowtow, hinting at the ancestor-worship aspects of these ceremonies, where kowtowing in front of the ancestral altar was, and still is, an essential part of the worship sequence.

3. "Wind and rain"; see Huard and Durand (1998: 94–100).

4. A friend told me that when he and his wife decided to get married, the *thay boi* told them that their chosen date was totally wrong. An assertive and modern man, he told me: "I laughed in the geomancer's face." According to his own testimony, the long-term outcome was disastrous: "Look, my marriage is a complete failure."

5. The number nine and its multiples are lucky because nine is the highest natural odd number, the essence of *duong,* and the favorite of the emperors. In contemporary Hoi An, nine and its products seem to be popular and lucky even if they are Gregorian, solar calendar dates.

6. In fact, "jungle meat" (*thit rung*) is a luxurious fare served in specialty restaurants that cater to men and offer alcohol as well as various degrees of female sexual services intended to accommodate and contain this excess of energy.

7. The mother of one friend reared some hundred chicks in her backyard in preparation for his sister's wedding. He told me that on the morning of the wedding, the yard looked like a killing field, with blood and feathers everywhere.

8. These two kinds of interrelations, reciprocity vs. economic exchange, are also the norm in the contemporary Hoianese rice-farming system. Xuan told me that while

she has a reciprocal work arrangement with her father-in-law and some neighbors, those outside this social circle who request her help have to pay her daily wages.

9. Choosing an ex-ARVN officer as the family representative was a political act. Hung, the bride's father, had also been recruited to the ARVN during the war. Though neither a fervent anti-Communist, nor a supporter of the Southern regime, he had been persecuted by the regime after reunification, and spent a few months in a reeducation camp. Although he seldom talks about it, I know that he feels some bitterness, which is generally well hidden. During his daughter's engagement, he was clearly making a political statement concerning his feelings about the current state of affairs. Though usually cautious, in this case he allowed himself to choose as his representative (somewhat similar to the best man in Western weddings) someone clearly out of favor with the current regime.

10. For a comprehensive discussion of the subject, see Illouz (2002). On the notion of weddings symbolizing sexual exclusivity, see Ember and Ember (1990: 174).

11. Indeed, a pre-wedding meal intended to induce intimacy among the parties is hardly unique to Hoi An. When I inquired about the henna ceremony in Israel that preceded my sister-in-law's wedding, I was told by her grandmother that "this party is very important because the two families meet in a merry atmosphere, eat, sing, and dance, and thus wouldn't arrive at the wedding as complete strangers."

12. Versions of this mixture are popular throughout South and Southeast Asia (e.g., the Indian *paan masala*). Though the habit of chewing *trau cau* is on the decline in Vietnam, the cultivation of areca palms has become a lucrative business in Hoi An in recent years, as the nuts are exported directly to Taiwan and southern China; the gentle palm now characterizes the Hoianese countryside.

13. The legend of the betel quid (Schultz 1994: 106) concerns marriage (although it emphasizes the precedence of sibling relations over spousal relations, and, like so many Vietnamese legends, ends tragically). Huu (1998: 668) suggests that this legend is resonant of the shift from polyandrous–matriarchal marriages to patriarchal–monogamous ones. He also stresses the antiquity of betel chewing, which is pre-Chinese.

14. Vietnamese men are heavy smokers and it is rare to find one who does not smoke at all. Yet several male friends said that they smoke "only when it is absolutely necessary," that is, in social situations in which refusing the cigarettes would offend the other party or imply aloofness. Interestingly, it is commonly agreed that green tea counters the dangers of smoking. Sitting one afternoon with Hung and his friends in a café, I told him that he would kill himself smoking so much. One of his friends, a physician and a smoker himself, told me: "Don't worry, Hung will not get sick because he drinks green tea." Though green tea is indeed a powerful antioxidant, I was told by a French physician that "smoking is presently the number-one killer of Vietnamese men."

15. The cream puffs were bought in one of the two bakeries in town that at the time offered French-style pastries and sweets, muffins, frozen yogurt, custard, and even cream cakes. In 2004, Hoi An boasted more than ten tourist-oriented and sophisticated bakeries, some operated by French chef-conditors (bakers).

16. I was told that this custom has to do with the fact that until not so long ago, many brides hardly knew their future husbands and were forced to leave their homes

and move into those of complete strangers. Brides were often terrified during the procession in which they were taken away from their families, and the presence of their parents might have aggravated the situation and unleashed a storm of crying and lamenting, which could bring bad luck.

17. A Central Highlands province, the home of many hill-tribe people, currently undergoing a process of economic "colonization" by Kinh and considered a wild frontier zone.

18. In Hoi An, cooking and serving the feast at home is always cheaper than having the food catered. Furthermore, a widely accessible system supports do-it-yourself feasts, as cheap rental of furniture and utensils is widely available. In every village or neighborhood there are businesses that rent tables, chairs, and cutlery for home-arranged feasts. The going price in Hoi An in year 2000 was approximately one U.S. dollar for a table with ten stools and some 50 cents for a set of ten bowls and serving trays.

19. The multicourse diachronic meal is actually a Russian custom, imported to France from tsarist Russia (Tannahill 1973).

20. The addition of noodles to ancestor-worship feast menus makes for the following culinary statement: the bird-and-egg dish stands for proper parenthood and kin relations, pork and chicken stand for prosperity, and noodles for longevity. Together they make for the aspired Vietnamese ideal of *Phuc Loc Tho:* happiness (symbolized by children, implied by the bird-and-egg dish), prosperity (pork and chicken), and longevity (noodles).

21. It should be noted that when specific dishes are more sought after, whether because they are tastier or because their portions are limited (e.g., meat dishes or the more luxurious desserts), guests at buffet meals are expected to be considerate of the others and to eat with restraint. However, as social control is weaker under such circumstances, it is often the case that an attendant is charged with distributing such dishes. Thus, when informal social control is weaker, there arises the need for institutional control.

22. For a similar analysis of the introduction of buffet meals into postwar West German cuisine, see Wildt (2001: 67–68).

23. "Passive resistance" and "selective adaptation" are the general cultural schemes with which the Vietnamese face changes imposed by external forces or foreign powers. While the elderly refuse to modify themselves and demand strict adherence to the traditional customs (e.g., the refusal of the Nguyen nobility to cooperate with the French and their tendency to retreat to their villages and detach themselves from the public sphere), some of the younger and the more progressive selectively adopt some of the new ideas, readapting them to the Vietnamese cultural framework (e.g., the inclusion of Communist war heroes, including Ho Chi Minh, into the traditional cult of heroes, and see Malarney 2002: 201).

24. Often, these are "minor wives" (*vo nho*), women who enter permanent relationships with married men, which include financial support and, sometimes, children. While there is often a wedding ritual, formalities are problematic for both Vietnamese and *Viet Kieu,* as polygamy is illegal both in Vietnam and in most countries where Vietnamese immigrants have settled.

6. FOOD AND IDENTITY IN COMMUNITY FESTIVALS

1. "Clan" is the accepted translation for the Vietnamese term *toc* (Huard and Durand 1998: 125; Nguyen 1995: 20).

2. The main building is a traditional wood-and-brick structure with a low, tiled roof, dedicated to the Tran clan ancestors and thus considered a *nha tho* ("house of worship"). This structure is included in the UNESCO World Heritage list of significant buildings (UNESCO, n.d., appendix 7b, p. 3, available at http://whc.unesco.org/en/list/948). Mr. Li and his wife and daughters live in a small new annex. Though the youngest male of twenty-four (!) brothers and sisters (his Chinese father had two Vietnamese wives, each of whom bore twelve children), Li is the only family member living in the house, and one of the few siblings left in Hoi An.

3. Extended family (*gia dinh*) worship has become popular in Hoi An in recent years, however. Several urban families have set up or reconstructed small *nha tho* (worship houses) and Hoi An's countryside is now dotted with dozens of such structures. I was told that there is a lot of money involved, and even that this has become a way of channeling money from relatives who live overseas.

4. A term coined by Fine (1996) in his ethnography of restaurant kitchens. While Fine refers only to cooking methods, I use this term in a broader sense, to include all manner of culinary strategies intended to reduce the effort involved.

5. This turbid and odorous fermented fish mash, before being filtered for the finer *nuoc mam,* is mixed with chili, sugar, ginger, and lime juice into a powerful sweet-pungent-salty dip.

6. Leaders of a successful Jewish revolt against the Greek-Seleuks in the second century BC, which began when a patriarch refused an order by an officer to sacrifice a pig in his temple, killed the officer instead, and fled to the mountains with his sons to launch a full-scale rebellion (Kraemer 2007: 31).

7. The Protestant congregation has some five hundred members and a nonresident pastor (from Danang). There is a much larger Catholic community with a cathedral, a bishop, and several thousand members.

8. Huard and Durand (1998: 233–56) do not even mention beef in their account of animals eaten in the 1930s.

9. There are a few places selling it in Hoi An, but no one would deny that this is a local specialty of Dien Ban, nor that it tastes much better there.

10. Many Hoianese Catholics have ancestor altars in their homes. Though some of these altars do display photographs of their deceased ancestors, icons of Jesus and Mary are always displayed *above* these photographs. Buddhists often arrange their altars in a similar way, placing the icon of Buddha on the highest level of the altar, yet displaying/worshiping their ancestors too. As for the Hoianese Protestants, some do have altars, yet generally speaking, they do not worship their ancestors.

11. The rejection of pork and the mentioning of the Macabees are relevant to my position as a Jewish anthropologist researching food. My contacts with the Christians in town, and especially with the close-knit Protestant community, were problematic. That Christmas Day, when the priest had invited me to hand the presents to the best

students of the Sunday school, I had felt embarrassed, feeling that I was deceiving my hosts. A week later, when I was invited to a Protestant wedding and was asked by the pastor to say the blessings, I responded that I was Jewish and didn't know the prayers. Though pretending that everything was OK, my hosts were surprised and uncomfortable. Why was it easier for me to participate in Buddhist, Cao Dai, or ancestor-worship ceremonies than in Christian ones? I suppose that, as with the Hoianese Protestants, my Jewish identity presented greater awkwardness in facing its "traditional foes" but "close relatives," the Christians, than those belonging to totally different spiritual worlds.

12. *Xoi dau xanh* is sometimes served at the altar (but not at the table) in ancestor-worship rituals, probably as a traditional dish and a favorite of the ancestors. Alternatively, as sticky rice (*nep*) is considered the "real" rice (see chapter 1), its ceremonial role can be explained in terms of its ancestral position as the origin of all rice.

13. The syncretist, spiritualistic Cao Dai ("High Tower" or "Supreme Palace") religion is one of several that appeared in Vietnam in the early twentieth century in the context of French colonial rule (Marr 1981: 303) and played a central role in the pre-1975 politics of the South. There are two Cao Dai temples in Hoi An, although neither seems very active. According to my informants, the community numbers some two hundred at most.

14. Marking the Taoist, Buddhist, and Confucian sects respectively.

15. A cheap and popular street snack: sticky-rice flour batter is steamed in small clay saucers and served with an orange gravy made of shrimp paste. A portion usually includes some dozen units, which are eaten with a unique wooden utensil that looks somewhat like a knife. At the Cao Dai feast, the orange gravy was made of pumpkin, and the cakes were served on a plate and eaten with chopsticks.

16. Here again, see Cohen's (2001) distinction between the plain food eaten in the temples and the conspicuous consumption of vegetarian food in commercial venues, which mushroom around town during the festival.

17. Tay Ninh, a town in the Mekong Delta on the Cambodian border (some 1,000 km from Hoi An), is the site of the religious and administrative headquarters of Caodaism. Its majestic noontime ceremony is a tourist attraction and a must for any visitor to the South, Vietnamese and foreign alike. For a literary description of the ceremony, see Graham Greene (1954).

18. Caodaism, like the other religious sects in Vietnam, was suppressed by the Communist government after reunification. As an erstwhile political and military foe, it was singled out. Moreover, unlike Christianity and Buddhism, Caodaism had no international support and was easier to suppress. Since *doi moi*, the government has eased its restrictions, returned some of the confiscated property, allowed the restoration of the ritual, and the reinstating of the clergy. I suspect that this turnaround by the state not only reflected the desire to appease the population and the international community, but also the realization that Caodaism, with its colorful temples and ceremonies, is a major tourist attraction.

19. In order to check the status of Caodaism in the area, I went to the huge Cao Dai temple in the neighboring city of Danang, but there too, I encountered only a handful

of participants at a none-too-impressive ceremony. The only spectators were a dozen high-school pupils having a rest in the well-tended garden.

20. These were the heads of six prominent Fujianese families that resisted the rule of the Qing Dynasty in the aftermath of the Ming collapse (Nguyen, V. X. 1998: 59) and eventually fled to Hoi An in 1697 (*Vietnam Cultural Window* 1998: 21).

21. Several deities are venerated in this temple. The one worshiped in the main hall is Bodhisattva Thien Hau, who, according to my informants, is "an incarnation of the Goddess of Mercy [Quan Am Bo Tat, the Chinese Guan Yin]. This goddess was born in *Phuoc Kien* and protects the fishermen and sailors. . . . She might be the Goddess of the Sea." To her left there was a model of a Chinese junk "like the one used by our ancestors to sail to Hoi An." This model is also worshiped. The main altar at the back room is dedicated to Luc Tanh Vuong Gia ("The Six Princes"), the ancestors of the community. The temple is dedicated to them as much as to Thien Hau. To their left is the altar of the "three goddesses and nine midwives," or "The Twelve Holy Midwives" (Sanh Thai Thap Tien Nuong [Nguyen 1998: 53]), who "teach babies the twelve essential human qualities, such as eating, crying or speaking." On the day of the festival, many women, most of them visibly pregnant, queued in front of this altar. Finally, the statue of a green dragon in the backyard is also worshiped. As is often the case in Vietnam, the icons in the back room, though located in an apparently secondary location, are not necessarily less important and may even surpass the central deity.

22. After kowtowing, the worshipers shook a numbered chip out of a bamboo container (there are usually ninety-nine chips). Then they approached the clerk, offered a donation, and received the appropriate "fortune" (according to the number of the chip): a slip of paper written in Chinese and Vietnamese. At about 10:00 AM, Hoi An's chief of police visited the temple and ordered the cessation of luck drawing. The organizers and worshipers were visibly upset, but they complied (for a similar incidence of police interference in the PRC, see Dean 1995: 99–117). Interestingly, the government lottery sellers who congregated by the gate of the temple continued to conduct their business throughout the day.

23. Also called Ma Tsu (Schipper 1993: 39) or Mazu (Dean 1995: 31).

24. In Fujian, Thien Hau is the patron of fishermen, but in Hoi An she is the protector of maritime trading, as suggested by a huge mural on the temple wall, where she is depicted flying to save a drowning merchant ship. Thus, the goddess herself has been adapted to the Hoianese context.

25. When, at a different worship, I asked why pieces of the entrails and blood were placed on top of the head of the pig, I was told that "the entire pig must be offered."

26. For a detailed description of the ritual killing of sacrificial animals, see Condominas (1977), whose description was magnificently reconstructed by Francis Ford Coppola in *Apocalypse Now*, or Lee (1990 [1969]: 34).

27. This feast featured a platter of cold cuts, corn soup with quail eggs, pork stomach in salt and lemon, steamed stuffed duck, beef curry, and fruit. The menu is remarkably similar to that of the Phuoc Kien feast. The menus, as well as the eating arrangements, were almost identical in the other Hoianese-Chinese community festivals I attended.

28. My interviewees often stressed the fact that pork is Chinese and that the Chinese prefer fatty food, cooked with pork lard, as opposed to the Kinh preference for vegetal oil.

7. RICE CAKES AND CANDIED ORANGES

1. As Tet is used throughout the book to only refer to the Vietnamese New Year, in this chapter the other two will be referred to exclusively by their translated names, the Summer Festival and Mid-Autumn Festival, respectively.

2. Other writers concur: see for instance, Huu and Cohen (1997: 6), Florence and Storey (1999: 96–99), Kamm (1996: 203–205), Ellis (1995: 163), and Crawford (1965: 190).

3. The Vietnamese calendar (adopted from the Chinese) is luni-solar. The 355-day lunar year must be amended to keep pace with the 365-day solar year. Thus, a thirteenth month is added every three years, between the third and the fourth months (Huard and Durand 1998: 106; Ellis 1995: 159).

4. Oddly enough, Do, in her description of the traditional festivals in the Red River Delta (1995: 7), claims that Tet is celebrated in the middle of the rice-farming period when the rice seedlings "have already been transplanted and are waiting for the appropriate weather to develop." In any case, the important point is that this is a transitional period.

5. For the structure and role of this totemic talisman, see Huu and Cohen (1997: 19–20). I was told that this custom is still common among the hill-tribe minorities. The only Tet pole I did see in Hoi An was erected by the culture department in the People's Park. Hickey (1967: 131) points out that this custom was already fading in the late 1950s.

6. Huu and Cohen (1997: 38) also mention the pomegranate as a fruit appropriate for the ancestor altar in Tet because "many seeds [stand for] many children." One of the Jewish New Year key symbols is the pomegranate, which is eaten in order to enhance one's good deeds and virtues in the coming year, and also to ensure fertility and prosperity.

7. Vietnamese bonsai gardens, unlike the diminutive Japanese ones, are made up of fairly large potted trees and shrubs.

8. Legend has it that two good genii once lived in a peach tree and protected villagers from evil spirits. They too would ascend home to heaven each year for Tet, leaving their earthly charges unprotected. The genii suggested that each family place a branch from the peach tree by their front doors, as the mere sight of it would terrify and ward off evil spirits. Hence, it is a custom to present a blossoming peach branch during Tet to protect the house (Huu and Cohen 1997: 41–42). In the North, people decorate their houses with pink peach blossoms (*hoa dao*). In the warmer-climate Center and South, the people use yellow apricot flowers (*hoa mai*). Interestingly, in recent years, the choice of Tet flowers in Hoi An has become a political signal: families of those who fought for the North opt for the pink blossoms, while those who served in the ARVN often prefer the yellow ones.

9. I joked with co Dung that the red watermelon seeds are probably hand-painted one by one. "They are not painted one by one," she replied seriously. "We dip them into bowls of red color."

10. Several families that I visited during Tet had both commercial and home-made *mut quat,* served alternately, according to the nature of their relations with the guests.

11. As in the legend of the betel quid, mentioned in the context of weddings, it is the inappropriate behavior of women in terms of conjugal relations and fidelity that causes the unavoidable tragedy.

12. In Hanoi, people release fish into lakes, ponds, and rivers to serve as the god's vehicle to heaven, but this is not practiced in Hoi An. I suspect that the low status of fish in Hoi An, as opposed to their higher status in Hanoi, underlies the prominence of paper horses and cooked chicken in the Hoianese worship.

13. Research into "the impacts of domestic technology . . . consistently reports that gender divisions remain stable (with women still doing most of the 'housework'. . . .), while 'labor-saving' inventions have not impacted upon the amount of time spent on domestic work" (Bell and Valentine 1997: 14).

14. Doubling a word/term is a grammatical Chinese mode of augmentation, and so the meaning of *du du* ("enough-enough") is "a lot."

15. In both houses where bananas and apples were presented on the altar (Thuy's and Nhan's), the color of the blossoming branch was pink, which identified the owners as Northerners or as "culturally inclined" toward the North.

16. The only place where I did see *banh day* prepared for Tet was in the vicinity of the Perfume Pagoda (Chua Huong) near Hanoi. Judging from the surprise and delight expressed by my Vietnamese companions, I suspect that the cakes were more of a novelty item produced for tourists than common New Year fare.

17. Though I could not find a reference to the written sources of this legend, it may have been first recorded in Chinese texts concerning Vietnam (Taylor 1983: 303). Even if it was compiled under Chinese rule, it refers to an independent pre-Chinese kingdom. In contemporary Vietnam, the legend is interpreted as clearly depicting a pre-Chinese culture (Huu 1998: 117).

18. In order to counterbalance this heroic rhetoric, it should be noted that Vietnamese history can also be read as oscillating between the unifying effects of the threat and/or conquest posed by foreign aggressors, and the internal struggle that bisected this society whenever the Vietnamese were left on their own. The twentieth-century Indochina wars, especially the American War (1965–1975), can be understood as a civil war between various Vietnamese parties. But even from this perspective, *banh Tet* as combat rations express the centrality of warfare in Vietnamese history and national identity.

19. *Chom-chom* is also strangely nicknamed *trai si da* or "the AIDS fruit." The round, prickly fruit is said to resemble the graphic depiction of "AIDS germs," as they are depicted in the anti-AIDS government propaganda posters visible everywhere. Here we encounter a process in which a recently introduced and, hence, nonmarked fruit (rambutan) is linked with a visual icon of a new and "modern" disease to create a

powerful symbol. However, as the fruit is appealing and popular, this linkage might lead to some sort of ambivalence regarding AIDS or, rather, expose the mixture of pleasure and fear that characterizes it.

20. Huu (1998: 128) suggests that there is another story about the scholars Luu and Nguyen, who went off to look for herbs in the mountains and disappeared in fairyland. Indeed, one of my informants mixed the two stories and told me about the herbalist Luu Nguyen, who went to look for herbs in the mountains and wandered into fairyland, where he stayed for one day. When he returned to his village, it turned out that a single day in fairyland is equivalent to 365 years on earth and thus, all his friends and relatives were long dead. He was told that his descendants still worshiped him on the day of his disappearance, the fifth of the fifth month. In despair, Luu Nguyen jumped into the river. I mention this version because despite the fact that it is clearly made up of two stories, the essential elements that explain the culinary customs of the festival remain coherent.

21. Tet Doan Ngo is celebrated in Hoi An right after the summer harvest. Since mid-spring, flocks of ducklings are reared alongside the main irrigation canals of Hoi An's rice villages of Cam Ha and Cam Chau. The ducks are fattest during the rice harvest when they are herded over the harvested fields to eat the chaff and residue. Thus, ducks are "in season" at Tet Doan Ngo only in Hoi An or, rather, in the Center and the South, where the rice harvest takes place just before the festival. Roasted duck is not mentioned by Huu (1998: 128) or Huu and Cohen (1997: 73) as characteristic of Tet Doan Ngo in the North.

22. The local and central authorities, as well as the locals independently, carefully preserve, promote, and even invent aspects of the Chinese identity of the town. A good example would be the establishing of a festival ("The New Festival of Old Hoi An") by the local government in August 1998, later turned into a monthly event ("Hoian Nights," celebrated every full-moon night). While this event features "Chinese elements," such as calligraphy and martial arts, the Hoianese Kinh developed an array of "Chinese artifacts," such as the "Chinese lanterns."

23. In fact, this is the night when the moon is at its furthest from earth (Huu and Cohen 1997: 74), yet when it rises, it appears reddish-orange on the horizon, large, and clear.

24. Huu and Cohen (1997: 75) suggest that purity and innocence, which are attributed to children, are the only means to get close to "the natural and sacred world." Thus, "by becoming like children, they can acquire attributes of innocence and purity" and become closer to the cosmic order.

CONCLUSION

1. Interestingly, Tan Chee Beng does not mention association by taste (as in "sweetheart," "he is so bitter," etc.), nor did my Hoianese informants. I must say that I still find it puzzling that while the Hoianese (and, apparently, the Chinese) use the colors, shapes, sounds, and textures of food to convey messages, they neglect taste, the most crucial sense when it comes to eating.

EPILOGUE

1. As pointed out earlier, all names in the book have been changed to protect privacy.

2. In fact, after a few months in Hoi An I conducted informal interviews in Vietnamese about matters such as religious practices and beliefs, or different perceptions of identity, and I could speak Vietnamese at a sufficient level for the discussion of such complex matters.

References

Adams, C. 1990. *The Sexual Politics of Meat: A Feminist-Vegetarian Critical Theory.* New York: Continuum.

Adrian, B. 2003. *Framing the Bride: Globalizing Beauty and Romance in Taiwan's Bridal Industry.* Berkeley: University of California Press.

Agar, M. H. 1980. *The Professional Stranger: An Informal Introduction to Ethnography.* Orlando: Academic Press.

Allison, A. 1991. "Japanese Mothers and Obentos: The Lunch Box as Ideological State Apparatus." *Anthropological Quarterly* 64 (4): 195–208.

Anderson, B. 1983. *Imagined Communities: Reflections on the Origins and Spread of Nationalism.* London: Verso.

Anderson, E. N. 1988. *The Food of China.* New Haven: Yale University Press.

———, and M. L. Anderson. 1977. "Modern China: South." In *Food in Chinese Culture: Anthropological and Historical Perspectives,* edited by K. C. Chang, 319–82. New Haven: Yale University Press.

Appadurai, A. 1988. "How to Make a National Cuisine: Cookbooks in Contemporary India." *Comparative Studies in Society and History* 30 (1): 3–24.

———. 1993. *Modernity at Large: Cultural Dimensions of Globalization.* Minneapolis: University of Minnesota Press.

Arieli, D. 2001. "Outsider in China: The World of Western Expatriates Living in Beijing in the End of the 90s." Ph.D. dissertation, The Hebrew University of Jerusalem.

Ashkenazi, M. 1991. "From Tachi-Soba to Naoray: Cultural Implications of the Japanese Meal." *Social Science Information* 30 (2): 287–304.

———, and J. Jacob. 2000. *The Essence of Japanese Cuisine: An Essay on Food and Culture.* Richmond: Curzon.

Atkinson, R. A. et al. 1989. *Introduction to Psychology.* 10th ed. San Diego: Harcourt Brace Jovanovich.

Baker, H. D. R. 1979. *Chinese Family and Kinship.* London: Macmillan.

Barthes, R. 1979 [1961]. "Toward a Psycho-sociology of Contemporary Food Consumption." In *Food and Drink in History,* edited by R. Foster and O. Ranum. Baltimore: Johns Hopkins University Press.

————. 1998 [1957]. *Mythologies.* Tel Aviv: Babel (in Hebrew).

Bauman, Z. 2000. *Liquid Modernity.* Cambridge: Polity.

Beardsworth, A., and T. Keil. 1996. *Sociology on the Menu: An Invitation to the Study of Food and Society.* London: Routledge.

Bélanger, D. 2000. "Regional Differences in Household Composition and Family Formation in Vietnam." *Journal of Comparative Family Studies* 31 (2): 171–89.

Belasco, W., and P. Scranton, eds. 2002. *Food Nations: Selling Taste in Consumer Societies.* New York: Routledge.

Bell, D., and G. Valentine. 1997. *Consuming Geographies: We Are Where We Eat.* New York: Routledge.

Ben-Ari, E. 2000. "Globalization, 'Folk Models' of the World Order and National Identity: Japanese Business Expatriates in Singapore." In *Japanese Influences and Presence in Asia,* edited by M. Soderberg and I. Reader, 51–76. Richmond: Curzon.

Bich, V. P. 1999. *The Vietnamese Family in Change: The Case of the Red River Delta.* Nordic Institute of Asian Studies Monograph Series. Richmond: Curzon.

Billig, M. 1995. *Banal Nationalism.* London: Sage Publications.

Bodnar, J. 2003. "Roquefort vs Big Mac: Globalization and its Others." *European Journal of Sociology* 44 (1): 133–44.

Bohannan, L. 1999 [1966]. "Shakespeare in the Bush." In *Conformity and Conflict: Readings in Cutural Anthropology,* edited by J. P. Spradley and D. W. McCurdy, 35–44, 7th ed. Boston: Little, Brown.

Bond, M. H. 1994. *Behind the Chinese Face.* Oxford: Oxford University Press.

Borton, L. 1995. *After Sorrow: An American among the Vietnamese.* New York: Kodansha International.

Boudarel, G. 2001. "Ba Den: The Black Lady Mountain." *Vietnamese Studies* 139: 11–16.

Bourdieu, P. 1980. "La Metamorfoses De Gost." In *But Who Produced the Producers? Works in the Sociology of Culture,* edited by I. Even-Zohar and G. Elgazi, 22–29. Tel Aviv: Tel Aviv University Press (in Hebrew).

————. 1984. *Distinction: A Social Critique of the Judgment of Taste.* London: Routledge and Kegan Paul.

Burns, P., and R. M. Brown. 1993. "Eleventh Century Cham-Philippine Foreign Affairs." In *Ancient Town of Hoi An* (Papers of the International Symposium on the Ancient Town of Hoi An, Da Nang, March 1990), 64–67. Hanoi: The Gioi.

Caplan, P., ed. 1997. *Food, Health and Identity.* London: Routledge.

Carruthers, A. 2004. "Cute Logics of the Mulitcultural and the Consumption of the Vietnamese Exotic in Japan." *Positions: East Asia Cultures Critique* 12 (2): 401–429.

Cerulo, K. A. 1997. "Identity Construction: New Issues, New Directions." *Annual Review of Sociology* 23: 385–409.

Chambers, E. 1987. "Applied Anthropology in the Post-Vietnam Era: Anticipations and Ironies." *Annual Review of Anthropology* 16: 309–337.

Chandler, D. P. 1993. *A History of Cambodia.* Chiang Mai: Silkworm.

Chang, K. C. ed. 1977. *Food in Chinese Culture: Anthropological and Historical Perspectives*. New Haven: Yale University Press.

Charlot, J. 1991. "Vietnamese Cinema: First Views." *Journal of Southeast Asian Studies* 22 (1): 33–62.

Cheung, S., and C. B. Tan. eds. 2007. *Food and Foodways in Asia: Resource, Tradition and Cooking*. London: Routledge.

Choo, S. 2004. "Eating Satay Babi: Sensory Perception of Transnational Movement." *Journal of Intercultural Studies* 25 (3): 203–213.

Clark, D. 2004. "The Raw and the Rotten: Punk Cuisine." *Ethnology* 43 (1): 19–31.

Cohen, E. 1972. "Toward a Sociology of International Tourism." *Social Research* 39 (1): 163–82.

———. 1979. "A Phenomenology of Tourist Experiences." *Sociology* 13 (2): 179–201.

———. 1987. "Hmong Cross: A Cosmic Symbol in Hmong (Meo) Textile Designs" *Journal of Anthropology and Aesthetics* 4 (Autumn): 27–45.

———. 1988. "Authenticity and Commodization in Tourism." *Annals of Tourism Research* 15 (3): 371–86.

———. 1992. "Tourist Arts." *Progress in Tourism, Recreation and Hospitality Management* 4: 3–32.

———. 1996. "The Study of Touristic Image of Native People: Mitigating the Stereotype of the Stereotype." In *Tourism Research: Critiques and Challenges*, edited by G. C. Pearce and R. W. Butler, 36–69. London: Routledge.

———. 2000. *The Commercialized Crafts of Thailand: Hill Tribes and Lowland Villages*. Richmond: Curzon.

———. 2001. *The Chinese Vegetarian Festival in Phuket: Religion, Ethnicity and Tourism on a Southern Thai Island*. Bangkok: White Lotus.

———, and N. Avieli. 2004. "Food in Tourism: Attraction and Impediment." *Annals of Tourism Research* 31 (4): 755–78.

Condominas, G. 1977. *We Have Eaten the Forest: Ethnography of the Mnong, Central Vietnam*. New York: Hill & Wang.

———. 1996. "Mnong Gar Alimentation and Cuisine." In Cuisines: Reflets des Sociétés, edited by Marie Claire Bataille-Benguigui and Françoise Cousin, 273–81. Paris: Editions Sépia-Musée de l'Homme.

Cooper, E. 1986. "Chinese Table Manners: You Are What You Eat." *Human Organization* 45 (2): 179–84.

Counihan, C. M. 1999. *The Anthropology of Food and Body: Gender, Meaning and Power*. New York: Routledge.

———. 2004. *Around the Tuscan Table; Food, Family and Gender in Twentieth Century Florence*. New York: Routledge.

———, and P. van Esterik. 1997. *Food and Culture: A Reader*. London: Routledge.

Crawford, A. C. 1965. *Customs and Culture of Vietnam*. Rutland, Vt.: Charles E. Tuttle.

Csordas, T. J. 1993. "Somatic Modes of Attention." *Cultural Anthropology* 8 (2): 135–56.

Cusack, I. 2000. "African Cuisines: Recipes for Nation-Building?" *Journal of African Cultural Studies* 13 (2): 207–225.

DaMatta, R. 1977. "Constraints and License: A Preliminary Study of Tow Brazilian National Rituals." In *Secular Ritual,* edited by S. G. Moore and B. Mayerhoff, 244–64. Assen: Van Gorcum.

Dang, N. V. 1997. "Culinary Traditions of the Viet in the Red River Delta." *Vietnamese Studies* 3 (125): 31–40.

———,T. S. Chu, and H. Luu. 2000. *Ethnic Minorities in Vietnam.* Hanoi: The Gioi.

Daniel, S. 1983. "The Toolbox Approach of the Tamil to the Issues of Moral Responsibility and Human Destiny." In *Karma,* edited by C. Keyes and V. Daniel, 27–62. Berkeley: University of California Press.

Dann, G. M. 1996. *The Language of Tourism: A Sociolinguistic Perspective.* Wallingford: CAB International.

Davis, D., and S. Harrell. eds. 1993. *Chinese Families in the Post-Mao Era.* Berkeley: University of California Press.

Dayan, M. 1977. *Vietnam Diary.* Dvir: Tel Aviv (in Hebrew).

Dean, K. 1995. *Taoist Rituals and Popular Cults of South-East China.* Princeton, N.J.: Princeton University Press.

Do, P. Q. 1995. *Traditional Festivals in Vietnam.* Hanoi: The Gioi.

Doan, T. T. 1993. "Hoi An Dialect." In *Ancient Town of Hoi An* (Papers presented at the International Symposium on the Ancient Town of Hoi An, Da Nang 1990), 93–100. Hanoi: The Gioi.

Dong, V. 1999. "The Cult of Holy Mothers in Central Vietnam." *Vietnamese Studies* 131: 73–82.

Douglas, M. 1957. "Animals in Lele Religious Symbolism." *Africa* 27: 46–58.

———. 1966. *Purity and Danger: An Analysis of Concepts of Pollution and Taboo.* London: Routledge and Kegan Paul.

———. 1972. "Deciphering a Meal." *Daedalus* 101 (1): 61–82.

———. 1975. *Implicit Meaning.* London: Routledge and Kegan Paul.

———. 1978. "Culture." In *Annual Report of the Russell Sage Foundation 1977–1978.* New York: Russell Sage Foundation.

———. 1984. *Food in the Social Order: Studies of Food and Festivities in Three American Communities.* New York: Russell Sage Foundation.

———, and J. Gross. 1981. "Food and Culture: Measuring the Intricacy of Rule Systems." *Social Science Information* 20 (1): 1–35.

———, and M. Nicod. 1974. "Taking the Biscuit: The Structure of British Meals." *New Society* 30 (637): 744–77.

Du-Bois, C., Tan Chee-Beng, and S. Mintz. 2008. *The World of Soy.* Chicago: University of Illinois Press.

Duong, T. H. 1995. *Novel Without a Name.* London: Picador.

———. 1998. *Paradise of the Blind.* Harmondsworth: Penguin.

Durkheim, E. 1915. *The Elementary Forms of Religious Life.* London: Allen & Unwin.

———, and E. Mauss. 1963 [1903]. *Primitive Classification.* London: Cohen and West.

Eisenstadt, S. N., and B. Giesen. 1995. "The Construction of Collective Identity." *Archives Sociologies* 36: 72–102.

Eliade, M. 1959. *The Sacred and the Profane.* New York: Harcourt Brace Jovanovich.

Elias, N. 1978 [1939]. *The Civilizing Process.* Oxford: Basil Blackwell.

Ellis, C. 1995. *Culture Shock Vietnam: A Guide to Customs and Etiquette.* Singapore: Times Books International.

Ember, C. R., and M. Ember. 1990. *Cultural Anthropology.* Englewood Cliffs, N.J.: Prentice Hall.

Engles, F. 1969 [1845]. *The Condition of the Working Class in England.* London: Granada.

Evans-Pritchard, E. E. 1982. *The Nuer.* Oxford: Oxford University Press.

Feld, S. 1991. "Sound as a Symbolic System: The Kaluli Drum." In *The Varieties of Sensory Experience: A Sourcebook in the Anthropology of Senses,* edited by D. Howes, 79–99. Toronto: University of Toronto Press.

Feldman, J. 1999. "It is My Brothers Whom I Am Seeking: Israel Ministry of Education Youth Voyages to Poland of the Shoah." Ph.D. dissertation, The Hebrew University of Jerusalem.

Fiddes, N. 1991. *Meat: A Natural Symbol.* London: Routledge.

Fine, G. A. 1996. *Kitchens: The Culture of Restaurant Work.* Berkeley: University of California Press.

Fischler, C. 1979. "Gastro-Nomie et Gastro-Anomie: " *Communications* 31: 189–210.

———. 1980. "Food Habits, Social Change and the Nature/Culture Dilemma." *Social Science Information* 19 (6): 937–53.

———. 1988. "Food, Self and Identity." *Social Science Information* 27 (2): 275–92.

Fjelstad, K., and Nguyen Thi Hien, eds. 2006. *Possessed by the Spirits: Mediumship in Contemporary Vietnamese Communities.* Ithaca: Cornell Southeast Asia Program Publications.

Florence, M., and R. Storey. 1999. *Vietnam: A Travel Survival Kit.* Melbourne: Lonely Planet.

Frazer, J. G. 1963 [1922]. *The Golden Bough.* New York: Macmillan.

Freidberg, S. 2003. "Not All Sweetness and Light: New Cultural Geographies of Food." *Social and Cultural Geography* 4 (1): 3–6.

Friedman, J. 1990. "Being in the World: Globalization and Localization." *Theory, Culture and Society* 7: 311–28.

de Garine, I. 2001. "Views about Food Prejudice and Stereotypes." *Social Science Information* 40 (3): 487–507.

Geertz, C. 1966. "Religion as a Cultural System." In *Anthropological Approaches to the Study of Religion,* edited by M. Banton, pp. 1–46. London: Tavistock.

———. *The Interpretation of Cultures.* 1973. New York: Basic Books.

General Statistical Office. 1999. *1999 Statistical Yearbook.* Hanoi: Statistical Publishing House.

Giddens, A. 1991. *Modernity and Self-Identity*. Cambridge: Polity Press.

Gobron, G. 1950. *History and Philosophy of Caodaism: Reformed Buddhism, Vietnamese Spiritism, New Religion in Euroasia*. Saigon: Tu-Hai.

Goffman, E. 1959. *The Presentation of Self in Everyday Life*. New York: Doubleday.

Goody, J. 1982. *Cooking, Cuisine and Class: A Study in Comparative Sociology*. Cambridge: Cambridge University Press.

Graburn, N. H. H. 1967. "The Eskimos and Airport Art." *Trans-Action* 14 (10): 28–33.

———. 1984. "The Evolution of Tourist Arts." *Annals of Tourism Research* 11: 393–419.

Greene, G. 1954. *The Quiet American*. Harmondsworth: Penguin.

Gronow, J. 1993. "What is 'Good Taste?'" *Social Science Information* 32 (2): 279–301.

Guggenheim, Y. K. 1985. *The Development of the Science of Nutrition from Ancient to Modern Times*. Jerusalem: The Hebrew University Magnes Press (in Hebrew).

Gvion-Rosenberg, L. 1990. "Why do Vegetarian Restaurants Serve Hamburgers? Toward an Understanding of a Cuisine." *Semiotica* 80 (1–2): 61–79.

Hall, C. C. I. 1995. "Asian Eyes: Body Image and Eating Disorders of Asian and Asian American Women." *Eating Disorders* 3 (1): 8–19.

Hall, S. 1996. "Introduction: Who Needs Identity?" In *Questions of Cultural Identity*, edited by S. Hall and P. Du Gay, 1–17. London: Sage Publications.

Handelman, D. 1997. "Rituals/Spectacles." *International Social Science Journal* 153: 388–98.

———. 1998. *Models and Mirrors: Towards an Anthropology of Public Events*. New York: Bergahn.

Hardy, A. 2005. *Red Hills: Migrants and the State in the Highlands of Vietnam*. Copenhagen: Nordic Institute of Asian Studies and Singapore: Institute of Southeast Asian Studies.

Harris, M. B. 1977. *Cannibals and Kings: The Origins of Cultures*. New York: Random House.

———. 1987. *The Sacred Cow and the Abominable Pig: Riddles of Food and Culture*. Tel Aviv: Massada (in Hebrew).

———. 1991. *Our Kind*. Tel Aviv: Ma'ariv Book Guild (in Hebrew).

Harvey, D. 1989. *The Condition of Postmodernity*. Oxford: Blackwell.

Helman, C. G. 2000. *Culture, Health and Illness*. 4th ed. Oxford: Butterworth-Heinemann.

Herr, M. 1991 [1968]. *Dispatches*. New York: Vintage.

Hickey, Gerald C. 1967. *Village in Vietnam*. New Haven: Yale University Press.

Higgs, P. 2003. "Footpath Traders in a Hanoi Neighborhood." In *Consuming Urban Culture in Contemporary Vietnam*, edited by L. Drummond and M. Thomas, 75–88. London: RoutledgeCurzon.

Hirschman, C., and V. M. Loi. 1996. "Family and Household Structure in Vietnam: Some Glimpses from a Recent Survey." *Pacific Affairs* 6: 229–50.

Hoa, M., and Huu N. 1997. *The Peasant, the Buffalo and the Tiger: Vietnamese Legends and Tales*. Hanoi: The Gioi.

Hoai, T., and C. Hoai. 1968 [1942]. *Thi Nhan Viet Nam* [Vietnamese Poets]. Saigon: 51–52.

Hoang, B. C., Pho D. T., and Huu N. 1999. "Overview of Traditional Vietnamese Medicine," 1–28. In *Vietnamese Traditional Medicine*. Hanoi: The Gioi.

Hoang, T. C. 1993. "On a Lingua Franca in Hoi An: Da Nang in the 18th Century." In *Ancient Town of Hoi An*, 101–108. Hanoi: The Gioi.

Hoang, V. K., and Lam M.D. 1993. "Ancient Coins Found in Hoi An and their Historical Periods." In *Ancient Town of Hoi An*, 68–71. Hanoi: The Gioi.

Hoang, V.T. 1996. *How South Vietnam was Liberated*. Hanoi: The Gioi.

Holtzman, J. 2006. "Food and Memory." *Annual Review of Anthropology* 35: 361–78.

Hoskins, J. 2007. "Caodai Exile and Redemption." In *Religion and Social Justice for Immigrants*, edited by P. Hondagneu–Sotelo. Piscataway, N.J.: Rutgers University Press.

Howell, S. 2003. "Modernizing Mansaf: The Consuming Contexts of Jordan's National Dish." *Food and Foodways* 11 (4): 215–43.

Huard, P., and M. Durand. 1998 [1954]. *Viet-Nam, Civilization and Culture*. Hanoi: École Francaise d'Extrême-Orient.

Hucker, C. O. 1978. *China to 1850: A Short History*. Stanford, Calif.: Stanford University Press (Hebrew trans., Tel Aviv: Dvir).

Hughes, G. 1994. "Authenticity in Tourism." *Annals of Tourism Research* 22 (4) 781–803.

Huu, N. 1997. "Buddhist Vegetarian Meals." *Vietnamese Studies* 3 (125): 89–106.

———. 1998. *Sketches for a Portrait of Vietnamese Culture*. Hanoi: The Gioi.

———, and B. Cohen. 1997. *Tet: The Vietnamese Lunar New Year*. Hanoi: The Gioi.

Hy Van Luong, and Diep D. H. 1991. "Culture and Capitalism in the Pottery Enterprises of Bien Hoa, South Vietnam (1878–1975)." *Journal of Southeast Asian Studies* 22 (1): 16–32.

Iacomo, B. 1998. "Cao Lau Noodles: History in the Taste." *Vietnam Cultural Window* [Cua So Vna Hoa Viet Nam] 6 & 7: 16–17.

Illouz, E. 2002. *Consuming the Romantic Utopia: Love and the Cultural Contradictions of Capitalism*. Haifa: University of Haifa and Zmora-Bitan (In Hebrew).

Jackson-Doling, A., T. T. Choi, M. Isaak and H. von Holzen. 1997. *The Food of Vietnam: Authentic Recipes from the Heart of Indochina*. Singapore: Periplus.

Jamieson, N. L. 1995. *Understanding Vietnam*. Berkeley: University of California.

Jun, J., ed. 2000. *Feeding China's Little Emperors*. Stanford, Calif.: Stanford University Press.

Kalka, I. 1991. "Coffee in Israeli Suburbs." *Leisure Studies* 10: 119–31.

Kamm, H. 1996. *Dragon Ascending: Vietnam and the Vietnamese*. New York: Arcade.

Karnow, S. 1984. *Vietnam: A History*. New York: Penguin.

Keyes, C. F. 1977. *The Golden Peninsula: Culture and Adaptation in Mainland Southeast Asia*. New York: Macmillan.

Khare, R. S., ed. 1992. *The Eternal Food: Gastronomic Ideas and Experiences of Hindus and Buddhists*. Delhi: Sri Satguru.

Kivinen, M., ed. 1998. *The Kalamari Union: Middle Class in East and West U.S.A.* Aldershot: Ashgate.

Kleinen, J. 1999. *Facing the Future, Reviving the Past: A Study of Social Change in a Northern Vietnamese Village.* Singapore: Institute of Southeast Asian Studies.

Kraemer, D. C. 2007. *Jewish Eating and Identity through the Ages.* New York: Routledge.

Krowolski, N., and T. Nguyen. 1997. "Some Notes on Vietnamese Alimentary Practices and Foreign Influences." *Vietnamese Studies* 3 (125): 151–90.

———, and I. Simon-Baruch. 1993. *Autour du Riz: Le repas chez quelques populations d'Asie du Sud-Est.* Paris: L'Harmattan.

Kuipers, J. C. 1991. "Matters of Taste in Weyewa." In *The Varieties of Sensory Experience: A Sourcebook in the Anthropology of Senses,* edited by D. Howes, 111–27. Toronto: University of Toronto Press.

Kulick, D., and M. Willson, eds. 1995. *Taboo: Sex, Identity and Erotic Subjectivity in Anthropological Fieldwork.* New York: Routledge.

Kwon, H. 2006. *After the Massacre: Commemoration and Consolation in Ha My and My Lai.* Berkeley: University of California Press.

Le, B. M., C. K. Nguyen, H. K. Ha, T. D. Tran, and Q. H. Vu. 2002. "Consumption of Food in Rural and Urban Areas in 2000." *Vietnamese Studies* 146 (4): 70–78.

Le, B. T. 1994. "Geographical Aspects of Pho Hien." In *Pho Hien: The Center of International Commerce in the XVII–XVIII Centuries* (collected papers of the seminar held in December 1992 by the Association of Vietnamese Historians), 23–28. Hanoi: The Gioi.

———. 1997. *Vietnam: The Country and its Geographical Regions.* Hanoi: The Gioi.

Le, D. P. 1997. "Some Eating and Drinking Rituals in Hue Imperial Court." *Vietnamese Studies* 3 (125): 75–88.

Le, K. L. ed. 2000. *The 30-Year War 1945–1975.* Hanoi: The Gioi.

Leach, E. R. 1974. "Oysters, Smoked Salmon and Stilton Cheese." In *Claude Lévi-Strauss: An Introduction,* 15–33. New York: Penguin Books.

Lee, R. B. 1990 [1969]. "Eating Christmas in the Kalahari." In *Conformity and Conflict: Readings in Cultural Anthropology,* edited by J. P. Spradly and D. W. McCurdy, 30–37. Boston: Little, Brown.

Levi-Strauss, C. 1966a. *The Savage Mind.* London: Weidenfeld & Nicolson.

———. 1966b. "The Culinary Triangle." *Partisan Review* 33: 586–95.

———. 1970. *The Raw and the Cooked* (Mythologies I). Trans. from the French by J. and D. Weightman. London: Jonathan Cape.

———. 1973. *From Honey to Ashes* (Mythologies II). Trans. from the French by J. and D. Weightman. New York: Harper & Row.

———. 1987. *The Origins of Table Manners* (Mythologies III). Trans. from the French by J. and D. Weightman. London: Jonathan Cape.

Lien, M., and B. Nerlich, eds. 2004. *The Politics of Food.* New York: Berg.

Littrell, M. A., L. F. Anderson, and P. J. Brown. 1993. "What Makes a Craft Souvenir Authentic?" *Annals of Tourism Research* 20: 197–215.

Loveday, L., and S. Chiba. 1985. "Partaking with the Divine and Symbolizing the Societal: The Semiotics of Japanese Food and Drink." *Semiotica* 56 (1–2): 115–31.

Lowenthal, D. 1985. *The Past is a Foreign Country*. Cambridge: Cambridge University Press.

Lu, S., and G. A. Fine. 1995. "The Presentation of Ethnic Authenticity: Chinese Food as a Social Accomplishment." *Sociological Quarterly* 36 (3): 535–53.

Lupton, D. 1996. *Food, the Body and the Self*. London: Sage Publications.

MacCanell, D. 1973. "Staged Authenticity: Arrangements of Social Space in Tourist Settings." *American Journal of Sociology* 79 (3): 589–603.

———. 1976. *The Tourist: A New Theory of Leisure Class*. New York: Schocken and McGlynn.

Malarney, S. K. 1997. "Culture, Virtue and Political Transformation in Contemporary Northern Viet Nam." *Journal of Asian Studies* 56 (4): 899–920.

———. 2001. "'The Fatherland Remembers Your Sacrifice'": Commemorating War Dead in North Vietnam." In *The Country of Memory: Remaking the Past in Late Socialist Vietnam,* edited by Hue-Tam Ho Tai. Berkeley: University of California Press.

———. 2002. *Culture, Ritual and Revolution in Contemporary Vietnam*. London: Routledge and Curzon Press.

Malinowski, B. 1935. *Coral Gardens and Their Magic: A Study of the Methods of Tilling the Soil and of Agricultural Rites in the Trobriand Islands*. New York: American Book Company.

Manderson, L. 1986. "Introduction: The Anthropology of Food in Oceania and Southeast Asia." In *Shared Wealth and Symbol: Food Culture and Society in Oceania and Southeast Asia,* edited by L. Manderson, 1–18. Cambridge: Cambridge University Press.

Marr, D. G. 1981. *Vietnamese Tradition on Trial, 1920–1945*. Berkeley: University of California Press.

———. 2000a. "Concepts of 'Individual' and 'Self' in Twentieth-Century Vietnam." *Modern Asian Studies* 34 (4): 769–98.

———. 2000b. "History and Memory in Vietnam Today: The Journal of Xua and Nay." *Journal of Southeast Asian Studies* 31 (1): 1–25.

Mauss, M. 1990. *The Gift: Forms and Functions of Exchange in Archaic Societies*. London: Routledge.

———. 2005 [1925]. *The Sociology of the Gift*. Tel-Aviv: Resling.

McIntosh, R. W., and R. Goeldner. 1990. *Tourism: Principles, Practices, Philosophies*. 6th ed. New York: Wiley.

Mennell, S. 1985. *All Manners of Food: Eating and Taste in England and France from the Middle Ages to the Present*. Oxford: Basil Blackwell.

———. 1989. *Norbert Elias: Civilization and the Human Self-Image*. Oxford: Basil Blackwell.

———, S., A. Murcott, and A. V. Otterloo. 1992. "The Sociology of Food: Eating, Diet and Culture." *Current Sociology* 40 (2).

Metcalf, P. 2002. *They Lie, We Lie: Getting On with Anthropology.* London: Routledge.

Minh, C., Ha V. T., and T. T. Nguyen. 1993. *Buddhism in Vietnam.* Hanoi: The Gioi.

Mintz, S. 1985. *Sweetness and Power: The Place of Sugar in Modern History.* New York: Viking.

———. 1996. *Tasting Food, Tasting Freedom.* Boston: Beacon Press.

———. 1997. "Afterward: Swallowing Modernity." In *Golden Arches East: McDonald's in East Asia,* edited by J. L. Watson, 183–202. Stanford, Calif.: Stanford University Press.

———. 2002. "Foreword: Food for Thought." In *The Globalization of Chinese Food,* edited by D. Wu and S. Cheung, xii-xx. Richmond Surrey: Curzon.

———, and D. Schlettwein-Gsell. 2001. "Food Patterns in Agrarian Societies: The 'Core-Fringe-Legume Hypothesis'." *Gastronomica* 1 (3): 41–52.

———, and C. M. Du Bois. 2002. "The Anthropology of Food and Eating." *Annual Review of Anthropology* 31: 99–119.

Mitchell, D. O., M. D. Ingco, and R. C. Duncan. 1997. *The World Food Outlook.* Cambridge: Cambridge University Press.

Momoki, S. 1994. "Japan and Vietnam in the Asian Trade System in the 17th–18th Centuries." In *Pho Hien: The Center of International Commerce in the XVII–XVIII Centuries* (collected papers of the seminar held by the Association of Vietnamese Historians in December 1992), 39–48. Hanoi: The Gioi.

Murcott, A. 1982. "On the Social Significance of the 'Cooked Dinner' in South Wales." *Social Science Information* 21(4–5): 677–95.

Narayan U. 1997. *Dislocating Cultures: Identities, Traditions and Third-World Feminism.* New York: Routledge.

Nemeroff, C., and P. Rozin. 1989. " 'You Are What You Eat': Applying the Demand-Free 'Impressions' Technique to an Unacknowledged Belief." *Ethos* 17: 50–69.

Ngoc, T. 2005. "New Developments Lure Visitors to Hoi An." *Viet Nam News,* 13 June, pp. 21.

Nguyen, D. D. 1993. "The Birth and Historic Evolution of Hoi An." In *Ancient Town of Hoi An,* 117–27. Hanoi: The Gioi.

Nguyen, D. N. 1993. "Markets and Villages." In *The Traditional Village in Vietnam,* 318–68. Hanoi: The Gioi.

Nguyen, H. H., and T. C. Tran. 1996. *Vietnamese Traditional Water Puppetry.* Hanoi: The Gioi.

Nguyen, K. T. 1993. "The Village: Settlement of Peasants in Northern Vietnam." In *The Traditional Village in Vietnam,* 7–43. Hanoi: The Gioi.

Nguyen, K. V. 1967. *An Introduction to Vietnamese Culture.* East Asian Cultural Studies Series, no. 10. Tokyo: Tokyo Press.

———. 1993. *Vietnam: A Long History.* Hanoi: The Gioi.

Nguyen, N. C., and D. Sachs. 2003. *Two Cakes Fit for a King: Folktales from Vietnam.* Honolulu: University of Hawai'i Press.

Nguyen, T. 1997. "Are There Regional Differences in Vietnam?" *Vietnamese Studies* 3 (125): 107–150.

Nguyen, T. C. 1993. "The Traditional Viet Village in Bac Bo: Its Organizational Structure and Problems." In *The Traditional Village in Vietnam,* 44–142. Hanoi: The Gioi.

Nguyen, T. T. 1997. *Nhung Mon An Viet Nam* [Vietnamese Dishes]. Ca Mau: Nha Xuat Ban Mui.

Nguyen, V. H. 1995 [1944]. *The Ancient Civilization of Vietnam.* Hanoi: The Gioi.

Nguyen, V. M., and D. P. Le. 1997. "Characteristics of Vietnamese Culinary Technique." *Vietnamese Studies* 3 (125): 41–50.

Nguyen, V. X. 1998. *Hoi An.* Danang: Danang Publishing House.

Nguyen, X. H. 2001. *Glutinous-Rice-eating Tradition in Vietnam and Elsewhere.* Bangkok: White Lotus.

Noguchi, P. H. 1994. "Savor Slowly: Ekiben—The Fast Food of High-Speed Japan." *Ethnology* 33 (4): 317–30.

Ohnuki-Tierney, E. 1987. *The Monkey as Mirror: Symbolic Transformations in Japanese History and Ritual.* Princeton, N.J.: Princeton University Press.

———. 1990. "The Ambivalent Self of the Contemporary Japanese." *Cultural Anthropology* 5: 197–218.

———. 1993. *Rice as Self: Japanese Identities Through Time.* Princeton, N.J.: Princeton University Press.

———. 1995. "Structure, Event and Historical Metaphor: Rice and Identities in Japanese History." *Journal of the Royal Anthropological Institute* 1: 227–53.

Olson, J. S., and R. Roberts. 1991. *Where the Domino Fell: America and Vietnam 1954 to 1990.* New York: St. Martin's Press.

Ong, A., and D. M. Nonini, eds. 1997. *Ungrounded Empires: The Cultural Politics of Modern Chinese Transnationalism.* New York: Routledge.

Orlove, B., and E. Schmidt. 1995. "Swallowing their Pride: Indigenous and Industrial Beer in Peru and Bolivia." *Theory and Society* 24: 271–98.

Ortner, S. B. 1973. "On Key Symbols." *American Anthropologist* 75(5): 1338–46.

———. 1974. "Is Female to Male as Nature is to Culture?" In *Women, Culture and Society,* edited by M. Z. Rosaldo and L. Louise, 67–87. Stanford, Calif.: Stanford University Press.

———. 1990. "Patterns of History: Cultural Schemas in the Founding of Sherpa Religious Institutions." In *Culture Through Time,* edited by E. Ohnuki-Tierney. Stanford: Stanford University Press.

Palazzoli, C. 1981. "Le Vietnam entre deux mythes." Paris: Economica. Trans. by N. Huu in *Sketches for a Portrait of Vietnamese Culture,* 555. Hanoi: The Gioi.

Palmer, C. 1998. "From Theory to Practice: Experiencing the Nation in Everyday Life." *Journal of Material Culture* 3 (2): 175–99.

Papin, P. 1997. "Food References and Monetary Equivalents in Ancient Village Conventions (huong uoc)." *Vietnamese Studies* 3 (125): 5–24.

Pham, V. B. 1999. *The Vietnamese Family in Change: The Case of the Red River Delta.* Nordic Institute of Asian Studies Monograph. Richmond: Curzon.

Phan, H. L., Q. N. Nguyen, and D. L. Nguyen. 1997. *The Country Life in the Red-River Delta.* Hanoi: The Gioi.

Pilcher, J. 1998. *Que Vivan los Tamales: Food and the Making of Mexican Identity.* Albuquerque: University of New Mexico Press.

——. 2001. "Mexico Pepsi Challenge: Traditional Cooking, Mass Consumption and National Identity." In *Fragments of a Golden Age: The Politics of Culture in Mexico since 1940,* edited by J. Gilbert, A. Rubenstein and E. Zolov, 71–90. Durham, N.C.: Duke University Press.

Pilleboue, J., and D. Weissberg. 1997. "Coffee-Culture in Vietnam." *Vietnamese Studies* 4 (126): 47–80.

Poe, T. N. 2001. "The Labor and Leisure of Food Production as a Mode of Ethnic Identity Building among Italian in Chicago, 1890–1940." *Rethinking History* 5 (1): 131–48.

Popkin, Samuel L. 1979. *The Rational Peasant: The Political Economy of Rural Society in Vietnam.* Berkeley: University of California Press.

Rabinaw, P. 1977. "Ali: An Insider's Outsider." In *Reflections on Fieldwork in Morocco,* 31–70. Berkeley: University of California Press.

Rabinowitz, D. 1995. "The Twisting Road for Saving Brown Women." *Theory and Criticism* 7 (Winter): 5–29 (in Hebrew).

Radcliffe-Brown, A. R. 1922. *The Andaman Islanders.* Cambridge: Cambridge University Press.

Rasmussen, S. 1996. "Matters of Taste: Food, Eating and Reflections on 'The Body Politic' in Tuareg Society." *Journal of Anthropological Research* 52: 61–83.

Reid, A. 1988. *Southeast Asia in the Age of Commerce 1450–1680.* Vol. I. *The Lands below the Wind.* New Haven: Yale University Press.

Richards, A. I. 1937. *The Food and Nutrition of African Natives.* London: International Institute for African Languages and Cultures.

——. 1939. *Land, Labor and Diet in Northern Rhodesia.* London: Oxford University Press.

——. 2004 [1932]. *Hunger and Work in a Savage Tribe: A Functional Study of Nutrition among the Southern Bantu.* London: Routledge.

——, and E. M. Widdowson. 1936. "A Dietary Study in Northeastern Rhodesia." *Africa* 9: 166–96.

Ritzer, G. 1993. *The McDonalization of Society: An Investigation into the Changing Character of Contemporary SocialLife.* Thousand Oaks: Pine Forge.

Rosaldo, R. 1980. *Ilongot Head Hunting 1883–1974: A Study in Society and History.* Stanford, Calif.: Stanford University Press.

——. 1989. *Culture and Truth: The Remaking of a Social Analysis.* Boston: Beacon.

Sahlins, M. D. 1976. *Culture and Practical Reason.* Chicago: University of Chicago Press.

——. 1982. "Poor Man, Rich Man, Big Man, Chief." In *Anthropology: Contemporary Perspective,* edited by D. E. Hunter and P. Whitter. Boston: Little Brown.

Sanday, P. R. 1986. *Divine Hunger: Cannibalism as a Cultural System.* Cambridge: Cambridge University Press.

Sasson-Levy, O. 2000. "Constructing Gender Identities within the Israeli Army." Ph.D. dissertation, The Hebrew University of Jerusalem.

de Saussure, F. 1960. *Course in General Linguistics.* London: Owen.

Schafer, J. C. 2000. "The Collective and the Individual in Two Post-War Vietnamese Novels." *Crossroads: An Interdisciplinary Journal of Southeast Asian Studies* 14 (2): 13–48.

Schipper, K. 1993. *The Taoist Body.* Berkeley: University of California Press.

Scholliers, P. 2001. *Food, Drink and Identity.* Oxford: Berg.

Schultz, G. F. 1994. *Vietnamese Legends.* Hanoi: The Gioi.

Sen, A. K. 1981. *Poverty and Famines: An Essay on Entitlement and Deprivation.* Oxford: Oxford University Press.

Seneviratne, H. L. 1992. "Food Essence and the Essence of Experience." In *The Eternal Food: Gastronomic Ideas and Experiences of Hindus and Buddhists,* edited by R. S. Khare, 179–200. Delhi: Sri Satguru.

Shapira, R., and D. Navon. 1991. "Alone Together: Public and Private Dimensions of a Tel-Aviv Cafe." *Qualitative Sociology* 14 (2): 107–125.

Sheehan, N., H. Smith, E. W. Kenworthy, and F. Butterfield. 1971. *The Pentagon Papers as Published by The New York Times.* New York: Bantam.

Simmel, G. 1991."The Sociology of the Meal." Trans. in M. Symons, *Eating into Thinking: Explorations into the Sociology of Cuisine.* Adelaide: Flinders University.

Skorupski, J. 1976. *Symbol and Theory: A Philosophical study of Theories of Religion in Social Anthropology.* Cambridge: Cambridge University Press.

Smith, V. L. 1977. "Eskimo Tourism: Micro-Models and Marginal Men." In *Hosts and Guests: The Anthropology of Tourism,* edited by V. L. Smith, 51–70. Philadelphia: University of Pennsylvania Press.

Solomon, H. 1993. "Blood Among the Beta-Israel and their Christian Neighbors in Ethiopia: Key Symbols in Inter-Group Context." Jerusalem Studies of Jewish Folklore. Jerusalem: Institute for Jewish Studies in the Hebrew University, 117–34 (in Hebrew).

Souchou, Y. 2002. *Confucian Capitalism: Discourse, Practice and the Myth of Chinese Enterprise.* London: RoutledgeCurzon.

Stein, R. 2008. *Itineraries in Conflict: Israelis, Palestinians and the Political Lives of Tourism.* Durham, N.C.: Duke University Press.

Sterling, R. 2000. *World Food: Vietnam.* Melbourne: Lonely Planet.

Strong, R. 2002. *Feast: A History of Grand Eating.* London: Random House.

Sutton, D. E. 1997. "The Vegetarian Anthropologist." *Anthropology Today* 13 (1): 5–8.

———. 2001. *Remembrance of Repasts: An Anthropology of Food and Memory.* Oxford: Berg.

Swidler, A. 1986. "Culture in Action: Symbols and Strategies." *American Sociological Review* 51: 273–86.

Tambiah, S. J. 1969. "Animals are Good to Think and Good to Prohibit." *Ethnology* 18: 423–89.

Tan, C. B. 1998. "Changing Chinese Food and Chinese Symbolism in Malaysia." Paper presented at the 5th symposium on Chinese Dietary Culture, The Chinese University of Hong Kong, June 1998. Hong Kong: The Chinese University of Hong Kong.

Tannahill, Reay. 1973. *Food in History.* London: Eyre Methuen.

Taylor, P. 2004. *Goddess on the Rise: Pilgrimage and Popular Religion in Vietnam.* Honolulu: University of Hawai'i Press.

———. 2007. *Cham Muslims of the Mekong Delta: Place and Mobility in the Cosmopolitan Periphery.* Singapore: National University of Singapore Press.

Taylor, W. K. 1983. *The Birth of Vietnam.* Berkeley: University of California Press.

———. 1998. "Surface Orientations in Vietnam: Beyond Histories of Nation and Region." *Journal of Asian Studies* 57 (4): 949–78.

———. 2004. How I Begun to Teach about the Vietnam War. *Michigan Quarterly Review* 43 (4): 637–47.

Teman, E. 2003. "The Medicalization of "Nature" in the "Artificial Body": Surrogate Motherhood in Israel." *Medical Anthropological Quarterly* 17 (1): 78–98.

Thomas, M. 2004. "Transitions in taste in Vietnam and the Diaspora." *Australian Journal of Anthropology* 15 (1): 54–76.

Touraine, A. 2002. "From Understanding Society to Discovering the Subject." *Anthropological Theory* 2 (4): 387–98.

Tran, H. D., and A. T. Ha. 2000. *A Brief Chronology of Vietnamese History.* Hanoi: The Gioi.

Tran, K. P. 1993. *Cham Ruins: Journey in Search of an Ancient Civilization.* Hanoi: The Gioi.

Tran, V. A., ed. 2000. *Van Hoa Am Thuc O Pho Co Hoi An* [The Culinary Culture of Ancient Hoi An]. Hanoi: Nha Xuat Ban Khoa Hoc Xa Hoi.

Trankell, B. I. 1995. *Cooking, Care and Domestication: A Culinary Ethnography of the Tai-Yong, Northern Thailand.* Uppsala: Uppsala University Press.

Truong, H. Q. 1994. "The Birth and Development of Pho Hien." In *Pho Hien: The Center of International Commerce in the XVII–XVIII Centuries,* 29–39. Hanoi: The Gioi.

Tu, N., and Le D. T. 2002. "Monitoring Nutrition in Vietnam." *Vietnamese Studies* 146 (2): 79–94.

Tuchman, B. W. 1983. *The March of Folly: From Troy to Vietnam.* Translated into Hebrew by Eshkol, Y. (1986). Tel Aviv: Maa'riv Library (in Hebrew).

Tuchman, G., and H. G. Levine. 1993. "New York Jews and Chinese Food: The Social Construction of an Ethnic Pattern." *Journal of Contemporary Ethnography* 22 (3): 382–407.

Turner, B. S. 1991. "Recent Developments of the Theory of the Body." In *The Body: Social Processes and Cultural Theory,* edited by M. Featherstone, M. Hepworth, and B. S. Turner, 1–35. London: Sage Publications.

Turner, V. W. 1960. "Mochuna the Hornet." In *In the Company of Man,* edited by J. Casagrande, 334–55. New York: Harper & Bros.

———. 1967. *The Forest of Symbols: Aspects of Ndembu Ritual.* Ithaca: Cornell University Press.

van den Berghe, P. L. 1984. "Ethnic Cuisine: Culture in Nature." *Ethnic and Racial Studies* 7 (3): 387–97.

Veblen, T. 1953 [1899]. *The Theory of the Leisure Class.* New York: Mentor.

Vietnam Cultural Window, ed. 1998. "Where the Chinese Can Meet." Nos. 6–7, pp. 20–21.

Visser, M. 1999. "Food and Culture: Interconnections." *Social Research* 66 (1): 117–30.

Vo, N. G. 1994. *Unforgettable Days.* Hanoi: The Gioi.

Vu, C. H. 1997. *Fruit-Trees in Vietnam.* Hanoi: The Gioi.

Vuong, X. T . 1997. "Social Behavior of the Viet in Kinh Bac Area with Regard to Eating and Drinking." *Vietnamese Studies* 3 (125): 63–74.

Warde, A. 1997. *Consumption, Food and Taste: Culinary Antinomies and Commodity Cultures.* London: Sage Publications.

———, and L. Martens. 2000. *Eating Out: Social Differentiation, Consumption and Pleasure.* Cambridge: Cambridge University Press.

Warner, E. T. C. 1984 [1922]. *Myths and Legends of China.* Singapore: Graham Brash.

Watson, J. 2000. "Food as Lens: The Past, Present and Future of Family Life in China." In *Feeding China's Little Emperors,* edited by J. Jun, 199–212. Stanford, Calif.: Stanford University Press.

———, and M. Caldwell. 2005. *The Cultural Politics of Food and Eating.* Oxford: Blackwell.

Watson, J. L., ed. 1997. *Golden Arches East: McDonald's in East Asia.* Stanford, Calif.: Stanford University Press.

Weber, M. 1976 [1909]. *The Agrarian Sociology of Ancient Civilizations.* London: New Left.

Werner, J., and D. Bélanger, eds. 2002. *Gender, Household and State: Doi Moi in Viet Nam.* Ithaca: Cornell Southeast Asia Series.

Wheeler, C. 2006a. "One History, Two Regions: Cham Precedents in the History of the Hoi An Region." In *Viet Nam: Borderless Histories,* edited by Nhung Tran and A. Reid, 163–93. Madison: University of Wisconsin Press.

———. 2006b. "Re-thinking the Sea in Vietnamese History: The Littoral Integration of Thuan-Quang, Seventeenth-Eighteenth Centuries." *Journal of Southeast Asian Studies* 17 (1): 123–53.

———. 2010. "Maritime Subversions and Socio-Political Formations in Vietnamese History: A Look from the Marginal Center (mien Trung)." In *New Perspectives on History and Historiography in Southeast Asia: Continuing Explorations,* edited by M. A. Aung-Thwin and K. Hall. London: Routledge.

White, D. G. 1992. "You Are What You Eat: The Anomalous Status of Dog-Cookers in Hindu Mythology." In *The Eternal Food: Gastronomic Ideas and Experiences of Hindus and Buddhists,* edited by R. S. Khare, 53–94. Delhi: Sri Satguru.

Wildt, M. 2001. "Promise of More: The Rhetoric of (Food) Consumption in a Society Searching for Itself: West Germany in the 1950s." In *Food, Drink and Identity,* edited by P. Scholliers, 63–80. Oxford: Berg.

Wilson, T. M., ed. 2006. *Food, Drink and Identity in Europe.* Amsterdam: Rodopi.

Wisensale, S. K. 2000. "Family Policy in Changing Vietnam." *Journal of Comparative Family Studies* 31 (1): 79–90.

Wu, D., and Tan C. B. 2001. *Changing Chinese Foodways in Asia.* Hong Kong: Chinese University Press.

——, and S. Cheung, eds. 2002. *The Globalization of Chinese Food.* Richmond Surrey: Curzon.

Yan, Y. 1997. "McDonald's in Beijing: The Localization of Americana." In *Golden Arches East: McDonald's in East Asia,* edited by J. L. Watson, 39–76. Stanford, Calif.: Stanford University Press.

——. 1999. "Of Hamburger and Social Space: Consuming McDonald in Beijing." In *The Consumer Revolution in China,* edited by D. Davis, 201–225. Berkeley: University of California Press.

Yang, K. C. 1965. *Chinese Communist Society: The Family and the Village. Part II: A Chinese Village in Early Communist Transition.* Cambridge, Mass.: M.I.T. Press.

Yudkin, J., and J. C. McKenzie. 1964. *Changing Food Habits.* London: MacGibbon and Kee.

Zilber-Rosenberg, I. 1996. *Nutrition, Food for Thought: Food and Nutrition in Health and Disease.* Tel Aviv: Open University Press (in Hebrew).

Index

NIR AVIELI is Lecturer in the Department of Sociology and Anthropology at Ben Gurion University in Israel. A cultural anthropologist, his primary research interests are food and tourism. He has conducted ethnographic fieldwork in Vietnam, Thailand, India, Singapore, and Israel.